Archæological Institute of America.

PAPERS

OF THE

American School of Classical Studies at Athens.

VOLUME I.

1882-1883.

BOSTON:
CUPPLES, UPHAM, AND CO.
1885.

PRESS OF
J. S. CUSHING & CO.,
115 HIGH STREET,
BOSTON.

PREFACE.

THE regulations of the AMERICAN SCHOOL OF CLASSICAL STUDIES AT ATHENS provide that "there shall be published annually a volume of Papers of the School, to be made up from the work of the Director and the students during the preceding school year." This volume, now issued in tardy compliance with the rule, represents portions of the work of the first school year, 1882–1883. The publication has been delayed by various unavoidable difficulties, among which must be mentioned those which have attended the preparation and the printing of two collections of Greek inscriptions. Even now it has been necessary to postpone the appearance of Dr. Crow's paper on the Pnyx: this, and probably one or two other papers belonging to the work of the first school year, will form part of the second volume, which, it is hoped, will be published before the end of the present year. One paper which will be included in the second volume, Dr. Sterrett's Preliminary Report of his journey in Asia Minor in 1884, with his collection of inscriptions (including those of forty-two Roman milestones), has been published already in a separate form.

The first place in the present volume is given to the Inscriptions of Assos, collected in 1881 and 1882 by the expedition sent out by the Archæological Institute of America. These have been edited by Dr. Sterrett, who went from Athens to Assos for that purpose in April, 1883. Although the actual historic gain to be derived from these inscriptions may not be great, still it is hoped that the glimpse which they give of the life of a quiet Greek town in Asia Minor, with its Senate and People passing decrees as grand as those of Athens, and with its local magnates, women as well as men, earning the public gratitude by their gifts, will be welcome to all scholars. Grammarians will rejoice that the Aeolic dialect has been enriched by one important verbal form (see page 6). Moreover, this publication of the first collection of Greek inscriptions ever made by an American expedition in classic lands marks an era in our national scholarship. The originals of many of the inscriptions of Assos are now in the Museum of Fine Arts in Boston. A list of these, with the numbers which they bear in the catalogue of the Museum, will be found on page 90. The second paper contains a collection of inscriptions copied by Dr. Sterrett and Mr. W. M. Ramsay at Tralles in Asia Minor during the summer of 1883, and first published by Dr. Sterrett in the *Mittheilungen* of the German Archæological Institute at Athens. The present paper, however, differs from the article in the *Mittheilungen* in many important respects, as is explained in various editorial notes. A valuable note on the Trallian Olympiads, which was kindly sent to the editors by Mr. Ramsay, is inserted in this paper (pp. 102-104); and several changes have been made in the text of the inscriptions and in the commentary, during the absence of Dr. Sterrett in Asia, by the advice of Mr. Ramsay, who was associated with Dr. Sterrett in copying these inscriptions.

The three papers which follow were written by Messrs. Wheeler, Bevier, and Fowler, in immediate connection with their work at Athens. The first drafts of these were read at meetings of the School; and they were presented to the Managing Committee after the end of the year, in their present form, as theses, in conformity to the rules of the School. These papers will give the friends of the School a general idea of the subjects to which our students have directed their attention. The last paper in this volume was read by the Director at one of the meetings at Athens.

The editors have generally confined themselves to the usual editorial duties of supervision and correcting the proofs. As the papers and the commentaries on the inscriptions were revised after the end of the school year by their authors, they alone are responsible for the opinions expressed by them and for the manner of presentation. Each writer, moreover, has followed his own views in expressing Greek proper names in English. An exception must be made in the case of the papers on the Trallian Inscriptions, as is explained above; and also in that of some of the Assos Inscriptions which are now in Boston but were inaccessible to Dr. Sterrett at Assos owing to the jealousy of the Turkish officials (see page 11).

The latest circular giving information about the School at Athens, issued in January, 1885, will be found at the end of this volume.

William W. Goodwin,
Thomas W. Ludlow, } *Editors.*

February, 1885.

AMERICAN SCHOOL OF CLASSICAL STUDIES AT ATHENS.

1882-1883.

MANAGING COMMITTEE.

John Williams White (*Chairman*), Harvard University, Cambridge, Mass.

Martin L. D'Ooge, University of Michigan, Ann Arbor, Mich.

Henry Drisler, Columbia College, 48 West 46th St., New York, N. Y.

Basil L. Gildersleeve, Johns Hopkins University, Baltimore, Md.

William W. Goodwin (of Harvard University), Director of the School, Athens, Greece (*ex officio*).

E. W. Gurney, Harvard University, Cambridge, Mass.

Albert Harkness, Brown University, Providence, R. I.

Thomas W. Ludlow (*Secretary*), Yonkers, N. Y.

Charles Eliot Norton (President of the Archæological Institute of America), Harvard University, Cambridge, Mass. (*ex officio*).

Lewis R. Packard, Yale College, New Haven, Conn.

Francis W. Palfrey, 255 Beacon St., Boston, Mass.

Frederic J. de Peyster (*Treasurer*), 7 East 42nd St., New York, N.Y.

William M. Sloane, College of New Jersey, Princeton, N. J.

W. S. Tyler, Amherst College, Amherst, Mass.

J. C. Van Benschoten, Wesleyan University, Middletown, Conn.

DIRECTOR OF THE SCHOOL.

WILLIAM W. GOODWIN, LL.D.

STUDENTS.

JOHN M. CROW, A.B. (Waynesbury College), Ph.D. (Syracuse University).

HAROLD N. FOWLER, A.B. (Harvard University).

PAUL SHOREY, A.B. (Harvard University), holder of the Kirkland Fellowship of Harvard University.

J. R. S. STERRETT, University of Virginia, Ph.D. (University of Munich).

FRANKLIN N. TAYLOR, Wesleyan University.

JAMES R. WHEELER, A.B. (University of Vermont), Graduate Student of Harvard University.

FRANK E. WOODRUFF, A.B. (University of Vermont), B.D. (Union Theological Seminary), holder of a Fellowship of the Union Theological Seminary.

LOUIS BEVIER, A.M. (Rutgers College), Ph.D. (Johns Hopkins University).

The seven who are first named entered as students for the full year. Mr. Woodruff, however, was called to the Professorship of Sacred Literature in the Andover Theological Seminary, and left Athens in March, 1883. The six others completed the full year of study in conformity to the regulations, and received the certificate of the School.

Dr. Bevier, although he was not a regular member, studied in Athens and took part in the exercises of the School during the greater part of the school year.

CONTENTS.

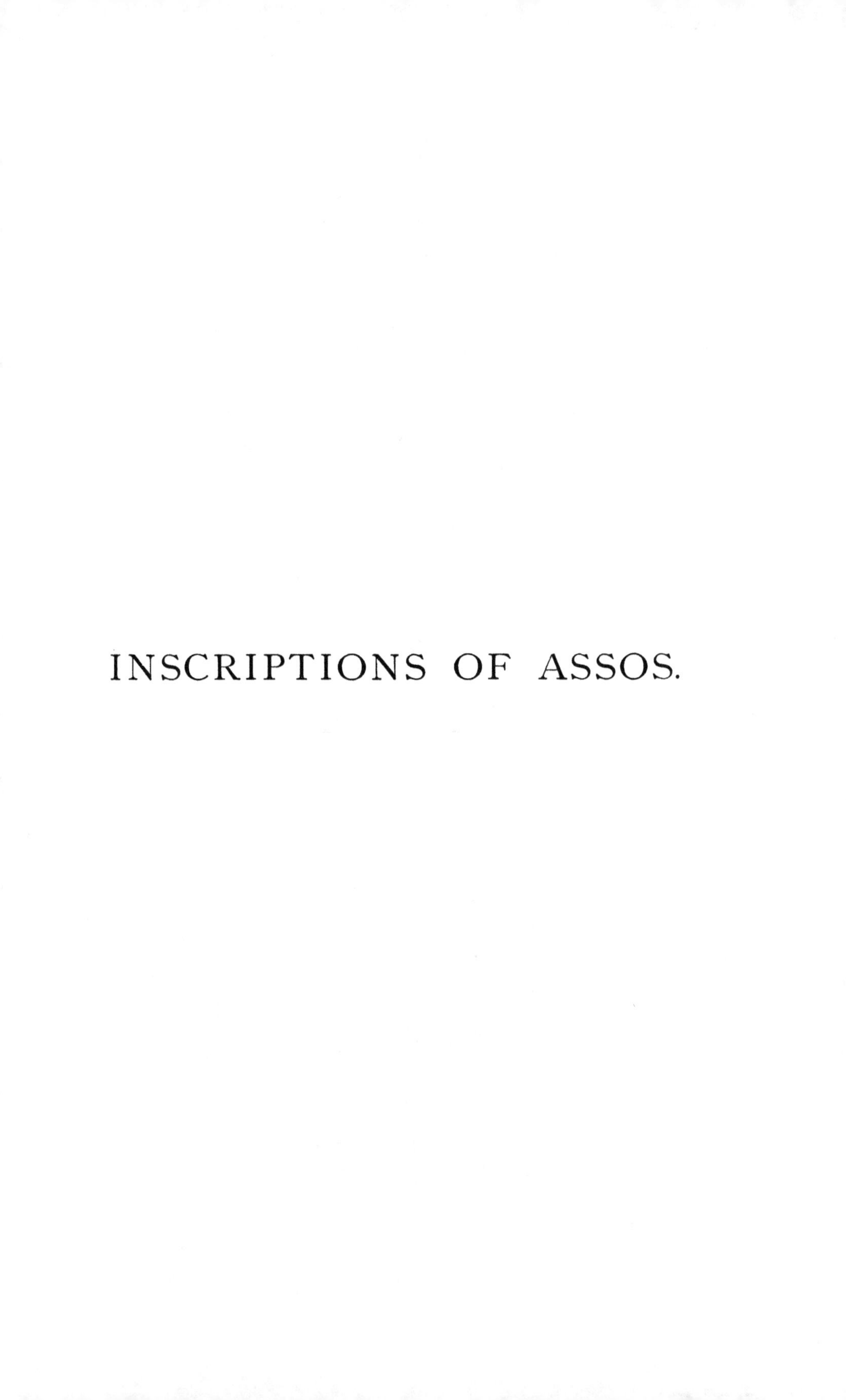

INSCRIPTIONS OF ASSOS.

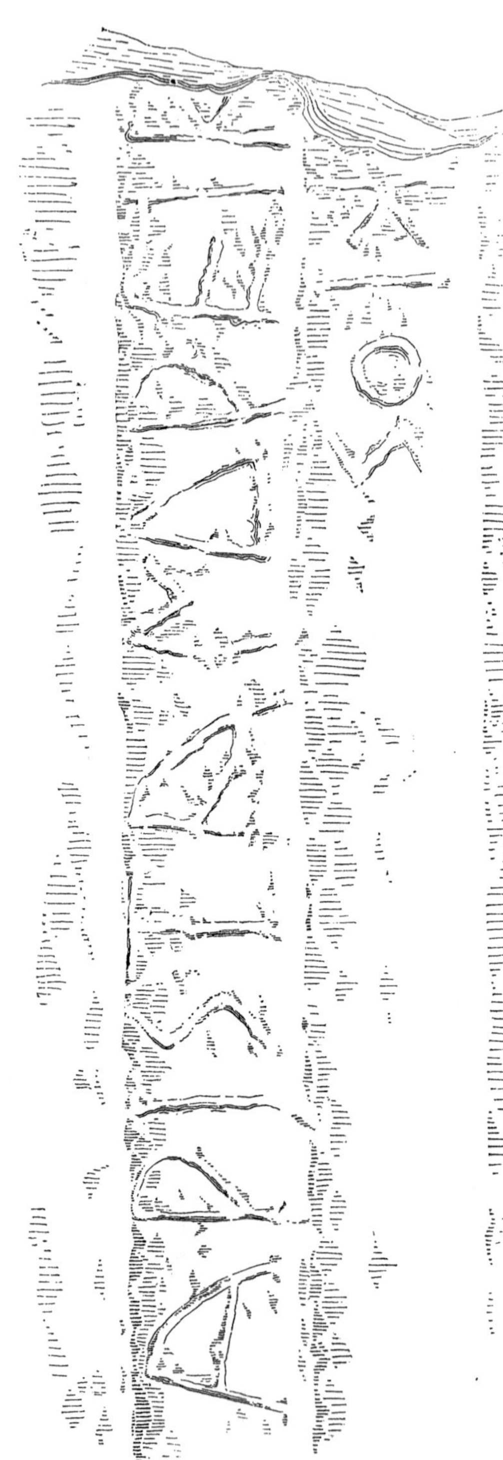

2

INSCRIPTIONS OF ASSOS.

No. I.

Boustrophedon inscription on two flutings of a broken proto-doric column, in the western Street of Tombs. (See plate.)

This inscription undoubtedly belongs to the sixth century before Christ, though none of the letters that are most important in deciding the age, such as Ξ, Ψ, Χ, occur in it. It has no special epigraphical value in its present mutilated condition, the letters ΑΡΙΣΤΑΝΔΡΕΙ(Α?) and the ending -ΚΙΟΣ alone remaining. The monument is, however, of importance in the early history of Greek architecture, as will be shown in Mr. Clarke's forthcoming *Report on the Excavations at Assos.*

No. II.

On a rock just within the city wall, on the south-west.

In the rock are hewn two niches for votive offerings, surmounted by pediments. Above the niches, upon the inclined upper surface of the rock, are the letters IΡΟΝ. The dotted appearance of the letters is due to the manner of working the stone with a coarse drill, of which all the lines, and especially the pediments, bear evidence. The archaic character of the inscription is noticeable in the forms of the letters. On the right of the niches are the letters ΑΤΕ, in ligature, = ATE, which are apparently of later date.

No. III.

Found May 10th, 1882, on the Acropolis, north of the temple, near the surface of the ground. (*See opposite page.*)

The upper part of the slab is well preserved. The end of the inscription is broken away, and has never been found. The inscription was published by Professor Frederic D. Allen in the *American Journal of Philology*, Vol. III., No. 12, p. 463, and was republished from that journal by Cauer in the second edition of his *Delectus inscriptionum Graecarum propter dialectum memorabilium*, No. 430, p. 285. Greatest height of slab, 0.18; width, 0.29 m.

[Τ]ὰ σκεύεά ἔσσι δαμόσια ἐπὶ
ἀγορανόμω Μεγιστία Σωγενεί-
ω· ἡμιμέδιμνοι χάλκιοι τρεῖς,
ἡμίεκτα ἔννεα, διχοίνικα δέ-
[κ]α, χοίνικες ἔπτα, τρίχοα
[χ]άλκια τέσσαρα, ἡμίχοον, ἄλ-
[λο ἡμ]ίχοον χῶναν ἔχον· στά-
[θμα χά]λκι[α·] τάλαντα τρί[α] . .
. . . . [π]εντάμνάον . . .

The inscription is interesting chiefly because we learn from this and the three following fragments that the language of Assos was the Aeolic of Lesbos. It is an inventory of measures, most probably

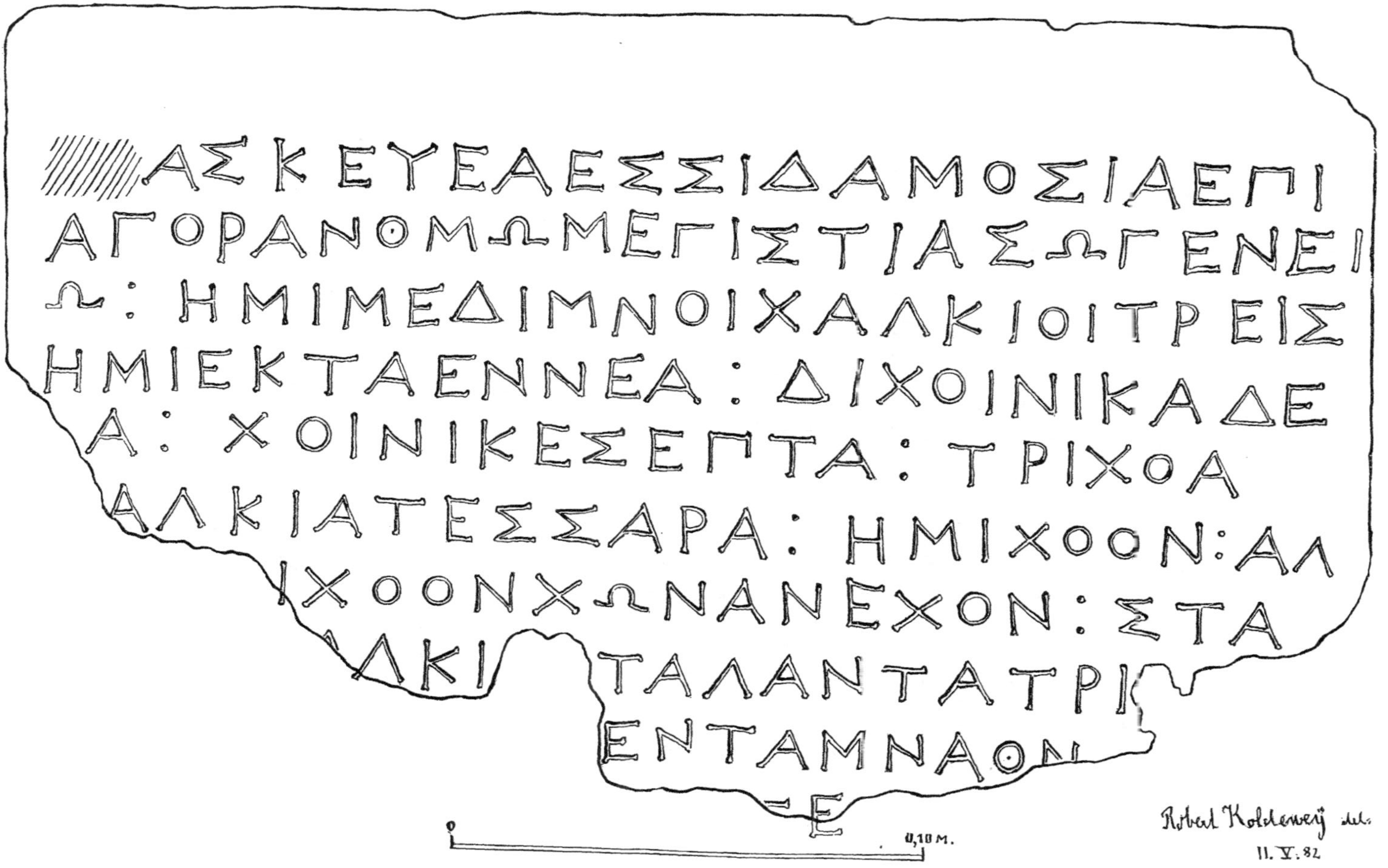

ΑΣΚΕΥΕΑΕΣΣΙΔΑΜΟΣΙΑΕΠΙ
ΑΓΟΡΑΝΟΜΩΜΕΓΙΣΤΙΑΣΩΓΕΝΕΙ
Ω:ΗΜΙΜΕΔΙΜΝΟΙΧΑΛΚΙΟΙΤΡΕΙΣ
ΗΜΙΕΚΤΑΕΝΝΕΑ:ΔΙΧΟΙΝΙΚΑΔΕ
Α:ΧΟΙΝΙΚΕΣΕΠΤΑ:ΤΡΙΧΟΑ
ΑΛΚΙΑΤΕΣΣΑΡΑ:ΗΜΙΧΟΟΝ:ΑΛ
ΙΧΟΟΝΧΩΝΑΝΕΧΟΝ:ΣΤΑ
ΛΚΙ ΤΑΛΑΝΤΑΤΡΙ
ΕΝΤΑΜΝΑΘΟΝ
Ε

0 — 0,10 M.

Robert Koldewey del.
11. V. 82

belonging to the temple of Athena, near which it was found. Such inventories were made by an official at the expiration of his term of office, for the use of his successor, and to show officially that there had been no maladministration of the goods and chattels of the temple during his term. Many such inventories have been found, —for instance, those of the property in the Parthenon (see *C. I. G.*, Vol. I., *Tabulae Magistratuum; C. I. A.*, Vol. I., pp. 48–78), and several lists of articles belonging to the Asklepieion at Athens.

The one letter wanting in line 1 is almost certainly T.

The inscription is of the greatest importance grammatically, because it clears up a point hitherto doubtful, to which Professor Allen called attention in the *American Journal of Philology* (above cited). Meister, in his *Griech. Dial.* I., p. 171, note 2, points out that the third person plural of the Aeolic ἔμμι has hitherto had no documentary voucher. In the inscription of Eresos, as published by Conze (*Reise auf der Insel Lesbos*, p. 35 sqq.), we find the form Ε≶ΤΙ as the third person plural of ἔμμι. For this Ε≶ΤΙ, Sauppe (*Commentatio de duabus inscriptionibus Lesbiacis*, in Göttinger Programm, 1871) suggested that ΕΝΤΙ be read, and he was followed by Cauer in the first edition of his *Delectus inscriptionum Graecarum propter dialectum memorabilium*, No. 123, and by Bechtel in *die inschriftlichen Denkmäler des aeolischen Dialekts*, in Bezzenberger's *Beiträge*, V., p. 138 sqq. This conjecture seemed to be but slightly supported by the words of Herakleides in *Eustathios*, 1557, 41: τῶν δ' αὐτῶν Δωριέων καὶ τὸ φρονοῦσι καὶ νοοῦσι φρονεῦντι λέγειν καὶ νοεῦντι ἐπὶ περισπωμένων δηλαδὴ, ἅπερ ἐξάρσει τοῦ ν λεγόμενα Αἰολικά ἐστιν οἷον φρονεῦτι· ἔτι δὲ καὶ εὖτι ἀντὶ τοῦ εἰσὶν, ὅπερ ἄλλως ἐντὶ λέγεται Δώριον ὁμοῦ ὂν καὶ Αἰολικόν. The correctness of φρονεῦτι, εὖτι, and ἐντί was disputed by Meister, who virtually demands the form Ε≶≶Ι,* which fortunately is established beyond doubt by our inscription.

Notice the dialectic patronymic Σωγένειος, which runs with Σωγένης = Σωσιγένης.

---

* Meister, *Griech. Dial.* I., p. 171, note 2: An die Richtigkeit von φρονεῦτι εὖτι ist nicht zu glauben, ἐντί ist böotisch, wie die gleich darauf "äolisch" genannten Formen οἴκεντι φίλεντι.—Nach dem Vorbilde ἴεισι äolisch εἶσι anzunehmen, erscheint bedenklich, da dem Part. Fem. μάτεισα nicht εἶσα sondern ἔσσα entspricht. Ich treffe desshalb keine Entscheidung.

No. IV.

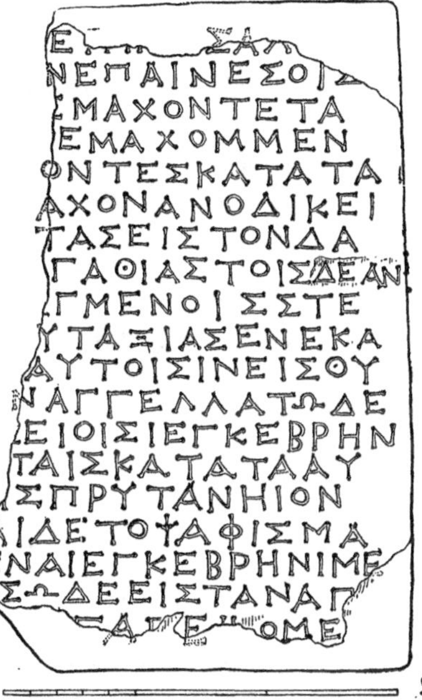

Fragment found near west end of Stoa. The left side is broken away. Holes were bored as marks for cutting the letters. Height, 0.257; greatest width, 0.165m.

The inscription is too fragmentary for even probable restoration, the left side being entirely wanting. It probably belongs to the third century before Christ, and is interesting solely on account of the dialect. Notice datives in -οισι, accusatives in -οις, ἀναγγελλάτω, ψάφισμα, and the patronymic Ἀνοδίκειος.

. . . . επαινεσοι
. . . . [Τηλέ]μαχον τετα-
[γμένον . . . . . . Τηλ]έμαχομ Μεν-
[άνδρω . . . . . . -οντες κατὰ τὰ
[αὐτὰ (πάτρια) . . . . Τηλέμ]αχον Ἀνοδίκει-
[ον] . . . . τᾶς εἰς τὸν δᾶ-
[μον εὐνοίας καὶ καλοκὰ]γαθίας· τοὶς δὲ ἀν-
[αγεγραμμένοις (?) καὶ τετα]γμένοις στε-
[φάνοις . . . . . . ε]ὐταξίας ἕνεκα
. . . . αὐτοῖσιν εἰς θυ-
[σίαν . . . . . . ἀ]ναγγελλάτω δὲ
. . . . [ἐν τοῖς . .]είοισι ἐγ Κεβρῆν-

[ι, ἐπαινέσαι δὲ τοὶς δικασ]ταὶς κατὰ τὰ αὐ-
[τὰ, καλέσαι δὲ αὐτοὶς εἰ]ς πρυτανήιον
[εἰς δεῖπνον, ἀναγράψ]αι δὲ τὸ ψάφισμα
[εἰς δύο στάλας καὶ τιθ]έναι ἐγ Κεβρῆνι μὲ-
[ν εἰς τὸ ἱρὸν τοῦ Διὸς, ἐν Ἄσ]σῳ δὲ εἰς τὰν ἀπ-
. . . .

No. V.

Fragment found below the agora wall. Rulings for the lines are still visible. Greatest length, 0.16 ; *greatest height to moulding,* 0.165 *m.*

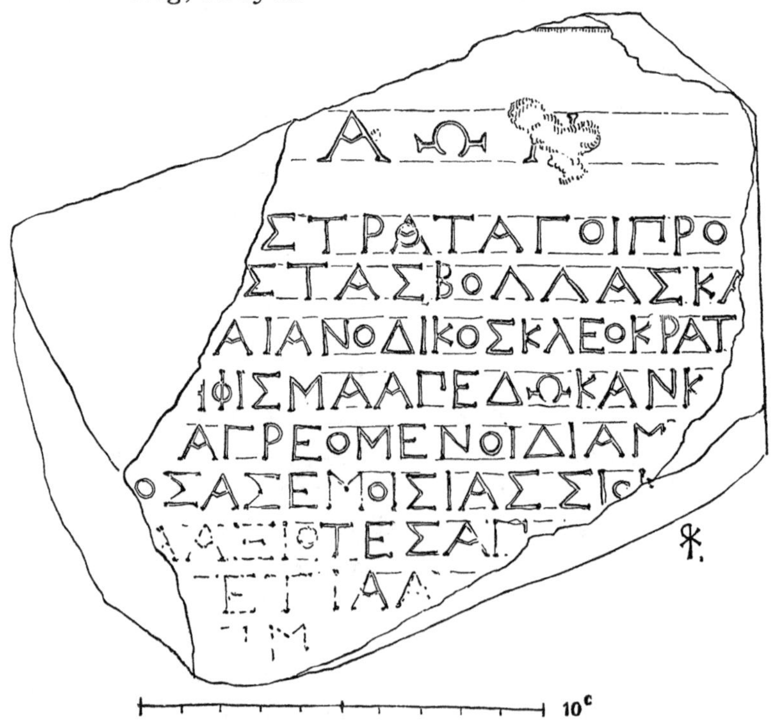

ΛΩΝ

στράταγοι Προ-
· · · · [γραμματεὺ]ς τᾶς βόλλας κα-
[ὶ τῶ δάμω · · · · κ]αὶ Ἀνόδικος Κλεοκράτ-
[εος or -η · · · τὸ ψά]φισμα ἀπέδωκαν κ-
[αὶ] · · · · · · · · ἀγρεόμενοι διὰ Μ ·
ὅσας ἔχουσι (?) Ἄσσιοι

A restoration is impossible. The inscription is interesting solely in a dialectic view. Compare the forms στράταγοι (see Cauer, *Delectus inscriptionum Graecarum propter dialectum memorabilium*, No. 431, p. 277), τᾶς βόλλας, Ἀνόδικος, Κλεοκράτ[εος], ἀπέδωκαν, ἀγρεόμενοι (*Cauer*, p. 286 : *ex vetustissima dialecto Lesbiaca videtur servatum esse;* cf. Meister, *Dial.* I. 177 sq.). It has small O and two forms of Λ.

Professor Allen (*American Journal of Philology*, 1882, p. 463) calls attention to the new name Ἀνόδικος, and Professor Gildersleeve adds this note: —

"Ἀνόδικος = Ἀναξίδικος would be tempting if it were not for the ο in Ἀνο. So Ἀνακλῆς runs with Ἀναξικλῆς rather than Ἀνάκλητος to which it is usually referred. Ἀναγόρα, the name of one of Sappho's friends (*Suidas*), has been crowded out by the Ἀνακτορία of Maximus Tyrius (see Swinburne's *Anactoria*), but Ἀναγόρα = Ἀναξαγόρα would have its masculine in Ἀναξαγόρας. Ἀνακρέων, if compounded with ἀνά, *up*, would be the only one of its group to be so compounded according to Fick (*Personennamen*, s. 121). Βασιλοδίκα, which is found *C. I. G.* 2448, 3, is a fellow to Ἀναξιδίκη."

No. VI.

Found at the portal entrance at the end of the agora; a mere fragment. Rulings for the lines are still visible. Length, about 0.23 m.; height, 0.17 m.

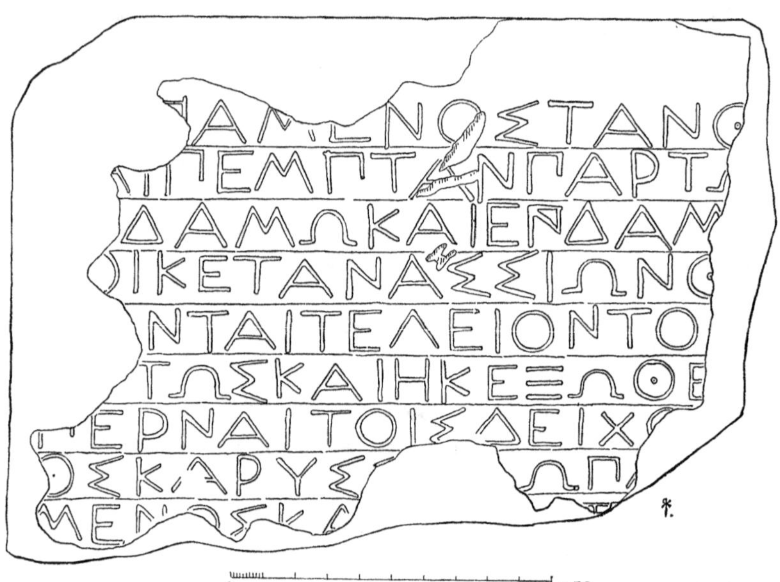

. . . . .]αμενος τὰν θ-
. . . . . . πέμπταν πὰρ τω
. . . . . δάμω καὶ [ἐν] δάμ[ῳ]
. . . . . οἰκέταν Ἀσσίων θ-
. . . . .]νται τέλειον το
. . . . . οὕ]τως καὶ ηκεξωθε
. . . . . π]ερναι τοις δειχθ[
. . . . . .]ος Καρυσ[τ . . . ωπ
. . . . .]μενος κα[ὶ . . . . .

No. VII.

Decree found September 5 *and* 6, 1881, *at the eastern end of the Stoa plateau, on two fragments of marble. Copied by* W. C. Lawton.

This inscription was published in Mr. Clarke's first *Report on the Investigations at Assos*, in 1882. The present editor was unable to see this or either of the two other long inscriptions published in that Report, because they were kept sealed during his stay in Assos by order of the Turkish officials, who could not be induced to open them for inspection. The following is taken from the introductory note of the former editor: —

"This inscription contains a decree, passed by some town whose name is lost, giving a crown and a vote of thanks to the town of Assos for sending judges to decide certain lawsuits, and giving the same distinctions to the judges themselves. The upper part of the inscription, with most of the preamble, is lost. Inscription No. 3568 f., in Boeckh's *Corpus Inscript. Graec.*, Vol. II., p. 1128, contains a similar vote of thanks sent by the town of Peltae to Antandros: Boeckh assigns this document to the third century B.C."

The following notes are added in Mr. Clarke's Report: —

"Line 8. Αὐλητῶν τῇ πρώτῃ ἡμέρᾳ: cf. Aeschines in *Ctes.*, § 45, κηρύττεσθαι τοῖς τραγῳδοῖς, and the spurious decree in Demosth. *Cor.*, § 118, Διονυσίοις, τραγῳδοῖς καινοῖς, with the corrupt expression, τραγῳδῶν τῇ καινῇ, *ibid.*, § 55.

"Line 12. ΣΤΕΦΑΝΩΝ is the stonecutter's mistake for ΣΤΕΦΑΝΩΙ.

"Line 13. ΙΣΣΩ must be a mistake for ΙΣΩΣ.

"Phonetic spellings, as τὴμ βουλήν (l. 15), τὸγ γραμματέα (l. 17), βουλὴγ καί (l. 23), will be noticed; as also occasional omission of I in HI and ΩI, and careless insertion of I after H and Ω." *

---

* The stone is now (June, 1884), in the Museum of Fine Arts in Boston; but the inscription has been much defaced since it was copied by Mr. Lawton in 1881, many words having become illegible. The traces of letters, however, amply confirm Dr. Sterrett's restoration of ἐπελθόντες in line 23, ΕΠΕΛΘ . . . ΕΣ being quite certain. In line 31 the form ΗΡΗΘΗΣΑΝ (for ᾑρέθησαν), as previously published, is not confirmed; the stone has ΗΡΕΘΗΣΑΝ. — W. W. G.

. . . . ΜΙΑ . . . .
. . . .
. . . . ΔΗΜΟΣΦΑΙΝΗΤΑΙΤΑΣΚΑ . . . .
. . . . ΤΟΙΣΚΑΛΟΙΣΚΑΙΑΓΑΘΟΙΣΤΩΝΑΝΔΡΩΝ
. . . . ΠΑΡΑΓΙΝΩΝΤΑΙΑΝΔΡΕΣΑΞΙΟΙΤΟΥΔΗΜΟΥΕΙΔ
. . . . ΠΑΡΧΟΥΣΑΝΕΥΧΑΡΙΣΤΙΑΝΔΕΔΟΧΘΑΙΤΗΙΒΟΥΛΗ ·
. . . . . . ΔΗΜΩΙΕΠΗΝΗΣΘΑΙΤΟΝΔΗΜΟΝΤΟΝΑΣΣΙΩΝΕΠΙΤ ·
. . . . . ΕΙ · ΕΧΕΙΠΡΟΣΗΜΑΣΚΑΙΣΤΕΦΑΝΟΥΣΘΑΙΑΥΤΟΝΕΝΤΟΙΣ
. . . . . ΤΟΙΣΔΙΟΝΥΣΙΟΙΣΑΥΛΗΤΩΝΤΗΙΠΡΩΤΗΙΗΜΕΡΑΙΧΡΥΣΩΙΣΤΕ
· ΑΝΩΙΕΠΙΤΩΑΠΟΣΤΕΙΛΑΙΔΙΚΑΣΤΑΣΚΑΛΟΥΣΚΑΓΑΘΟΥΣΚΑ ·
· ΡΑΜΜΑΤΕΑΕΠΗΝΗΣΘΑΙΔΕΚΑΙΤΟΥΣΔΙΚΑΣΤΑΣΤΟΥΣΠΑ
ΡΑΓΕΝΟΜΕΝΟΥΣΕΧΕΛΑΟΝΑΘΗΝΑΓΟΡΟΥΛΑΤΙΜΟΝΚΛΕΟΜΟΡ
· ΟΥΚΑΙΣΤΕΦΑΝΩΣΑΙΕΚΑΤΕΡΟΝΑΥΤΩΝΧΡΥΣΩΙΣΤΕΦΑΝΩΝΕΠ ·
· · ΙΤΑΣΜΕΝΔΙΑΔΙΚΑΣΑΙΤΩΝΔΙΚΩΝΙΣΣΩΚΑΙΔΙΚΑΙΩΣΤΑΣ
. . . . . ΥΣΑΙΑΠΟΠΑΝΤΟΣΤΟΥΒΕΛΤΙΣΤΟΥΥΠΑΡΧΕΙΝΔΕΑΥΤΟ · ·
. . . . ΜΒΟΥΛΗΝΚΑΙΤΟΝΔΗΙΜΟΝΠΡΩΤΟΙΣΜΕΤΑΤΑΙΕ
ΡΑΥΠΑΡΧΕΙΝΔ . . . Ο · · ΚΑΙΠΡΟΞΕΝΟΥΣΤΗΣΠΟΛΕΩΣΗΜΩΝΣΤΕ
ΦΑΝΩΙΣΑΙΔΕ · ΑΙΤΟΓΓΡ . . . . ΤΕΑΜΕΛΑΓΧΡΟΝΜΕΛΑΓΧΡΟΥΘΑΛΕ
ΡΩΙΣΤΕΦΑΝΩΙΕΠΙΤΩΠΑΡΑΣΧ · ΣΘΑΙΤΗΝΚΑΘΑΥΤΟΝΧΡΕΙΑΝΜΕΤΑ
ΠΑΣΗΣΦΙΛΟΤΙΜΙΑΣΤΗΣΤΕΑΝΑΓΓ · ΛΙΑΣΤΩΝΣΤΕΦΑΝΩΝΤΗΝΕΠ ·
. . . Σ . . ΠΟΗΣΑΣΘΑΙΤΟΥΣΑΓΩΝΟΘΕΤ · ΣΤΟΥΜΟΥΣΙΚΟΥΙΝΑΔΕΚΑ ·
ΑΣΣΙΟΙΕΙΔΗΣΩΣΙΝΤΗΝΤΕΤΩΝΑΝΔΡ · · ΚΑΛΟΚΑΓΑΘΙΑΝΚΑΙΤΗΝ
ΤΟΥΔΗΜΟΥΕΥΧΑΡΙΣΤΙΑΝΑΙΡΕΘΗΝΑΙΠΡΕΣΒΕΥΤΑΣΟΙΤΙΝΕΣΑΦΙΚΟ
ΜΕΝΟΙΠΡΟΣΑΥΤΟΥΣΕΠΕΛΘ . . . ΕΣ . . . ΤΕΤΗΝ · ΟΥΛΗΓΚΑΙΤΟΝΔΗ
ΜΟΝΤΟΤΕΨΗΦΙΣΜΑΑΠΟΔΩΣΟΥΣΙΝΑΥΤΟΙΣΚΑ · · ΟΦΑΝΙΟΥΣΙΝΤΗ ·
ΤΕΤΩΝΑΝΔΡΩΝΚΑΛΟΚΑΓΑΘΙΑΝΚΑΙΤΗΝΕΥΝΟΙΑΝ · ΝΕΧΟΜΕΝ
ΠΡΟΣΤΟΝΔΗΜΟΝΑΥΤΩΝΚΑΙΠΑΡΑΚΑΛΕΣΟΥΣΙΝΑΣΣΙΟΥΣΚΑΙΠΑ
ΡΑΥΤΟΙΣΠΟΗΣΑΣΘΑΙΤΗΝΑΝΑΓΓΕΛΙΑΝΤΩΝΣ · ΕΦΑ
ΝΩΝΥΠΟΤΟΥΚΑΤΑΣΤΑΘΗΣΟΜΕΝΟΥΑΓΩΝΟΘΕΤΟΥ · ΟΥ
ΜΟΥΣΙΚΟΥΑΓΩΝΟΣΠΡΟΝΟΗΣΑΙΔΕΙΝΑΚΑΙΤΟΨΗΦΙΣΜΑΑΝΑ . . .
ΦΗΙΕΙΣΤΗΛΗΝΛΙΘΙΝΗΝΚΑΙΑΝΑΤΕΘΗΠΑΡΑΥΤΟΙΣΕΝΤΩΙΕ
ΠΙΦΑΝΕΣΤΑΤΩΙΤΟΠΩΙΠΡΕΣΒΕΥΤΑΙΗΡΕΘΗΣΑΝΚΛΕΟΜΗ
ΔΗΣΗΓΙΑΣΑΓΟΡΟΥΑΝΑΞΑΓΟΡΑΣΔΙΟΝΥΣΙΟΥ

. . . . δῆμος* φαίνηται τὰς κα[ταξίας] [ἀποδιδοὺς χάριτας] τοῖς καλοῖς καὶ ἀγαθοῖς τῶν ἀνδρῶν, [καὶ οἳ ἂν ὕστερον] παραγίνωνται ἄνδρες ἄξιοι τοῦ δήμου εἰδ[ήσωσιν ὑ]πάρχουσαν εὐχαριστίαν, δεδόχθαι τῇ βουλῇ [καὶ τῷ] δήμῳ ἐπῃνῆσθαι τὸν δῆμον τὸν Ἀσσίων ἐπὶ τ[ῇ] [πίστ]ει [ῇ] ἔχει πρὸς ἡμᾶς, καὶ στεφανοῦσθαι αὐτὸν ἐν τοῖς . . . . τοις Διονυσίοις, αὐλητῶν τῇ πρώτῃ ἡμέρᾳ, χρυσῷ στε[φ]άνῳ, ἐπὶ τῶ ἀποστεῖλαι δικαστὰς καλοὺς κἀγαθοὺς κα[ὶ] [γ]ραμματέα, ἐπηνῆσθαι δὲ καὶ τοὺς δικαστὰς τοὺς παραγενομένους, Ἐχέλαον Ἀθηναγόρου, Λάτιμον Κλεομόρ[γ]ου, καὶ στεφανῶσαι ἑκάτερον αὐτῶν χρυσῷ στεφάνῳ, ἐπ[ὶ] [τῷ] τὰς μὲν διαδικάσαι τῶν δικῶν [ἴσως] καὶ δικαίως, τὰς [δὲ διαλ]ῦσαι ἀπὸ παντὸς τοῦ βελτίστου, ὑπάρχειν δὲ αὐτο[ῖς] [ἔφοδον ἐπὶ τὴ]μ βουλὴν καὶ τὸν δῆμον πρώτοις μετὰ τὰ ἱερά· ὑπάρχειν δ' [αὐτ]ο[ὺς] καὶ προξένους τῆς πόλεως ἡμῶν· στεφανῶσαι δὲ [κ]αὶ τὸγ γρ[αμμα]τέα, Μέλαγχρον Μελάγχρου, θαλερῷ στεφάνῳ, ἐπὶ τῶ παρασχ[έ]σθαι τὴν καθ' αὑτὸν χρείαν μετὰ πάσης φιλοτιμίας· τῆς τε ἀναγγ[ε]λίας τῶν στεφάνων τὴν ἐπ[ί][στασιν] πο(ι)ήσασθαι τοὺς ἀγωνοθέτας τοῦ μουσικοῦ· ἵνα δὲ κα[ὶ] Ἄσσιοι εἰδήσωσιν τήν τε τῶν ἀνδρ[ῶν] καλοκαγαθίαν καὶ τὴν τοῦ δήμου εὐχαριστίαν, αἱρεθῆναι πρεσβευτὰς οἵτινες ἀφικόμενοι πρὸς αὐτοὺς ἐπε[λθόντες ἐπί] τε τὴν [β]ουλὴγ καὶ τὸν δῆμον τό τε ψήφισμα ἀποδώσουσιν αὐτοῖς κα[ὶ ἀπ]οφανιοῦσιν τὴ[ν] τε τῶν ἀνδρῶν καλοκαγαθίαν καὶ τὴν εὔνοιαν [ἣ]ν ἔχομεν πρὸς τὸν δῆμον αὐτῶν, καὶ παρακαλέσουσιν Ἀσσίους καὶ παρ' αὐτοῖς πο(ι)ήσασθαι τὴν ἀναγγελίαν τῶν σ[τ]εφάνων ὑπὸ τοῦ κατασταθησομένου ἀγωνοθέτου [τ]οῦ μουσικοῦ ἀγῶνος· προνοῆσαι δὲ ἵνα καὶ τὸ ψήφισμα ἀνα[γρα]φῇ εἰ(ς) στήλην λιθίνην καὶ ἀνατεθῇ παρ' αὐτοῖς ἐν τῷ ἐπιφανεστάτῳ τόπῳ. Πρεσβευταὶ ἡρέθησαν Κλεομήδης Ἡγιασαγόρου, Ἀναξαγόρας Διονυσίου.

---

* The preamble must run somewhat as follows: —

[Ἔδοξεν τῇ βουλῇ· Ἐπειδὴ πεμφθέντος πρέσβεως πρὸς Ἀσσίους, ὄντας ἡμῶν φίλους καὶ εὔνους, περὶ αἰτήσεως δικαστῶν καὶ γραμματέως, Ἄσσιοι διὰ παντὸς πρόνοιαν ποιούμενοι περὶ δικαιοσύνης ἔπεμψαν δικαστὰς ἄνδρας καλοὺς καὶ ἀγαθοὺς καὶ πίστιν ἔχοντας καὶ κρίσιν ὑγιῆ προσφερομένους, Ἐχέλαον Ἀθηναγόρου, Λάτιμον Κλεομόργου, καὶ γραμματέα, Μέλαγχρον Μελάγχρου, οἳ καὶ παραγενόμενοι εἰς τὴν πόλιν ἡμῶν ἐδίκασαν τὰς δίκας ἴσως καὶ δικαίως μετὰ πάσης σωφροσύνης ἀκολούθως τοῖς τε νόμοις καὶ τοῖς ψηφίσμασιν· ὅπως οὖν καὶ ὁ]

"[*By decree of the Senate. Whereas after we had sent an ambassador to the Assians, our friends and well-wishers, to ask from them judges and a clerk, the Assians, who are ever full of forethought in matters of justice, have sent us judges, men of noble and good character, faithful men with sound judgments, to wit, Echelaos, son of Athenagoras, Latimos, son of Kleomorgos, and the clerk, Melanchros, son of Melanchros, who on their arrival in our city have judged the suits equitably and justly with all temperance according to the laws and the decrees: — now therefore in order that*] the people may appear [*duly grateful*] to noble and good men [*and that hereafter all who*] may come to us who are worthy of the people, may know that gratitude is in store for them, be it enacted by the senate and the people, that the people of the Assians be thanked [*for the good-will which*] they have for us, and be crowned with a golden crown at the . . . Dionysia, on the first day of the flute-players, inasmuch as they have sent us good and honorable judges, together with a clerk; and further that the judges who came to us, Echelaos, son of Athenagoras, and Latimos, son of Kleomorgos, be thanked and be crowned each with a golden crown, inasmuch as they gave judgment in some of the suits [*equitably*] and justly, and settled others amicably in the best possible manner; and that they be the first to have [*access to*] the senate and the people after the sacrifices, and that they be proxenoi of our city; further, that the clerk Melanchros, son of Melanchros, be crowned with a wreath of leaves, inasmuch as he has performed his duties with all zeal; and that the overseers of the musical contest be charged with the proclamation of the crowns. And in order that the Assians may be made aware of the noble character of these men and of the gratitude of our people, be it further enacted that ambassadors be appointed, who shall go to them, and, presenting themselves to their senate and people, shall deliver to them this decree, and shall make known to them the noble character of these men and the good-will which we have for their people, and shall invite the Assians to make proclamation of the crowns in their own city also, through the overseer who may be appointed to superintend the musical contest; and that the ambassadors further provide that this decree be cut upon a stone pillar, and set up in the most conspicuous place in their city. Kleomedes, son of Hegiasagoras, and Anaxagoras, son of Dionysios, were appointed ambassadors."

The custom of bringing judges in times of civil dissension from a distant but friendly city, to settle disputes and suits whose amicable adjustment by the home authorities had been despaired of, seems to have been not unknown even in comparatively early times. Herodotus (IV. 161; V. 28) speaks of mediators (*καταρτιστῆρες*) who were brought from Paros to Miletos, and from Mantineia to Kyrene, to act as umpires. Christ (*Sitzungsberichte der königlichen bayerischen Akademie der Wissenschaften*, 1866, p. 259 ff.) points out that, during the hegemony of Athens, the cities and islands which owed allegiance to the mistress of the seas had no right of jurisdiction in important suits and criminal processes, but had to lay them before Athenian courts for judgment. (See also M. H. E. Meier, *Die Privatschiedsrichter und die öffentlichen Diäteten Athens, so wie die Austrägalgerichte in den griechischen Staaten des Alterthums.*) Thus the force of habit created in these communities a feeling of dependence on others for the settlement of knotty cases, a feeling which outlasted the Athenian empire. From the testimony of inscriptions, it is clear that it was *for the most part* the communities belonging to the Athenian confederacy which were in the habit of calling upon other states for mediating Dikasts, although the practice was by no means confined exclusively to these communities. The judges were generally chosen from cities so distant that they might be presumed to know nothing of the suits upon which they would have to give judgment, so that they might approach their tasks with impartial and unprejudiced minds. Thus Antandros sends judges to the distant Peltai (*C. I. G.*, 3568 f.), Iasos in Karia sends to the island of Kalymna (*C. I. G.*, 2671), Assos sends to Stratonikeia in Karia (see below, No. VIII.). In regard to the time when this custom prevailed, it is noteworthy that the decrees in honor of Dikasts all belong to the period between the fall of the Athenian Confederacy and the subjugation of Greece by the Romans. The oldest decree of this kind is that of the Kalymnians (*C. I. G.*, 2671); the youngest is that of the Adramytteni (*C. I. G.*, 2349 *b*, Addenda), which falls in the year 69 or 70 B.C. (cf. Christ, *loc. cit.*).

The method of procedure on such occasions may be ascertained from Inscriptions VII. and VIII. An ambassador was sent by one state to another to request one or more judges and a clerk. After the lawsuits had been disposed of to the satisfaction of all concerned, the city which sent the judges and the judges themselves were honored by special decrees. At first, simple praise was bestowed upon the judge, the clerk, and the city sending them. Afterwards, besides crowns of gold, statues and portraits were given, along with the right of holding property, of being proxenos, etc. Later on, the city (Demos) ceases to participate in the honors, which are heaped on the judge and his clerk. The honors conferred on the clerk were the same in kind as those of the judge, but less in degree. The people of Adramyttion (*C. I. G.*, 2349 *b.*) and of Peltai (*C. I. G.*, 3568 *b.*) honor the judge with a crown and a statue, while the clerk must be content with a crown and portrait. The proclamation of the honors conferred was first made at some festival of the city whose suits had been adjudged, whereupon a special ambassador was sent to the other city to request a similar proclamation. The official decree conferring the honors was then engraved, and set up in a temple or some other prominent and frequented place in *both* cities. Frequently the person is named who is to have charge of the erection of the stele; sometimes, too, a certain maximum sum is fixed to defray all expenses connected with the proclamation of the honors, the crown, and the engraving, and erection of the stele or statues. Our inscription belongs probably to the second century before Christ. The honors decreed to the judges seem to be genuine, and the crowns of gold were probably actually given as decreed. But during the Roman period, honors absolutely disproportionate to the services rendered were often decreed by cities to individuals. Such honors were of course purely formal, a fact which did not prevent them from being sought after. Nay, decrees bestowing honors on private citizens were sometimes actually bought by ambitious persons, or by the kinsmen of a deceased man of wealth. For an example of this, see an inscription of Synnada, published by W. M. Ramsay in the *Bulletin de Correspondance Hellénique*, 1883, p. 302.

Assos was said to have been founded by a colony from Mytilene or Methymna; we should therefore expect to find the same names at Assos that are usual in the island of Lesbos.

Echelaos, one of the judges, bears the name of the son of Penthilos, who founded Mytilene (Plut. *Septem Sap. Conv.*, 20; *Paus.* III., 2, 1; *Strab.* XIII., p. 582; Aristot. *Pol.* V., 10, p. 1311, ed. Boruss. Acad.). The name (Ἐχέλαος, Ἐχέλας, Ἔχελος, Ἔχελλος) seems to have been popular in Lesbos (cf. Ahrens, *Dial.* II., p. 497, 499; Le Bas, *Inscriptions Grecques et Latines*, fasc. V., No. 119).

One of the tyrants of Mytilene bore the name of *Melanchros*, the clerk in our inscription (cf. *Strab.* XIII., p. 617; *Diog. Laert.* I., 4, 1; *Suid. s.v.* Πίττακος).

The name *Latimos* is found on a coin of Smyrna (*Mionnet* III., 203), and Pape conjectures that Λάτιμος must be restored in Mionnet VI., 314, and in *C. I. G.*, 2138, where Boeckh reads Ἄλτιμος.

Kleomorgos and *Hegiasagoras* are entirely new names. Ἡγιασαγόρας = Ἀγιασαγόρας (also Ἁγιασαγόρας); Ionic Ἡγίης, Ἡγίας, Ἧγις = Ἀγίας (Ἁγίας), Ἆγις. Κλεόμοργος = Κλεο + μόργος: μόργος, *purifier*, from μόργνυμι = ὀμόργνυμι.

No. VIII.

Marble stele found underneath the altar of the Byzantine apse which was built upon the foundations of the temple in antis at the western end of the agora. (*See plate, pp.* 18, 19.)

It contains a decree of the town of Stratonikeia, conveying the public thanks and a vote of a crown to Assos for sending a judge, of the same character as No. VII. The stone was not used as part of the pavement, but was thrown in with the debris to raise the level of the floor of the apse. The top is lost with the preamble of the decree, which is restored conjecturally below. The width varies from 0.405 to 0.415 metres; the greatest height is 0.53 m., the smallest is 0.47 m.

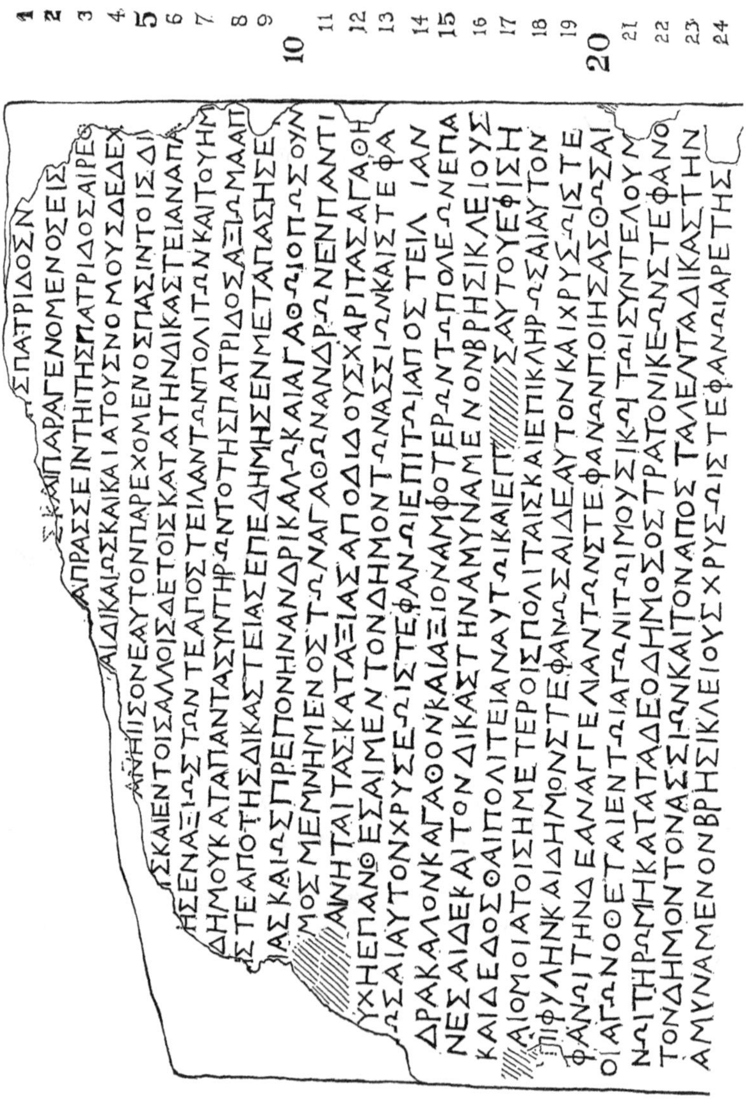

ΣΠΑΤΡΙΔΟΣΝ
ΣΚΑΙΠΑΡΑΓΕΝΟΜΕΝΟΣΕΙΣ
ΑΠΡΑΣΣΕΙΝΤΗΙΤΗΣΠΑΤΡΙΔΟΣΑΙΡΕΘ
ΑΙΔΙΚΑΙΩΣΚΑΙΚΑΙΑΤΟΥΣΝΟΜΟΥΣΔΕΔΕΧ
ΑΝΗΙΙΣΟΝΕΑΥΤΟΝΠΑΡΕΧΟΜΕΝΟΣΠΑΣΙΝΤΟΙΣΔΙ
ΣΚΑΙΕΝΤΟΙΣΑΛΛΟΙΣΔΕΤΟΙΣΚΑΤΑΤΗΝΔΙΚΑΣΤΕΙΑΝΑΠΑ
ΗΣΕΝΑΞΙΩΣΤΩΝΤΕΑΠΟΣΤΕΙΛΑΝΤΩΝΠΟΛΙΤΩΝΚΑΙΤΟΥΗΜ
ΔΗΜΟΥΚΑΤΑΠΑΝΤΑΣΥΝΤΗΡΩΝΤΟΤΗΣΠΑΤΡΙΔΟΣΑΞΙΩΜΑΑΠ
ΣΤΕΑΠΟΤΗΣΔΙΚΑΣΤΕΙΑΣΕΠΕΔΗΜΗΣΕΝΜΕΤΑΠΑΣΗΣΕ
ΑΣΚΑΙΩΣΠΡΕΠΟΝΗΝΑΝΔΡΙΚΑΛΩΚΑΙΑΓΑΘΩΙΟΠΩΣΟΥΝ
ΜΟΣΜΕΜΝΗΜΕΝΟΣΤΩΝΑΓΑΘΩΝΑΝΔΡΩΝΕΝΠΑΝΤΙ
ΑΝΗΤΑΙΤΑΣΚΑΤΑΞΙΑΣΑΠΟΔΙΔΟΥΣΧΑΡΙΤΑΣΑΓΑΘΗ
ΥΧΗΕΠΑΝΘΕΣΑΙΜΕΝΤΟΝΔΗΜΟΝΤΩΝΑΣΣΙΩΝΚΑΙΣΤΕΦΑ
ΩΣΑΙΑΥΤΟΝΧΡΥΣΕΩΙΣΤΕΦΑΝΩΙΕΠΙΤΩΙΑΠΟΣΤΕΙΛ ΙΑΝ
ΔΡΑΚΑΛΟΝΚΑΓΑΘΟΝΚΑΙΑΞΙΟΝΑΜΦΟΤΕΡΩΝΤΩΠΟΛΕΩΝΕΠΑ
ΝΕΣΑΙΔΕΚΑΙΤΟΝΔΙΚΑΣΤΗΝΑΜΥΝΑΜΕΝΟΝΒΡΗΣΙΚΛΕΙΟΥΣ
ΚΑΙΔΕΔΟΣΘΑΙΠΟΛΙΤΕΙΑΝΑΥΤΩΙΚΑΙΕΓΓ [illegible] ΣΑΥΤΟΥΕΦΙΣΗ
ΑΙΟΜΟΙΑΤΟΙΣΗΜΕΤΕΡΟΙΣΠΟΛΙΤΑΙΣΚΑΙΕΠΙΚΛΗΡΩΣΑΙΑΥΤΟΝ
ΠΙΦΥΛΗΝΚΑΙΔΗΜΟΝΣΤΕΦΑΝΩΣΑΙΔΕΑΥΤΟΝΚΑΙΧΡΥΣΩΙΣΤΕ
ΦΑΝΩΙΤΗΝΔΕΑΝΑΓΓΕΛΙΑΝΤΩΝΣΤΕΦΑΝΩΝΠΟΙΗΣΑΣΘΩΣΑΙ
ΟΙΑΓΩΝΟΘΕΤΑΙΕΝΤΩΙΑΓΩΝΙΤΩΙΜΟΥΣΙΚΩΙΤΩΙΣΥΝΤΕΛΟΥΜ
ΝΩΙΤΗΡΩΜΗΚΑΤΑΤΑΔΕΟΔΗΜΟΣΟΣΤΡΑΤΟΝΙΚΕΩΝΣΤΕΦΑΝΟ
ΤΟΝΔΗΜΟΝΤΟΝΑΣΣΙΩΝΚΑΙΤΟΝΑΠΟΣΤΑΛΕΝΤΑΔΙΚΑΣΤΗΝ
ΑΜΥΝΑΜΕΝΟΝΒΡΗΣΙΚΛΕΙΟΥΣΧΡΥΣΩΙΣΤΕΦΑΝΩΙΑΡΕΤΗΣ

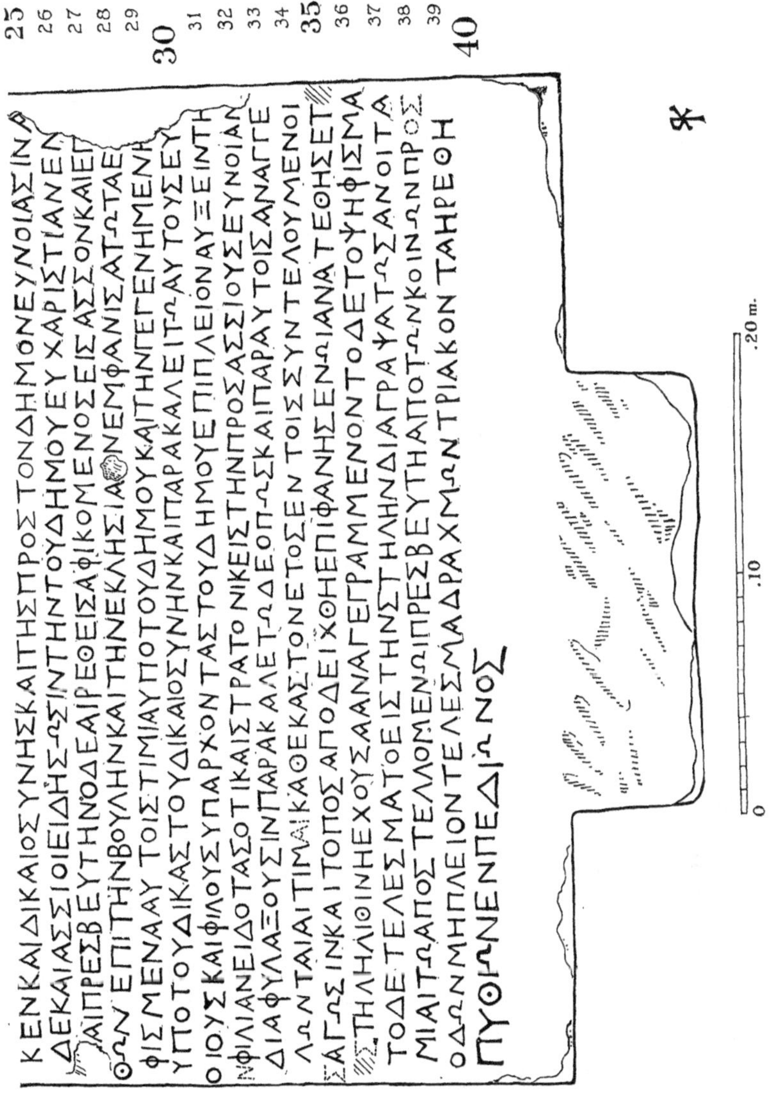
ΚΕΝΚΑΙΔΙΚΑΙΟΣΥΝΗΣΚΑΙΤΗΣΠΡΟΣΤΟΝΔΗΜΟΝΕΥΝΟΙΑΣΙΝΑ
ΔΕΚΑΙΑΣΣΙΟΙΕΙΔΗΣΩΣΙΝΤΗΝΤΟΥΔΗΜΟΥΕΥΧΑΡΙΣΤΙΑΝΕΝ
ΑΙΠΡΕΣΒΕΥΤΗΝΟΔΕΑΙΡΕΘΕΙΣΑΦΙΚΟΜΕΝΟΣΕΙΣΑΣΣΟΝΚΑΙΕΠ
ΘΩΝΕΠΙΤΗΝΒΟΥΛΗΝΚΑΙΤΗΝΕΚΛΗΣΙΑΝΕΜΦΑΝΙΣΑΤΩΤΑΕ
ΦΙΣΜΕΝΑΑΥΤΟΙΣΤΙΜΙΑΥΠΟΤΟΥΔΗΜΟΥΚΑΙΤΗΝΓΕΓΕΝΗΜΕΝΗ
ΥΠΟΤΟΥΔΙΚΑΣΤΟΥΔΙΚΑΙΟΣΥΝΗΝΚΑΙΠΑΡΑΚΑΛΕΙΤΩΑΥΤΟΥΣΕΥ
ΟΙΟΥΣΚΑΙΦΙΛΟΥΣΥΠΑΡΧΟΝΤΑΣΤΟΥΔΗΜΟΥΕΠΙΠΛΕΙΟΝΑΥΞΕΙΝΤΗ
ΝΦΙΛΙΑΝΕΙΔΟΤΑΣΟΤΙΚΑΙΣΤΡΑΤΟΝΙΚΕΙΣΤΗΝΠΡΟΣΑΣΣΙΟΥΣΕΥΝΟΙΑΝ
ΔΙΑΦΥΛΑΞΟΥΣΙΝΠΑΡΑΚΑΛΕΤΩΔΕΟΠΩΣΚΑΙΠΑΡΑΥΤΟΙΣΑΝΑΓΓΕ
ΛΩΝΤΑΙΑΙΤΙΜΑΙΚΑΘΕΚΑΣΤΟΝΕΤΟΣΕΝΤΟΙΣΣΥΝΤΕΛΟΥΜΕΝΟΙ
ΣΑΓΩΣΙΝΚΑΙΤΟΠΟΣΑΠΟΔΕΙΧΘΗΕΠΙΦΑΝΗΣΕΝΩΙΑΝΑΤΕΘΗΣΕΤ
ΣΤΗΛΗΛΙΘΙΝΗΕΧΟΥΣΑΑΝΑΓΕΓΡΑΜΜΕΝΟΝΤΟΔΕΤΟΨΗΦΙΣΜΑ
ΤΟΔΕΤΕΛΕΣΜΑΤΟΕΙΣΤΗΝΣΤΗΛΗΝΔΙΑΓΡΑΨΑΤΩΣΑΝΟΙΤΑ
ΜΙΑΙΤΩΑΠΟΣΤΕΛΛΟΜΕΝΩΙΠΡΕΣΒΕΥΤΗΑΠΟΤΩΝΚΟΙΝΩΝΠΡΟΣ
ΟΔΩΝΜΗΠΛΕΙΟΝΤΕΛΕΣΜΑΔΡΑΧΜΩΝΤΡΙΑΚΟΝΤΑΗΡΕΘΗ
ΠΥΘΙΩΝΕΝΠΕΔΙΩΝΟΣ
0
.10
.20 m.

[Ἔδοξεν τῇ βουλῇ· Ἐπειδὴ ὁ δῆμος ὁ Ἀσσίων ἔν τε τοῖς πρότερον χρόνοις εὔνους ὢν καὶ φίλος τῷ δήμῳ τῷ Στρατονικέων, καὶ νῦν, πρεσβεύοντος τοῦ δήμου τοῦ Στρατονικέων καὶ
ἀξιοῦντος διδόναι ἄνδρα δικαστήν, ὁ δῆμος ὁ Ἀσσίων, διὰ παντὸς πρό-]
[νοιαν ποιούμενος περὶ δικαιοσύνης, κατὰ τοὺς τῆ]ς πατρίδος ν[όμους]
[ἔπεμψεν Ἀμυναμενὸν Βρησικλείους ὃ]ς καὶ παραγενόμενος εἰς [Στρα-]
[τονίκειαν ἐσπούδασεν ἀκόλουθ]α πράσσειν τῇ τῆς πατρίδος αἱρέ-
[σει (?) · · · · · δικάζων ἴσως κ]αὶ δικαίως καὶ κατὰ τοὺς νόμους [ἃς διέλ-]
[υσεν δίκας, ἵνα φ]ανῇ ἴσον ἑαυτὸν παρεχόμενος πᾶσιν τοῖς δι-
[καζομένοι]ς, καὶ ἐν τοῖς ἄλλοις δὲ τοῖς κατὰ τὴν δικαστείαν ἅπα-
[σιν ἐπεδήμ]ησεν ἀξίως τῶν τε ἀποστειλάντων πολιτῶν καὶ τοῦ ἡμ-
[ετέρου] δήμου, κατὰ πάντα συντηρῶν τὸ τῆς πατρίδος ἀξίωμα, ἀπ-
[ολυθεί]ς τε ἀπὸ τῆς δικαστείας ἐπεδήμησεν μετὰ πάσης ε[ὐ-]
[νο]ίας καὶ ὡς πρέπον ἦν ἀνδρὶ καλῷ καὶ ἀγαθῷ· ὅπως οὖν
[καὶ ὁ δῆ]μος μεμνημένος τῶν ἀγαθῶν ἀνδρῶν ἐν παντὶ
[καιρῷ φ]αίνηται τὰς καταξίας ἀποδιδοὺς χάριτας· Ἀγαθῇ
[τ]ύχῃ· ἐπα(ιν)έσαι μὲν τὸν δῆμον τ(ὸ)ν Ἀσσίων καὶ στεφα-
[ν]ῶσαι αὐτὸν χρυσέῳ στεφάνῳ ἐπὶ τῷ ἀποστεῖλ[α]ι ἄνδρα καλὸν κἀγαθὸν καὶ ἄξιον ἀμφοτέρων τῶ(ν) πόλεων· ἐπα-
[ι]νέσαι δὲ καὶ τὸν δικαστὴν Ἀμυναμενὸν Βρησικλείους
καὶ δεδόσθαι πολιτείαν αὐτῷ καὶ ἐγγ[όνοι]ς αὐτοῦ ἐ[φ'] ἴσῃ
[κ]αὶ ὁμοίᾳ τοῖς ἡμετέροις πολίταις καὶ ἐπικληρῶσαι αὐτὸν
[ἐ]πὶ φυλὴν καὶ δῆμον, στεφανῶσαι δὲ αὐτὸν καὶ χρυσῷ στε-
φάνῳ· τὴν δὲ ἀναγγελίαν τῶν στεφάνων ποιησάσθωσαν
οἱ ἀγωνοθέται ἐν τῷ ἀγῶνι τῷ μουσικῷ τῷ συντελουμέ-
νῳ τῇ Ῥώμῃ κατὰ τάδε. ὁ δῆμος ὁ Στρατονικέων στεφανο[ῖ]
τὸν δῆμον τὸν Ἀσσίων καὶ τὸν ἀποσταλέντα δικαστὴν
Ἀμυναμενὸν Βρησικλείους χρυσῷ στεφάνῳ ἀρετῆς [ἕνε-]
κεν καὶ δικαιοσύνης καὶ τῆς πρὸς τὸν δῆμον εὐνοίας. ἵνα
δὲ καὶ Ἄσσιοι εἰδήσωσιν τὴν τοῦ δήμου εὐχαριστίαν, ἑλ[έσ-]
[θ]αι πρεσβευτήν· ὁ δὲ αἱρεθεὶς ἀφικόμενος εἰς Ἄσσον καὶ ἐπ[ελ-]
θὼν ἐπὶ τὴν βουλὴν καὶ τὴν ἐκ(κ)λησίαν ἐμφανισάτω τὰ ἐ[ψη-]
φισμένα αὐτοῖς τίμια ὑπὸ τοῦ δήμου καὶ τὴν γεγενημένη[ν]
ὑπὸ τοῦ δικαστοῦ δικαιοσύνην, καὶ παρακαλείτω αὐτοὺς εὐνοίους καὶ φίλους ὑπάρχοντας τοῦ δήμου ἐπὶ πλεῖον αὔξειν τ[ὴ-]
[ν] φιλίαν, εἰδότας ὅτι καὶ Στρατονικεῖς τὴν πρὸς Ἀσσίους εὔνοια[ν]

διαφυλάξουσιν. παρακαλε(ί)τω δὲ ὅπως καὶ παρ' αὐτοῖς ἀναγγέλωνται αἱ τιμαὶ καθ' ἕκαστον ἔτος ἐν τοῖς συντελουμένοι[ς] ἀγῶσιν, καὶ τόπος ἀποδειχθῇ ἐπιφανὴς ἐν ᾧ ἀνατεθήσετ[αι] [σ]τήλη λιθίνη ἔχουσα ἀναγεγραμμένον τόδε τὸ ψήφισμα. τὸ δὲ τέλεσμα τὸ εἰς τὴν στήλην διαγραψάτωσαν οἱ ταμίαι τῷ ἀποστελλομένῳ πρεσβευτῇ ἀπὸ τῶν κοινῶν πρ[οσ]όδων μὴ πλεῖον τέλεσμα δραχμῶν τριάκοντα. ᾑρέθη Πυθίων Ἐνπεδίωνος.

["*By decree of the Senate. Seeing that the people of Assos have been well disposed and friendly to the people of Stratonikeia, both in former times and now, when the people of Stratonikeia had sent an embassy to request them to grant a judge, the people of Assos, being ever zealous in the cause of justice, according to the laws*] of their country [*have sent Amynamenos, son of Bresikles,*] who, upon his arrival in [*Stratonikeia, has striven*] to justify by his acts [*the choice*] of his country, [*judging the suits which he settled equitably,*] justly, and according to the laws, [*in order that*] he might appear just to all those [*for whom he judged*]. And in all other matters connected with his mission he showed himself during his stay with us worthy of the citizens who sent him and of our people as well, inasmuch as he preserved the dignity of the country in all respects. And after the duties of his mission had been discharged, he sojourned among us with all good-will and as was becoming to an honorable and good man. Now therefore, in order that the people may appear to be at all times mindful of good men by returning becoming thanks, be it resolved as follows, with the blessing of Fortune: —

That the people of Assos receive our thanks and be crowned with a golden crown for having sent an honorable and good man, one worthy of both the cities. And that the judge Amynamenos, son of Bresikles, be thanked, and that the freedom of the city be given to him and his descendants, on fair and equal terms with our own citizens, and that he be assigned to tribe and deme, and also be crowned with a golden crown. And let the directors of the contest make proclamation of the crowns, in the musical contest which is celebrated in honor of Rome, in the following words: 'The people of Stratonikeia crown the people of Assos and Amynamenos, son of

Bresikles, the judge sent to us, with a golden crown, on account of their excellence, justice, and good-will towards our people.'

"And in order that the Assians also may know the gratitude of our people, let an ambassador be chosen, and let the ambassador-elect, immediately upon his arrival at Assos, present himself to the senate and the assembly of the people, and make known the honors herein voted to them, as well as the justice which was meted out by their judge, and let him request them, as they are already well-wishers and friends of our people, to increase their friendship, knowing that the people of Stratonikeia will ever preserve their good-will for the Assians. Let him request that the honors be proclaimed at Assos also every year at the celebration of the games, and that a prominent place be set apart in which a stone stele having this decree engraved upon it may be set up. Let the treasurers pay to the ambassador who is sent the sum expended upon the stele, which must not exceed thirty drachmas, from the public revenues. Pythion, son of Empedion, was chosen ambassador."

Line 13. ΕΠΑΝΘΕΣΑΙ is the stonecutter's mistake for ΕΠΑΙΝΕΣΑΙ.

Line 14. The uncontracted form of *χρύσεος* occurs not infrequently in Ionic inscriptions, *e.g.*, in an inscription of Stratonikeia published in the *Bulletin de Corr. Hell.*, 1881, p. 183.

Line 16. Βρησικλείους. The ending -ειοὺς of the genitive occurs rather frequently as the termination for nouns in -κλης all along the western seaboard of Asia Minor. So at Miletos (*C. I. G.* 2856–57, Πασικλείους), at Teos (*C. I. G.* 3089, Ἀγαθοκλείους; 3114, Σωσικλείους), at Erythrai (Christ in *Sitzungsberichte der Königl. bayer. Akademie*, 1866, p. 247, Ἰατροκλείους and Ἰατροκλήους), at Smyrna (*C. I. G.* 3141, Διονυσοκλείους, Μενεκλείους, Ἀθηνοκλείους), and in the interior at Aphrodisias (*C. I. G.* 2747, 2776, Ἀριστοκλείους). Both forms -ειους and -ηους may be explained from -κλεϝους. To compensate for the digamma the ε was either expanded to ει or lengthened to η.

Lines 30–31. The form εὐνοίους for εὔνους is probably a mistake of the stonecutter, who no doubt thought at first that he had to carve some form of εὔνοια.

Line 32. Stratonikeia was founded on the site of the ancient Idrias by Antiochos Soter (280 to 261 B.C.) in honor of his wife Stratonike; consequently our inscription must date after that event. Both the character of the letters and other considerations that will appear below make it clear that the inscription dates before the year 84 B.C., the year of the pacification of the Eastern provinces by the Romans.

The name Βρησικλῆς (cf. Βρῆσος: Conze, *Reise auf der Insel Lesbos*, plate XVII. 1) is the Lesbian and Assian turn given to Διονυσικλῆς.* The Lesbian promontory Βρῆσσα, a name still to be recognized in the modern Βρησσιά, was the seat of the cult of Dionysos, who took from the name of the place the epithet Βρησεύς.† A variation of the epithet must be recognized in Βρησαγενής, which occurs in an inscription of Βρησσιά published in the *Bulletin de Corr. Hell.*, 1880, pp. 445, 446 (Διονύσῳ Βρησαγενεῖ).‡ From Lesbos the cult of Διόνυσος Βρησεύς passed over to Smyrna, as is known from several inscriptions of that city (*C. I. G.* 3160, 3161, 3176, 3190). It was popular also at Mytilene (see *Bull. de Corr. Hell.*, 1880, p. 441) and Methymna (*Bull. de Corr. Hell.*, 1883, p. 40).

It was quite natural that Dionysos Breseus should establish himself at Assos, for the local cults of the mother country were usually continued in the colony. There is no direct evidence to prove the existence of this cult at Assos, but certainly the name Βρησικλῆς of our inscription proves that Διόνυσος Βρησεύς was not unknown there.

---

* This form occurs occasionally in inscriptions, and once in Pausanias (6. 17. 1). Cf. also *Hermes*, 1870, p. 203. Διονυσιοκλῆς occurs in Athenaios (3. 96*d*, 116*d*, 118*d*) and in an inscription of Karystos (*C. I. G.* 2152*b*). The more correct form, Διονυσοκλῆς, although found in inscriptions and in Strabo (14. 649), does not seem to have been more in use than the less correct forms.

† Meister, *Griechische Dialekte*, p. 107: "Βρῆσσα ist aus Ϝρηκια von ῥήγνυμι (vgl. Ῥήγιον) entstanden, wie der Stamm Ϝρηκ- auch der boeotische Name Βρεικίδας (für Ϝρηκίδας) zeigt. Die Schreibungen mit einfachem σ, Βρήση, Βρησεύς, Βρισαῖος u. s. w., erklären sich durch später eingetretene Vereinfachung der Gemination. Auf diesen Dionysosbeinamen geht auch der lesbische Kurzname Βρῆσος Βρήσω auf der Inschrift 34, 2, Zurück." See Conze, *Reise auf d. Ins. Lesbos*, plate XVII. 1. See also Ahrens *de dial. graec.*, i. p. 34. For the explanations of the epithet Βρησεύς by the ancient writers, see Columella, xii. 39. 2; Macrobius, *Sat.* i. 18; Persius, *Sat.* i. 76.

‡ Βρησαγενής is regularly formed, as the writer in the *Bulletin* points out, and may be compared with Κρηταγενής (Κρητογενής), an epithet of Zeus (cf. Steph. Byz. s.v. Γάζα; Eckhel. *Doct. Num.* 2. 301 *d*; *C. I. G.* 2554), and with Μελησιγενής, an epithet of Homer (cf. Pseud. Plut. *Vit. Hom.* I. 2; Luc. *Demosth. enc.* 9; Procl. *Chrest.* 1; *Suid.* s.v. Ὅμηρος). The epithet Βρησεύς was spelled in different ways, through the ignorance or carelessness of stonecutters. Thus

The fact that the cult of personified Rome is mentioned (in line 22) gives a hint, but only a hint, in regard to the date of the inscription, for unfortunately the date of the introduction of the worship of Dea Roma at Stratonikeia can never be known except by inference. But certainly its early introduction was made possible by the well-known adulation and servility of the Greeks.

Rhodes obtained a commercial treaty from Rome in the year 306–7 B.C., at a time when Carthage was hard pressed by the daring invasion of Africa by Agathokles, tyrant of Syracuse.* Both Pergamon and Rhodes early espoused the cause of Rome against Philip of Macedonia, and Dea Roma was certainly worshipped at both places; but there is no evidence to show that the cultus was introduced at a specially early time.

With Smyrna and Alabanda the case is different, for positive proof exists of the early introduction of the cult at these places. In the year 26 A.D. the people of Smyrna boast of the fact that they were the first to erect a temple in honor of Dea Roma, and state that this temple was built during the consulship of M. Porcius Cato (*i.e.* 195 B.C.). At this time Rome was great, it is true, but still it was before she had reached the acme of her power, nay, even before the destruction of Carthage and the subjugation of the kings who ruled in Asia.† This was the year after Greece had been proclaimed free by Flamininus at the celebration of the Isthmian games. This fact makes plausible the assumption that the temple was erected to Dea Roma in recognition of that event, as well as to take time by the forelock by a marked exhibition of friendliness to all-conquering

---

alongside of Βρησεύς (*C. I. G.* 3160, 3161) we find Βρεισεύς (*C. I. G.* 3176, 3190), Βρησσαῖος (Hesych. s.v.), Βρησαῖος (Etym. Mag.), Βρισαῖος (Steph. Byz. and Etym. Mag.); cf. also *C. I. G.* 2042.

* Polyb. xxx. 5, 6: *οὕτως γὰρ ἦν πραγματικὸν τὸ πολίτευμα τῶν Ῥοδίων ὡς σχεδὸν ἔτη τετταράκοντα πρὸς τοῖς ἑκατὸν κεκοινωνηκὼς ὁ δῆμος Ῥωμαίοις τῶν ἐπιφανεστάτων καὶ καλλίστων ἔργων οὐκ ἐπεποίητο πρὸς αὐτοὺς συμμαχίαν.* Droysen, *Diadochen*, Drittes Buch, p. 154, says in regard to this: "Polybios handelt von diesen Dingen bei Gelegenheit der zweiten rhodischen Gesandschaft des Jahres 587 (v. Chr. 167), die *θερείας ἀρχομένης* nach Rom kam." Accordingly, 167 + 140 = 307.

† Tac. *Ann.* 4, 56 *seq.*: [Smyrnaeos] primos templum urbis Romae statuisse, M. Porcio consule, magnis quidem iam populi Romani rebus, nondum tamen ad summum elatis, stante adhuc Punica urbe et validis per Asiam regibus.

Rome.* In the year 170 B.C. Alabanda, which lies just north of Stratonikeia, erected a temple, and instituted yearly games (Ῥώμαια) in honor of Dea Roma.† This was no doubt done in commemoration of the defeat and humiliation of Antiochos III., the Great, and of the success of the Roman arms against Perseus of Macedonia.

It is very probable that the cultus of Dea Roma was introduced at Stratonikeia about the same time as at the neighboring Alabanda, so that we may safely assign the year 150 B.C. as an approximate date for this inscription, a date which is made almost certain by the character of the letters.

Both *Amynamenos* and *Bresikles* are new names. Amynamenos belonged to the Larichos family (see below, Nos. xlviii–liii). Compare Ἀμύνανδρος, Ἀμυνόμαχος; see Fick, *Personennamen*, p. 9. For Bresikles see Fick, p. 20.

---

* Smyrna was proud of this temple : policy perhaps demanded it. Certainly at the time this boast was made (26 A.D.) the coins of Smyrna had a temple on the obverse with the legend Τιβέριος Σεβαστός, and on the reverse Σεβαστή and Σύνκλητος (see Mionnet, iii. 219, vi. 330, and Eckhel *Doct. Num.* ii. 547). Coins of Smyrna bearing the legend *templum Romae et Augusti* are quite common; the legend remains the same, but in the temple may be seen the image of the emperor during whose reign the coin was struck (Preller, *Römische Mythologie*, 776, note 2).

† Liv. 43. 6: Alabandenses templum Urbis Romae se fecisse commemoraverunt ludosque anniversarios ei divae instituisse.

No. IX.

Carian wreaths on a Dikast Stele, surmounted by pediment; found below the Bouleuterion.

Λάνθην Προδίκου δικάσαντα.

Μυλασεῖς. Ἀλαβανδεῖς.

Λάνθης is probably Λα + ανθης: see Fick, *Personennamen*, pp. 50, 154.

No. X.

Dikast Stele found in the Agora. The inscription is broken away.

Below the moulding of the top is the word ΑΙΓΑΕΩΝ, and below it is a wreath encircling a goat's head. This is equivalent to the coat of arms of the city of Aigaiai, being a play on the word *αἶξ*. Assos seems to have sent a judge to Aigaiai, which city bestowed upon him the honors customary in such cases.

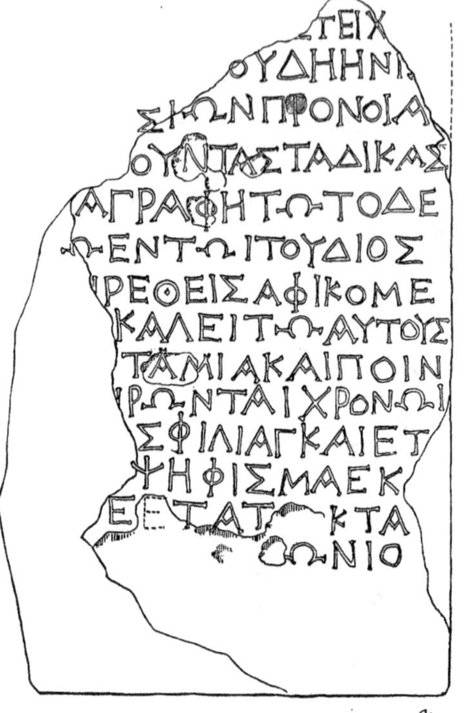

No. XI.

Fragment of gray marble, found in the Bouleuterion; the right edge is nearly perfect. Lines have been ruled for the letters, and are still visible. Greatest height, 0.21 *m.; greatest width,* 0.115 *m.*

*

-τειχ
ουδη ηνι
[τὸν δῆμον τὸν Ἀσ]σίων π[ρ]όνοια[ν]
[ποιούμενον] · · · · · ου[ν]τας τὰ δικασ-
[τήρια · · · · · · ἀν]αγρα[φ]ήτω τόδε
[τὸ ψήφισμα ἐν Ἄσσ]ῳ ἐν τῷ τοῦ Διὸς
[ἱερῷ· ὁ δὲ αἱ]ρεθεὶς ἀφικόμε-
[νος εἰς Ἄσσον παρα]καλείτω αὐτοὺς
[εἰς φιλίαν · · · · · τ[αμ]ια καὶ ποιν-
· · · · · · · [ᾧ ἂν χ]ρῶνται χρόνῳ
· · · · · · · [εἰ]ς φιλίαγ καὶ ἑτ-
[αιρείαν · · · · τὸ]ψήφισμα ἐκ
· · · · · · · · · ε τατ · · κτα
· · · · · · · · · [αἰ]ώνιο[ν]

No. XII.

Found in Byzantine rooms south of the subterranean passage below the Bouleuterion. The slab has been broken through the centre of the inscription, the right side only being preserved. Length, 0.53 *m.; width,* 0.20 *m.*

ΞΟΔ
ΙΙΓΑΡΙΣΤΩΒΑΚΧΩ
ΑΑΙΑΜΠΕΛΟΙΑΙΕΝΤΩΡΟΔΙ
ΞΙΩΙΙΑΞΙΑΙΚΑΙΙΓΑΙΛΙΣΕΑΡΙΑΔ
ΗΚΑΙΠΙΟΛΝΟΝ · Α · ΜΑΤΙΣΜΟΝ
ΑΞΙΑΞ ΤΗΡΩΝΟΓΔΟΗΚΟΝΤΑ
ΤΑΣΠΡΟΣΟΔ ΑΣ
ΛΟΙΣΙΤΑΔΥΟΜΕΡΗΤΩΠΑΤΙ
ΑΣΟΙΣΙΔΕΚΑΙΤΟΕΞΡΤΩΝΠΑ
ΚΑΤΑΝΜΑΤΕΡΑΜΕΓΙΣΤΩ

ἀρίστω Βάκχω
αἱ ἄμπελοι αἱ[ἐ]ν τῷ Ῥοδι
Νάξιαι καὶ Ἀριαδ
καὶ πι[θα]νὸν
ἄξια [στα]τήρων ὀγδοήκοντα
τὰς προσόδ[ους] ἃς
τὰ δύο μέρη
. . . .
τὰν ματέρα Μεγιστῷ

From the character of the letters, the inscription cannot be later than 150 B.C. The beginning is gone, and the letters, which are small, are often hopelessly worn. This is to be regretted, because, judging from the few words which can be made out, the inscription seems to have been an important document.

Ῥοδι-, in line 2, probably has nothing to do with the little river Rhodios (see *Mittheilungen des Deutschen Archaeologischen Instituts in Athen*, 1881, p. 217 ff.), but must be referred to the island of Rhodes.

No. XIII.

Found walled into the very late diagonal masonry at the north-east corner of the Bouleuterion. The inscribed side was outwards, but in an enclosed position, unfavorable to being read.

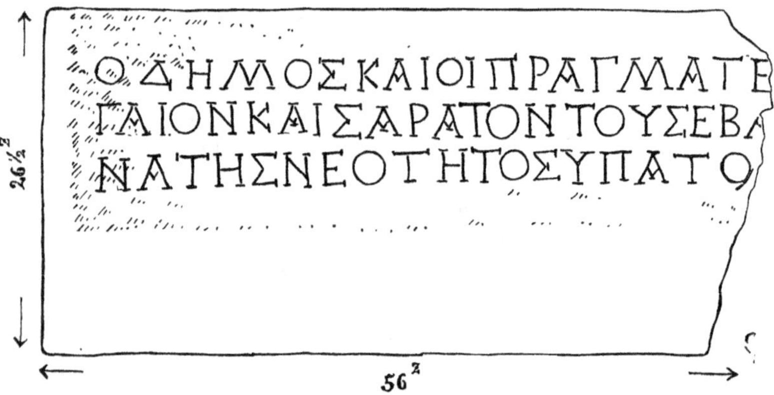

Ὁ δῆμος καὶ οἱ πραγματε[υόμενοι παρ' ἡμῖν Ῥωμαῖοι]
Γαῖον Καίσαρα τὸν τοῦ Σεβα[στοῦ υἱὸν καὶ πάτρω-]
να τῆς νεότητος, ὕπατο[ν τῆς Ἀσίας, ἀνέθηκαν]

"The people and the Roman merchants established among us have erected a statue of Caius Caesar, son of Augustus, *princeps iuventutis*, and consul (proconsul) of Asia."

The stone is remarkable as being a *palimpsest*, so to speak; there has been a hasty erasure of earlier letters, leaving a rough surface.

Dr. Schliemann found a similar inscription at Ilium (*Ilios*, p. 633).

Caius Caesar and his brother Lucius, sons of M. Vipsanius Agrippa, and Julia, daughter of Augustus, were both adopted by Augustus. Caius was appointed *princeps iuventutis* and consul in the year 5 B.C., but this latter appointment was not to take effect for five years.

Accordingly he was consul in the year 1 A.D., and his name appears in the fasti for that year. As consul he went in the year 1 A.D. to Asia, accompanied by his tutor, M. Lollius (grandfather of Lollia Paullina), and spent the year 2 A.D. in preparations for war against Phraates IV., king of Parthia. He doubtless touched at Assos; but whether this is so or not, our inscription certainly dates from the year 2 A.D.

Roman merchants were settled in various places in Greece and Asia. Such resident merchants are mentioned in inscriptions of the following places: at Prymnessos (*Mittheilungen des Deutschen Archaeologischen Instituts in Athen*, 1882, p. 127); at Akmonia (*C. I. G.*, 3874); at Apameia (Le Bas et Waddington, *Inscriptions de l'Asie Mineure*, 746); at Erythrai (*Bulletin de Correspondance Hellènique*, 1880, p. 161); at Delos (*Bull. de Corr. Hell.*, 1879, p. 148; *C. I. G.*, 2285 b, 2286–2288; *Bull. de Corr. Hell.*, 1877, p. 284, etc.); at Kibyra (*Bull. de Corr. Hell.*, 1878, p. 598, No. 5, and p. 599, No. 6); at Argos (*C. I. L.*, 595, 596; Foucart, *Inscriptions du Peloponnèse*, 123, 124, 124 a; *C. I. G.*, 1137); at Mantineia (*Bulletino dell' Instituto di Corrispondenza Archeologica*, 1854, p. 35); at Edessa (Foucart, *Inscriptions, etc.*, 1345); at Berrhoea (Foucart, *Inscriptions, etc.*, 1330 a); at Tralleis (*Bull. de Corr. Hell.*, 1881, p. 347; *C. I. G.*, 2927, 2930); at Salamis in Cyprus (Le Bas et Waddington, *Asie Mineure*, 2754); at Mytilene (*Bull. de Corr. Hell.*, 1880, p. 433; *C. I. L.*, III. 450; *Orelli-Henzen*, 4111); at Sestos (*Bull. de Corr. Hell.*, 1880, p. 516); at Kyzikos (*Mittheilungen, etc.*, 1881, p. 41, —cf. also *Revue Arch.*, XXXII., p. 268; *C. I. G.*, 3689 = *C. I. L.*, III. 372; *Hamilton*, 315 = *C. I. L.*, 373); at Pergamon (*Die Ergebnisse der Ausgrabungen zu Pergamon*, 1880–1881, p. 50). To this list must now be added Assos, and probably Ilium (*C. I. G.*, 3598 b). As a parallel to the Roman πραγματευόμενοι in Greece and Asia Minor, may be cited the merchants of Egypt and Kition in Cyprus, who were resident at the Peiraieus (see *Hermes*, 1871, p. 352, where Köhler says: *Die Kitier und Aegypter treten in der Inschrift als geschlossene Körperschaften auf, ähnlich wie in späteren Inschriften die Italici oder cives Romani qui Argeis, qui Mityleneis negotiantur*; see above). See *Bull. de Corr. Hell.*, 1884 (*Delos*).

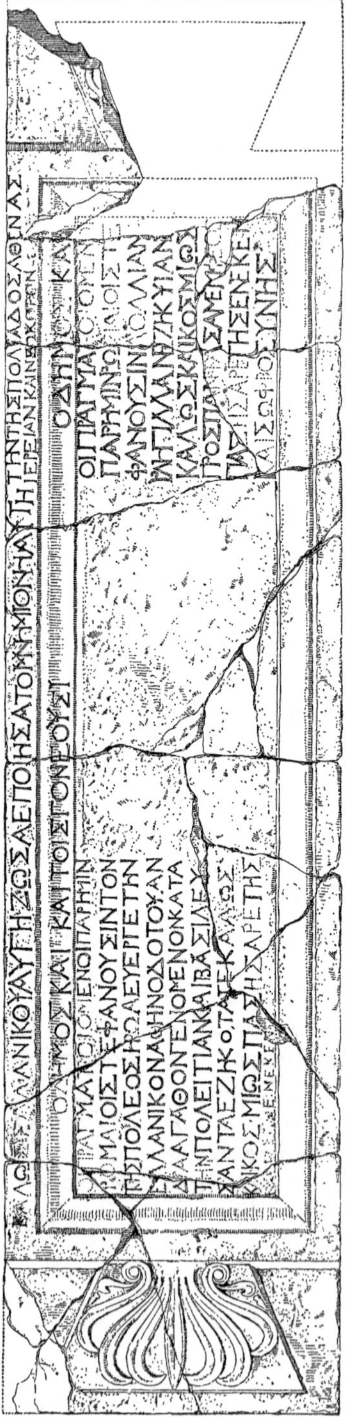

No. XIV.

Marble slab from above a tomb in the western Street of Tombs.

I.

Ὁ δῆμος καὶ οἱ πραγματευόμενοι παρ' ἡμῖν Ῥομαῖοι στεφανοῦσιν τὸν τῆς πόλεος ἥρωα εὐεργέτην, Ἑλλάνικον Ἀθηνοδότου, ἄνδρα ἀγαθὸν γενόμενον κατὰ τὴν πολιτείαν καὶ βασιλεύσαντα ἐζηκότα τε καλῶς καὶ κοσμίως, πάσης ἀρετῆς ἕνεκεν.

"The people and the Roman merchants established among us crown, in recognition of his perfect virtue, the hero of the city, the benefactor Hellanikos, son of Athenodotos, who has shown his excellence in the government of the state and as one of our hereditary kings, and who has lived honorably and discreetly."

II.

Ὁ δῆμος καὶ οἱ πραγματευόμενοι παρ' ἡμῖν Ῥωμαῖοι στ[ε]φανοῦσιν [Λ]ολλίαν ['Α]ρλήγιλλαν ἐζηκυῖαν καλῶς καὶ κοσμίως πρὸς πά[ντ]ας ἀμέμ[πτως] πάσ[ης ἀρε]τῆς ἕνεκεν κ[αὶ σωφρο]σύνης.

"The people and the Roman merchants established among us crown, in recognition of her perfect virtue and her prudence, Lollia Arlegilla, who has lived honorably, discreetly, and blamelessly before all men."

III. (*continuation of* II.).

τὴν τῆς Πολ[ι]άδος 'Αθενᾶς ἱέρειαν καὶ νεωκόρον.

"The priestess of Athena Polias, and keeper of her temple."

IV.

[Ἑλ]λῶ[πις] Ἑλλανίκου αὐ(τ)ὴ ζῶσα ἐποίησα τὸ μνημῖον ἡαυτῇ καὶ τοῖς γονεοῦσι.

"I, Hellopis, daughter of Hellanikos, have erected this memorial to myself and my parents during my lifetime."

These inscriptions are interesting in many respects. Originally the slab contained simply two honorary inscriptions of an official character, side by side, surrounded by an elaborate moulding. I. occupies the left of the panel; II. the right. The persons honored in them were man and wife (see the note to the following inscription). Hellanikos belonged to the ancient royal family of Assos. In the next inscription (No. XV.) we learn that this family officiated as priests of Augustus and Zeus Homonoos, whereas in this inscription Lollia Arlegilla is priestess and neokoros of Athene Polias alone. Now this seems to indicate that Hellanikos and Lollia Arlegilla lived when Rome was still a republic, before the "Imperial Cultus" was instituted. Had the Imperial Cultus died out or been ignored after it had once been introduced at Assos, such neglect would have brought down condign punishment on the Assians for *incuria caerimoniarum Augusti* (see Marquardt's *Cyzicus,* p. 82, and No. XV. below). III. is engraved on the moulding immediately above II., to which it is simply an explanatory addition.

But if I., II., and III. are thrown back to a pre-Augustan time, how is IV. to be accounted for, seeing that the style of the inscription is such that it probably must be separated from the rest by a long period ?

The facts of the case may have been the following. The Hellopis of IV. lived at a time when Greek civilization at Assos had fallen from its high estate. She claims to be the daughter of Hellanikos : but he can hardly have been the Hellanikos of I. Hellopis may have found the ancient slab containing the above inscriptions neglected ; the name of the man honored in one of them happened, luckily enough, to be Hellanikos, and the thought may have occurred to her to make use of the slab in the tomb which she erected for herself and her parents during her lifetime. Accordingly she had her inscription carved on the moulding above I. It is done in a rough, careless way, and in a miserable language, well in keeping with the spirit of the times in which she lived.

Of her name only two letters are certain, ΛΩ, while ΛΛΩ is highly probable. The name may therefore be ΥΛΛΩΝΙΣ, or ΥΛΛΩΠΙΣ, or ΕΛΛΩΝΙΣ, or ΕΛΛΩΠΙΣ. The preference must be given to Π over Ν, and ΕΛΛΩΠΙΣ is more probable than ΥΛΛΩΠΙΣ. After ΕΛΛΑΝΙΚΟΥ the stone certainly reads ΑΥΓΗ, but this is a mistake for ΑΥΤΗ. After ΜΝΗΜΙΟΝ the stone reads ΗΑΥΤΗ, which stands for ΕΑΥΤΗ ; the same blunder is to be found in *Mittheilungen des Deutschen Archaeologischen Instituts in Athen*, 1881, p. 124 ; and αἱαυτῇ occurs in an inscription of Apameia (*Bulletin de Correspondance Hellénique*, 1883, p. 307).

No. XV.

Fragments of an inscription previously published, found in the Gymnasium.

The inscription, so far as it is now recovered, reads: —

ΟΙΕΡΕΥΣΤΟΥΣΕΒΑΣΤΟΥΘ
ΕΟΥΚΑΙΣΑΡΟΣΟΔΕΑΥ·
ΟΣΚΑΙΠΑΤΡΙΟΣΒΑΣΙΛΕΥ
ΣΚΑΙΙΕΡΕΥΣΤΟΥΔΙΟΣΤ
ΟΥΟΜΟΝΩΟΥΚΑΙΓΥΜ
ΝΑΣΙΑΡΧΟΣ · ΚΟΙΝΤΟΣΛΟ
ΛΛΙΟΣΦΙΛΕΤΑΙΡΟΣΤΗΝ
ΣΤΟΑΝΑΝΕΘΗΚΕΝΘΕΩΙΚ
ΑΙΣΑΡΙΣΕΒΑΣΤΩΙΚΑΙΤΩΙΔΗ
ΜΩΙ · · · · · · · ΚΑ
ΙΤΟΥΣ · · · · · · · ·
ΕΧΟΜΕΝΟΥΣ

Ὁ ἱερεὺς τοῦ Σεβαστοῦ Θ-
εοῦ Καίσαρος, ὁ δὲ αὐ[τ-]
ὸς καὶ πάτριος βασιλεὺ-

ς καὶ ἱερεὺς τοῦ Διὸς τ-
οῦ Ὁμονώ(ι)ου, καὶ γυμ-
νασίαρχος, Κοΐντος Λό-
λλιος Φιλέταιρος τὴν
στοὰν ἀνέθηκεν θεῷ Κ-
αίσαρι Σεβαστῷ καὶ τῷ δή-
μῳ . . . . κα-
ὶ τοὺς . . . .
ἐχομένους . . . . . .

"The priest of the God Caesar Augustus, himself likewise hereditary king, priest of Zeus Homonoos, and gymnasiarch, Quintus Lollius Philetairos, has dedicated the Stoa to the God Caesar Augustus and the people." . . . .

This inscription, as published by Boeckh (*C. I. G.*, 3569) from the early travellers (Hunt, Walpole, Richter, Leake, Raczynski, and Fellows), begins with what is really the ninth line, and reads as follows: —

ΑΙΣΑΡΙΣΕΒΑΣΤΩΙΚΑΙΤΩΙΔ
ΟΙΕΡΕΥΣΤΟΥΣΕΒΑΣΤΟΥΘ
ΕΟΥΚΑΙΣΑΡΟΣΟΔΕΑΥ
ΟΣΚΑΙΠΑΤΡΙΟΣΒΑΣΙΛΕΥ
Σ · ΚΑΙΙΕΡΕΥΣΤΟΥΔΙΟΣΤ
ΟΥΟΜΟΝΩΟΥΚΑΙΓΥΜ
ΝΑΣΙΑΡΧΟΣοΚΟΙΝΤΟΣΔΟ

Waddington (*Voyage Arch.*, No. 1033) rightly puts Boeckh's first line in the seventh place, and adds the fragments of three other lines found by Duthoit in 1865, as follows: —

ΟΙΕΡΕΥΣΤΟΥΣΕΒΑΣΤΟΥΘ
ΕΟΥΚΑΙΣΑΡΟΣΟΔΕΑΥ
ΟΣΚΑΙΠΑΤΡΙΟΣΒΑΣΙΛΕΥ

ΣΚΑΙΙΕΡΕΥΣΤΟΥΔΙΟΣΤ
ΟΥΟΜΟΝΩΟΥΚΑΙΓΥΜ
ΝΑΣΙΑΡΧΟΣ · ΚΟΙΝΤΟΣΛΟ
ΑΙΣΑΡΙΣΕΒΑΣΤΩΚΑΙΤΩΙΔΗ
ΜΩΙ *espace vide* ΚΑ
ΙΤΟΥΣ *espace vide*
ΕΧΟΜΕΝΟΥΣ

The two lines now unearthed fill the gap between the sixth and seventh lines. These are of great importance in restoring the inscription, showing that Quintus Lollius Philetairos, the hereditary king, dedicated the Stoa, which was itself brought to light by our expedition.

We are now in possession of three other inscriptions (see Nos. XVI.–XVIII.) relating to Quintus Lollius Philetairos or his family. The πάτριος βασιλεύς is, as Boeckh points out (*C. I. G.*, 3569), the lineal descendant of the ancient kings of the Aeolic city of Assos. After their deposition they still retained the title of king, along with certain rights and privileges, mainly of a priestly nature, which ensured to them an honorable position in society.* Among such rights, Strabo mentions the presidency of the games, the right to wear the royal purple, to carry a σκίπων instead of the σκῆπτρον, etc.†

A similar state of affairs existed at Pergamon.‡ At Athens, after the abolition of the monarchy, the kingly dignity was replaced by that of the Archons, who originally were limited or constitutional kings; the archonship at first was held for life, and was for many

---

* Concerning the βασιλεύς, or *rex sacrificulus*, in Lesbos and the adjoining provinces of Asia Minor, see *Hermes*, 1878, p. 386: *Mittheilungen des deutschen archaeologischen Institutes in Athen.*, 1881, p. 51.

† Strabo, XIV. pp. 632, 633: ἄρξαι δέ φησιν Ἄνδροκλον τῆς τῶν Ἰώνων ἀποικίας, ὕστερον τῆς Αἰολικῆς, υἱὸν γνήσιον Κόδρου τοῦ Ἀθηνῶν βασιλέως, γενέσθαι δὲ τοῦτον Ἐφέσου κτίστην. διόπερ τὸ βασίλειον τῶν Ἰώνων ἐκεῖ συστῆναί φασι, καὶ ἔτι νῦν οἱ ἐκ τοῦ γένους ὀνομάζονται βασιλεῖς ἔχοντές τινας τιμάς, προεδρίαν τε ἐν ἀγῶσι καὶ πορφύραν ἐπίσημον τοῦ βασιλικοῦ γένους, σκίπωνα ἀντὶ σκήπτρου, καὶ τὰ ἱερὰ τῆς Ἐλευσινίας Δήμητρος.

‡ *C. I. G.*, 2189: τὰν ἐπώνυμον ἀπὺ βασιλέων πρυτανήΐαν, on which Boeckh (No. 3569) remarks: reges non dynastae illi Attalici sunt, sed urbis regis antiquissimi, ab his igitur ille genus derivabat ideoque creatus etiam prytanis eponymus erat, quod munus Pergami competivisse regum posteris patet.

generations hereditary in the family of Medon, the son of the last king, Codrus. Even in later times the Second Archon was still called *βασιλεύς*.

Kyzikos offers a parallel to this family of Assos, of which it may not be out of place to mention the main points.* It seems that Antonia, the eldest daughter of the triumvir Mark Antony by his second wife, Antonia, was married to the rich Asiarch Pythodoros in the year 34 B.C. Her daughter Pythodoris married Polemon, king of Pontus, and became the mother of Antonia Tryphaena, the queen of Kotys. Something similar happened in the ancient royal family of Assos. A Lollia, perhaps connected with the Lollii of Sicily (see Cicero, *Verr.* III. 25; B.C. 73) or with the A. Lollius of *C. I. L.*, III. 388 (?), must have married the *πάτριος βασιλεύς* of Assos (cf. last inscription, of Lollia Arlegilla and Hellanikos), and the offspring of this marriage was Quintus Lollius, the person mentioned in No. XVIII. as the father of our Quintus Lollius Philetairos. The family tree was presumably the following: —

Hellanikos — Lollia Arlegilla.
|
Quintus Lollius.
|
Q. Lollius Philetairos — Lollia Antiochis.

In Kyzikos, the Princess Antonia Tryphaena, before her marriage with Kotys, is priestess both of Athena Polias and of Livia-Julia, who, in imitation of Athena, is called Σεβαστὴ Νικηφόρος. In Kyzikos, Livia-Julia is *σύνναος* with Athena Polias, and is in every respect the peer of the Olympic Goddess.

At Assos, we find that Quintus Lollius Philetairos is priest both of Zeus Homonoos and of Augustus. This circumstance leads to the belief that the God Augustus was associated with Zeus at Assos in exactly the same manner as the Goddess Livia-Julia with Athena

* See Millingen in Ὁ ἐν Κωνσταντινουπόλει Ἑλληνικὸς Φιλολογικὸς Σύλλογος, 1872, p. 23 ff., and the plates at the end of the volume; Curtius in *Monatsberichte der Königlichen preussischen Akademie der Wissenschaften*, 1874, p. 7 ff.; Mommsen in *Ephemeris Epigraphica*, 1875, pp. 254, 255; Mordtmann in *Mittheilungen des deutschen archaeologischen Institutes in Athen*, 1881, p. 55; Reinach in *Bulletin de Correspondance Hellénique*, 1882, p. 613.

Polias at Kyzikos. The worship of the new Gods who sat on the imperial throne, which was a symbol of Roman dominion, seems to have been distasteful to the people of Kyzikos; and Augustus, who had confirmed them in the privileges granted to the city by Pompey, found himself compelled to punish neglect of his cult by depriving them for a season of these very privileges. Thus spurred on to good works, the Kyzikans began in a surly humor to build a temple to Augustus.* But the matter was dropped as soon as Augustus died, and thus Kyzikos incurred the displeasure of Tiberius, who punished the city on account of *incuria caeremoniarum Augusti* (Tac. *Ann.* IV. 36). The royal family, of which Antonia Tryphaena was a member, espoused the cause of the new Gods, and this lady was especially zealous. As a maiden princess (*Monatsberichte,* as above, inscription No. III.) she is priestess of Athena Polias and Livia-Julia during the troublous times consequent on the neglect of the new cult; in inscription No. IV. she is Queen Dowager, and her exertions to establish the Imperial Cultus have been crowned with complete success, for the people of Kyzikos are not only not disinclined to pay divine honors to the *dead* emperor, but they even worship willingly the *living* Caligula as Helios, and his sister Drusilla as νέα Ἀφροδίτη.

We do not know that the Assians were unfriendly to the imperial cultus, but the representative of the ancient kings of Assos certainly curried favor by supporting it and by himself becoming the priest of Augustus.

This inscription and the three following must be referred to the reign of Tiberius, as the θεῷ Καίσαρι Σεβαστῷ proves; see also No. XVII., and the note on θεός in No. XXVI.

---

* *Dio Cass.*, LVII. 24; Marquardt, *Cyzicus*, p. 82.

No. XVI.

Dedicatory inscription of Bath; evidently set in the wall; found in six pieces at different times near the Bath; marble very white. Whole length of slab, 1.20 *m.; whole height,* 0.48 *m.; length within moulding,* 0.765 *m.; height within moulding,* 0.345 *m.; thickness,* 0.08 *m.*

Λ]ολλ[ία Ἀντιο[χὶς, ἡ γυ]νὴ ἡ Κοΐ[ν]του
Λ]ολλί[ου] Φιλεταίρου, βασιλεύσα-
σα] κατὰ τὰ πάτρια, πρώτ[η] γυναικῶν, τὸ βαλανῆον καὶ τὰ ἑπόμενα τῷ βαλανήῳ ἀνέθηκεν
Ἀφροδείτῃ Ἰουλίᾳ καὶ τῷ δήμῳ.

"Lollia Antiochis, wife of Quintus Lollius Philetairos, first of women, who was queen in accordance with ancestral customs, dedicated this Bath and its belongings to Julia Aphrodite and the people."

See note to No. XVII.

No. XVII.

Epistyle inscription from Bath in ten pieces, some of which were free lintels, some embedded in the wall. Height of epistyle, 0.38 *m.*

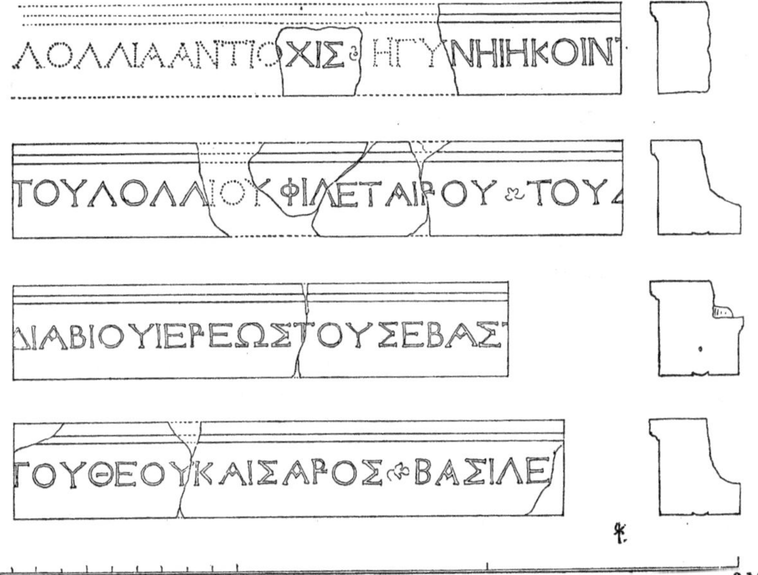

Λολλία Ἀντιο]χὶς, [ἡ γυ]νὴ ἡ Κοΐν-
του Λολλ[ίου] Φιλεταίρου τοῦ
διὰ βίου ἱερέως τοῦ Σεβαστοῦ θεοῦ Καίσαρος, βασιλε[ύσασα
κατὰ τὰ πάτρια, πρώτη γυναικῶν,
τὸ βαλανῆον καὶ τὰ ἑπόμενα τῷ
βαλανήῳ ἀνέθηκεν Ἀφροδείτῃ
Ἰουλίᾳ καὶ τῷ δήμῳ.]

"Lollia Antiochis, wife of Quintus Lollius Philetairos, priest for life of Divus Caesar Augustus, [first of women], who was queen [in accordance with ancestral customs, dedicated this Bath and its belongings to Julia Aphrodite and the people.]"

Mr. W. C. Lawton calls attention to the fact that Antiochis is a Roman surname,* and hence need not be connected with any particular Antiochis or Antiochia.

Concerning Quintus Lollius Philetairos, see note to No. XV. Philetaerus occurs as the name of a freedman of Augustus.† Phileterus is also found *C. I. L.*, II. 4122; III. 4815; IV. 653, 2192. The Julian family was held in high honor in the Troad for mythological reasons. Livia, wife of Augustus, was adopted into the Gens Julia by Augustus, and assumed the name of Julia Augusta after his death.‡ On coins of the period she appears as Julia Augusta, § and Ἰουλία Σεβαστή or Ἰουλία θεὰ Σεβαστή; on coins of Ephesos she is Ἄρτεμις Σεβαστή,¶ and perhaps also Aphrodite, as in our inscription.‖ For the cultus of Livia at Kyzikos as Σεβαστὴ Νικηφόρος, see No. XV. In Lampsakos she is Ἑστία, νέα Δημήτηρ (*C. I. G.*, 3642).

The only other Julia to whom our inscription could possibly refer is the unhappy daughter of Augustus, wife of M. Vipsanius Agrippa and Tiberius. Indeed, various facts in regard to her seem to make very plausible the assumption that she is here referred to as Julia Aphrodite. The character of Aphrodite suits Julia much better than Livia, for she was witty, beautiful, and young, while Livia had only faded beauty to boast at the time when our inscription was carved. Again, when in the year 17 B.C. Agrippa was sent by Augustus to the east with supreme power, Julia accompanied him. On his return from the excursion to the Pontus with Herod the Great, in 16 B.C., he spent some time on the western seaboard of Asia Minor; and while they were in the Troad, Julia and her immediate servants narrowly escaped being drowned in the Scamander. The inhabitants of Ilion made no attempt to rescue her from the threatened death. Agrippa was enraged, and mulcted them in a heavy fine, which

---

* Gruter, p. DCLXXXIX: Julia Euhemeris mater et Julia Antiochis avia, etc., found at Rome; cf. p. DCCLV.

† Gruter, p. DLXXXII: Philetaero Aug. lib. praepos., etc.

‡ Liviam in familiam Juliam, nomenque Augustae adsumebatur. Tac. *Ann.* 1, 8; cf. also Eckhel, *Doct. Num.*, VI. pp. 146–158.

§ Eckhel, *Doct. Num.*, VI. pp. 147, 157; Orelli, 613–618, 1320, 1328, 1724, 2937; Rasche, II. pp. 1784–1792.

¶ Eckhel, *Doct. Num.*, VI. p. 152; Rasche, II. p. 1792.

‖ Rasche, II. p. 1328.

was finally remitted at the intercession of Herod the Great and Nikolaos Damaskenos.* If this inscription refers to Julia, it might be brought into connection with her narrow escape in the Scamander.

In spite of her profligacy, Julia was always a great favorite with the people, both at Rome and in the provinces. Inscriptions in her honor have been found at several places in the provinces: at Delos (*Bull. de Corr. Hell.*, 1878, p. 400); at Eresos, on the island of Lesbos (*ibid.*, 1880, p. 443); at Sestos (*ibid.*, 1880, p. 517), erected after her death, as Ἰουλίαν θεάν proves; at Thasos (*Revue Archéologique*, 1879, p. 283).

From these scraps of evidence we might be inclined to refer the inscription to Julia; but still it is more probable that Livia is meant, because the inscription dates after the death of Augustus, when Julia was in greater disgrace than ever, owing to the hatred of Tiberius.

---

* Nikolaos Dam., who was an eye-witness, relates the matter, and boasts of the philanthropy shown by himself in appeasing the wrath of Agrippa. Nic. Dam. in Müller's *Frag. Hist. Graec.*, III. 350: Ἰλιεῖς γάρ, ἀφικνουμένης νύκτωρ ὡς αὐτοὺς Ἰουλίας τῆς Καίσαρος μὲν θυγατρὸς, γυναικὸς δὲ Ἀγρίππα, καὶ τοῦ Σκαμάνδρου μεγάλου ῥυέντος ὑπὸ χειμάρρων πολλῶν, κινδυνευούσης περὶ τὴν διάβασιν ἀπολέσθαι, οὐκ ᾔσθοντο. Ἐφ' οἷς ἀγανακτήσας ὁ Ἀγρίππας, ὅτι οὐ παρεβοήθησαν οἱ Ἰλιεῖς, δέκα μυρίασιν ἐζημίωσεν ἀργυρίου. Οἱ δὲ ἀπόρως ἔχοντες, καὶ ἅμα οὐ προϋπειδόμενοι τὸν χειμῶνα, οὐδὲ ὅτι ἔξιοι ἡ παῖς (she was twenty-three years old at this time), Ἀγρίππᾳ μὲν οὐδοτιοῦν εἰπεῖν ἐτόλμησαν, ἥκοντ[ος] δὲ τ[οῦ] Νικολά[ου] δεόμενοι παρασχεῖν αὐτοῖς Ἡρώδην βοηθὸν καὶ προστάτην. Josephus (*Ant. Jud.*, XVI. 22: Ἰλιεῦσι μὲν γὰρ αὐτὸν διήλλαξεν ὀργιζόμενον) relates that Agrippa forgave them, and rescinded the fine at the intercession of Herod.

No. XVIII.

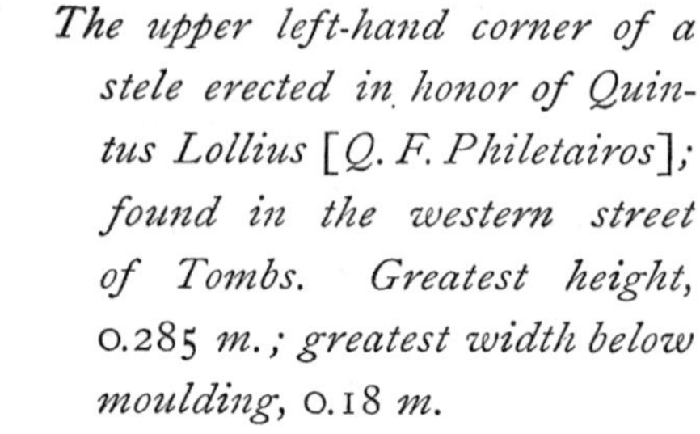

The upper left-hand corner of a stele erected in honor of Quintus Lollius [Q. F. Philetairos]; found in the western street of Tombs. Greatest height, 0.285 m.; greatest width below moulding, 0.18 m.

Q. Lollius [Q. F. Philetaerus]
Ὁ δῆμος [ἐτίμησεν Κοΐντον]
Λόλλιον Κο[ΐντου υἱὸν Φιλέταιρον]
χρυσῷ στ[εφάνῳ καὶ εἰκόνι χαλκῇ (?) καὶ]
εἰκόνι γραπ[τῇ καὶ εἰκόνι μαρ-]
μαρίνῳ . . . . . .

"Quintus Lollius, Quinti filius, Philetaerus. The people have honored Quintus Lollius Philetairos, the son of Quintus Lollius, with a golden crown, and with portraits [of himself in bronze (?)], in painting, and in marble" . . . . .

A Quintus Lollius is mentioned in a Latin inscription of Alexandria Troas (*C. I. L.*, III. 388).

The slab has mouldings on both sides, showing that both sides were to be exposed to view. On the rear side, the corner of a slightly sunken panel is visible, which makes it probable that this side contained the marble portrait (in bas-relief) mentioned in the inscription. The ΛΟΛΛΙΟΝΚΟ of line 3 makes the restoration of lines 1, 2, and 3 certain.*

Objection may be made to the restoration of the last three lines on account of the number of εἰκόνες bestowed upon Lollius; but it was by no means unusual to bestow even a greater variety of portraits upon persons who had been of service to a city. Thus the ἔφηβοι and νέοι of Teos honor Aischrion (*C. I. G.*, 3085) στεφάνῳ χρυσῷ καὶ εἰκόνι γραπτῇ καὶ εἰκόνι γραπτῇ τελείᾳ καὶ εἰκόνι χαλκῇ καὶ ἀγάλματι μαρμαρίνῳ καὶ εἰκόνι χρυσῇ.

* For an elaborate discussion of εἰκὼν γραπτή in all its bearings, see *C. I. G.*, 3068.

No. XIX.

Marble block found in Gymnasium, 0.83 *m. by* 0.51 *m. The inscription has been mostly chiselled off, so that nothing satisfactory remains.*

ΟΔΗΜΟΣΚΑΙΟΙΠΡΑΓΜΑ
ΘΕΑΝΑΡΗΟΥΙΑΙΝΙΙΡΑΝΝ
ΓΡΗΝΤΟΥΣΕΒΑΣΤΟΥΘΕ

ὁ δῆμος καὶ οἱ πραγμα[τευόμενοι παρ' ἡμῖν Ῥωμαῖοι]
θεὰν . . . .
τὴν τοῦ Σεβαστοῦ Θε[οῦ ἱέρειαν or θυγατέρα ?]

No. XX.

This is published by Mr. Waddington in *Voy. Arch.*, 1034 *a*. It never comprised more than two lines.

ΠΡΑΓΜΑΤΕΥΟΜΕΝΟΙΡΩ
ΗΝΕΥΕΡΓΕΤΙΝΤΟΥΚΟΣΜ

[οἱ ἐν Ἄσσῳ] πραγματευόμενοι Ῥω[μαῖοι]
[τ]ὴν εὐεργέτιν τοῦ κόσμ[ου]

Mr. Waddington thinks that "the benefactress of the world" is Livia, the wife of Augustus.

No. XXI.

Three fragments from western Street of Tombs.

Two of the fragments fit together in the following manner: —

I. ΙΓΜΑΤΙ
ΙΣΤΕΦΑ
ΩΝΙΟΙ

II. ΝΒΑΣΙ/
ΟΣΥΝΗΣΙ
ΑΤΡΙΔΙΡ

The third is from the left edge of the inscription, and looks thus: —

Ι
III. ΑΙΘ
ΚΑ

I give the following attempt at a restoration for what it is worth. In regard to the length of the lines, I have been guided solely by Mr. Bacon's estimate of the space occupied by the inscription.

Ὁ δῆμος καὶ οἱ πρ]αγματ[ευόμενοι παρ' ἡμῖν Ῥωμαῖοι
στεφανοῦσι χρυσῷ] στεφά[νῳ τὸν τῆς πόλεως ἥρωα
Ἀπολλώνιον Ἀπολλ]ωνίου, [ἄνδρα καλὸν καὶ ἀγαθὸν γενόμενον καὶ πάτριο]ν βασιλ[έα ἐζηκότα καλῶς καὶ κοσμίως κ-]
αὶ θ[εοφιλῶς, φιλοφρ]οσύνης κ[αὶ πάσης ἀρετῆς ἕνεκεν]
κα[ὶ εὐχρηστίας τῇ π]ατρίδι

"On account of his kindliness, general excellence, and usefulness to his country, the people and the Roman merchants established among us crown with a golden crown Apollonios, son of Apollonios, the hero of the city, a noble and good man, who as hereditary king has lived among us honorably, decently, and with piety towards the Gods."

No. XXII.

From the western entrance of the Agora. Length of block, 1.45 m. This and the two following inscriptions were probably identical in form.

ΕΚΤΗΣΠΡΟΣΟΔΟΥΤΩΝΑΓΡΩΝ
ΚΛΕΟΣΤΡΑΤΟΣΥΙΟΣ///ΟΛΕΩΣ

Ἐκ τῆς προσόδου τῶν ἀγρῶν [ὧν ἀπέλιπεν εἰς ἐπισκευὴν τῆς πόλεως] Κλεόστρατος, υἱὸς [π]όλεως, [φύσει δὲ Ἀπελλικῶντος, ἐπεσκευάσθη.]

This is probably Waddington's No. 1033 *a* (*Voy. Arch., Asie Mineure*), and has been mutilated since it was first copied by Duthoit.

No. XXIII.

On three narrow stones (resembling the edges of a sill), which formed a band in the wall; dug from debris covering the street south of the Greek Bath.

ΕΚΤΗΣΠΡΟΣΟΔΟΥΤΩΝΑΓΡΩΝΩΝΑΠΕΛΙΠΕΝ
ΩΣΚΛΕΟΣΤ ΟΛΕΩΣΦΥΣΕΙΔΕ
ΑΠΕΛΛΙΚΩΝΤΟΣ

ἐκ τῆς προσόδου τῶν ἀγρῶν ὧν ἀπέλιπεν [εἰς ἐπισκευὴν τῆς πόλε]ως Κλεόστ[ρατος, υἱὸς π]όλεως, φύσει δὲ Ἀπελλικῶντος, [ἐπεσκευάσθη].

This must be Boeckh's No. 3570 (*C. I. G.*).

No. XXIV.

Rim of the marble basin of fountain next the entrance of the underground passage south of the Bouleuterion. Found in cistern beneath.

ΩΝΑΠ

[Ἐκ τῆς προσόδου τῶν ἀγρῶν] ὧν ἀπ[έλιπεν εἰς ἐπισκευὴν τῆς πόλεως Κλεόστρατος, υἱὸς πόλεως, φύσει δὲ Ἀπελλικῶντος, ἐπεσκευάσθη].

"This has been restored from the rents of the lands which Kleostratos, son of the city, but by nature son of Apellikon, bequeathed for the restoration of the city."

Kleostratos had evidently bequeathed to the city of Assos certain lands, the proceeds of which were to be used for repairs and restorations.

The phrase υἱὸς πόλεως occurs frequently in inscriptions (Le Bas and Waddington, *Asie Mineure*, 525, 881, 1592; *C. I. G.*, 2719, 3082, 3173, 3570, 3874); and on coins (Mionnet, *Phrygie*, 442, 445; Supplement, *Carie*, 131, *Phrygie*, 196). Waddington remarks that such adoptions by the city may be compared with the purses given in France, England, and Scotland to promising sons of poor parents, to enable them to pursue a course of study.

No XXV.

Slab in a fountain south of village of Pasha Kieui, about five miles directly north of Assos. Cut for fountain niche. The stone is broken away on left side. Height of slab, 0.42 m.; width, 0.42 m. The inscription certainly belongs to Assos, but it is quite unintelligible.

\ONIONENIAYIONEIΣIIAΣH
NTEΔΩPEANΔIANEIMANTA
ƆNKAIMONONKAITONΣEITΩ
ΠOPONΠΛHPΩΣANTAEKTΩ
IΣΔHNAPIAMYPIA · ΣEITΩNH
ΔEΠOΛΛAKIΣKAIAΓOPAΣANTA
ITOYTONMEΔI ˀNΔHNAPI
KAIΠOIHΣAN OYE
OYΔ ΠYPP
NΘH/ EΠI
AΣΠΛ ¯ΠIΣH
¯AKA IΩNA
- - ∩

· · · · [ὅλ]ον τὸν ἐνιαυτὸν εἰς παση
· · · · τε δωρεὰν διανείμαντα
· · [πρῶτ]ον καὶ μόνον καὶ τὸν σειτω-
[νηθησόμενον σ]πόρον πληρώσαντα ἐκ τῶ-
[ν ἰδίων · · · ε]ἰς δηνάρια μύρια σειτωνή-
[σαντα · · ·] δὲ πολλάκις καὶ ἀγοράσαντα
τὸν μέδι[μν]ον δηνάρι-
[α] · · · καὶ ποιήσαν[τα] · · · ·

No. XXVI.

A decree of the town of Assos, passed on the accession of the Emperor Caligula in 37 A.D., engraved on a bronze tablet (0.54 m. × 0.38 m.), of which a fac-simile is given in the opposite plate. Published in Mr. Clarke's first Report on the Investigations at Assos.

Ἐπὶ ὑπάτων Γναίου Ἀκερρωνίου Πρόκλου καὶ Γαΐου Ποντίου Πετρωνίου Νιγρίνου.

Ψήφισμα Ἀσσίων γνώμῃ τοῦ δήμου.

Ἐπεὶ ἡ κατ' εὐχὴν πᾶσιν ἀνθρώποις ἐλπισθεῖσα Γαΐου Καίσαρος Γερμανικοῦ Σεβαστοῦ ἡγεμονία κατήνγελται, οὐδὲν δὲ μέτρον χαρᾶς εὕρηκ[ε]ν ὁ κόσμος, πᾶσα δὲ πόλις καὶ πᾶν ἔθνος ἐπὶ τὴν τοῦ θεοῦ ὄψιν ἔσπευκεν, ὡς ἂν τοῦ ἡδίστου ἀνθρώποις αἰῶν[ος] νῦν ἐνεστῶτος,

Ἔδοξεν τῇ βουλῇ καὶ τοῖς πραγματευομένοις παρ' ἡμῖν Ῥωμαίοις καὶ τῷ δήμῳ τῷ Ἀσσίων κατασταθῆναι πρεσβείαν ἐκ τῶν πρώτων καὶ ἀρίστων Ῥωμαίων τε καὶ Ἑλλήνων τὴν ἐντευξομένην καὶ συνησθησομένην αὐτῷ δεηθησομένην τε ἔχειν διὰ μνήμης καὶ κηδεμονίας τὴν πόλιν, καθὼς καὶ αὐτὸς μετὰ τοῦ πατρὸς Γερμανικοῦ ἐπιβὰς πρώτως τῇ ἐπαρχείᾳ τῆς ἡμετέρας πόλεως ὑπέσχετο.

Ὅρκος Ἀσσίων.

Ὄμνυμεν Δία Σωτῆρα καὶ θεὸν Καίσαρα Σεβαστὸν καὶ τὴν πάτριον ἁγνὴν παρθένον εὐνοήσειν Γαΐῳ Καίσαρι Σεβαστῷ καὶ τῷ σύμπαντι οἴκῳ αὐτοῦ, καὶ φίλους τε κρινεῖν οὓς ἂν αὐτὸς προαιρῆται καὶ ἐχθροὺς οὓς ἂν αὐτὸς

ΕΠΙΥΠΑΤΩΝΓΝΑΙΟΥΑΚΕΡΡΩΝΙΟΥ
ΠΡΟΚΛΟΥΚΑΙΓΑΙΟΥΠΟΝΤΙΟΥΠΕΤΡΩ
ΝΙΟΥΝΙΓΡΙΝΟΥ

ΨΗΦΙΣΜΑΑΣΣΙΩΝΓΝΩΜΗΙΤΟΥΔΗΜΟΥ

ΕΠΕΙΗΚΑΤΕΥΧΗΝΠΑΣΙΝΑΝΘΡΩΠΟΙΣΕΛΠΙΣΘΕΙΣΑΓΑΙΟΥ
ΚΑΙΣΑΡΟΣΓΕΡΜΑΝΙΚΟΥΣΕΒΑΣΤΟΥΗΓΕΜΟΝΙΑΚΑΤΗΝΓΕΛΤΑΙ
ΟΥΔΕΝΔΕΜΕΤΡΟΝΧΑΡΑΣΕΥΡΗΚΗΝΟΚΟΣΜΟΣΠΑΣΑΔΕΠΟΛΙΣ
ΚΑΙΠΑΝΕΘΝΟΣΕΠΙΤΗΝΤΟΥΘΕΟΥΟΨΙΝΕΣΤΙΕΥΚΕΝΩΣΑΝΤΟΥ
ΗΔΙΣΤΟΥΑΝΘΡΩΠΟΙΣΑΙΩΝΟΥΝΥΝΕΝΕΣΤΩΤΟΣ

ΕΔΟΞΕΝΤΗΙΒΟΥΛΗΙΚΑΙΤΟΙΣΠΡΑΓΜΑΤΕΥΟΜΕΝΟΙΣΠΑΡΗΜΙΝ
ΡΩΜΑΙΟΙΣΚΑΙΤΩΙΔΗΜΩΙΤΩΙΑΣΣΙΩΝΚΑΤΑΣΤΑΘΗΝΑΙΠΡΕΣ
ΒΕΙΑΝΕΚΤΩΝΠΡΩΤΩΝΚΑΙΑΡΙΣΤΩΝΡΩΜΑΙΩΝΤΕΚΑΙΕΛΛΗ
ΝΩΝΤΗΝΕΝΤΕΥΞΟΜΕΝΗΝΚΑΙΣΥΝΗΣΘΗΣΟΜΕΝΗΝΑΥΤΩΙ
ΔΕΗΘΗΣΟΜΕΝΗΝΤΕΕΧΕΙΝΔΙΑΜΝΗΜΗΣΚΑΙΚΗΔΕΜΟΝΙΑΣ
ΤΗΝΠΟΛΙΝΚΑΘΩΣΚΑΙΑΥΤΟΣΜΕΤΑΤΟΥΠΑΤΡΟΣΓΕΡΜΑΝΙΚΟΥ
ΕΠΙΒΑΣΠΡΩΤΩΣΤΗΙΕΠΑΡΧΕΙΑΙΤΗΣΗΜΕΤΕΡΑΣΠΟΛΕΩΣ
ΥΠΕΣΧΕΤΟ

ΟΡΚΟΣ ΑΣΣΙΩΝ

ΟΜΝΥΜΕΝΔΙΑΣΩΤΗΡΑΚΑΙΘΕΟΝΚΑΙΣΑΡΑΣΕΒΑΣΤΟΝΚΑΙΤΗΝ
ΠΑΤΡΙΟΝΑΓΝΗΝΠΑΡΘΕΝΟΝΕΥΝΟΗΣΕΙΝΓΑΙΩΙΚΑΙΣΑΡΙΣΕΒΑΣ
ΤΩΙΚΑΙΤΩΙΣΥΜΠΑΝΤΙΟΙΚΩΙΑΥΤΟΥΚΑΙΦΙΛΟΥΣΤΕΚΡΙΝΕΙΝ
ΟΥΣΑΝΑΥΤΟΣΠΡΟΑΙΡΗΤΑΙΚΑΙΕΧΘΡΟΥΣΟΥΣΑΝΑΥΤΟΣΠΡΟΒΑ
ΛΗΤΑΙΕΥΟΡΚΟΥΣΙΝΜΕΝΗΜΙΝΕΥΕΙΗΕΦΙΟΡΚΟΥΣΙΝΔΕΤΑΕΝΑΝ
ΤΙΑ

ΠΡΕΣΒΕΥΤΑΙΕΠΗΝΓΕΙΛΑΝΤΟΕΚΤΩΝΙΔΙΩΝ

ΓΑΙΟΣΟΥΑΡΙΟΣΓΑΙΟΥΥΙΟΣΟΥΟΛΤΙΝΙΑΚΑΣΤΟΣ

ΕΡΜΟΦΑΝΗΣ	ΖΩΙΛΟΥ
ΚΤΗΤΟΣ	ΠΙΣΙΣΤΡΑΤΟΥ
ΑΙΣΧΡΙΩΝ	ΚΑΛΛΙΦΑΝΟΥΣ
ΑΡΤΕΜΙΔΩΡΟΣ	ΦΙΛΟΜΟΥΣΟΥ

ΟΙΤΙΝΕΣΚΑΙΥΠΕΡΤΗΣΓΑΙΟΥΚΑΙΣΑΡΟΣΣΕΒΑΣΤΟΥΓΕΡΜΑΝΙΚΟΥ
ΣΩΤΗΡΙΑΣΕΥΞΑΜΕΝΟΙΔΙΙΚΑΠΙΤΩΛΙΩΙΕΘΥΣΑΝΤΩΙΤΗΣΠΟΛΕ
ΩΣΟΝΟΜΑΤΙ

B. del.

BRONZE TABLET FOUND AT ASSOS. SEPT. 24th 1881

προβά[λ]ληται. Εὐορκοῦσιν μὲν ἡμῖν εὖ εἴη, ἐφιορκοῦσιν δὲ τὰ ἐναν[τία].

Πρεσβευταὶ ἐπηνγείλαντο ἐκ τῶν ἰδίων·

Γάϊος Οὐάριος, Γαΐου υἱὸς, Οὐολτινία, Κάστος,
Ἑρμοφάνης Ζωΐλου,
Κτῆτος Πισιστράτου,
Αἰσχρίων Καλλιφάνους,
Ἀρτεμίδωρος Φιλομούσου,

οἵτινες καὶ ὑπὲρ τῆς Γαΐου Καίσαρος Σεβαστοῦ Γερμανικοῦ σωτηρίας εὐξάμενοι Διὶ Καπιτωλίῳ ἔθυσαν τῷ τῆς πόλεως ὀνόματι.

"In the Consulship of Gnaeus Acerronius Proculus and Gaius Pontius Petronius Nigrinus.

A Decree of the Assians by Vote of the People.

Since the supremacy of Gaius Caesar Germanicus Augustus, for which all men have hoped with eager longing, has been proclaimed, and the world has known no bounds to its delight, and every city and every nation is eager to behold the face of the God, feeling that the most delightful age for mankind is now begun, —

It is enacted by the Senate, and the Roman merchants established among us, and the people of Assos, that an embassy be appointed from the first and best Romans and Greeks to meet and congratulate him, and to entreat him that he will hold our city in remembrance and under his protection, even as he himself promised when with his father Germanicus he first set foot in our city's province.

OATH OF THE ASSIANS.

We swear by Zeus Soter and the Deity Caesar Augustus, and by the pure Virgin whom our fathers worshipped, that we will be faithful to Gaius Caesar Augustus and all his house, and that we will consider those our friends whom he shall prefer, and those our enemies whom he shall declare. May it be well with us if we are true to our oaths, and may it be otherwise if we are false to them.

These offered themselves as ambassadors at their own expense : —

> Gaius Varius Castus, son of Gaius, of the tribe Voltinia,
> Hermophanes, son of Zoïlos,
> Ktetos, son of Pisistratos,
> Aischrion, son of Kalliphanes,
> Artemidoros, son of Philomousos.

These also invoked Jupiter Capitolinus for the preservation of Gaius Caesar Augustus Germanicus, and made sacrifice in the name of the city."

The People are usually mentioned immediately after the Senate, ἡ βουλὴ καὶ ὁ δῆμος being the standing formula in Greek inscriptions. Departures from this rule are so rare that there must be unusual and weighty reasons therefor. It is noteworthy that the Roman merchants are mentioned in our inscription immediately after the Senate and before the δῆμος. We may regard this either as a piece of politeness towards the Romans on the part of the Assians on this special occasion, or else we may infer that the Roman merchants were both wealthy and powerful, and that, as they belonged to the ruling class, their arrogance demanded that they be named in official documents before the subject class, the δῆμος.

The resident Romans were doubtless well hated everywhere; and it is known from the ancient writers that any maltreatment of this class by the native citizens was thoroughly avenged by the emperors (Marquardt, *Cyzicus*, p. 82).

After the recall of Germanicus from Germany in 17 A.D., the Senate assigned to him the Eastern provinces with the highest imperium; and in the year 18 A.D. he visited the Troad and Assos. Caligula was then only six years old; and the promise referred to in our inscription could not have been made by him in the character of heir presumptive to the imperial throne, since he was then by no means certain of the succession. Germanicus and Agrippina were both held in high honor in the Troad and in Lesbos. The inscriptions of Ilium Novum in *C. I. G.*, 3610, and Le Bas and Waddington, *Asie Mineure*, 1039, were doubtless set up at the time of the visit of Germanicus to the Troad. Germanicus is θεός in inscriptions of Lesbos (*C. I. G.*, 2183, 3528; *Bull. de Corr. Hell.*, 1880, p. 432;

Plehn, *Lesbiaca*, p. 82), and Agrippina is θεὰ Σεβαστὰ Αἰολὶς καρποφόρος on coins and in inscriptions of Mytilene (*C. I. G.; Bull. de Corr. Hell.*, and Plehn, as above).

It is not Tiberius, but Octavianus, who is referred to under the title of Καῖσαρ Σεβαστός. The title of Tiberius in Greek inscriptions is Τιβέριος Καῖσαρ Σεβαστός; and Octavianus, alone of all the emperors, was called simply Καῖσαρ Σεβαστός. Dittenberger has proved (in an article entitled *Kaiser Hadrians erste Anwesenheit in Athen*, in Hermes, 1873, p. 213 sqq.) that, whenever reference is made in Greek inscriptions to a dead emperor, his name is prefaced by the word θεός, as if θεός were a praenomen, θεός being a simple translation of *divus*. When a living emperor is mentioned, the word θεός regularly comes after his other titles; for instance, Αὐτοκράτορα Καίσαρα Νέρουαν Τραϊανὸν Σεβαστὸν Γερμανικὸν Δακικὸν θεὸν, θεοῦ υἱὸν, κ.τ.λ. But in Attic inscriptions θεῖος or θειότατος was the more popular title for the living emperor.

The deity by whom the Assians swear as "the pure Virgin whom our fathers worshipped," is Athena Polias, in whose honor they had erected the Doric temple which crowned the Acropolis of Assos. See Nos. III., XIV. Athena Polias was worshipped at various places in Asia Minor: at Priene (*C. I. G.*, 2904), at Teos (*C. I. G.*, 3048), at Pergamon (*C. I. G.*, 3553, and several inscriptions in *Die Ergebnisse der Ausgrabungen zu Pergamon*, 1880 and 1881), at Kyzikos (*Monatsberichte der Königl. preuss. Akademie der Wissenschaften*, 1874, p. 16).

Of the names in this inscription three seem to have been popular in Aeolic districts. A *Hermophanes* is mentioned on a coin of the Aeolic city Kymai (*Mionnet*, III. 11).

A *Zoilos* is mentioned, is an inscription of Methymna (Le Bas, *Inscriptions Grecques et Latines*, fasc. 5, No. 191 b.; Ahrens, *Dial.*, II. 496).

An epic poet named *Aischrion*, a friend and companion of Alexander the Great, was a native of Mytilene (Müller, *Fragmenta Historicorum Graecorum*, II., pp. xix., xx., and Tzetzes, *Chil.*, 8, 406).

Gaius Varius Castus was probably a kinsman of *Publius Varius*, whose tomb is still in existence on the western street of tombs (see Nos. LXX., LXXI.).

No. XXVII.

From the epistyle of the little temple (prostylos) next the Bath; height of epistyle, 0.35 m.

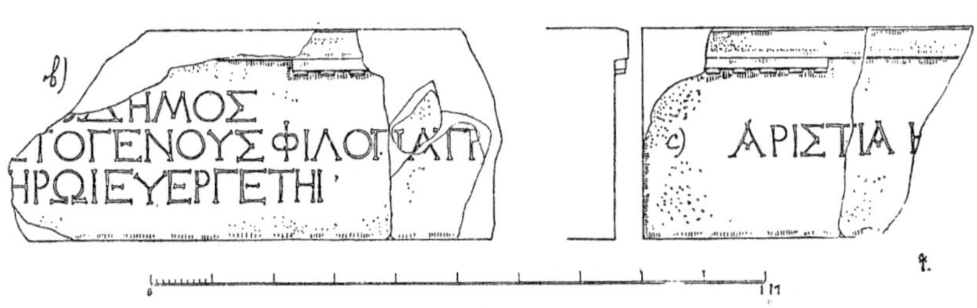

(*a*) Ὁ δῆμος
Καλλισθένει Ἡφαιστογένους ἥρωι.

(*b*) [Ὁ] δῆμος
[Καλλισθένει Ἡφαισ]τογένους φιλοπάτ[ριδι],
ἥρωι εὐεργέτῃ.

(*c*) [Ὁ δῆμος] Ἀριστίᾳ Ἡ[φαιστογένους].

(*a*) "The people to the hero Kallisthenes, son of Hephaistogenes."

(*b*) "The people to the hero-benefactor, lover of his country, Kallisthenes, son of Hephaistogenes."

(*c*) "The people to Aristias, son of Hephaistogenes."

Hephaistogenes is a new name.

No. XXVIII.

Fragment of a decree of the Roman period, entitled περὶ τοῦ μὴ καθίστασθαι πράκτορας, *published in Mr. Clarke's first Report. We have chiefly the preamble, of which the last lines are imperfect. The inscription has the late forms* Ϲ *and* W *for* Ʃ *and* Ω, *and omits* Ι *in* ΗΙ *and* ΩΙ.*

ΔΟΓΜΑΠΕΡΙΤΟΥΜΗΚΑΘΙϹΤΑϹΘΑΙΠΡΑΚΤΟΡΑϹ
ΓΝWΜΗΒΟΥΛΗϹΤΕΚΑΙΔΗΜΟΥΛΑΧΟΝΤWΝΔΟ
ΓΜΑΤΟΓΡΑΦWΝΕΠΑΝΘΟΥϹΤΟΥΕΡΜΟΓΕΝΟΥϹ
ΕΡΜΟΓΕΝΟΥϹΤΟΥΕΠΑΝΘΟΥϹΚΡΑΤΗϹΙΝΕΙ
ΚΟΥΤΟΥΜΕΝΕϹΘΕWϹ. ΕΠΕΙΔΗΟΚΟΙΝΟϹΑΠΑΝ
ΤWΝΕΚΠΡΟΓΟΝWΝΕΥΕΡΓΕΤΗϹΤΙ*ΚΛ*ΝΕΙΚΑ
ϹΙϹϹΥΝΑΠΑϹΙΝΟΙϹΑΛΛΟΙϹΕΥΕΡΓΕΤΙΤΗΝΠΑ
ΤΡΙΔΑΚΟϹΜWΝΤΟΕΑΥΤΟΥΓΕΝΟϹΕΝΠΑΝΤΙΚΑΙ
ΡWΕΝΔΕΙΚΝΥΜΕΝΟϹΤΗΝΕΙϹΤΗΝΠΑΤΡΙΔΑΕΥ
ΝΟΙΑΝΚΑΙΤΗϹΗΜΕΡΟΝΗΜΕΡΑΒΕΒΟΥΛΗΤΑΙ
ΝΟΜΟΘΕΤΗϹΕΙϹΤΟΝΑΙWΝΑ   ΤΑΕϹΤΗΝΛΙΤΗϹ
ΚΟΙΝΗϹΕΥΕΡΓΕϹΙΑϹΚΑΙΠΙΚΡ   ΜΕΓΑΛΟΥΦΟΡ
ΤΙΟΥΤΗΝΠΑΤΡΙΔΑΚΟΥ   ΟϹΑΝΑΔΕΧΟ
ΜΕΝΟϹΤΗΝΤWΝΠΟΛ   ΚΤΟΡWΝΠΡΑ
ΞΙΝΔΕΔΟΧΘΑΙΤΗ   ΗΜWΚΑΙΤΟΙϹ
ΠΡΑΓΜΑΤΕΥΟΜ   WΜΑΙΟΙϹΕΠΗ
ΝΗϹΘΑΙΜΕΝ*Τ   ΤΟΝΑΡ\oΝ
ΤΑΛΕΓΟΝΤΑ   ΟΛΕWϹ
ΤΑΚΑΛΛΙϹΤ   ΥϹΤΑΕ
ΠΙΚΕΦΑ   ΤΟΝ
ϹΤΡΑ   ΤΗΓΙ
ΑΓΝΟΜΟ   ΟΥ
ΤΗΝΚΑΤΟΡΘ
ΠΡΑΚΤΟΡ
ΞΕΝΙΚ
ΤΟΥΤ
ΤΟ

* This is one of the inscriptions which were kept sealed by the Turkish officials (see p. 11), and could not be seen by Dr. Sterrett. An inspection of the stone (now in the Museum of Fine Arts in Boston) shows that in line 11 what was read at Assos . . **ΤΑΕϹΤΗΝΛΙΤΗ** · (τὰ ἐς τὴν λιτη ·) is meant for . . **ΤΑϹϹΤΗΝΑΙΤΗϹ,** *i.e.* [κα]τα(σ)στῆν(α)ι τῆς; and that **ΑΡ[Χ]ΟΝ** is the true reading at the end of line 17. — W. W. G.

Δόγμα περὶ τοῦ μὴ καθίστασθαι πράκτορας.

Γνώμη βουλῆς τε καὶ δήμου, λαχόντων δο-
γματογράφων Ἐπάνθους τοῦ Ἑρμογένους,
Ἑρμογένους τοῦ Ἐπάνθους, Κρατησινεί-
κου τοῦ Μενεσθέως. Ἐπειδὴ ὁ κοινὸς ἁπάν-
των ἐκ προγόνων εὐεργέτης Τι. Κλ. Νεικά-
σις, σὺν ἅπασιν οἷς ἄλλοις εὐεργέτι τὴν πατρίδα, κοσμῶν τὸ ἑαυτοῦ γένος, ἐν παντὶ και-
ρῷ ἐνδεικνύμενος τὴν εἰς τὴν πατρίδα εὔνοιαν, καὶ τῇ σήμερον ἡμέρα βεβούληται
νομοθέτης εἰς τὸν αἰῶνα [κα]τα(σ)στῆν(α)ι τῆς
κοινῆς εὐεργεσίας, καὶ πικρ[οῦ καὶ] μεγάλου φορ-
τίου τὴν πατρίδα κου[φίσαι, αὐτ]ὸς ἀναδεχό-
μενος τὴν τῶν πολ[ιτικῶν πρα]κτόρων πρᾶ-
ξιν, δεδόχθαι τῇ [βουλῇ καὶ τῷ δ]ήμῳ καὶ τοῖς
πραγματευομ[ένοις παρ᾽ ἡμῖν Ῥ]ωμαίοις ἐπηνῆσθαι μὲν Τ[ι. Κλ. Νεικάσιν] τὸν ἄρ[χ]ον-
τα, λέγοντα   τῆς π]όλεως
τὰ κάλλιστ[α   ο]υς τὰ ἐ-
πικεφά[λαια   τὸν
στρα[τηγὸν   στρα]τηγί-
α(ς) νομο[θεσίας]   ου
τὴν κατόρθ[ωσιν
πράκτορ[ας
ξενικ
τουτ
το

"A decree to suspend the appointment of Tax-gatherers.

By vote of the senate and people, when Epanthes, son of Hermogenes, Hermogenes, son of Epanthes, and Kratesineikes, son of Menestheus, held the office of decree-writers.

Whereas Tiberius Claudius Neikasis, who inherits from all his ancestors the title of public benefactor, besides all the other services which he has rendered to the country, to the honor of his own family, on all occasions showing his good-will towards the country, has this day further manifested his desire to become a lawgiver (*i.e.* a model?) for all time to our public benefactors,* and to relieve the country of a great and grievous burden by taking upon himself the functions of the civil tax-gatherers, — therefore be it resolved by the senate, the people, and the Roman merchants established among us, that Ti. Cl. Neikasis, the magistrate, be publicly thanked, etc."

The name Tiberius Claudius shows that Neikasis (*i.e.* Νικάσιος) was probably born during the reign of Tiberius. The names *Epanthes* and *Kratesineikes* are new. *Hermogenes* seems to have been a common name in Lesbos (see Le Bas, *Inscriptions*, V. n. 191).

The word δογματογράφος seems to have been confined to Aeolic districts. It occurs elsewhere only in an inscription of Mytilene published by Carl Curtius (*Hermes*, 1873, p. 407, sqq.), and afterwards by Δ. Μαρκόπουλος (in the Μουσεῖον καὶ Βιβλιοθήκη τῆς ἐν Σμύρνῃ Εὐαγγελικῆς Σχολῆς, 1876–1878, p. 12). According to the analogy of λογογράφος, it refers to officials whose duty it was to prepare decrees, and to have them engraved and published after their passage. In other cities this duty belonged to other officials, for instance, to the γραμματεῖς at Athens (Franz, *Elementa*, p. 316).

In Sparta (*C. I. G.*, 1239) and Smyrna (*C. I. G.*, 3137) the superintendent of such matters was called γραμματοφύλαξ.

---

* The expression *νομοθέτης εἰς τὸν αἰῶνα τῆς κοινῆς εὐεργεσίας* is strange and obscure. Neither the explanation given above nor any other that has been suggested is satisfactory. The titles *νομοθέτης* and *εὐεργέτης* were sometimes conferred on distinguished men by vote of a city. See *C. I. Gr.*, No. 5752, *ὑπὲρ εὐεργεσίας καὶ προξενίας*; and No. 2777, *Ἀσίας ἀρχιερῆ, νομοθέτην, γυμνασίαρχον δι' αἰῶνος, τὸν εὐεργέτην ἡ πατρίς*. The title of our inscription seems to show that the expression in question refers to the assumption by Neikasis of the functions of the *πράκτορες*. Is the painfully restored [κα]τα(σ)στῆν(α)ι after all incorrect?

Dr. Sterrett, of course, is not responsible for the translation of the inscription, after the many changes in the text (see note on p. 55). — W. W. G.

No. XXIX.

Found at the western entrance of the Agora, on a stone from the pedestal of a statue, afterwards used as a building-stone with another block of the same pedestal. Length, 0.687 *m.; height,* 0.43 *m.*

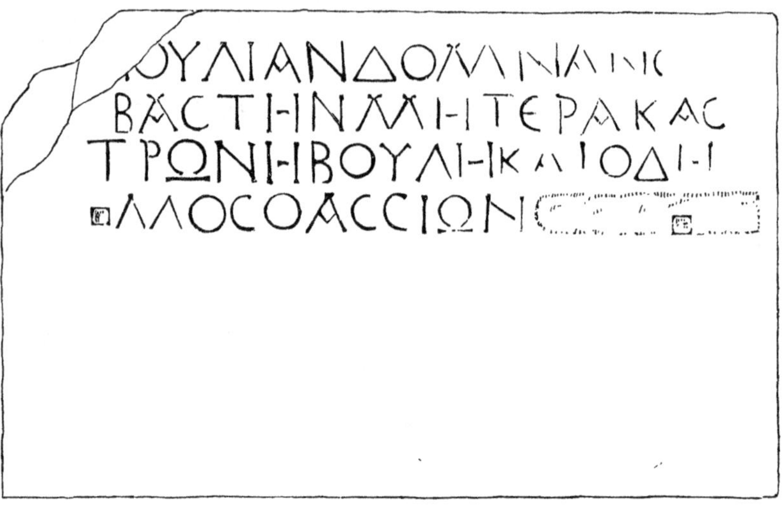

Ἰουλίαν Δόμναν Σ[ε-]
βαστὴν, μητέρα κάσ-
τρων, ἡ βουλὴ καὶ ὁ δῆ-
μος ὁ Ἀσσίων [ἀνέθηκαν]

"The Senate and the people of Assos [*have erected a statue of*] Julia Domna Augusta, mother of the camps."

The last word has been erased. It was probably the intention to erase the whole, and replace it with a new inscription in honor of the lady to whom the statue was rededicated. After the word ἀνέθηκαν had been erased, it was determined to cover this inscription with a bronze tablet bearing the new one. The dowel holes for the metallic attachments may still be seen.

Julia Domna was wife of Septimius Severus, who was emperor from 103 to 211 A.D. She was called *mater castrorum*, which in Greek inscriptions was usually translated into μήτηρ στρατοπέδων (*C. I. G.*, 1075, 1216, 3771, 4701 *b*, 6829); but she is often called μήτηρ κάστρων, as in our inscription (*C. I. G.*, 2972; add. 3882 *a*; Le Bas and Waddington, *Asie Mineure*, 1707; *Bull. de Corr. Hell.*, 1878, p. 597, 1882, p. 182), while in *C. I. G.*, 4343, add., she is called μήτηρ τῶν ἱερῶν κάστρων.

Assos coins of Julia Domna frequently occur.

No. XXX.

Great pedestal block of bluish-gray marble, found at the western end of the Agora. It is so massive and heavy that all attempts to break it for lime-burning or to split it for building purposes were in vain. It is badly battered, as if by a heavy hammer, and is nearly cut in two by a saw; the mouldings are well designed and cut. Breadth below mouldings, 0.645 *m.; whole height, including mouldings,* 1.35 *m.; height between mouldings,* 0.94 *m.*

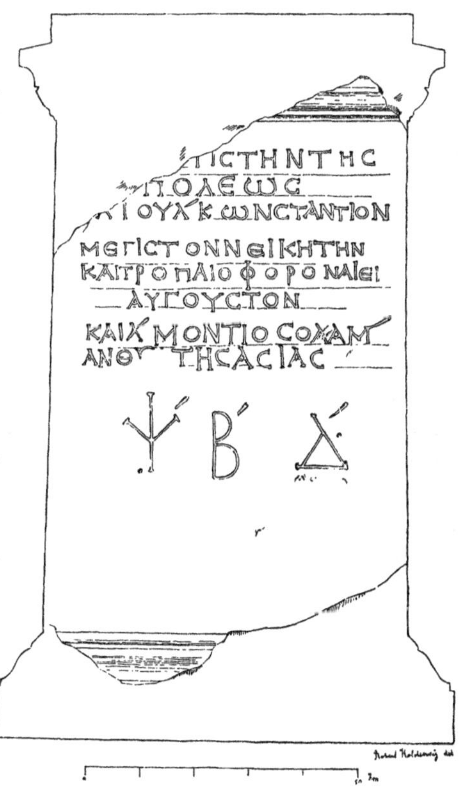

[Τὸν κτ]ίστην τῆς
πόλεως
Φλ(άουιον) Ἰούλ(ιον) Κωνστάντιον
μέγιστον νεικητὴν
καὶ τροπαιοφόρον αἰεὶ
Αὔγουστον
Καίλ(ιος) Μόντιος ὁ λαμ(πρότατος)
ἀνθύ(πατος) τῆς Ἀσίας.
Ψ(ηφίσματι) β(ουλῆς), δ(ήμου).

"Caelius Montius, the most illustrious proconsul of Asia, [*has erected this statue of*] Flavius Julius Constantius, the founder of the city, the greatest conqueror and trophy-bearer, forever Augustus. By decree of the Senate and People."

Constantius II., Flavius Julius, was emperor from 337 to 361 A.D. It is interesting that he is called κτίστης τῆς πόλεως, but the special occasion to which the title refers will probably never be known. With Caelius Montius another is added to the list of proconsuls of Asia (see Waddington, *Fastes des Provinces Asiatiques de l'Empire Romain*). Very little is known of Caelius Montius, except that he was murdered by Gallus Caesar, the cousin of Constantius.

Constantius, before his departure on his expedition against Magnentius, had appointed his cousin, Gallus Caesar, commander-in-chief of the eastern army, which was operating against the Persians. Upon the return of Constantius to Constantinople from his victorious campaign in the west, he found that Gallus Caesar had been guilty of maladministration, and two commissioners, Domitianus (praefectus praetorio Orientis, see *Notitia dignitatum*, chap. II.) and Caelius Montius (quaestor palatii, see *Notitia dignitatum*, chap. XII.), were sent to Antioch, the residence of Gallus Caesar, to make inquiries concerning his conduct of affairs. These commissioners were instructed to ensnare him with diplomatic craft and intrigue; but so far from acting prudently, they behaved with such arrogance and haughtiness towards Gallus that he became enraged at the insults thus offered to an imperial prince, and so excited the soldiery and populace against the commissioners that they were forthwith put to death.

This murder occurred towards the close of the year 353 A.D., the same year in which Constantius, by his great and decisive victories over Magnentius, had reunited the whole of the immense Roman empire under his rule. The words μέγιστον νεικητήν in our inscription will scarcely admit of its being assigned to any other year than 353 A.D., the only objection to this date being that all the historians of the events that culminated in the murder of Montius mention him as *quaestor* and not as *proconsul.* The inscription, on the contrary, affirms that he was proconsul when he erected the statue of Constantius.

Concerning the title "proconsul Asiae," see the *Notitia dignitatum*, chap. XX.

No. XXXI.

Roman milestone (formerly an altar) found at the principal gateway opening upon the western Street of Tombs. Height of altar, 1.13 *m.; width of base and top mouldings,* 0.49 *m.; height between mouldings,* 0.70 *m.; height of mouldings,* 0.32 *m.*

DDDNNN
FFFIIIVALENTIN
THEODOSIOET
ARCADIODIISFE
CIBVSVICTORIBVS
ETTRIVMFATORI
BVSSEMPERAVG
ADSOLACIVMLA
VORISAEFESTI
NATIONIS

"(Tribus) D(ominis) n(ostris) f(elicibus) I(mperatoribus), Valentin(iano), Theodosio, et Arcadio, diis fe[li]cibus victorib[us e]t triumfatoribus semper Aug(ustis) ad solacium la(b)ori[o]sae festinationis (?)."

This inscription dates, we think, between the years 383 and 385 A.D. In 383 A.D., when Valentinianus II. and Theodosius I. were emperors, Arcadius was proclaimed Augustus by his father, Theodosius. The fact that among their other titles that of *diis felicibus* is given them would seem to place the inscription before the year 385 A.D., the year in which Theodosius prohibited sacrifices, after which the title of *God* would scarcely be given to the emperors.

I have no explanation to offer of the last lines.

An inscription very similar to this was copied by Mr. Ramsay "in a fountain at the café on the pass of Belcaive," near Sardeis. It was recently published by Mommsen in the *Ephemeris Epigraphica*, 1884, p. 64, and reads: (*Quattuor*) *d*(*ominis*) *n*(*ostris*) *Fl*(*aviis*) *Gratiano*, [*Va*]*lentin*[*i*]*ano*, *Th*[*e*]*o*[*do*]*sio*, *et* [*Arcadi*]*o* [*v*]*i*[*ctoriosi*]*ssi*[*m*]*is sempe*[*r Augustis*]. It dates from the year 383 A.D.

No. XXXII.

Inlaid in the mosaic floor of the Byzantine Church. Diameter of octagon, 0.98 *m. Attention is called to* Ε *in last line.*

Σατορνίλος σχολαστικὸς ὑπὲρ εὐχῆς ἑαυτοῦ ἐποίησεν.

"Satornilos, the scholar, made this in accordance with his vow."

Satornilos may possibly be the *comes domesticorum* (see *Notitia dignitatum*, I. 14–16, but especially chap. XV.), a man of wealth and rank, who was put to death by the Empress Eudokia in the year 444 A.D., a deed which greatly incensed her husband, the Emperor Theodosius II., who took revenge by depriving her of the state and rank of empress. This *comes domesticorum* is generally called Saturninus by the historians of the period, but Priskos Panetes and Sokrates Scholastikos use the grecized form Satornilos (*Priskos Panetes* in Müller, *Fragmenta historicorum graecorum*, IV., pp. 93, 94: καὶ πρὸς τοῦτο ἐπένευσε βασιλεὺς, καὶ Σατορνίλου περιουσίᾳ καὶ γένει κοσμουμένου θυγατέρα εἰρήκει δώσειν. Τὸν δὲ Σατορνίλον ἀνῃρήκει Ἀθηναῒς ἡ καὶ Εὐδοκία). He was consul with Merobaudes in the year 383 A.D., the year in which Arcadius was proclaimed Augustus by his father, Theodosius I. (Socratis Scholastici, *Historiae Ecclesiasticae*, 5, 10, 5: τότε δὴ ὁ βασιλεὺς τὸν υἱὸν Ἀρκάδιον Αὔγουστον ἀνηγόρευσε κατὰ τὴν ὑπατείαν Μερογαύδου τὸ δεύτερον καὶ Σατορνίλου, τῇ ἑκκαιδεκάτῃ τοῦ Ἰανουαρίου μηνός).

Ὑπὲρ εὐχῆς is analogous to the formula ὑπὲρ νίκης or ὑπὲρ νίκης καὶ σωτηρίας, which corresponds to the Latin *pro salute* and *pro salute et victoria* (*Mittheilungen d. Deutsch. Arch. Inst.*, 1881, p. 312).

No. XXXIII.

In mosaic pavement of Byzantine Church. Length, 0.81 *m.*

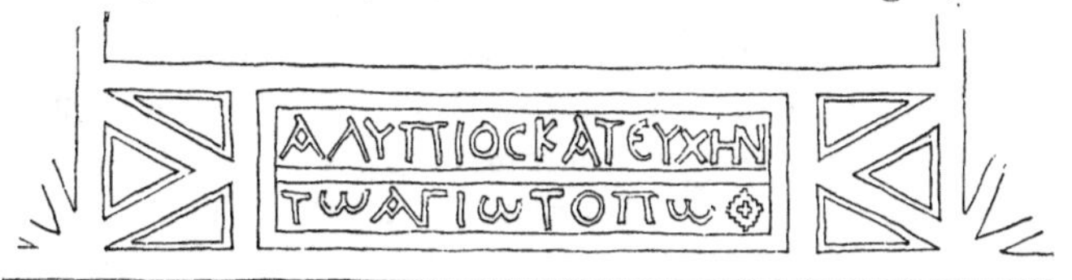

Ἀλύπιος κατ' εὐχὴν τῷ ἁγίῳ τόπῳ.

"Alypios to the Holy Place, according to his vow."

Alypios was a common name for bishops. See Le Quien, *Oriens Christianus*, I. 201, 376, 552; II. 154, 205, 551, 761, 1019, etc.

No. XXXIV.

Christian inscription above door of mosque; published in C. I. G., *No.* 8804, *and in facsimile on plate XIV. at end of Vol. IV. See opposite plate.*

Ναοῦ τὸ σαθρὸν κήρυκος Κορνηλίου εἰς κάλλος ἦρεν σὺν πόθω τε κὲ μόχθω αἰτῶν ἀμοιβὴν λύσιν πολλῶν σφαλμάτων Ἄνθιμος ὁ πρόεδρος Σκαμάνδρου πόθω· ναοῦ τὸ τερπνὸν, τὴν [θ]έσιν, τὸ πο[ικ]ίλον, ὑπερφυῆ τε λανπρότητα πᾶς βλέπων τούτου νεουργὸν Ἄνθιμον λάτρι(ν) νόει, καὶ λύσιν ἐτοῦ (i.e., αἰτοῦ) πτεσμάτων τῶν ἐν βίω.

"Anthimos, the president of Skamandros, earnestly praying for the forgiveness of his many sins as his reward, has with zeal and labor restored to beauty the unsound parts of the Church of the Herald Cornelius. Let every one who looks upon the delightsomeness of the church, its situation, its mosaic, its marvellous splendor, think of the servant (of the Lord) Anthimos, the restorer of this, and pray for the forgiveness of the sins of his life."

St. Cornelius, the Centurion (see *Acts of the Apostles*, chap. X.), was the first of the Gentiles to be baptized by St. Peter. He became a missionary to the Troad, says tradition, founded a church at Skepsis, died and was buried there. According to Le Quien (*Oriens Christianus*, I., p. 784), Skepsis afterwards changed its name to Ἅγιος Κορνήλιος, and *Philippus Cyprius* mentions Hagios Cornelios as a bishopric.

Skamandros was a town of the Troad in later times. It is mentioned in the list of Hierokles (*Synecdemus*, 672, 10, ed. Parthey, Berlin, 1866), and *Pliny*, 5, 124, says *Scamandria civitas Troadis.*

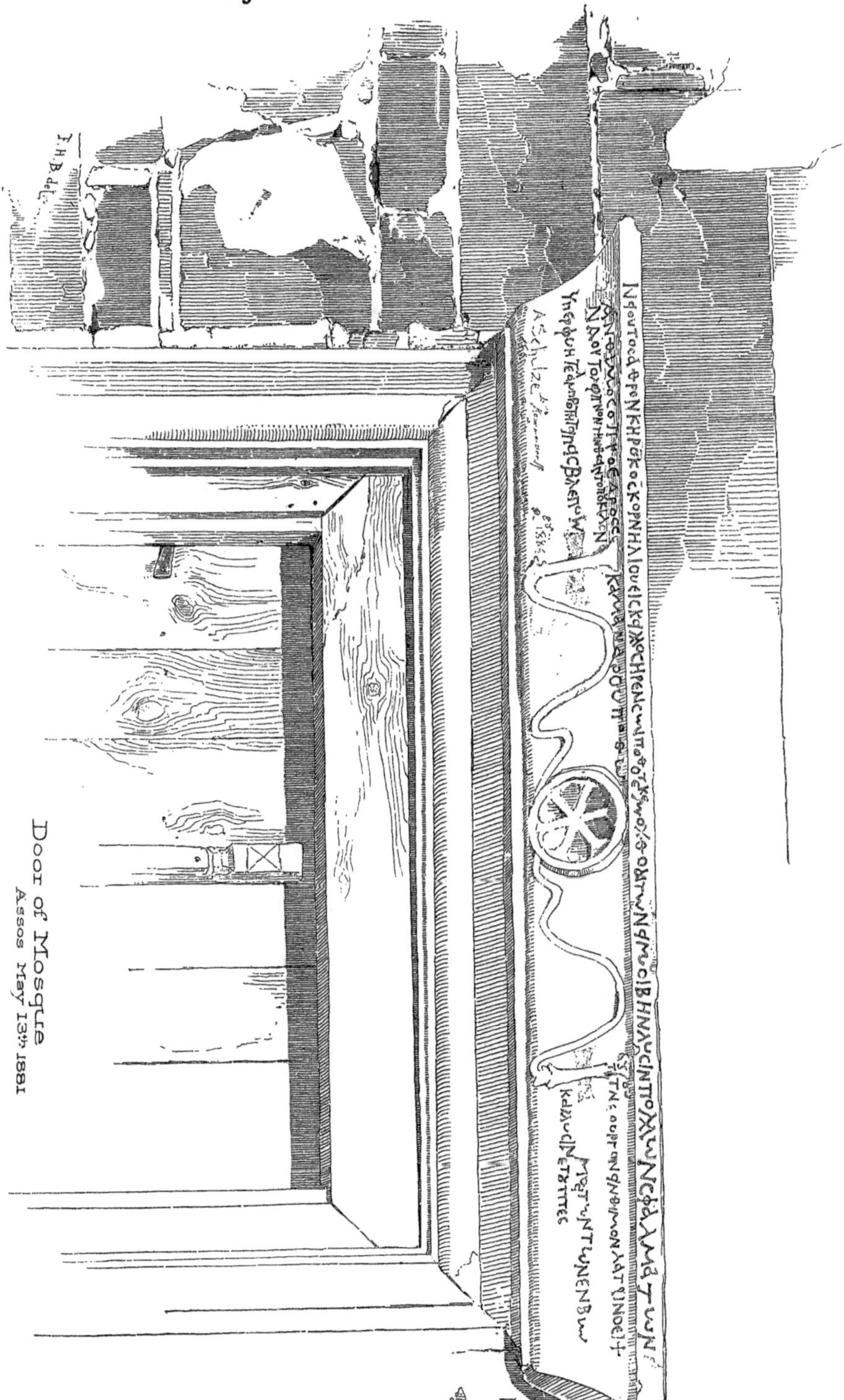

F. H. B. del.

Door of Mosque
Assos May 13th 1881

No. XXXV.

Christian inscription upon door-jamb of one of the chambers of the Greek Bath. Breadth, 0.585 m.

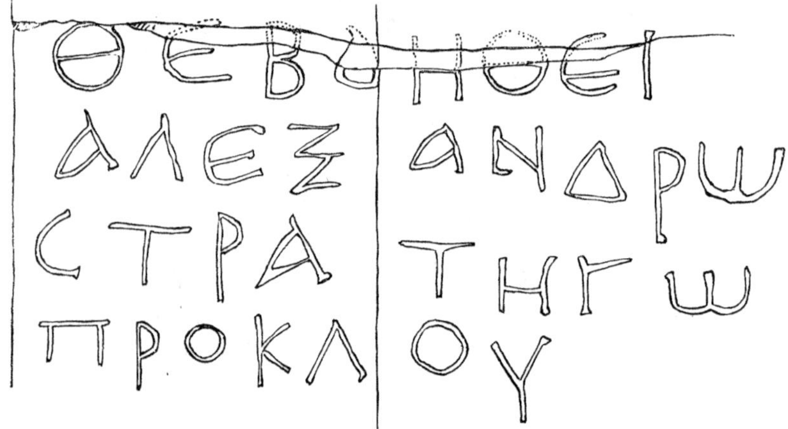

Θε(ὲ) βοήθει ’Αλεξάνδρω στρατηγῶ Πρόκλου.

"O God, help Alexander the general, son of Proklos."

The inscription perhaps indicates that this special room of the Bath was used as a tomb for Alexander the General, who must have been a man of prominence at Assos at a late period, when ancient Greek civilization had declined to such an extent that even the use of the baths had been forgotten.

No. XXXVI.

Graffito very roughly scratched on plaster of division wall of eastern chamber of later (lower) Roman Bath. The letters are deep enough to make it possible to take a plain impression. The stucco background is painted red and black.

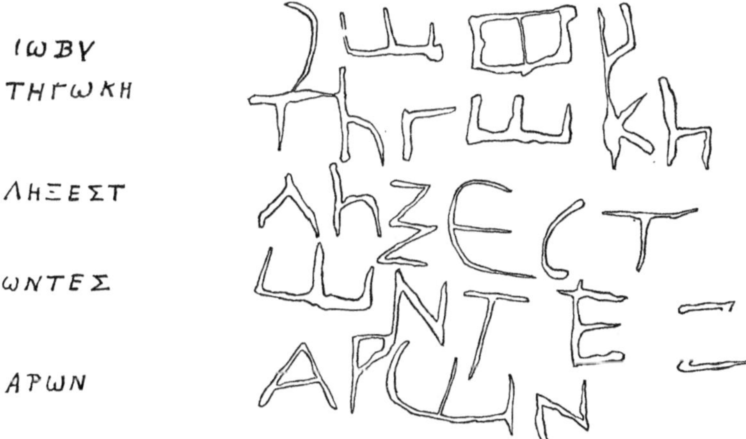

NOTE. — All the letters appear plain except the third, which can hardly be B as given in the margin of the plate. The meaning of the inscription is wholly uncertain. The beginning may be some proper name in the dative, or in the genitive in ω, perhaps preceded by the interjection Ἰώ. After this, κήλη ξεστῶν τε(σ)άρων might mean a *tumor of* (*containing*) *four pints!*

Mr. W. M. Ramsay now (December, 1884) suggests that the third character may be π, and the eighth ιᴟ for ια, and that a numeral (δύω or τρία) may be concealed in the first two characters; so that we might possibly read . . πυτήρια· κήληξ [ξ]εστῶν τε(σ)άρων, *i.e.* . . ποτήρια· κύλιξ ξεστῶν τεσσάρων. — EDD.

FRAGMENTARY INSCRIPTIONS.

No. XXXVII.

On fragment of block near entrance of Gymnasium. Height 0.40 m.; breadth at top, 0.50 m.; at bottom, 0.65 m.

TATP

[π]άτρ[ιος βασιλεύς]

No. XXXVIII.

Block of an epistyle lying on the seashore at the harbor of Assos. Beneath the crowning moulding the front is divided into three facets, on the upper two of which are the inscriptions. Length, 1.45 m.; height, 0.35 m.; thickness, 0.45 m.

SDESVAPECVN
ϽΑΝΤΕΘΥ ΙΔΩ

[· · · u]s de sua pecun[ia]

No. XXXIX.

From epistyle of Gymnasium.

Ο Ν Α Σ Δ

The fragment does not belong to the Stoa inscription, as appears from the size of the epistyle. The letters are very similar to those of the Stoa epistyle (see No. XV., p. 35), and are very nearly of the same height, but further apart.

No. XL.

Roman builder's brick with stamp. Letters beautifully cut. Found near the summit of the Acropolis.

INΘBA

Possibly the stamp indicates the conformity of the tile to an official standard, like that which forms one of the most curious discoveries of the excavations of 1882, and which will be illustrated by Mr. Clarke in his Report.

Nos. XLI. and XLII.

Fragments found in the debris accumulated beneath the retaining wall of the Agora.

(41) DIVI · F · AV
T T T

(42) ΩNTOΣ
OMΩN
Ⅎ

No. XLIII.

Four fragments of the same inscription, from the southern part of the western Street of Tombs.

Fragments 1 and 2 fit together thus:

ETEI
TATPON
OYΓON
YAΓΩNO

The first letter in line 2 may be T or Π, not Γ. In line 4, [το]ῦ ἀγῶνο[ς] is certain.

(3) K
M
AΣ

(4) I

No. XLIV.

Found on the plan of the small temple in antis, at the western end of the Agora.

NTO<

No. XLV.

On a fragment of a marble epistyle found in the Greek Bath; belongs to the interior epistyle.

TANE
ΘΑΥΗ

In line 2, a second Α has been erased, and Υ put in in its place.

No. XLVI.

On block of Anta (0.66 *m. broad,* 0.31 *high*), *near entrance to Gymnasium. Badly mutilated; central portion entirely destroyed.*

The whole Anta was probably covered by the inscription, as the top and bottom lines are too near the bond lines to admit of the inscription being complete on this one stone. Seven lines may be traced; but I can lay hold of nothing tangible on which to base a restoration.

Ι Ω		/ ΟΙϽΩ
		ΔΟ
ΚΟΜΤΟΙ		ΛΡΙΟΥ
ΙΚΛΙ Ͻ		C ΤΗΤΑΥ
ΤΗΤΗΑΩ	Ν	ϽΑΤЄ
ΓΟЄΦΩΙ		ΔΩCΙ
ΘЄΛCΟΥ	ΘΤΕΙΒΙ	ΓЄC

No. XLVII.

Fragment of athlete inscription in wall of mosque of Pademlee.

ΙΙΑΞ
ΝΕΙΚΗΣ,
ΠΑΝΚΡΑΤΙϹ
ΠΑΥΛΙΙΑΙΣ
ΣΕΙΓΙΝΡ
ΙΝ

νεικήσ[αντα ἐνδόξως]
[ἀνδρῶν] πανκράτιο[ν]

EPITAPHS.

THE gravestones of Assos are peculiar. I have seen nothing like them elsewhere in Asia Minor, if I except a single stone at Tralleis (see Tralleis Inscriptions, below, No. XIX.). They are about one foot high, and about two feet square in plan. The inscription on the side consists generally of the name of the deceased, with the name of his father in the genitive; but the name of the father is sometimes omitted. On one stone (No. LIX.) there are as many as four names.

In Asia Minor gravestones differ widely in character, a kind which occurs constantly in one locality being entirely absent in another. In Phrygia the panelled door is the rule, except in the upper Maeander valley, where the horned altar occurs. In other localities the stele slab with pediment is found.

The Epitaphs which follow are mostly dialectic. A-stems have the genitive in -α; ο-stems have the genitive in -ω; and the genitive of the sigma-stems is in -η. This genitive in -η is not susceptible of explanation; and, in fact, it has been doubted by Gustav Meyer * on the ground that Le Bas' inscription is too fragmentary to justify the assumption of such a genitive from it alone. This would be quite true if it rested solely on Le Bas' inscription. But Conze found and published several new examples of this genitive in his *Reise auf der Insel Lesbos*. Of these Θεόκλη (plate XIV. 3), Ἐχεκράτη (page 14), Ζώη (plate XVI. 1), are certain; but Θεογένη (plate VI. 3) might be disputed. Meister, in his *Griechische Dialekte*, does not

* *Griechische Grammatik*, p. 288, note 1: Dass die Formen Πολυδεύκη Εὐαγένη Ἑρμογένη, die auf einer in Delos gefundenen lesbischen Inschrift (Le Bas, *Inscriptions Grecques et Latines*, fasc. 5, No. 191) stehen, genitive sind, wie *Ahrens*, 2, 510, und nach ihm, Wald, *Additamenta ad dialectum et Lesbiorum et Thessalorum cognoscendam*, 24, annehmen, ist nicht zu erweisen, da der Text ganz lückenhaft ist.

hesitate to accept this Aeolic genitive in -η on the strength of the above evidence. But all doubts will be dissipated by the fresh and certain evidence of our epitaphs. No. LV. has Ποσείδιππος Διοφάνη; No. LVI. has Διοφάνης Διοφάνη; No. LVIII. has Τιμάνθα Ἐρατογένη; No. LXV. has Λυκομήδης Ἀναξάν[θ]η.

The corresponding dative and accusative are -ῃ and -ην.*

Note the fem. patronymic adjectives in -εια in No. XLIX., Ἀσίννω Ἀνοδικεία; and in No. LI., Ἀλέκτρα Λαριχεία, corresponding to the masculine patronymic adjectives Σωγένειος (No. III.) and Ἀνοδίκει[ος] (No. IV). Ἀσίννω Ἀνοδικεία in XLIX. is one person.

Nos. XLVIII.-LIV.

From Larichos Burial Enclosure in Western Street of Tombs.

Larichos seems to have been a very common name in Aeolic districts. Sappho's brother bore that name; and a Mytilenaean named Larichos was the father of Erigyos, one of the generals of Alexander the Great.

XLVIII. — *Andesite pedestal,* 0.79 *m. square in plan. Letters very irregularly cut; alpha bar straight.*

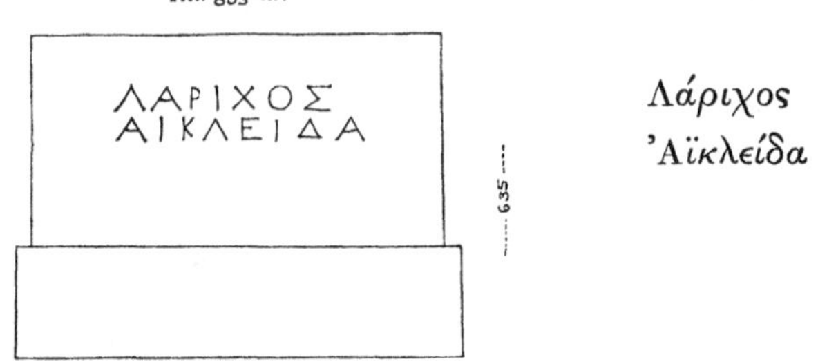

Λάριχος
Ἀϊκλείδα

* Meister, *Griechische Dialekte*, I., p. 154: Entsprechend diesen auch anderwärts vorkommenden Accusativen auf -ην, hat sich die ganze nachgewiesene Flexion der äolischen Eigennamen (-ης, -η, -ηι, (-η), -ην) nach Analogie der männlichen α-Stämme (-ᾱς, -ᾱ, -ᾱι (-ᾱ), -ᾱν) gebildet.

XLIX. — *Block* 0.79 *m. square; straight alpha bar; letters carelessly cut.*

Α≶ΙΝΝΩ	Ἀσίννω
ΑΝΟΔΙΚΕΙΑ	Ἀνοδικεία

Ἀσι- belongs to ἕαδον, ἅσ-μενος: see Fick, *Personennamen*, p. 16. For Ἀνοδικεία, patronymic adjective from Ἀνόδικος, see note to No. V.

L. — *Block* 0.785 × 0.745 *m.; straight alpha bar; letters carelessly cut.*

ΑΙΚΛΕΙΔΑ≶	Ἀϊκλείδας
ΛΑΡΙΧΩ	Λαρίχω

LI. — *Block* 0.78 *m. square; broken and straight alpha bar; letters very regularly cut.*

ΑΛΕΚΤΡΑ	Ἀλέκτρα
ΛΑΡΙΧΕΙΑ	Λαριχεία

LII. — *Block* 0.79 *m. square; broken alpha bar; letters very regularly cut.*

ΛΑΡΙΧΟ≶	Λάριχος·
ΑΙΚΛΕΙΔΑ	Ἀϊκλείδα

LIII. — *Block in plan* 0.82 × 0.785 *m.; broken alpha bar; letters well cut.*

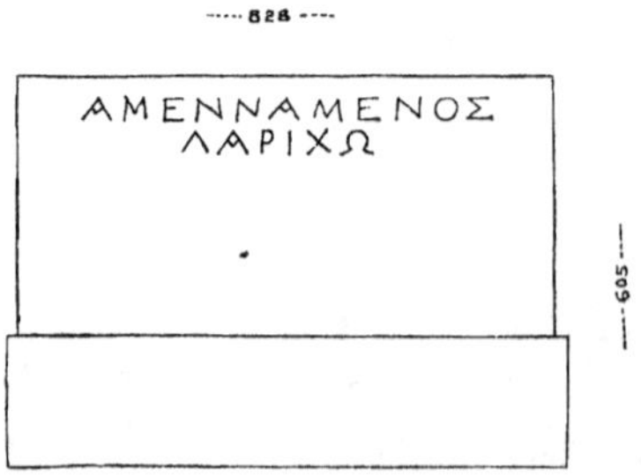

828

ΑΜΕΝΝΑΜΕΝΟΣ
ΛΑΡΙΧΩ

605

Ἀμεννάμενος
Λαρίχω

Prof. F. D. Allen (*American Journal of Philology*, 1882, p. 464) refers Ἀμεννάμενος to Ἀμεινάμενος.

LIV. — *Block* 0.625 *m. square; broken alpha bar; letters deeply cut; stone not carefully smoothed.*

ΑΔΕΑ	Ἀδέα
ΗΡΟΙΔΑ	Ἡροΐδα

The daughter of Kynane, who married Philip Arrhidaios under the name of Eurydike, was first named Adea. Heroites occurs as the name of a man on a coin of Kymai (*Mionnet*, VI. 7). In Conze (*Reise auf d. Insel Lesbos*, p. 36, l. 37) we find the name Ἡρωΐδα.

No. LV.

Pedestal near ornamented sarcophagus, on the east; like those of the Larichos Burial Enclosure. Straight alpha bar; block 0.60 *m. square.*

[Π]ΟΣΕΙΔΙΠΠΟΣ	[Π]οσείδιππος
ΔΙΟΦΑΝΗ	Διοφάνη

No. LVI.

Near ornamented sarcophagus. Straight alpha bar; block 0.55 *m. square.*

ΔΙΟΦΑΝΗΣ	Διοφάνης
ΔΙΟΦΑΝΗ	Διοφάνη

No. LVII.

On threshold of exedra, near ornamented sarcophagus in western Street of Tombs. Letters deeply but roughly cut. It is the end of an inscription.

ωΠΛΟC

No. LVIII.

Altar from "Timantha Exedra" in western Street of Tombs. In plan, 0.50 × 0.32 *m.*

TIMANΘA	Τιμάνθα
EPATOΓENH	Ἐρατογένη

With Τιμάνθα cf. Τιμάνθης: Fick, *Personennamen*, p. 154.

No. LVIX.

In western Street of Tombs. Original breadth, 0.585 *m.; height,* 0.26 *m.*

NIK · Δ	Νικ[ό]δ[ημος]
ΠΠΟΜΕΔΩΝ	[Ἱ]ππομέδων
XYPIΩNOΣ	Χυρίωνος
ΦΙΛΙΚΕΑΑΡΙΣΤΩΝ	Φιλικ[έ]α Ἀρίστων
ΜΙΔΑ	Μίδα

The stone had suffered in antiquity, especially in the first name. It was further maltreated by the wantonness of the Turks after it had been brought to light by our excavations. Thus have perished the ΦΙ of the fourth line and the ΙΔ of the fifth; but, fortunately, not until the inscription had been copied by Mr. Koldewey.

In line 4, Mr. Koldewey reads K where I think I could see E; thus, according to him, the name would be ΦΙΛΙΚΚΑ.

Four persons seem to have been buried in this grave: Nikodemos and Hippomedon, sons of Chyrion; and Philikea and Ariston, children of Midas. Χυρίωνος is possibly a mistake of the stonecutter for Κυρίωνος.

No. LX.

Inscription on sarcophagus in western Street of Tombs, near the great gateway.

It has been so hacked and battered that it is illegible. It begins with ΠΟΛ; the second line ends with ΕΡΧ; in the fifth line may be distinguished ΔΙω; but the inscription is forever lost.

No. LXI.

In western Street of Tombs; 0.78 m. square.

Α Ξ Ω Ν	Ἄξων
ΑΜΥΝΝΑΜΕΝΩ	Ἀμυνναμένω

Ἄξων perhaps = Ἄσων: Fick, *Personnenamen*, p. 16.

No. LXII.

In western Street of Tombs; 0.675 m. square.

ΚΛΕΙΤΟΜ Α	Κλειτομ[άχ]α

No. LXIII.

In western Street of Tombs; badly battered. Breadth, 0.45 m.; height, 0.27 m.

ΑΡΙΣΤΙΑΣ	Ἀριστίας

No. LXIV.

In western Street of Tombs. In plan, 0.555 × 0.525 m.

ΕΡΗΤ	Ἐρητ[υμένης?]

No. LXV.

From the eastern Street of Tombs, near and on the right of two standing columns belonging to an ancient Greek tomb. It lies in the bushes, near the footpath which turns off to the right from the columns. Alpha bar broken. Block 0.65 m. square; height, 0.315 m.

ΛΥΚΟΜΗΔΗΣ	Λυκομήδης
ΑΝΑΞΑΝΘΗ	Ἀναξάν[θ]η

With Ἀναξάνθης cf. Ἐριάνθης, Κλεάνθης: Fick, *Personennamen*, p. 154.

No. LXVI.

From eastern Street of Tombs. Block 0.68 *m. square; height,* 0.33 *m. Alpha bar straight.*

The inscription is old, its archaic character being noticeable chiefly in the unequal-legged Ͷ. Letters exactly *στοιχηδόν*. Letters of first line are deeply cut; those of the second line are not so deep, and are more weathered; but all are still distinct.

ΟͶΥΜΑΗΣ	Ὀνυμάης
ΕΓΜΕΙΤΙΣ	Ἔγμειτις

Ὀνυμάης = Ὀνόμας (Arr. *Anab.* 3, 24, 4); cf. Ὀνόμαστος = Ὀνύμαστος (Keil, *Inscrip. Boeot.* x. 4); Ahrens, *de dial. graec.*, 518, 521. Ἔγμειτις, perhaps ἐν + μῆτις (?): Fick, *Personennamen*, p. 56.

No. LXVII.

Pedestal found in field outside of the principal eastern gateway, near the head of the torrent. Block 0.60 *m. square;* 0.545 *m. high.*

ΑΡΙΣΤΙΑΣ	Ἀριστίας
ΔΑΦΑΟΥ	Δαφάου

Δάφαος: Δαο-, Δαϊ-, Δηι-, Δηϊο-; cf. Δάοχος: Fick, *Personennamen*, pp. 22, 137.

No. LXVIII.

In bushes on eastern Street of Tombs, directly east of the principal eastern gateway. 0.705 *m. square.*

ΜΟΡΜΩΤΤΟΣ	Μόρμωττος

No. LXIX.

Late Byzantine sarcophagus from middle of western Street of Tombs.

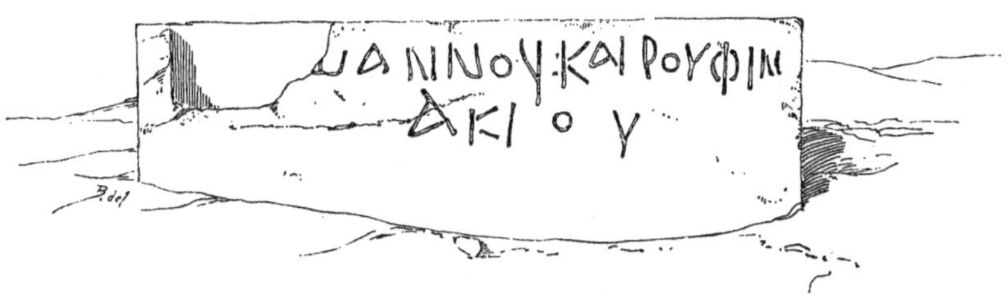

[Iω] ANNoYKAIPoYΦIN
AKIoY

[᾿Ιω]άννου καὶ ῾Ρουφινακίου.

No. LXX.

Sepulchral inscription found Sept. 12, 1881, *on a large trachyte block at the beginning of the western Street of Tombs. Published in Mr. Clarke's first Report.*

ΠΟΠΛΙΩΙΟΥΑΡΙΩΙ
ΠΟΠΛΙΟΥΥΙΩΙΑΝΙΗΝΣΙΣ
ΑΚΥΙΛΑΙ

i.e.

Ποπλίῳ Οὐαρίῳ
Ποπλίου υἱῷ ᾿Ανιῆνσις
᾿Ακυίλᾳ

P. Vario
P. F. Aniensis
Aquilae

It is now known that this inscription stood over the door of the large tomb of which the plan and section are given in Mr. Clarke's first Report, plate 32. On the left exedra of the tomb is the Latin inscription

P · VARIO · P · F · ANI · · · · ·
AQVILAE

᾿Ανιῆνσις in the Greek inscription represents the Latin genitive *Aniensis*. Members of the *tribus Aniensis* seem to have been settled in various parts of the Troad, *e.g.*, at Adramyttion (*Bull. de Corr. Hell.*, 1878, p. 129) and at Ilium (Le Bas and Waddington, *Asie Mineure*, No. 1037).

No. LXXI.

Found in the tomb of P. Varius Aquila, of which No. LXX. is the dedicatory inscription.

The stone is broken into seventeen pieces. The whole of the right side of the slab is preserved, and line 9, which is complete, shows the full length of the inscription. Length of slab, 1.68 m.; breadth, 0.84 m. The letters are large (0.04 × 0.037 m.); but the inscription is nevertheless extremely difficult to read. Hearty thanks are due to Mr. W. M. Ramsay, who, during a brief stay at Assos, gave me material help in the task of deciphering it.

ΙΟΝΙΑΝΥΠΟ..ΡΜΙ ΟΝΤΑΠΑΘωC
ωΜΑΓΓωΔЄЄΥCЄΒΙΙΥCΙΝΠΡΟΙΡЄΙ
ΔΥCΚΟΛΟΝΓΑΡЄCΤΙΝΑΤΟΝΑΛΛΟ..
ΑΤΟΝЄΜΟΝΘΑΝΑΤΟΝЄΙCΤΗΝΑΥΤΗΝΝΑΡ
ΗCΓΥΝΑΙΚΟCΜΟ Δ' CΤЄΘЄΙCΠΑΡΑΤΙ
ΝΗΜΑΗΜωΝΓι ΟΡΙΙΙΠΛΟΥΤωΝΙΠΡΟC
ΗΔΕΝΑΤΟΛΜΗCΑΙΜΗΤΕΑΦΑΙΜΑΤΟCΜΗΤЄΑΛΛΟ
ΡΙΟΝΧΡΗCΑCΘΑΙΛ ΜΗΤЄΔΥΝΗΘΗΝΑΙΤΙΝΑ
ΜЄΤΑΤΗΝЄΜΗΝЄΝΤΑΦΗΝ ΝΟΙΞΑΙΤΟ ΑΜΑΡΙΟΝ
ΑΙЄΙΙΙΒΟωΙΟΥCΤΙΒΟωΝΘΜΑΚΑΚΑΙΑΧΘΟ C
ΥCЄΙΤΙCΤΟΛΜΗCЄΙЄΞ ΚЄΙΝωΝΑΥΤΟΥCΠΑ
Ο · Ο · ΘΗCΑΙΚΟΛΑCΙΝ

. . . .

[σ]ῶμα [ἐ]γὼ δὲ
δύσ[κ]ολον γάρ ἐστιν (??)
[μετ]ὰ τὸν ἐμὸν θάνατον εἰς τὴν αὐτὴν νάρ-
[θηκα τ]ῆς γυναικός μο[υ]
[μ]νῆμα ἡμῶν Πλουτῶνι· πρὸς
[δὲ μ]ηδένα τολμῆσαι μήτε ἀφ' αἵματος μήτε ἀλλό-
[τ]ριον χρησάσθαι λ[ηνῷ] μήτε δυνηθῆναί τινα
μετὰ τὴν ἐμὴν ἐντάφην [ἀ]νοῖξαι τὸ [κ]αμάριον.
[κ]αὶ ἐ[π]ιβοῶ [τ]οὺς κα[τ]αχθο[νίους]
[θεο]ὺς, εἴ τις τολμήσει ἐξ [ἐ]κείνων, αὐτο[ῖ]ς πᾶ-
[σιν βαρεῖαν προσ]θῆσαι κόλασιν.

Line 7. In regard to *μήτε ἀφ' αἵματος*, compare *τοῖς τέκνοις ἐκ τοῦ αἵματός μου* (*Bull. de Corr. Hell.*, 1883, p. 310) and *τὸ ἀπὸ τοῦ αἵματος αὐτοῦ* (*Bull. de Corr. Hell.*, 1883, p. 312; and Mr. Ramsay's note in *Journal of Hellenic Studies*, 1883, p. 400).

Line 8. The usual word for sarcophagus is *σορός*, but *ληνός* is also found in inscriptions of Thessalonike (*C. I. G.*, 1979, 1981, 1983). It occurs also in this signification in a metrical inscription recently found on the Hohenstiefel, near Coblenz, and published by Mommsen in the *Wochenschrift für Klassische Philologie*, 1884, No. I., pp. 26, 27. Mommsen thinks this use of the word is sufficient reason to claim Thessalonike as the home of Tychikos, the man over whose grave the epitaph once stood. But it occurs also in an inscription of Mytilene, published in the *Bull. de Corr. Hell.*, 1880, p. 423. Pollux (10, 150) makes this remark: *σοροποιοῦ σκεύη σορὸς, πυελὸς, κιβωτὸς, ληνός*. The restoration *ληνός* seems certain.

Line 9. *ἐντάφη* was found for the first time in a dialectic inscription of Kymai (*C. I. G.*, 3524, 11); next in an inscription of Tralleis (see Tralleis Inscriptions, below, No. XVII.).

καμάριον is the diminutive of *καμάρα*, *a vaulted chamber*, frequent in inscriptions in the sense of *tomb*. In this signification *καμάρα* is confined strictly to Asia Minor, and is found in inscriptions of Smyrna, Ephesos, Chios, Teos, Thyateira, Hierapolis, Telmissos, Palmyra, and once in an inscription found in Rome (*C. I. G.*, 6341), which was no doubt the epitaph of a man from Asia Minor. The exact meaning of *καμάρα* is best illustrated by an inscription of Tralleis published in the *Bull. de Corr. Hell.*, 1881, p. 346: Ἡ *σορὸς καὶ ἡ περὶ αὐτὴν καμάρα καὶ ὁ παρακείμενος βωμὸς καὶ ἡ παρεστῶσα στήλη, κ.τ.λ.*

We are justified in assuming that the inscription was erected by P. Varius Aquila, in whose tomb it was found, and that it occupied the interior back wall, so that it was the first object to strike the eye of a person entering.

No. LXXII.

Inscription on a sarcophagus in the field at the extreme north of western Street of Tombs. (*See opposite page.*) *Published by Boeckh,* C. I. G., 3573.

The original inscription reads : —

ΑΝΓΟϹΚΛΑΥ	Ἄνγος Κλαυ(δίου)
ΜΑΚΕΔΟΝΟϹ	Μακεδόνος
ΚΑΙΚΛ · ΝΕΙΚΗϹ	καὶ Κλ(αυδίας) Νείκης,
ΠΕΡΙΟΥΚΑΙΔΙ	περὶ οὗ καὶ δι-
ΑΤΑΞΙϹΕΝΤΟΙϹ	άταξις ἐν τοῖς
ΑΡΧΕΙΟΙϹΑΠΟ	ἀρχείοις . ἀπό-
ΚΕΙΤΑΙ	κειται

" Coffin of Claudius Makedon and Claudia Nike, concerning which a legal document is deposited in the archives."

The inscription by the side of the original one,

+ΛΟΥΚΙΑΝΟΥΠΡΕϹΒ +Λουκιανοῦ πρεσβ(υτέρου),

tells us that the sarcophagus was afterwards appropriated by Loukianos (or Lucian), an elder of the Christian church of Assos.

Our excavations have shown that such appropriation of others' tombs was very common at Assos, as many as five or six bodies often being found in one grave. This, too, was in defiance of the imprecations and penalties invoked upon the heads of violators of tombs by the original owners. It was customary to invoke the vengeance of the Gods on those who should dare to remove the body from the tomb or to place another there. Usually a sum of money was indicated in the epitaph, which was to be paid to the family of him whose tomb had thus been violated, or to the municipal treasury, or to both. Besides curses and threats of fines, the epitaph not infrequently goes

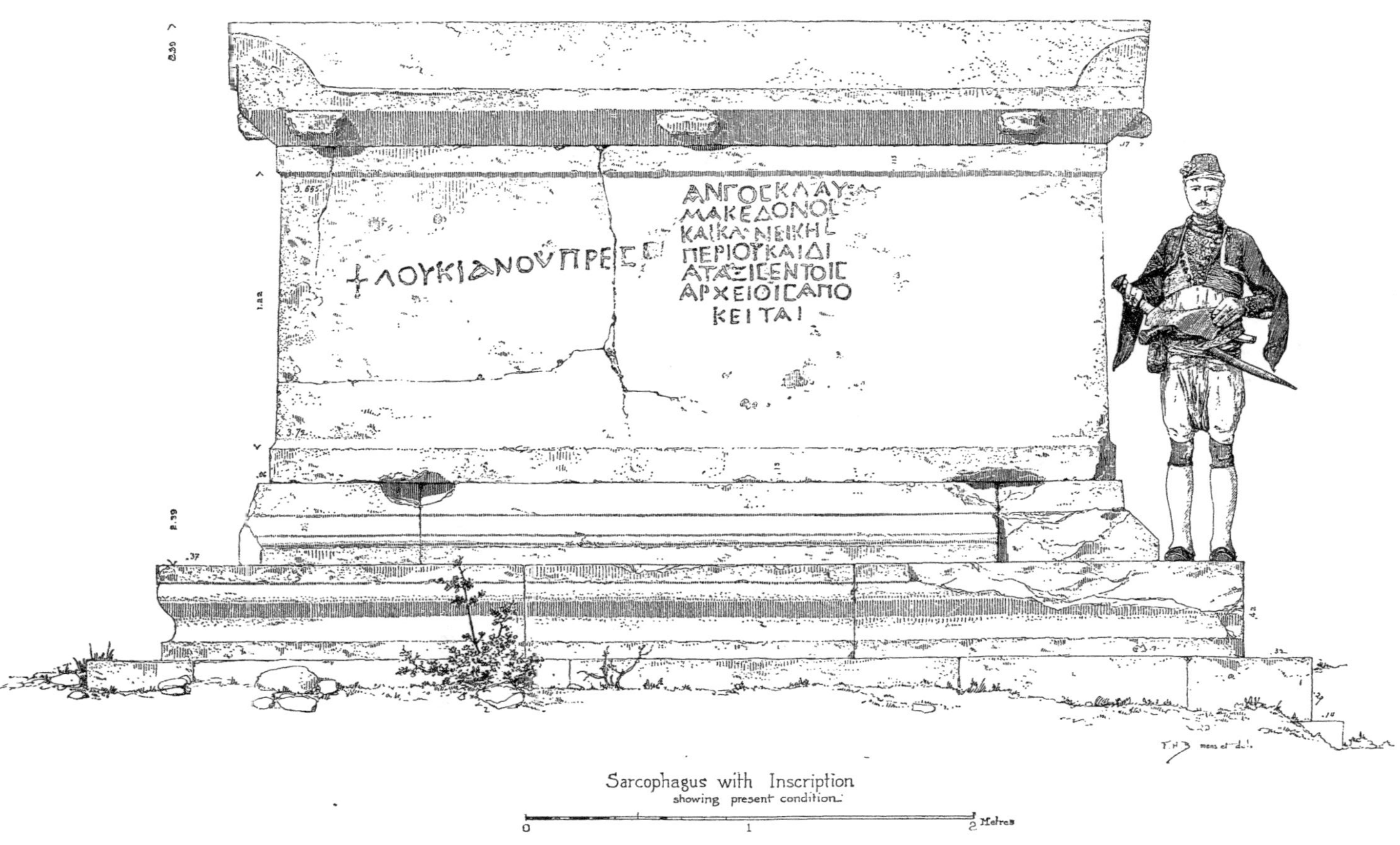

Sarcophagus with Inscription
showing present condition.

on to state that the document has been registered officially, and deposited in the archives of the city, to ensure that transgressors shall be prosecuted to the full extent of the law. The penalty for violation of the tomb is not mentioned in our inscription, but that it existed in the archives is clear from the words *περὶ οὗ καὶ διάταξις ἐν τοῖς ἀρχείοις ἀπόκειται.**

---

* The Gods were called upon to wreak vengeance on tomb-violators in manifold ways, of which the following (*C. I. G.*, 3915) may serve as a specimen: *ὃς δὲ ἂν ἐναντίον τι ποιήσει τοῖς προγεγραμμένοις, ἔσται μὲν ὑπεύθυνος τοῖς προστείμοις, καὶ μήτε τέκνων μήτε βίου ὄνησις εἴη μηδὲ γῆ βατὴ μηδὲ θάλασσα πλωτή, ἀλλὰ ἄτεκνος καὶ ἄβιος καὶ προώλης σὺν τῷ σπέρματι παντὶ ἀποθάνοι· καὶ μετὰ θάνατον δὲ λάβοι τοὺς ὑποχθονίους θεοὺς τιμωροὺς καὶ κεχολωμένους.*

The Christian curses yield but little in point of fierceness to the pagan. Usually, in Christian inscriptions, we find that the tomb-violator *shall reckon it out with God*, *ἔσται αὐτῷ πρὸς τὸν θεόν*; but this formula is subject to a number of variations, most of which have been collated by Mr. Ramsay in the *Journal of Hellenic Studies*, 1883, p. 400. Thus we find *ἔσται αὐτῷ πρὸς τὸ μέγα ὄνομα τοῦ θεοῦ* (*C. I. G.*, 3902); *ἔσται αὐτῷ πρὸς τὸν ζῶντα θεὸν καὶ νῦν καὶ ἐν τῇ κρισίμῳ ἡμέρᾳ* (*C. I. G.*, 3902 *r*); *λήψεται παρὰ τοῦ ἀθανάτου θεοῦ μάστειγα αἰώνιον* (*C. I. G.*, 3891); *ἔσται αὐτῷ πρὸς τὴν χεῖρα τοῦ θεοῦ* (*C. I. G.*, 3963); *ἔσται αὐτῷ πρὸς τὸν κριτὴν θεόν* (*Bull. de Corr. Hell.*, 1883, pp. 310, 312); *ἐνορκιζόμεθα τὸ μέγεθος τοῦ θεοῦ καὶ τοὺς καταχθονίους δαίμονας μηδένα ἀδικῆσαι τὸ μνημεῖον* (*Bull. de Corr. Hell.*, 1882, p. 516: in the *Journal of Hellenic Studies*, as cited above, Mr. Ramsay asks in regard to this, "Are the *δαίμονας* devils, or is the inscription a mixture of pagan and Christian phraesology?"); *ἔσται ἐπικατάρατος παρὰ θεῷ εἰς τὸν αἰῶνα* (*Journal of Hellenic Studies*, 1883, pp. 400, 408); *ἔσται αὐτῷ πρὸς τὸν Χριστόν* (*C. I. G.*, 3902: Boeckh doubts this, but the stone is still in the cemetery of Eumenia, and the reading is certain; see *Journal of Hellenic Studies*, 1883, pp. 433, 401); *ὃς ἂν ταύτῃ τῇ σορῷ κακοεργέα χεῖρα προσοίσει, δώσει τῷ θεῷ λόγον τῷ μέλλοντι κρείνειν ζῶντας κὲ νεκρούς* (*Journal of Hellenic Studies*, 1883, p. 435).

No. LXXIII.

Stone built into an arch of the church south of the Greek Bath. Published by Le Bas and Waddington, Asie Mineure, 1034 d, *from Duthoit's imperfect copy. Height of panel,* 0.33 *m.; length of panel,* 0.71 *m.*

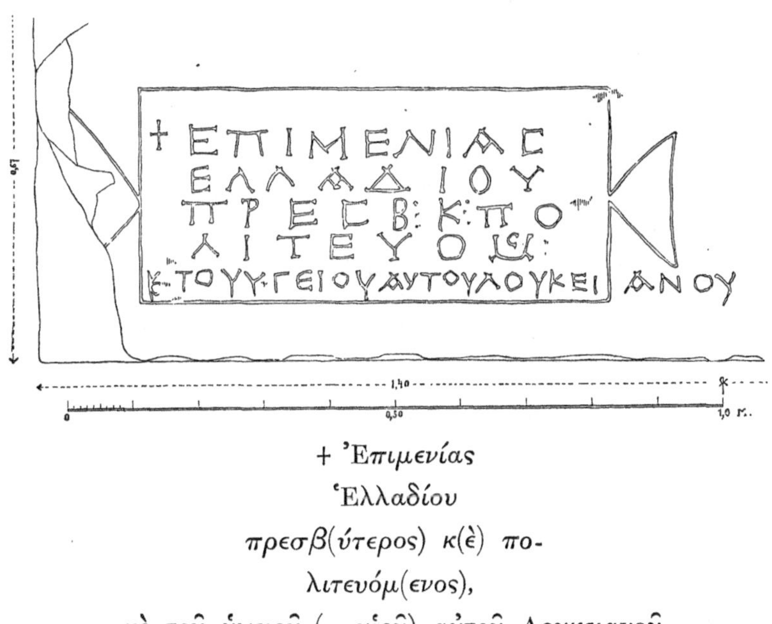

+ Ἐπιμενίας
Ἑλλαδίου
πρεσβ(ύτερος) κ(ὲ) πο-
λιτευόμ(ενος),
κὲ τοῦ ὑγειοῦ (= υἱοῦ) αὐτοῦ Λουκειανοῦ.

"Epimenias, son of Helladios, elder and statesman, and his son Loukianos."

The panel was intended originally only for the epitaph of Epimenias; but later, when his son Loukianos died, his name was added for reasons of economy. It will be seen that the family were as economical of grammar as of money.

For πολιτευόμενος see *C. I. G.*, 2059, 2152 *b*, 2671, 2693 *d*, 2811 *b*; and *Bull. de Corr. Hell.*, 1878, p. 599, 1883, p. 17.

No. LXXIV.

Sarcophagus inscription from middle of western Street of Tombs. Measurements, 0.90 × 0.75 *m.*

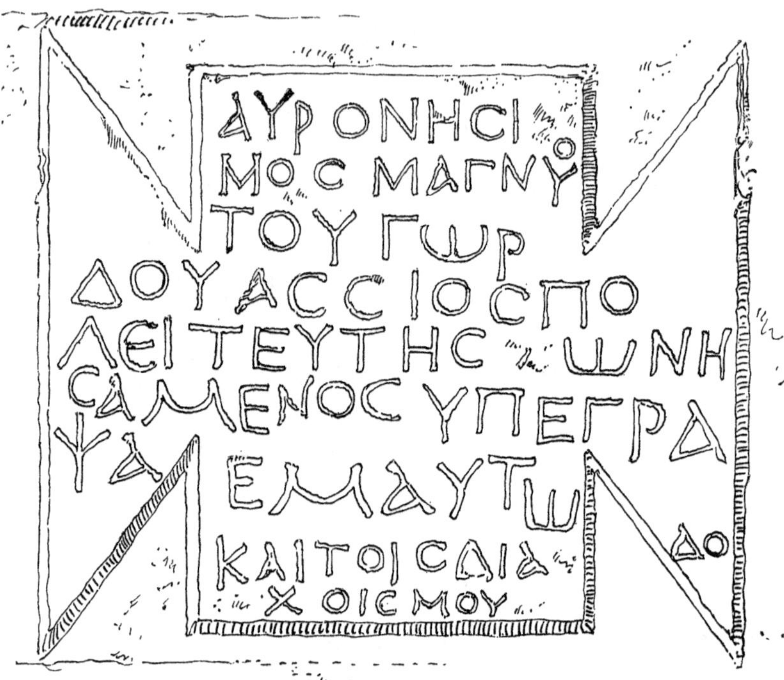

Αὐρ(ήλιος) Ὀνήσιμος Μάγνου τοῦ Γώρδου, Ἄσσιος πολειτευτὴς, ὠνησάμενος ὑπέγραψα ἐμαυτῷ καὶ τοῖς διαδόχοις μου.

"I, Aurelius Onesimos, son of Magnus, the son of Gordos, an Assian statesman, have bought (this tomb) and subscribed (a document devoting ?) it to myself and my successors."

Here ὑπέγραψα probably refers to a legal document (διάταξις) intended to secure the tomb for his family, and deposited in the archives, as in No. LXXII. Gordos is a new name.

ADDITIONAL NOTE.

On a base at the eastern end of the Stoa, which is certainly not of earlier date than the buildings around it, Koppa appears as one of the many masons' marks. Masons' marks occur on nearly all the buildings of Assos, as well as on the more recent fortification walls; but none have been found on the most ancient walls.

LIST OF NAMES OCCURRING IN THE ASSOS INSCRIPTIONS.

[*The names marked with an asterisk are new.*]

I. — GREEK NAMES.

'Αδέα, LIV.
'Αθηναγόρας, VII.
'Αθηνόδοτος, XIV.
* 'Αϊκλείδας, XLVIII., L., LII.
Αἰσχρίων, XXVI.
'Αλέκτρα, LI.
'Αλέξανδρος, XXXV.
Ἄλύπιος, XXXIII.
* 'Αμεννάμενος, LIII.
* 'Αμυναμενός, VIII.
* 'Αμυννάμενος, LXI.
'Αναξαγόρας, VII.
* 'Αναξάνθης, LXV.
Ἄνθιμος, XXXIV.
* 'Ανοδικεία, XLIX.
* 'Ανοδίκειος, IV.
* 'Ανόδικος, V.
* Ἄξων, LXI.
'Απελλικῶν, XXII., XXIII., XXIV.
['Απολλ]ώνιος (?), XXI.
'Αριστίας, XXVII., LXIII., LXVII.
'Αρίστων, LIX.
'Αρτεμίδωρος, XXVI.
* 'Ασίννω, XLIX.
* Βρησικλῆς, VIII.
* Γῶρδος, LXXIV.
* Δάφαος, LXVII.
Διονύσιος, VII.
Διοφάνης, LV., LVI.
* Ἔγμειτις, LXVI.
'Ελλάδιος, LXXIII.
'Ελλάνικος, XIV.
* 'Ελλῶπις (?), XIV.
* 'Επάνθης, XXVIII.
'Εμπεδίων, VIII.
* 'Επιμενίας, LXXIII.
'Ερατογένης, LVIII.
'Ερητ[υμένης ?], LXIV.
'Ερμογένης, XXVIII.
'Ερμοφάνης, XXVI.
'Εχέλαος, VII.
Ζωΐλος, XXVI.
* 'Ηγιασαγόρας, VII.
* 'Ηροΐδας, LIV.
* 'Ηφαιστογένης, XXVII.
'Ιππομέδων, LIX.
'Ιωάννης, LXIX.
Καλλισθένης, XXVII.
Καλλιφάνης, XXVI.
Κλειτομάχα, LXII.

II. — ROMAN NAMES.

(*a*) Emperors and Empresses.

(*b*) Consuls.

(*c*) PROCONSULS.

Caelius Montius, XXX.

Satornilos (perhaps), XXXII.

(*d*) OTHER ROMAN NAMES.

St. Cornelius, XXXIV.
Lollia Antiochis, XVI., XVII.
Lollia Arlegilla, XIV.
Quintus Lollius, XVIII.
Quintus Lollius Philetairos, XV., XVI., XVII.
Magnus, LXXIV.
Gaius Varius Castus, XXVI.
Publius Varius Aquila, LXX.

THE following Assos inscriptions are now in the MUSEUM OF FINE ARTS in Boston.

They are here designated by the numbers under which they stand in the Museum Catalogue. S. denotes *Stone Register;* P. denotes *Pottery Register.*

No. in this volume.	No. in Museum Register.
III.	S. 1123.
IV.	S. 1124.
V.	S. 1125.
VI.	S. 1122.
VII.	S. 1131.
VIII.	S. 1132.
IX.	S. 1133.
X.	S. 1141.
XI.	S. 1126.
XII.	S. 1127.
XIII.	S. 1136.
XIV.	S. 1140.
XVI.	S. 1139.
XVIII.	S. 1129.
XXI., i., ii.	S. 1137. *a, b, c.*
" iii. (Now in four fragments.)	S. 1117.
XXIV.	S. 1119.
XXVII., *a* (*b* and *c* are not in the Museum.)	S. 1177.
XXVIII.	S. 1134.
XL.	P. 4168.
XLI.	S. 1116.
XLII.	S. 1023.
XLIII. (Now in five fragments.)	S. 1111, *a, b, g, j, d.*
XLV. (In three fragments.)	S. 1135.
LXXI. (In seventeen fragments.)	S. 1138.

INSCRIPTIONS OF TRALLEIS.

EDITED BY

J. R. S. STERRETT.

INSCRIPTIONS OF TRALLEIS.

THE following inscriptions are a part of the results of the work carried on during the summer of 1883, by means of the ASIA MINOR EXPLORATION FUND, which was subscribed in England under the auspices of the "Society for the Promotion of Hellenic Studies."

During a great part of the summer I accompanied Mr. W. M. Ramsay on his expedition into Asia Minor. Tralleis is so easy of access by railway from Smyrna that we did not expect to find inscriptions there; in fact, we went on other business preparatory to our expedition into the interior. But brought incidentally into contact with the inscriptions below, we copied them as a matter of course. Scholars have long known of and coveted the six inscriptions which are built into the wall of the great ruin known now as the Utch Geuz, the Three Eyes or Arches. Frequent attempts have been made to read them with a glass from the time of Pococke to the present day; but such attempts have either been very unsatisfactory or have failed entirely owing to the smallness of the letters of the inscriptions and the great height of the stones above the ground. Convinced by trial of the utter hopelessness of gaining satisfactory readings with a glass, we determined to make a ladder long enough to reach them. The construction of the ladder was accomplished through the very great kindness of Mr. Urquhart of Aidin, who furnished us with the necessary materials, seventeen working men, and two carpenters. But, even with the help of the ladder, the undertaking was attended with great difficulty and considerable danger. The impossibility of taking impressions of the stones under such circumstances will be evident to all.

In the preparation of this paper I have received material help from Mr. Ramsay. It was first published in the *Mittheilungen des deutschen archäologischen Institutes in Athen*, 1883, pp. 320–338; and it is here reprinted with some changes and additions, the most important of which are in Nos. VI., XI., XIV., and XV.

No. I.

At Tralleis, on front of Utch Geuz. Copied by J. R. S. S.

Λ Ο Λ Λ Ι Α Ν Ο Ν
ΤΟΝΛΑΜΠΡΟΤΑΤΟΝ
Τ Η Σ Α Σ Ι Α Σ
ΑΝΘΥΠΑΤΟΝΤΟΓ
ΛΑΜΠΡΟΤΑΤΗΚΑΙΣΑΡΕΩΝ
ΤΡΑΛΛΙΑΝΩΝΠΟΛΙΣΤΟΝΕΜ
ΠΑΣΙΝΕΑΥΤΗΣΕΥΕΡΓΕΤΗΝ
ΠΡΟΝΟΗΣΑΜΕΝΩΝ
ΤΗΣΑΝΑΣΤΑΣΕΩΣΤΩΝΤΙΜΩΝ
ΤΦΑΔΙΑΔΟΥΤΙΕΝΟΥΝΚΑΙΜΑΥΡ
ΕΠΑΓΑΘΟΥΔΙΟΝΥΣΙΟΥΚΑΙΜΑΥΡ
ΧΑΡΙΤΩΝΟΣΝΚΑΙΠΟΛΟΥΚΙΛΙΟΥ
ΜΟΥΝΑΤΙΟΥΚΛΩΔΙΑΝΟΥΚΑΙΠΛΓ
ΚΙΝΝΙΟΥΓΛΥΠΤΟΥΙΕΡΕΩΝΤΩΝ
ΓΡΑΜΜΑΤΕΩΝΤΟΥΔΗΜΟΥ *

Λολλιανὸν τὸν λαμπρότατον τῆς Ἀσίας ἀνθύπατον τὸ γ΄ [ἡ] λαμπροτάτη Καισαρέων Τραλλιανῶν πόλις τὸν ἐμ πᾶσιν ἑαυτῆς εὐεργέτην· προνοησαμένων τῆς ἀναστάσεως τῶν τιμῶν [Τ]. Φ[λ](αουίου) Διαδου[μ]ένου ν(εωτέρου) καὶ Μ. Αὐρ. Ἐπαγάθου Διονυσίου καὶ Μ. Αὐρ. Χαρίτωνος ν(εωτέρου) καὶ Πο(πλίου) Λουκιλίου Μουνατίου Κλωδιανοῦ καὶ Π. Λ[ι]κιννίου Γλύπτου ἱερέων τῶν γραμματέων τοῦ δήμου.

---

* The ligatures that occur in this and the following inscriptions cannot be given in type.

Boeckh has written at some length on the proconsulship of Lollianus (ad *C. I. G.*, 3516), and Waddington has collected the inscriptions and passages of authors which bear upon the proconsulships of Lolliani (*Fastes des provinces Asiatiques de l'Empire Romain*, Nos. 165 and 173; and *Bull. de Corr. Hell.*, 1882, p. 291). To the data of M. Waddington may be added a passage from the *Acta Sanctorum Leonis et Paregorii* in *AA. SS.*, Feb. III., p. 59: *Illis vero diebus contigit Proconsulem Lollianum, electum ab Imperatoribus, venire usque ad eos, cum eo tempore penes Procuratorem urbis, qui erat Pataris, regimen foret.* Three proconsuls of Asia Minor bore the name of Lollianus: Lollianus Gentianus, Lollianus Avitus, and Egnatius Lollianus. The Lollianus of this inscription must be the third, inasmuch as neither of the others could properly be called simply Lollianus. The second proconsulate of Egnatius Lollianus is mentioned in an inscription of Thyateira (*C. I. G.*, 3517); his third proconsulate in one of Alexandria Troas (*C. I. L.*, III., 468). The date of Lollianus is still uncertain; it appears from the *Acta Sanctorum* that two emperors were reigning during part of his term of office, and from the inscription of Thyateira that there was only one emperor during his second proconsulate.

We gather from this inscription that there was a board of five γραμματεῖς τοῦ δήμου in Tralleis.

A Tiberius Claudius Glyptos is mentioned in an inscription of Tralleis (*C. I. G.*, 2926; Le Bas and Waddington, *Voy. Arch.*, No. 604). He was doubtless a kinsman of the Glyptos of our inscription, who in all probability was the clerk of Tralleis mentioned on coins of Septimius Severus and Caracalla (cf. Mionnet, *Lydie*, 1095, 1099, 1100).

Mounatios was perhaps son of the critic of Tralleis, a friend of Herodes Atticus (Philostratos, *Vit. Soph.*, p. 231: ξυμπίπτοντα δὲ αὐτῷ Μουνάτιον τὸν κριτικόν· ὁ δὲ ἀνὴρ οὗτος ἐκ Τραλλέων, κ.τ.λ.).

No. II.

In wall of cotton factory of Anastasios Kokkalas in Aidin. Copied by W. M. R. and J. R. S. S. Published in the Ὅμηρος *(a periodical of Smyrna),* 1874, *p.* 29, *but inaccurately.*

ΗΒΟΥΛΗΚΑΙΟΔΗΜΟΣ
ΚΑΙΗΓΕΡΟΥΣΙΑΕΤΕΙΜΗΣΑΝ
ΤΙΒΕΡΙΟΝΚΛΑΥΔΙΟΝΤΙΒΕΡΙ
Ο////ΛΑΥΔΙΟΥΗΦΑΙΣΤΙΩΝΟΣ
ΥΙΟ\ΚΥΡΕΙΝΑΗΦΑΙΣΤΙΩΝΑ
ΕΠ////ΓΟΝΙΑΝΟΝΓΥΜΝΑΣΙΑ////
ΧΗΣΑΝΤΑΤΩΝΤΡΙΩΝΓΥ
ΜΝΑΣΙΩΝΤΗΝΠΡΩΤΗΝΤΕ
ΤΡΑΜΗΝΟΝΕΚΤΩΝΙΔΙΩΝΚΑΙ
ΘΕΝΤΑΕ\ΛΙΟΝΔΙΟΛΗΣΗ
ΜΕΡΑΣΖΗΣΑΝΤΑΣΩΦΡΟΝΩΣ
ΚΑΙΚΟΣΜΙΩΣ
ΚΛΑΥΔΙΑΕΠΙΓΟΝΟΥΤΕΤΡΑΚΙΣ
ΟΛΥΜΠΙΟΝΕΙΚΟΥΘΥΓΑΤΗΡ
ΙΙΓΡΙΓΕΝΙΣΤΟΝΙΔΙΟΝΥΟΝΓΕΝΟ
ΜΕΝΟΝΦΙΛΟΜΗΤΟΡΑ

Ἡ βουλὴ καὶ ὁ δῆμος καὶ ἡ γερουσία ἐτείμησαν Τιβέριον Κλαύδιον, Τιβερίο[υ Κ]λαυδίου Ἡφαιστίωνος υἱό[ν], Κυρείνᾳ, Ἡφαιστίωνα Ἐ[πιγ]ονιανόν, γυμνασια[ρ]-χήσαντα τῶν τριῶν γυμνασίων τὴν πρώτην τετράμηνον ἐκ τῶν ἰδίων καὶ θέντα ἔ[λα]ιον δι' ὅλης ἡμέρας, ζήσαντα σωφρόνως καὶ κοσμίως. Κλαυδία, Ἐπιγόνου τετράκις Ὀλυμπιονείκου θυγάτηρ, [Περιγ]ενὶς τὸν ἴδιον υ(ἱ)ὸν γενόμενον φιλομήτορα.

Tiberius Claudius Hephaistion, being named in honor of Tiberius, was probably not born before Tiberius became emperor, so that his birth can hardly have taken place before the year 14 A.D. If we allow twenty-five years for him to grow to manhood and become a father, the birth of his son, Tiberius Claudius Epigonianos, would fall about the year 39 A.D. Supposing then that Epigonianos was forty years old when he held the office of gymnasiarch, we obtain as the earliest probable date for our inscription the year 79 A.D. Tiberius Claudius is a popular name through all Trallian history, and our inscription is perhaps as late as the year 150 A.D. Assuming that the mother, Claudia Perigenis, was nineteen years old at the birth of her son, Tib. Cl. Hephaistion Epigonianos, the earliest probable date for her birth is the year 20 A.D. She belonged to a distinguished Trallian family, the Epigoni, which Cicero* says was well known even in Rome, and she brought this name into the family of the Hephaistiones.

No. III.

At Tralleis, on front of Utch Geuz. Copied by J. R. S. S.

ΕΥΤΥΧΗ
ΤΟΝΑΞΙΟΛΟΓΩΤΑΤΟΝ
ΔΙΟΛΟΥΤΟΥΕΤΟΥΣ
ΜΟΝΟΝ
ΑΓΟΡΑΝΟΜΟΝ
ΗΣΥΝΤΕΧΝΙΑ
ΤΩΝΛΙΝΥΦΩΝ

Εὐτύχη τὸν ἀξιολογώτατον δι' ὅλου τοῦ ἔτους μόνον ἀγορανόμον ἡ συντεχνία τῶν λινύφων.

This inscription is in a state of perfect preservation. Le Bas attempted to read it with a glass, but with very indifferent success, as a glance at Le Bas and Waddington (*Voy. Arch.*, No. 606) will show.

Eutyches is here honored by the guild of linen weavers as the only ἀγορανόμος, *director of the market*, for a whole year. He is clearly identical with Μάρκος Νώνιος Εὐτύχης, who is handed down to memory in an *official* inscription of the city of Tralleis (*C.I. G.*, 2929). Among other things, it is there recorded that he was the first and only ἀγορανόμος for a whole year (καὶ δι' ὅλου τοῦ ἔτους πρῶτον καὶ μόνον ἀγορανομήσαντα). The municipal officers were elected for a term of four months (τετράμηνος), and Eutyches held this office for three terms, or through the whole year.

* *Pro Flacco*, 22: Ubi erant illi Pythodori, Archidemi, Epigoni, ceteri homines apud nos noti, inter suos nobiles?

No. IV.

At Tralleis, on side of Utch Geuz. Copied by J. R. S. S.

\ΝΜΑΥΡΣΩΤΗΡΙΧΟΝ
ΛΟΤΕΙΜΟΤΑΤΟΝ
ΑΡΧΟΝΚΑΙΔΙΑΠΑΣΗΣ
ΕΚΠΡΟΓΟΝΩΝΕΝ
\ΞΙΝΛΕΙΤΟΥΡΓΟΝ

[Οἱ (νέοι, γέροντες, λίνυφοι?) ἐτείμησ]αν Μ. Αὐρ. Σωτήριχον [τὸν φι]λοτειμότατον [βούλ]αρχον καὶ διὰ πάσης [κρίσεως?] ἐκ προγόνων ἐν [πᾶσ]ιν λειτουργόν.

This inscription was published by Boeckh (*C. I. G.*, 2928) from Pococke, and afterwards by Waddington (*Voy. Arch.*, No. 608) from Le Bas' more careful copy. A closer inspection of the stone has brought to light only a few more letters. I am convinced that a down stroke (\), like that of an A, preceded the N in the first line. This would seem to demand a plural verb, whose subject might be νέοι, γέροντες, λίνυφοι, or something similar.

No. V.

At Tralleis, on front of Utch Geuz. Copied by J. R. S. S.

ΗΒΟΥΛΗΚΑΙΟΔΗΜΟϹΕΤΙ
ΜΗϹΕΝΜΑΥΡΕΥΑΡΕϹΤΟΝ
ΒΟΥΛΑΡΧΗϹΑΝΤΑΑΓΟΡΑΝΟΜΗ
ϹΑΝΤΑΕΙΡΗΝΑΡΧΗϹΑΝΤΑϹΤΡΑ
ΤΗΓΗϹΑΝΤΑΔΕΚΑΠΡΩΤΕΥϹΑΝ
///ΑϹΕΙΤΩΝΗϹΑΝΤΑΤΑΜΙΕΥϹΑΝΤΑ
ΑΝΑΘΕΝΤΑΤΗΚΡΑΤΚLΒΟΥΛΗ
ΕΙϹΝΟΜΗΝΕΠΙΤΗΓΕΝΕΘΛΙΩΗΜΕ

Η
ΡΑΗΤΙϹΕϹΤΙΝΜΠΕΡΕΙΤΙΟΥΘ̄✱ΓΤΛΙ

ΠΡΟΝΟΗϹΑΜΕΝΟΥΤΗϹΑΝΑϹΤΑϹΕ
ΩϹΤΟΥΑΝΔΡΙΑΝΤΟϹΜΑΥΡϹΩΤΗΡΙ
///ΟΥΤΟΥΥΙΟΥΑΥΤΟΥΒΟΥΛΗϹΔΗ
///ΟΥΓΕΡΟΥϹΙΑϹΓΡΑΜΜΑΤΕΩϹ

Ἡ βουλὴ καὶ ὁ δῆμος ἐτίμησεν Μ. Αὐρ. Εὐάρεστον, *βουλαρχήσαντα, ἀγορανομήσαντα, εἰρηναρχήσαντα, στρατηγήσαντα, δεκαπρωτεύσαν[τ]α, σειτωνήσαντα, ταμιεύσαντα, ἀναθέντα τῇ κρατ(ίστῃ)* Κλ(αυδίᾳ) Βουλῇ *εἰς νομὴν ἐπὶ τῇ γενεθλίῳ ἡμέρᾳ, ἥτις ἐστὶν μη(νὸς)* Περειτίου *ἐννάτῃ, δηνάρια γτλ[γ΄]· προνοησαμένου τῆς ἀναστάσεως τοῦ ἀνδριάντος* Μ. Αὐρ. Σωτηρί[χ]*ου, τοῦ υἱοῦ αὐτοῦ, βουλῆς, δή[μ]ου, γερουσίας γραμματέως.*

This inscription is almost perfectly preserved. It was first examined by Fellows with a glass, and was published by Boeckh (*C. I. G.*, 2930 *b*) from Fellows' *Lycia*. It was afterwards copied more successfully, but still very imperfectly, by Le Bas (*Voy. Arch.*, No. 610). The stone is about fifty-five feet from the ground, and the letters of the inscription are so small that it is impossible to read it accurately, even with the best glass.

The Euarestos of this inscription bears the name of Marcus Aurelius, so that he could hardly have been born before the year 161 A.D. He was probably the son of the Euarestos, who is frequently mentioned as clerk of Tralleis on coins of Marcus Aurelius, Lucius Verus, and Commodus (Mionnet, *Lydie*, 1079–1090), *i.e.*, from 161 A.D. to 180 A.D.

M. Aur. Euarestos could hardly have held all the offices mentioned in the inscription before his forty-fifth year; and assuming that he was born in the year in which Marcus Aurelius became emperor (161 A.D), we get the year 206 A.D. as an approximate date for our inscription.

M. Aur. Soterichos, son of the preceding, is the person honored in the last inscription (No. IV.).

No. VI.

In Aidin, in pavement of the public street in front of a doorway. Copied by W. M. R. and J. R. S. S.

ΙΟΥΘ _Αι
ΚΡΑΤΟΡΟΣΑΝΤΩΝ
ΙΟΥΕΚΤΩΝΚΛΑΥΔ
ΑΝΟΥΔΑΜΑΠΟΡΩΝ
Κ̊ · ΙΟΥ · ΑΡΤΕΜΙΔΩΡΙΩΝΑ
ΤΡΑΛΛΙΑΝΟΝΕΙΚΗϹΑΝ
ΤΑΑΝΔΡΩΝΠΑΝΚΡΑΤΙΟΝ
ΟΛΥΜΠΙΑΔΑΝϚ
ΑΡΧΙΕΡΑΤΕΥΟΝΤΟϹΚ
ΑΓΩΝΩΘΕΤΟΥΝΤΟϹ
Γ · ΙΟΥ · ΦΙΛΙΠΠΟΥ Υ
ΒΟΥΛΗϹΑΡΧΙΕΡΕϚ
ϹΙΑϹΚΑΙΑΓΩΝΟΘΓ
ΔΙΑΒΙΟΥ
ΑΛΥΤΑΡΧΟΥΙ
Π̊ΚΛΑΜΕΛΙΤ
ΠΙΜΕΛΗΘΕ
ΙΟΥΧΡΥϹΕΡϚ

['Ανατεθέντα ὑπὸ τ]οῦ θ[ειοτάτου] α[ὐτο]κράτορος 'Αντων[είν]ου ἐκ τῶν Κλαυδ[ι]ανοῦ Δαμᾶ πόρων Κό(ϊντον) 'Ιού(λιον) 'Αρτεμιδωρίωνα Τραλλιανὸ(ν), νεικήσαντα ἀνδρῶν πανκράτιον 'Ολυμπι[ά]δα ν[ϛ′], ἀρχιερατεύοντος καὶ ἀγων(ο)θετοῦντος [τὸ β′] Γ. 'Ιου. Φιλίππου, υ[ἱοῦ] βουλῆς, ἀρχιερέω[ς 'Α]σίας κ[αὶ] ἀγωνοθέ[του] διὰ βίου, ἀλυταρχοῦ[ντος] Πο(πλίου) Κλ(αυδίου) Μελίτ[ωνος καὶ ἐ]πιμεληθέ[ντος Γ(αΐου)] 'Ιου(λίου) Χρυσέρ[ωτος].

Gaius Julius Philippus is mentioned in an inscription of Aphrodisias (*C. I. G.*, 2790) which Boeckh, arguing from the name Julius Philippus, places in the time of the two Philippi (244–249 A.D.). Boeckh thought this theory strengthened by the fact that G. Jul. Philippus was *procurator Augustorum* (ἐπίτροπος τῶν Σεβαστῶν, *C. I. G.*, 2933; *Voy. Arch.*, No. 605); and the Augusti, on his theory, could be no other than the two Philippi. But an inscription of Tralleis (Le Bas, *Voy. Arch.*, No. 1652 *c*), makes G. Jul. Philippus flourish *during the lifetime* of an emperor Antoninus.* The same is the case in our inscription, which dates from the fifty-sixth Trallian Olympiad. But G. Jul. Philippus lived also during the reign of two joint emperors (see above). Accordingly, this Antoninus can be no other than Antoninus Pius, who was succeeded by the joint emperors, Marcus Aurelius and Lucius Verus. As Antoninus Pius died in March, 161 A.D., fifty-sixth Trallian Olympiad must fall between 141 A.D. (the first Olympic year after his accession in 138 A.D.) and 157 A.D. (the last before his death).

The inscription on the sepulchre of a servant of G. Jul. Philippus is published in the *Bull. de Corr. Hell.*, 1881, p. 346.

A Meliton was clerk of Tralleis under Domitia Augusta (see Mionnet), and may have been the father or grandfather of the Meliton here mentioned.

The following has been received from Dr. Sterrett, dated at Smyrna, May 20, 1884: "Mr. Ramsay has called my attention to a dated inscription of Olympia, published in the *Archaeologische Zeitung*, 1880, p. 62, No. 353. It proves so conclusively that the above reasoning concerning the date is correct, that I insert it here with Dittenberger's note: Ἡ Ὀλυμπικὴ βουλὴ Γ(άϊον) Ἰούλιον Φίλιππον Τραλλιανὸν, τὸν Ἀσιάρχην, ἠθῶν ἕνεκα, Ὀλυμπιάδι σλβ'. 'Die Datirung aus der 232 Olympiade (149 n. Chr.) lässt nicht den geringsten Zweifel dass dies derselbe Asiarch Philippos aus Tralles ist, der bei Gelegenheit des von Waddington (*Fastes des provinces Asiat.*, p. 221) auf den 23 Februar, 155 n. Chr., gesetzten Martyriums des Polycarp vorkommt. Vgl. Marquardt, *Ephem. Epigr.*, I. p. 221, n. 2.'" — EDD.

---

* This inscription is given in full on p. 103, below. Le Bas, from a bad copy, assigned it to Trallian Olympiad 50. Dr. Sterrett assigns No. VI. to Olympiad 53, reading ΝΓ for ΝϚ in line 10. But Mr. Ramsay, in his later note (pp. 102–104), shows that both of the inscriptions in question belong to Trallian Olympiad 56. This, by the above argument, must fall within the period 141–157 A.D., and is fixed by Mr. Ramsay on other grounds at 153 A.D. — EDD.

Since these pages were in type (December, 1884), the editors have received from Mr. W. M. Ramsay, of Exeter College, Oxford, the following note on the Olympic festivals of Tralles, which will be welcomed as a valuable contribution to our knowledge of a most obscure and perplexing subject: —

The emperor P. Aelius Hadrianus Olympius left Athens, which he had just enriched with the magnificent temple of Zeus Olympius, and came to Asia Minor in the autumn of 129 A.D. He landed at Ephesus, where the games mentioned on coins as ΑΔΡΙΑΝΑ ΟΛΥΜΠΙΑ were founded in his honor. He continued his journey through Magnesia to Tralles. Soon after this visit we begin to hear of Olympian games at Tralles, and of an *ἀνανέωσις* of these games. The suspicion at once arises that this *ἀνανέωσις* is connected with the visit of the Emperor. The inscriptions which mention the *ἀγωνοθεσία* of G. Julius Philippus furnish a criterion to convert this suspicion into comparative certainty. Two of these inscriptions are already published, one by M. Waddington (Le Bas, No. 1652 *c*) from an exceedingly bad copy, and one (No. VI. above) by Mr. Sterrett. The latter, which I also have seen, is engraved on a mutilated stone; and though all the most important facts remain distinct, yet one interesting point has been lost. The fifty-sixth Trallian Olympiad was the second at which Philip had been *ἀγωνοθέτης*. The following inscription on a stone in the Hebrew cemetery, within the limits of ancient Tralles, makes it possible to complete Mr. Sterrett's inscription, and to restore almost the whole of the fragment of which a copy was sent to M. Waddington. We are indebted for it to M. Pappaconstantinos, who had already deserved so well of all students of Trallian antiquities. In his company I visited the cemetery, and compared his copy with the stone itself. The stone is broken both at top and at bottom.

ΟΤΑΤΟΥΑΥΤΟΚΡΑΤΟ
ΑΝΤΩΝΕΙΝΟΥ///ΚΤΩΝ
ΚΛΑΥΔΙΑΝΟΥΔΑΜΑ
ΠΟΡΩΝ
ΑΣΚΛΗΠΙΑΚΟΝΔΙΟ
ΓΕΝΟΥΣΠΕΡΓΑΜΗΝΟΝ
ΝΕΙΚΗΣΑΝΤΑΟΠΛΟΝ
ΟΛΥΜΠΙΑΔΑΝϚ
ΑΡΧΙΕΡΑΤΕΥΟΝΤΟΣΚΑΙ
ΑΓΩΝΟΘΕΤΟΥΝΤΟΣΤΟΒ
ΓΙΟΥΦΙΛΙΠΠΟΥΥΟΥ
ΒΟΥΛΗΣΑΡΧΙΕΡΕΩΣΑ
ΣΙΑΣΚΑΙΑΓΩΝΟΘΕΤΟΥ
ΔΙΑΒΙΟΥ
ΑΛΥΤΑΡΧΟΥΝΤΟΣ
///ΚΛΜΕΛΙΤΩΝΟΣ

['Ανατεθέντα ὑπὸ τοῦ θει]ο-
τάτου αὐτοκράτο[ρος] 'Αντωνείνου [ἐ]κ τῶν Κλαυδιανοῦ Δαμᾶ
πόρων 'Ασκληπιακὸν Διογένους
Περγαμηνὸν νεικήσαντα ὅπλον
'Ολυμπιάδα νϚ', ἀρχιερατεύοντος καὶ ἀγωνοθετοῦντος τὸ β' Γ.
'Ιου. Φιλίππου, ὑ(ι)οῦ βουλῆς,
ἀρχιερέως 'Ασίας καὶ ἀγωνοθέτου διὰ βίου, ἀλυταρχοῦντος
[Πο.] Κλ. Μελίτωνος, [ἐπιμελη-
θέντος Γ. 'Ιου. Χρυσέρωτος]

For the sake of completeness, I shall now add the full text of the third inscription relating to this subject (Le Bas, No. 1652 *c*). It obviously belongs to the same year; and though the badness of the copy led M. Waddington to restore the fragment differently, there can now remain no doubt that the names of the officials are the same in all three.

['Ανατεθέντα] ὑπὸ τοῦ θειοτάτου αὐτοκράτορος 'Αντωνείνου ἐκ τ[ῶν] Κλαυδιανοῦ Δα[μᾶ] πόρων Γάϊον Φιλαδέλ[φου],* νεικήσαντα ἀνδρῶ[ν] πύγμην 'Ολυμπιάδα ν[ϛ'], ἀρχιερατεύοντος καὶ ἀγωνοθετοῦντος [τὸ β'] Γ. 'Ιου. Φιλίππου, ὑ[ι]οῦ βουλῆς, ἀρχιερέως 'Ασίας καὶ ἀγωνοθέτου διὰ βίου, ἀλυταρχοῦντος [Πο.] Κλ. Μ[ε]λίτωνος, ἐπιμ[ελ]ηθέντος Γ. 'Ιου. Χρυσέρωτος.

These three inscriptions record the names of the victors in the pancration, the boxing contest, and the race in armor, at the fifty-sixth Trallian Olympiad. G. Julius Philippus, the agonothete at these games, was at the same time High Priest of Asia. Now it has been established by M. Waddington that the martyrdom of Polycarp, which took place at the games in Smyrna, presided over by Philip as High Priest of Asia, is to be dated 155 A.D. Again, we know from an Olympian inscription (p. 101, end) that Philip was Asiarch at some time during the two hundred and thirty-second Elean Olympiad (149–152 A.D.); and the identity of the titles Asiarch and High Priest of Asia seems to me indisputable, in spite of M. Waddington's arguments against it. It is possible to reconcile these data only on the supposition that the highpriesthood of Asia, like almost all such offices *in that province*, was a penteteric office.† Philip was High Priest from 152 to 155 A.D. In 153 A.D. he presided over the fifty-sixth Olympian festival at Tralles. The fiftieth Olympiad at Tralles was in 129 A.D., the year when the emperor Hadrian visited the city. It is probable that the Trallians, when the Olympia were instituted in honor of this visit, sought to give them a spurious antiquity by the fiction that they were already fifty penteterides old. M. Waddington has published an inscription of Tralles which probably belongs to the

* M. Waddington restores [τὸν δεῖνα Περ]γαῖον Φιλαδελ[φέα]; but the preceding inscription shows that πόρων occupied an entire line, and that there is no gap before Γάϊον. This inscription has been so badly copied that it is justifiable to suppose that a line has been omitted by the copyist. The other two inscriptions mention the πατρίς of the victor, and I believe that this was also done in the present inscription. I would restore

Γάϊον Φιλάδελ[φον]
[τοῦ δεῖνος Τραλλιανόν]

† The Bishop of Durham will treat the questions connected with the Asiarchate with his usual learning and copiousness of illustration in a forthcoming work on St. Polycarp.

first century A.D., but purports to be of the fifth century B.C.; so that such patriotic frauds were evidently familiar in the city.

If, as I think probable, the restoration of Mr. Sterrett's inscription No. VIII., line 6, is correct, the Olympiad called η' μετὰ τὴν ἀνανέωσιν will be that of 161 A.D., which took place a few months after the death of Antoninus, who therefore bears the title θεός. — W. M. R.

No. VII.

In wall of cotton factory of Anastasios Kokkalas in Aidin. Copied by W. M. S. and J. R. S. S. Published in Ὅμηρος, 1873, *p.* 49, *and afterwards in the* Μουσεῖον καὶ βιβλιοθήκη *of the Smyrna Evangelical School,* 1876, *p.* 48, *but inaccurately.*

ΠΟΛΙΣΕΚΤΩΝ
ΝΩΝΠΡΟΣΟΔ
ΙΟΝΥΣΙΟΝΣΩ
ΣΕΛΕΥΚΕΑΝΕΙ
ΣΑΝΤΑΠΑΙΔΩΝ
ΠΑΛΗΝΟΛΥΜΠΙ
ΑΔΑ ΝΑ
ΑΛΥΤΑΡΧΟΥΝΤΟΣ
ΑΙΛΙΟΥΚΛ · ΑΡΙΣ
ΤΟΚΛΕΟΥΣΜΑΙΟΡΟΣ

[Ἡ] πόλις ἐκ τῶ[ν κοι]νῶν [π]ροσόδ[ων] [Δ]ιονύσιον Σώ[του] Σελευ[κ]έα νει[κή]σαντα παίδων πάλην Ὀλυμπιάδα να', ἀλυταρχοῦντος Αἰλίου Κλ(αυδίου) Ἀριστοκλέους Μαΐορος.

The letters at the end of the third line are much defaced.

The date of the inscription (Olymp. 51), according to Mr. Ramsay's note on No. VI., is 133 A.D. — EDD.

No. VIII.

At Tralleis, on side of Utch Geuz. Copied by J. R. S. S. Published by Boeckh (C. I. G., 2934) *from Pococke's exceedingly bad copy; it reads somewhat better in Le Bas and Waddington* (Voy. Arch., *No.* 611).

ΘΕΝΤΑΥΠΟΘΕ
ΝΕΙΝΟΥΕΚΤΩΝ
ΟΡΩΝΔΙΟΝΥCΙΟΝ
ΛΑΟΔΙΚΕΑΝΕΙΚΗ
ΑΙΔΩΝΠΥΓΜΗΝΟΛΥΜ
ΗΜΕΤΑΤΗΝΑΝΑΝΕ
ΡΧΙΕΡΑΤΕΥΟΝΤΟC
ΟΘΕΤΟΥΝΤΟCΤΟ
ΑΠΟΛΩΝΙΔΟΥΙΕΡΟ
ΠΑΡΑΔΟΞΟΥ · ΑΛΥ
ΤΟCCΕΞΤΟΥΛ · ΕΥΛ
ΡΕCΤΟΥ
ΘΕΝΤΟCΤΩΝΑΝΔΡΙ
ΟΥΑΡΧΙΕΡΕΩC

['Ανατε]θέντα ὑπὸ θε-
[οῦ 'Αντων]είνου ἐκ τῶν
[Κλ. Δαμᾶ π]όρων Διονύσιον
. . . . Λαοδικέα νεική-
[σαντα π]αίδων πυγμὴν 'Ολυμ-
[πιάδα] η' μετὰ τὴν ἀνανέ-
[ωσιν, ἀ]ρχιερατεύοντος
[καὶ ἀγων]οθετοῦντος τὸ
[β'] 'Απολ(λ)ωνίδου ἱερο-
[νείκου] παραδόξου, [ἀ]λυ-
[ταρχοῦν]τος Σέξτου [δ'? Ε]ὐ[α-]
ρέστου
[ἐπιμελη]θέντος τῶν ἀνδρι-
[άντων τ]οῦ ἀρχιερέως.

This Euarestos perhaps may be the father of the clerk of Tralleis mentioned on coins of M. Aurelius, L. Verus, and Commodus (cf. Mionnet, *Lydie*, 1079–1090, and No. V. above). Dionysius of Laodikeia is here victor in the παίδων πυγμήν "in the eighth Olympiad after the ἀνανέωσις." *

No. IX.

At Tralleis, on front of Utch Geuz. Copied by J. R. S. S. Published very imperfectly in Le Bas and Waddington (Voy. Arch., *No.* 609).

ΑϹϹΜΥΡ
ΤΡΑΛΙΑ
ΓΕΙΟϹ
ΟϹΝΕΙ
ϹΥΠΟ
ΟΥϹ · Α
ΥΘΙΑ
ΕϹΙΝ
c
ↃΨΑϹΠΙΔΑ
ↃΙΝΑ · Α
ΑΡΔΕϹΙΝ
ΤΟΝΤΗϹ
ΚΑΙϹΑΡΕΙΑ
ΜΩΠΟΙΗϹΑϹ
ΕΡΑΝΕΝΤΗ
ΟΥΠΑΤΡΙΔΙ
ΝΑ ↃΛΥΜΠΙΑ

* According to Mr. Ramsay's computation (p. 104), this date, that of the fifty-eighth Trallian Olympiad, is the year 161 A.D. — EDD.

[Αὐρ.? Δαμ?]ᾶς Σμυρ-
[ναῖος καὶ] Τρα(λ)λια-
[νὸς καὶ Ἀρ]γεῖος
[καὶ Λάτμι]ος νει-
[κήσας τοὺ]ς ὑπο-
[γεγραμμέν]ους ἀ-
[γῶνας· Π]ύθια
[τὰ ἐν Σάρδ]εσιν,
[τὴν ἐξ Ἄργο]υς ἀσπίδα
[δίς, τὰ κ]οινὰ Ἀ-
[σίας ἐν Σ]άρδεσιν,
. . . τον τῆς
[Νύσης?], Καισάρεια
[τὰ ἐν Λάτ]μῳ, ποιήσας
[. . . δευτ]έραν ἐν τῇ
[ἰδίᾳ ἑαυτ]οῦ πατρίδι
[καὶ ἀγῶ]να Ὀλυμπια-
[κόν].

This inscription could be read only very imperfectly by Le Bas (*Voy. Arch.*, No. 609) with a glass. The left side of the inscription has been purposely defaced; and the edge of the stone is broken and jagged, so that it is not possible to determine how many letters have been lost. Inscriptions are not rare in which the same man is mentioned as citizen of several cities; for instance, *C. I. G.*, Nos. 3425, 3426. The second inscription, after naming several cities of which Artemidoros was citizen, adds that he was citizen of many other cities (καὶ ἄλλων πολλῶν πόλεων πολείτης).

Damas, if that is the name of the athlete honored in our inscription, was originally a citizen of Smyrna, and was an adopted citizen of the other cities mentioned. He gained a victory at Tralleis (see last lines) and several other places. His πατρίς included all places of which he was citizen.

Tralleis claimed to be a colony of Argos (Strabo, p. 649); and for this reason the Trallians probably took special interest in the games of Argos.

No. X.

On column in Turkish cemetery at Aidin. Copied by W. M. R. and J. R. S. S.

Ι▨ΙC▨ΟΝΚΛΑΥΔΙΑΝΟΝΤΟΝ
ΣΤΕΦΑΝΗΦΟΡΟΝΚΑΙΓΡΑΜΜΑΤΕΑ
ΤΟΥΔΗΜΟΥΒΟΥΛΑΡΧΗΣΑΝΤΑ
ΕΙΡΗΝΑΡΧΗΣΑΝΤΑΑΓΟΡΑΝΟΜΗ
ΣΑΝΤΑΣΙΤΩΝΗΣΑΝΤΑΑΠΟ
▨ΝΔΡΕΙΑΣΔΙΣΧΡΥΣΟΦΟ
ΡΗΣΑΝΤΑ▨ΡΑΦΥΛΑΞΑΝΤΑ
ΠΑΝ▨ΥΡΙΑΡΧΗΣΑΝΤΑΑΡΓΥΡΟ
ΤΑΜΙΕΥΣΑΝΤΑΔΕΚΑΠΡΩΤΕΥΣΑΝΤΑ
ΓΡΑΜΜΑΤΕΥΣΑΝΤΑΚΑΙΤΗΣΦΙΛΟΣΕΒΑΣΤΟΥ
ΓΕΡΟΥΣΙΑΣΚΑΙΤΩΝΦΙΛΟΣΕΒΑΣΤΩΝ
ΝΕΩΝΚΑΙΡΩΜΑΙΩΝΥΠΟΣΧΟΜΕΝΟΝ
ΚΑΙΕΙΣΤΗΝΑΓΟΡΑΝΚΙΟΝΑΣΕΙΚΟΣΙ
ΣΚΟΥΤΛΩΣΑΝΤΑΔΕΚΑΙΜΟΥΣΩΣΑΝΤΑ
ΚΑΙΤΑΥΤΗΝΤΗΝΕΞΕΔΡΑΝΑΝΤΟΥΔΕΝΟΣ
ΑΝΑΘΕΝΤΑΚΑΙΤΗΙΚΛΑΥΔΙΑΙΒΟΥΛΗΙ
ΛΡ▨Ρ▨ΟΥΩΣΤΕΛΑΜΒΑΝΕΙΝΚΑΘΕ
ΚΛ▨ΟΝ▨ΤΟΣΕΝΘΑΔΕΕΚΑΣΤΟΝΒΟΥ
▨ΕΥ▨Ν▨ΤΟΥΗΜΕΡΑ✱ΣΝ
▨ΣΤΑΣΕΩΣΤΗΣ
▨ΤΗΣ▨ΛΥΔΙΑΣΒΟΥΛΗΣ
▨ΤΟΥΒΑΣΣΟΥΤΟΥΒΟΥΛΕΥΤΟΥ

[Γ(αῖον) Ἰούλι]ον Κλαυδιανὸν τὸν στεφανηφόρον καὶ γραμματέα τοῦ δήμου, βουλαρχήσαντα, εἰρηναρχήσαντα, ἀγορανομήσαντα, σιτωνήσαντα ἀπὸ [Ἀλεξα]νδρείας, δὶς χρυσοφορήσαντα, [πα]ραφυλάξαντα, παν[ηγυ]ριαρχήσαντα, ἀργυροταμιεύσαντα, δεκαπρωτεύσαντα, γραμματεύσαντα καὶ τῆς φιλοσεβάστου γερουσίας καὶ τῶν φιλοσεβάστων νέων καὶ Ῥωμαίων, ὑποσχόμενον καὶ εἰς *τὴν ἀγορὰν κίονας εἴκοσι, σκουτλώσαντα δὲ καὶ μουσώσαντα καὶ ταύτην τὴν ἐξέδραν ἀντ' οὐδενὸς, ἀναθέντα καὶ τῇ Κλαυδίᾳ Βουλῇ (ἀ)ρ[γυ]ρ[ί]ου ὥστε λαμβάνειν καθ' ἕκ[αστ]ον [ἔ]τος ἐνθάδε ἕκαστον βου[λ]ευ[τὴ]ν [πρώτῃ ἐνιαυ]τοῦ ἡμέρᾳ δηνάρια διακόσια πεντήκοντα· [προνοησαμένου τῆς ἀνα]στάσεως τῆς [στήλης ὑπὲρ] τῆς [Κλα]υδίας Βουλῆς [Σέξ]του Βάσσου τοῦ Βουλευτοῦ.*

This inscription was published by M. P. Constantinos in the Μουσεῖον καὶ Βιβλιοθήκη, 1875, p. 126, but inaccurately. Notwithstanding the fact that the city of Tralleis was very populous, it seems astonishing that the fabulously fertile valley of the Maeander could not supply the people with corn. Yet we know from the testimony of other inscriptions (*C. I. G.*, 2927: σειτωνήσαντα δὲ καὶ τὸν ἀπὸ Αἰγύπτου σεῖτον, etc.; 2930: σειτωνήσαντα ἀπὸ Αἰγύπτου, etc.) that Tralleis was, at least at times, compelled to bring corn from Egypt. It is also clear from this that the Alexandria from which Claudianus brought his corn can be no other than the Alexandria of Egypt.

In line 14, the reading σκουτλώσαντα is certain. In *Stephani Thesaur.*, s.v. σκούτλωσις, the following is given: "*Scutulatio, vestis praetextura, instita, ornatura in ima vestis parte.*" Hero in Isagog. περὶ εὐθυμετρικῶν: Εὐθυμετρικὸν μὲν οὖν ἐστιν πᾶν τὸ κατὰ μῆκος μόνον μετρούμενον, ὥσπερ ἐν ταῖς σκουτλώσεσιν οἱ στροφίολοι καὶ ἐν τοῖς ξυλικοῖς τὰ κυμάτια καὶ ὅσα πρὸς μῆκος μόνον μετρεῖται. It seems probable from this that the lower part of the wall of the Exedra was ornamented with a pattern. Dindorf, in *Steph. Thesaur.*, gives to μουσόω the meaning "*to adorn with mosaic,*" "*opere musivo orno.*" It appears then that Claudianus ornamented the Exedra with a *dado* and a mosaic pavement at his own expense, and that this stone, bearing the inscription in his honor, was placed in the Exedra.

No. V. gives great assistance in restoring the latter part of this inscription. In line 17, εἰς νομήν seems very plausible and appropriate; but Mr. Ramsay has noted in his copy the possibility of a Λ at the commencement of the line.*

---

* ΑΡ··Ρ·ΟΥ, *i.e.* (ἀ)ρ[γυ]ρ[ί]ου, is given above on the authority of Mr. Ramsay (December, 1884). — EDD.

No. XI.

In wall of cotton factory of Anastasios Kokkalas in Aidin. Copied by W. M. R. and J. R. S. S.

. . . .
ΤΗΣΚΑΙΦΙΛΟΣΕΒΑΣΤΟΣΜ
ΑΥΡΗΛΙΟΝΣΩΤΗΡΑΒΟΥΛΕΥ
ΤΗΝΚΑΙΦΙΛΟΣΕΒΑΣΤΟΝΤΟΝ
ΥΙΟΝΑΔΕΛΦΟΝΜΑΥΡΗΛΙ
ΟΥΑΜΜΙΑΝΟΥΒΟΥΛΕΥΤΟΥ
ΚΑΙΦΙΛΟΣΕΒΑΣΤΟΥΚΑΙ
ΓΡΑΜΜΑΤΕΩΣΤΟΥΔΗΜΟΥ
ΝΙΚΗΣΑΝΤΑ
ΤΟΝΙΕΡΟΝΑΓΩΝΑΤΩΝΣΠΑΡ
ΤΙΑΤΩΝΚΑΙΤΟΝΙΕΡΟΝ
ΑΓΩΝΑΤΩΝΗΡΑΚΛΕΙΩΝ
ΠΑΙΔΩΝΠΑΓΚΡΑΤΙΟΝ
ΚΑΙΙΣΑΓΩΓΟΝΤΩΝΟΛΥΜΠΙΩΝ
ΕΠΙΙΕΡΕΩΣΔΙΑΒΙΟΥΤΟΥΔΙ
ΟΣΤΟΥΛΑΡΑΣΙΟΥΦΛΑΟΥΙΟΥ
ΚΛΕΙΤΟΣΘΕΝΟΥΣΤΟΥΚΡΑΤΙ
ΣΤΟΥΔΙΣΑΣΙΑΡΧΟΥΠΡΩΤΟΙ
ΑΣΙΑΣΠΑΤΡΟΣΥΠΑΤΙΚΟΥΚΑ
ΠΑΠΠΟΥΣΥΝΚΛΗΤΙΚΩΝΤΗΣ
Θ ΑΥΤΟΥΠΕΝΤΑΕΤΗΡΙΔΟΣ

[Καθιέρωσεν ὁ δεῖνα βουλευ]τὴς καὶ φιλοσέβαστος Μ. Αὐρήλιον Σωτῆρα βουλευτὴν καὶ φιλοσέβαστον τὸν υἱὸν, ἀδελφὸν Μ. Αὐρηλίου Ἀμμιανοῦ βουλευτοῦ καὶ φιλοσεβάστου καὶ γραμματέως τοῦ δήμου, νικήσαντα τὸν ἱερὸν ἀγῶνα τῶν Σπ[α]ρτιατῶν καὶ τὸν ἱερὸν ἀγῶνα τῶν Ἡρακλείων παίδων παγκράτιον, κ[α]ὶ ἰσαγωγὸν τῶν Ὀλυμπίων ἐπὶ ἱερέως διὰ βίου τοῦ Διὸς τοῦ Λαρασίου Φλαουίου Κλειτοσθένους τοῦ κρατίστου δὶς Ἀσιάρχου, πρῶτο[υ] Ἀσίας, πατρὸς ὑπατικοῦ κα[ὶ] πάππου συν-κλητικῶν τῆς ἐννάτης αὐτοῦ πενταετηρίδος.*

The Herakleia of Tralleis are mentioned in *C. I. G.*, 2936; the ἀγὼν τῶν Σπαρτιατῶν seems to be mentioned here and in No. XII. for the first time.

In Tralleis, Zeus was worshipped under the name of Larasios, the priest of Zeus Larasios being one of the principal dignitaries of state (cf. Le Bas and Waddington, *Voy. Arch.*, No. 604). This last seems also clear from the fact that Flavius Kleitosthenes is priest for life of Zeus Larasios besides holding the high office of Asiarch.

This inscription belongs to the end of the second or the beginning of the third century A.D. The grandsons of Kleitosthenes are mentioned as having attained to senatorial rank, and Greeks were rarely admitted to the Roman Senate before the time of Marcus Aurelius.

---

* M. Pappadopoulos-Kerameus, *Chargé d'une mission paléographique en Orient par le Syllogue Littéraire Grec de Constantinople*, has had the goodness to send me the following letter in regard to Nos. XI. and XII. One cannot reasonably be expected to be acquainted with all that is published in the newspapers of Smyrna; still I am happy to make amends for my shortcomings in this respect by inserting the letter of M. Pappadopoulos-Kerameus in full.

Ἐν Κωνσταντινουπόλει, 24 Φεβρ. 1884.

Ἐλλογιμώτατε Κύριε,—Ἐν τῷ τελευταίῳ τεύχει τῶν Mittheilungen, 4 Heft, σ. 332, δημοσιεύετε ὑπ' ἀριθ. 11, ἐπιγραφὴν ἐκ Τράλλεων ἀντιγραφεῖσαν ὑφ' ὑμῶν καὶ τοῦ κοινοῦ φίλου κ. W. M. Ramsay. Ἀλλὰ τὴν ἐπιγραφὴν ταύτην τὴν ἀφορῶσαν τὸν Αὐρήλιον Σωτῆρα καὶ τὸν Κλειτοσθένην ἐδημοσίευσα τὸ πρῶτον ἐγὼ αὐτὸς, τὴν 31 Ἰουλίου, 1874, ἐν τῇ Σμυρναϊκῇ ἐφημερίδι "Ἀμάλθεια," No. 2061. Τὸ ὑμέτερον ἀντίγραφον οὐδεμίαν ἔχει διαφορὰν πρὸς τὴν ἐμὴν ἔκδοσιν· μόνον δὲ εἰς τὴν 18ην, γραμμὴν ἀνέγνωσα ΥΠΑΤΙΚΩΝ, καὶ ἡ ἀνάγνωσις φαίνεταί μοι προτιμοτέρα, τὸ δὲ Ι τοῦ ΚΑΙ ἀνεγινώσκετο κάλλιστα τότε.—Ἐν τῷ αὐτῷ τεύχει κατεχωρίσατε ὑπ' ἀρθ. 12 τεμάχιον ὁμοίας φύσεως ἐπιγραφῆς, δι' οὗ διορθοῦτε τὴν ἔκδοσιν "'Ομήρου" (1874, σ. 39). Ἀλλ' ἐν τῷ αὐτῷ "'Ομήρῳ" (1877, σ. 175–176), ἐδημοσίευσα καὶ ἐγὼ δοκίμιον διορθώσεως τοῦ ἐν λόγῳ τεμαχίου πραγματευόμενος τὰ κατὰ τὴν Ἐφεσίαν Λάρισσαν καὶ τὴν παρὰ Τράλλεσι Λάρασσαν.

Καίτοι δὲν ἔσχον τὸ εὐτύχημα νὰ γνωρίσω ὑμᾶς προσωπικῶς, ἔκρινα ὅμως καλὸν νὰ κοινοποιήσω ὑμῖν τ' ἀνωτέρω καὶ συνάμα νὰ συγχαρῶ ὑμᾶς διὰ τὰς σπουδαίας μελέτας καὶ ἐρεύνας τῆς ἀρχαιολογικῆς Ἀμερικανικῆς σχολῆς, ἧς ἀποτελεῖτε ἔξοχον μέλος.

Πεποιθὼς λοιπὸν ὅτι θ' ἀποδεχθῆτε εὐχαρίστως τὰς ἐμὰς σημειώσεις καὶ ὅτι θὰ εὐαρεστηθῆτε νὰ ποιήσητε αὐτῶν χρῆσιν ὅπου δεῖ,

διατελῶ μετὰ τιμῆς καὶ ὑπολήψεως

Ἀ. Παππαδόπουλος-Κεραμεύς.

The word εἰσαγωγός (line 13), for εἰσαγωγεύς, occurs only in one other place (*C. I. G.*, 2932), and then in an inscription of Tralleis. But in neither case does the context show whether the word means the *founder* or simply the *marshal* of the games. But that the latter is the meaning here is evident; for in the sense of *founder* it could not refer even to the ἀνανέωσις in 129 A.D. (see p. 103), which was at least half a century earlier than our inscription. It appears from τῆς ἐννάτης αὐτοῦ πενταετηρίδος that Kleitosthenes held the priesthood nine successive periods of four years (p. 103).

No. XII.

In wall of cotton factory of Anastasios Kokkalas in Aidin. Copied by W. M. R. and J. R. S. S. Published in Ὅμηρος, *1874, p. 39.*

. . . .
YIONNIKHCANTA
TEPONTONCΠAPTIATH
AΓΩNAΠAIΔΩNΠAΛHN
NIKHCANTAΔEKAITONIE
PONAΓΩNATΩNAΛEIΩN
EΠIIEPEΩCΔIABIOYTOYΔIOC
TOYΛAPAΓIOYΦΛAOYIOY
. . . .

[Ὁ δεῖνα καθιέρωσεν τὸν δεῖνα] υἱὸν νικήσαντα [τὸν] (ἱ)ερὸν τὸν Σπαρτιά[την] ἀγῶνα παίδων πάλην, νικήσαντα δὲ καὶ τὸν ἱερὸν ἀγῶνα τῶν Ἀλείων ἐπὶ ἱερέως διὰ βίου τοῦ Διὸς τοῦ Λαρα[σ]ίου, Φλαουίου [Κλειτοσθένους τοῦ κρατίστου δὶς Ἀσιάρχου, πρώτου Ἀσίας,] etc. See No. XI.

In line 2, the reading TEPON is certain, but T is clearly a mistake for I, and hence τὸν ἱερόν must be restored.

The ἀγὼν ὁ Σπαρτιάτης is mentioned in No. XI.; indeed, the two inscriptions are contemporary, as the name of the priest of Zeus Larasios indicates.

Games called Ἄλεια were also celebrated at Philadelphia (*C. I. G.*, 3416, 3427, 3428), and at Rhodes (*C. I. G.*, 3208, 5913).

No. XIII.

In wall of cotton factory of Anastasios Kokkalas in Aidin. Copied by W. M. R. and J. R. S. S. Published in Ὅμηρος, 1873, *p.* 490.

ΟΝΤΟΝΚΡΑΤΙΣΙΟΝ
ΘΥΠΑΤΟΝΕΥΕΡΓΕΤΗΝ
ΠΡΟΓΟΝΩΝΤΗΣΕΑΥ
ΠΑΤΡΙΔΟΣ · ΗΛΑΜ
ΟΤΑΤΗΜΗΤΡΟΠΟΛΙ
ΙΣΑΣΙΑΣΚΑΙΝΕΩΚΟ
ΣΤΩΝΣΕΒΑΣΤΩΝΚΑ
ΡΕΩΝΤΡΑΛΛΙΑΝΩΝ
ΠΟΛΙΣ

· · · · ο]ν τὸν κράτισ[τ]ον [ἀν]θύπατον, εὐεργέτην [ἐκ] προγόνων τῆς ἑαυ[τοῦ] πατρίδος, ἡ λαμ[προ]τάτη μητρόπολι[ς τῆ]ς Ἀσίας καὶ νεωκ[όρος] τῶν Σεβαστῶν Κα[ισα]ρέων Τραλλιανῶν πόλις.

Tralleis is called νεωκόρος on coins of Caracalla, but not on those of his successors.

No. XIV.

On a milestone, now built into a garden wall about two miles west of Aidin. First copied in 1880 *by W. M. Ramsay, who published the last two lines in the Journal of Hellenic Studies,* 1881, *p.* 47. *The whole was published by Mommsen, from Mr. Ramsay's copy, in the* Ephemeris Epigraphica, 1884, *p.* 65. *It was afterwards copied by J. R. S. S. in* 1884.

… CI … ON
CAISAPA … CC …
MANICV …
MAXIM …
IMP · XXII · P · P · COS
MI ΛΑ

. . . .

Caisar A[u]g(ustus) G[er]-
manicu[s Pontifex]
Maxim[us], ...
Imp(erator) XXII., P(ater) P(atriae), Co(n)s(ul) . . .
Μί(λια) τριάκοντα ἕν.*

The stone is badly defaced. It is the thirty-first milestone on the Roman road from Ephesos to Tralleis, and is still near its ancient site. The thirtieth milestone on the same road still exists at Dedekieui, about two miles west of Tralleis, and its inscription has been published, incorrectly by Le Bas (*Voy. Arch.*, 1652 *c*), correctly in the Μουσεῖον, etc., of the Smyrna School, 1876–78, p. 48.

No. XV.

In wall of cotton factory of Anastasios Kokkalas in Aidin. Copied by W. M. R. and J. R. S. S.

NERVA
////P · P
ESIMVS
ARVMCE
DARIAMC
LLIANOR\
RNATAM · AD
VOBVS
KPATOPINE
ATPIΠATPI∠
ΞIMOΣAΠE
OΣΛATOME
ΓYMNAΣI

* The text is given according to the latest copy, sent by Dr. Sterrett from Aidin, May 22, 1884. This differs essentially from that published in the *Mittheilungen*. Mr. Ramsay, in April, 1884, read CI · · DI, *i.e.* Cl[au]di[us], in line 1. — EDD.

This inscription was published in the Ὅμηρος, 1873, p. 537; but the stone has been considerably mutilated since, four fragments of lines, which are given in the Ὅμηρος, having been broken off at the end. These four lines are important for the restoration of the inscription. They read:

ΛΙΑΝΟΙΣΤΗΙΠΟ
ΛΙΟΩΝΚΟΣΜΗΣ
ΟΥΣΕΝΑΥΤΩ
ΚΑΘΙΕΡΩΣ

Also in line 12, Ὅμηρος has ΤΡΟΠΟΣΟΛΑΤΟΜΙ, which gives a hint in regard to the restoration. There is, however, no Ο between the Σ and Λ.

[Imp(eratori)] Nerva[e Caes(ari)]
[Aug(usto)] P(atri) P(atriae)
[On]esimus, [Aug(usti) l(ibertus), proc(urator)]
[lapicaedin]arum, ce[llam]
[cali]dariam g[ymnasii in]
[usum Tra]llianor[um]
[ex]ornatam ad
· · · [d]uobus [dedicavit]
[Αὐτο]κράτορι Νέ[ρουᾳ Καίσαρι]
[Σεβαστῷ π]ατρὶ πατρί[δος]
[Ὀνήσ]ιμος ἀπε[λεύθερος Σεβαστοῦ,]
[ἐπίτροπ]ος λατομε[ίων,]
[τὸ θερμὸν τοῦ γ]υμνα[σίου]
[παρὰ Τραλ]λιανοῖς τῇ πό[λει]
· · · · λίθων (?) κοσμησ
· · · · ους ἐν αὐτῷ · · ·
· · · καθιέρωσ[εν]

Since the publication of the inscription in the *Mittheilungen*, it has been published by Th. Mommsen in the *Ephemeris Epigraphica*, 1884, p. 61, from a copy sent him by Mr. Ramsay. On line 7, Mommsen remarks: "Possis supplere *templis* et 15, 16 [να]ούς, scilicet ut ea non comprehensa fuerint ipsa cella, sed ad eam aliquo modo adiuncta"; and on lines 14, 15: "Deest praeterea vocabulum quoddam respondens *incrustationi*."

The stone was probably a broad one, and for this reason a restoration is difficult; still the general tenor of the inscription may be made out.* Marcus Aurelius Onesimus is mentioned in another inscription of Tralleis (Le Bas and Waddington, *Voy. Arch.*, No. 612).

No. XVI.

Slab in Turkish cemetery in Aidin. Copied by W. M. R. and J. R. S. S.

ΣΑ[illegible]ΔΡΟΥΣ
ΑΝ[illegible]ΟΝ[illegible]Ε[illegible]ΑΣΤ
ΙΕΡΕΑΜ
ΑΡΧΙΚΗ
/ΤΟΚΡ
ΛΟΣ

ΝΤΟ
\Μ
ΛΝ
ΑΤ

[Καί]σα[ρα] Δρουσ[ον Γερμ-]
αν[ικ]ὸν [Σ]ε[β]αστ[όν,]
[ἀρχ]ιερέα μ[έγιστον,]
[δημ]αρχικῆ[ς ἐξουσίας]
[αὐ]τοκρ[άτορα,]
[ἡ βουλὴ καὶ ὁ δῆμ]ος
[καθιέρωσεν].

The slab has been worn smooth by the action of water. The inscription refers most probably to the celebrated Germanicus, to whom the Senate assigned the whole of the Eastern provinces with the highest imperium.

---

* Dr. Sterrett, in his latest copy, reads in lines 7, 8, [ex]ornatam ad[iectis simulacris d]uobus [dedicavit]; and in lines 15–17, · · · λίθων (?) κοσμήσ[ας καὶ τ]οὺς ἐν αὐτῷ [δύο ἀνδριάντας προσθεὶς] καθιέρωσ[εν]. — Edd.

No. XVII.

In wall of cotton factory of Anastasios Kokkalas in Aidin. Copied by W. M. R. and J. R. S. S.

ƆMNHME▨ONIAΣO
NOΣTOYAPXETEIMOY
KAIIAΣONOΣTCYIAΣONOΣ
ZΩ TOYAPXETEIMOYEΞOY ΣIN
ΣINΔEENTAΦHNTPYΦE
PINHΓYNHAYTOYKAI
EIKONINHΘEPEΠ▨HMOY

[Τὸ] μνημε[ῖ]ον Ἰάσο-
νος τοῦ Ἀρχετείμου
καὶ Ἰάσονος τ[ο]ῦ Ἰάσονος
ζῶ- τοῦ Ἀρχετείμου· ἕξου- σιν
σιν δὲ ἐντάφην Τρυφε-
ρὶν ἡ γυνὴ αὐτοῦ καὶ
Εἰκονὶν ἡ θρέπ[τ]η μου.

Possibly Jason may be connected with the Jason who was a tragic actor of Tralleis. The nominatives Τρυφερίν and Εἰκονίν are of singular nature. For ἐντάφη, see *C. I. G.*, 3524, 11, and Assos Inscriptions (above), No. LXI.

No. XVIII.

In wall of cotton factory of Anastasios Kokkalas in Aidin. Copied by J. R. S. S. Published in Ὅμηρος, 1873, *p.* 537.

MAIANΔPIAIEPOΦΩNTOΣ
ΓYNHΔEEΠAINETOY
AΠOΛΛΩNIOΣAPTEMIΔΩPOY

Μαιάνδρια Ἱεροφῶντος,
γυνὴ δὲ Ἐπαινέτου.
Ἀπολλώνιος Ἀρτεμιδώρου.

Two persons, probably of one family, were buried in the same grave.

Apollonios, son of Artemidoros, is mentioned in the list of πρόξενοι (Le Bas and Waddington, *Voy. Arch.*, No. 599 *b*, line 24).

No. XIX.

In yard of Turkish hut on the western outskirts of Aidin. Copied by J. R. S. S. Published in Ὅμηρος, 1883, *p.* 491.

ΑΡΤΕΜΙΔΩΡΟΣΜΗΝΟΔΩΡΟΥ
ΗΡΩΕΣΧΡΗΣΤΟΙΧΑΙΡΕΤΕ

Ἀρτεμίδωρος Μηνοδώρου.
Ἥρωες χρηστοὶ, χαίρετε.

The plural indicates that at least one other person was buried in the tomb with Artemidoros, but the name was never on this stone.

No. XX.

On two unfluted columns, which now support the vestibule of the Eski Yeni Djamessi in Aidin. Copied by J. R. S. S.

On the right of the entrance :

Μ
ΟΥΑΛΕΡΙΟΥ
ΒΕΙΤΑΛΙΟΥ

On the left of the entrance :

ΤΕΤΤΙΟΥ
ΣΚΑΡΤΟΥ

No. XXI.

Found on the land of Etem Bey Djan Zade Djanoglou, on the western outskirts of Aidin. Copied by J. R. S. S.

[illegible]	. . . .
[illegible]ΤΗΣΣΟΡ	. . . τῆς σορ[οῦ]
[illegible]	. . . .
ΟΕΙΣΠΟ	ὁ εἰς πο . . . .
ΚΟΣΕΣΤΗΝ[illegible]CI[illegible]	κος ἐς τὴν . . .
ΕΤΗΣ, ΥΝΑΙΚΟ	ε τῆς [γ]υναικό[ς]

No. XXII.

In the Liquorice Factory. Copied by W. M. R.

```
.        ЬΑ
ιΚ       ΣΙΙΞΛ
ΣΛΊ     ΛΤΕΣΤ
ΑΡ,     Ω
ΙLΙΤΛΙΓΗ<ΙΗ
ΑΙΕΩΝΚΑΙΘ
 ΧΟΙΡΟΣΘΗΛ
```

This fragment is given, because the rest of the stone, which is at present built into a wall surrounding the factory, may be uncovered at some future time.

ADDENDUM.

AIDIN, May 22, 1884.

A large round base, recently unearthed at Tralleis, has the following inscription, the beginning of which is wanting:—

ΚΛ · ΜΙΘΡΙΔΑΤΟΥΠΑΤΡΩΝΟΣ · ΑΙΙΟΥΛ ·
ΕΡΑΣΤΟΥΚΑΙΦΟΙΒΟΥΤΩΝΑΡΧΟΝΤΩΝ
ΑΥΤΗΣ

J. R. S. STERRETT.

THE

THEATRE OF DIONYSUS.

BY

JAMES R. WHEELER.

Θέατρον ἀξιόλογον, μέγα καὶ θαυμαστόν.

— Ps. Dicaearchus.

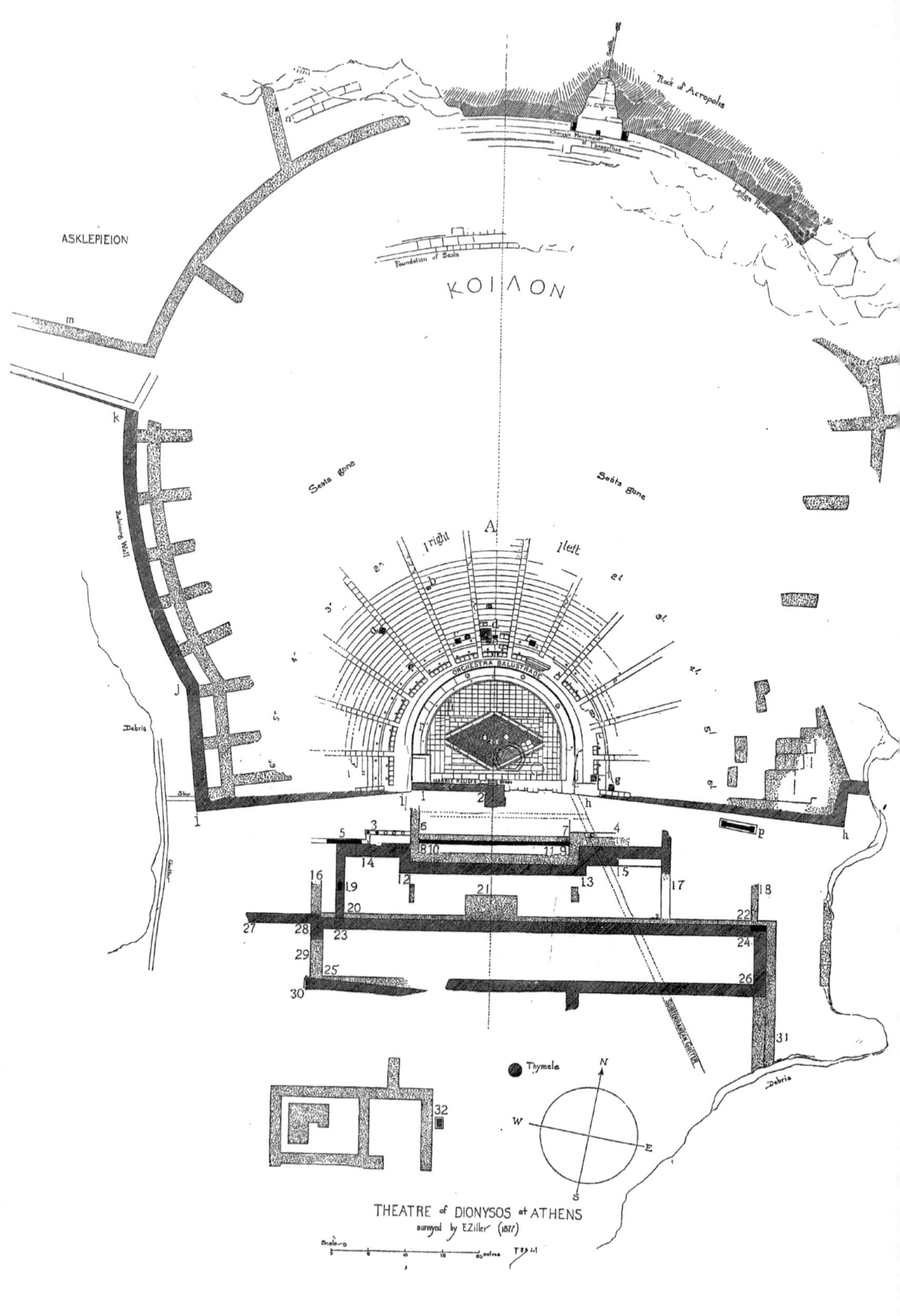

THEATRE of DIONYSOS at ATHENS
surveyed by E. Ziller (1877)

INTRODUCTORY NOTE.

It is somewhat strange that, although more than twenty years have passed since excavations upon the Dionysiac Theatre were begun, no paper has yet appeared in English which gives anything like a thorough account of these most important ruins. The chapter in Dyer's *Ancient Athens* is the only treatise on the subject of which the author knows; and in this Mr. Dyer has omitted all mention of the scene-structure, and of the reliefs in the hyposcenium of Phaedrus. Other parts of the theatre, moreover, he has not treated with great thoroughness; but exhaustive consideration of a special subject is perhaps not to be expected in a general work like *Ancient Athens*. Even the list of German works upon the theatre is an exceedingly short one; an article of Dr. Wilhelm Vischer in the *Neues Schweizerisches Museum* (1863), republished in Vischer's *Kleine Schriften*, II. pp. 324–390, and one by Dr. Leopold Julius in the *Zeitschrift für bildende Kunst*, Vol. XIII. (1877), being the only two which present the subject in a manner that approaches completeness. The former article was written when the excavations were unfinished; and while it is exceedingly valuable in some respects, it is naturally deficient in others. The article by Dr. Julius, on the other hand, is comparatively new; and although he occasionally seems inclined to make the ruins fit a preconceived theory, as in his views concerning the function of walls 12–13, 14, and 15 of the scene-structure,* the author unhesitatingly acknowledges the great

* See the Plan of the Theatre.

help that he has obtained from this admirable article in preparing the present paper. Dr. Julius, however, has viewed the theatre, as he himself states, chiefly from an architect's point of view, and has omitted much which belongs to a complete history of the building. The present article has been written after a stay in Athens of several months, during which the author made it a special work to study carefully the ruins of the theatre. He has made no startling discoveries, and does not lay claim to any great originality, though he believes that some facts have been brought to light which other students have overlooked. The object of this essay will, however, be attained if it provides American students with the means of forming a better idea of the greatness and magnificence of the Athenian Theatre. The accompanying plan of the theatre is essentially a copy of that made from a survey of Ernst Ziller, which was published, together with Dr. Julius's article, in the *Zeitschrift für bildende Kunst* for 1877.

PART I.

ACCORDING to Suidas,* the Athenians began to build the Dionysiac Theatre, on the south slope of the Acropolis, in the 70th Olympiad (500–496 B.C.), when the wooden seats of a previous structure gave way under the weight of the audience which was assembled to witness a contest between Aeschylus, Choerilus, and Pratinas. Whether this structure shared the fate of many other important buildings at Athens during the Persian invasions cannot be determined in the absence of records; but that there is work among the present ruins which dates from the fifth century B.C. there can be no doubt. We are therefore justified in assuming that even if the Persians destroyed the theatre in its unfinished state, it was soon afterwards rebuilt; though its completion was delayed until the beginning of the Macedonian period. We have no record of the condition of the building after the Persian wars, during the fifth century or the first half of the fourth century B.C.; but these are periods which witnessed the rise, perfection, and decline of the Athenian tragedy and older comedy; and even though the theatre at that time may have been largely built of wood, it is impossible to suppose that it could have been in a very rough or unfinished condition.

The first record of work done upon the theatre, later than that noticed by Suidas, is in a decree of the Athenian Assembly of Olympiad 109, 2 (343–342 B.C.),† commending the Senate for caring for the adornment of the theatre; while from another

* Suidas, under Πρατίνας: ἀντηγωνίζετο δὲ (sc. Πρατίνας) Αἰσχύλῳ τε καὶ Χοιρίλῳ, ἐπὶ τῆς ἑβδομηκοστῆς Ὀλυμπιάδος, καὶ πρῶτος ἔγραψε Σατύρους. ἐπιδεικνυμένου δὲ τούτου συνέβη τὰ ἰκρία ἐφ' ὧν ἑστήκεσαν οἱ θεαταὶ πεσεῖν. καὶ ἐκ τούτου θέατρον ᾠκοδομήθη Ἀθηναίοις.

† *C. I. A.*, II. 1, No. 114: ἐπε[μελήθη τῆ]ς εὐκοσμίας τοῦ θεάτρου. See Wachsmuth, *Stadt Athen*, p. 593, N. 5; see also on this whole point, C. Curtius in the *Philologus*, XXIV. p. 272, "Zum Redner Lykurgos." For the inscription especially, cf. Philistor, I. p. 190; and A. Riedmauer in *Verhandl. d. philol. Ges. in Würzburg*, 1862, p. 77, col. 1.

inscription of about the same date we learn that a certain Cephisophon had charge of work which was going on there.* Another decree † of the Assembly, passed upon the motion of the orator Lycurgus in Olymp. 112, 3 (330–329 B.C.), records that a certain Eudemus of Plataea made large donations to the city at that time, including a gift to the theatre. This would seem to show that the building was not even then entirely finished. Its completion was certainly the work of the orator Lycurgus; of this the Pseudo-Plutarch, Hypereides, and Pausanias give ample testimony, even were the decree of Stratocles wanting.‡ The language of the decree in honor of Eudemus seems to leave it uncertain whether the work upon the theatre had been finished at the time of its passage. It shows, at least, that the building was not finished before 330–329 B.C., and we know that it was finished before the death of Lycurgus in 325–324 B.C. §

The next record is a passage in Vitruvius ¶ (about the Christian era), who speaks of the Stoa of Eumenes ‖ at Athens as an example of a method of construction in theatrical architecture, which provided

---

* ἐπὶ τὸ θεατρικόν· Κηφισοφῶν Κεφαλίωνος Ἀφιδναῖος. Cf. Wachsmuth, *l. c.*, and especially *Philologus*, XXIV. p. 272. For the inscription itself, cf. *Verhandl. d. philol. Ges. in Würzburg*, 1862, p. 88, col. B′.

† Cf. Wachsmuth, *S. A.*, 599, N. 2, with references: καὶ νῦν [ἐπ]ι[δέδ]ω[κεν] εἰς τὴν ποίησιν τοῦ σταδί[ου] καὶ τοῦ θεάτρου τοῦ Παναθη[ναι]κοῦ χίλια ζεύγη καὶ ταῦτα πέπομφεν ἅπαντα π[ρὸ Π]αναθηναίων καθὰ ὑπέσχετο, wo τοῦ Παναθηναικοῦ von seiner richtigen Stelle nach σταδίου nur durch ein Versehen des Steinmetzen verschlagen ist. See *C. I. A.*, II. 1, No. 176.

‡ Plut. *Vit. X. Oratt.*, 841 c: τὸ ἐν Διονύσου θέατρον ἐπιστατῶν ἐπετέλεσεν (sc. Λυκοῦργος). In 852 the decree of Stratocles is given (ψήφισμα Γ′): see § 5, ἡμίεργα παραλαβὼν τούς τε νεωσοίκους καὶ τὴν σκευοθήκην, καὶ τὸ θέατρον τὸ Διονυσιακὸν ἐξειργάσατο. For the actual fragments of the decree of Stratocles, see *C. I. A.*, II. 1, No. 240 (see line 5), and *Philol.*, XXIV. pp. 83–114. Hyper., fragm. 121 (Blass): ᾠκοδόμησε δὲ τὸ θέατρον. Paus., I. 29, 16: οἰκοδομήματα δὲ ἐπετέλεσε μὲν τὸ θέατρον ἑτέρων ὑπαρξαμένων.

§ See Wachsmuth, *Stadt Athen*, p. 599, N. 2, especially the remarks at the end of the note.

¶ Vitruv., V. 9: Post scaenam porticus sunt constituendae, uti, cum imbres repentine interpellaverint, habeat populus quo se recipiat ex theatro choregiaque laxamentum habeant ad comparandum. Uti sunt porticus Pompeianae itemque Athenis porticus Eumeniae (word emended) ad theatrum Patrisque Liberi fanum.

‖ As to the interest taken by Eumenes in Athens, cf. Herzberg, *Griechenland unter Rom*, I. pp. 178, 479; also Plutarch, *Vit. Anton.*, 60, whence we know that he was honored by a statue on the Acropolis: ἡ δ' αὐτὴ θύελλα καὶ τοὺς Εὐμενοῦς καὶ Ἀττάλου κολοσσοὺς ἐπιγεγραμμένους Ἀντωνείνους Ἀθήνησιν ἐμπεσοῦσα μόνους ἐκ πολλῶν ἀνέτρεψεν.

for a portico behind the scene-structure (post-scaenam), that the audience might have a place to betake themselves in inclement weather, and that there might be space for the formation of the chorus. This Eumenes is probably Eumenes II. of Pergamus, and the elder brother of Attalus II., who built the Stoa at Athens which is called after his name.* He reigned from 197 to 159 B.C. The information, however, in regard to this Stoa of Eumenes is so scanty, and the text of Vitruvius so corrupt, that it is impossible to come to any certain conclusion as to the position of the building. It may have been in immediate connection with the scene-structure on the south, a view which Dr. Ulrich Koehler seems to hold;† but there are strong arguments for placing it between the theatre and the Odeum of Herodes Atticus. The inscription upon the flight of steps ‡ which leads up from the orchestra to the present stage furnishes us with the only record that we have of further additions to the theatre. This inscription, of which we shall speak below at greater length, is commonly assigned to the reign of Septimius Severus (193–211 A.D.). At this point all traces of the history of the theatre are lost; and during the middle ages § it disappeared so completely from view that

* Cf. Wachsmuth, *S. A.*, p. 642, N. 3.

† *Mittheilungen d. deutsch. archäol. Inst. in Athen*, III. p. 151.

‡ Wachsmuth, *S. A.*, p. 704, N. 2.

§ Cf. Mommsen's *Athenae Christianae*, c. V., in regard to the various structures erected in different parts of the theatre during the middle ages.

Mention is made of the theatre in a passage in one of three fragments in Müller's *Fragmenta Historicorum Graecorum*, II. p. 254, which are ascribed to Dicaearchus (B.C. 320). After describing the entrance to the city by the Sacred Way from Eleusis, the writer enumerates several of the more important buildings in the city, beginning: Ὠδεῖον τῶν ἐν τῇ οἰκουμένῃ κάλλιστον· θέατρον ἀξιόλογον, μέγα καὶ θαυμαστόν. Müller, however, in his commentary points out that there is great doubt of the authenticity of the fragment. Wachsmuth (*S. A.*, pp. 44, 45) absolutely rejects it, on the ground that it is chronologically impossible for the passage to be as old as Dicaearchus, since in it the Olympieium is spoken of as ἡμιτελές, which could not have been its condition until after the time of Antiochus IV., Epiphanes (175–164 B.C.). Wachsmuth refers the fragment with probability to Heracleides Criticus, who is quoted by the Apollonius whose writings form a part of the collection entitled Παραδοξογράφοι, edited by Westermann (Braunschweig, 1839). Cf. Pauly, *R. Encycl.*, I. 2, p. 1321, and Smith, *Dict. Gr. and R. Biog. and Myth.*, I. p. 239 (*b*). Apollonius (c. 19) quotes from this Heracleides, περὶ τῶν ἐν Ἑλλάδι πόλεων, a passage which is found almost exactly in another of the three fragments ascribed to Dicaearchus. See Müller, II. p. 232.

the travellers of the seventeenth and eighteenth centuries are hopelessly in the dark even as to its site. Stuart, for instance, writes of the Odeum of Regilla under the name of the "Theatre of Bacchus," while he mistakes the true site of the theatre for that of the Odeum of Pericles.* Richard Chandler was the first to recognize the true site; and Leake, by calling attention to the now well-known coin of the Payne-Knight collection in the British Museum, removed all doubt on the subject. This coin, although valueless in its details, at least proves conclusively that the theatre lay at the eastern end of the south side of the Acropolis, since otherwise the eastern front of the Parthenon could not have been represented on it.†

Excavations were first made upon this spot by Athenian archaeologists shortly before 1860, but these led to no other result than the uncovering of the steps which are hewn in the rock near the former site of the choragic monument of Thrasyllus. Early in the year 1862, the German architect Strack came to Athens; and, after some delay in obtaining permission from the owners of the soil, excavations were begun under his supervision on the seventeenth of March. On the twenty-second of March, step 17 of *κερκὶς* 1 (left)‡ was uncovered; and on the third of April, the double throne bearing the inscriptions *κήρυκος* and *στρατηγοῦ* was also laid bare. Soon after, the discovery of the row of marble chairs which enclose the orchestra, and of the orchestra itself, made it clear that important remains were waiting to be uncovered. On the third of June, Strack left Athens; and, after this time, all the excavations were under the direction of the Archæological Society of Athens. With some interruptions, the work, so well begun, was continued until 1865, when the theatre was left substantially in its present condition. That part of the western retaining wall which is near the Acropolis, however, was not uncovered until the excavations of 1877 laid bare the contiguous Asclepieion.

The Athenian archæologists Rhousopoulos and Koumanoudes have given reports of the excavations made in 1862, the former in the

---

* *Antiquities of Athens*, II. p. 23.

† This coin is figured in Dyer's *Ancient Athens*, and in Smith's *Dict. of Geog.*, I. p. 285.

‡ By reference to the plan, the numbering of the *κερκίδες* in the *κοῖλον* will be made clear. See also the first note on p. 149 (below).

'Αρχαιολογικὴ 'Εφημερίς, the latter in the Φιλίστωρ, Voll. III. and IV. In 1863, Dr. Vischer of Bâle wrote the excellent paper above mentioned, with a more general treatment of the subject, in the *Neues Schweizerisches Museum*. The only plan of the theatre which existed before the year 1870 was the somewhat incomplete one by the architect Ernst Ziller, which was published in the 'Αρχαιολογικὴ 'Εφημερίς for 1862. In 1870, however, more complete drawings were made by the same architect; and these, with some additions, were published in 1877 in the *Zeitschrift für bildende Kunst*, XIII., accompanied by the paper of Julius, already mentioned. Two short articles, by Professor Fr. Christian Kirchhoff, in the *Programme des Königlichen Christianeums zu Altona* for 1882 and 1883, complete the list of publications which treat of the theatre: the title of the former is, *Vergleichung der Ueberreste vom Theater des Dionysos zu Athen aus dem 5ten Jahrhundert vor Christi mit den Regeln des Vitruv für die Erbauung griechischer Theater und mit meiner orchestischen Hypothese;* that of the lattter is, *Neue Messungen der Ueberreste vom Theater des Dionysos in Athen, nebst einigen Bemerkungen.*

PART II.

A Greek theatre consists of three parts: the scene-structure (with the stage), the orchestra, and the κοῖλον or auditorium. These parts are so distinct that they must be discussed separately. First, we shall consider the ruins of the scene-structure.

THE SCENE-STRUCTURE.*

As a preface to any explanation of the complicated lines of wall which lie upon the south side of the theatre, it should be said that the problem which they present is no easy one, and that, outside of certain quite distinct limits, definite statements concerning them must rest chiefly on uncertain theories. It is, however, possible to make out the foundations of the oldest or Hellenic scene and of the postscenium wall at the back of it with a high degree of certainty; and we may also feel sure of the position of the ancient parascenia, though their exact limits cannot be defined. Some traces also remain of work which probably belongs to the time of Lycurgus. The additions to the theatre made in Roman times, however, make many points uncertain, though we can generally distinguish the Roman from the Hellenic work both by construction and by position.

The lines of wall 10–11, 6–8 and 7–9 (at right angles with 10–11), and 20–22, form the skeleton, as it were, of the whole building. We shall later see reason, however, for thinking that 20–22 originally had the support and covering of a contiguous wall on the south, which was probably narrower than the present Piraic-stone wall 23–24. All the walls first mentioned are built of conglomerate stone, and are of care-

* See the plan of the theatre. The dotted parts represent conglomerate stone; and those which are "cross-hatched" denote that Piraic stone is used, or that evidence exists of its former presence.

ful and solid construction; though at present the wall 20–22 has fallen a good deal out of line, probably because for centuries it has been without support, except from the surrounding earth, for a height varying from five to ten feet. There can be little doubt that these older walls date from the erection of the first permanent theatre; that is, from the fifth century before Christ.

The wall 10–11 is the foundation of the scene (σκηνή);* in front of this, and connected with it, was the stage (λογεῖον), supported upon its outer or northern side by the wall of the hyposcenium (ὑποσκήνιον). No remains of any hyposcenium dating from Hellenic times have been found; but it is obvious that any such structure must have been removed in Roman times to make room for the larger stage, which, according to the fashion of the day,† was carried far forward into the orchestra. The cross-walls, 6–8 and 7–9, are the foundations of the inner walls of the parascenia (παρασκήνια); and, according to Leopold Julius, 16 and 17 are the foundations of their outer walls.‡ Much of the wall 16 is destroyed; but its construction is by no means good enough to put it on a par with such walls as 10–11, 20–22, 6–8, and 7–9. Little can be said with confidence of the wall 17; it is much destroyed, and has evidently served its day as part of a Roman structure. I do not believe, therefore, that these walls 16 and 17 are part of the original Hellenic structure, though they doubtless occupy very nearly the position of the original walls of the parascenia. All traces of the front wall of the parascenia are gone, and it is impossible to say how far both the walls 6–8 and 7–9, with the outer walls corresponding to them, originally extended; probably, however, they reached very nearly to the line on which now the little stylobates with Doric columns stand, at 3 and 4. §

I must confess myself unable to solve the problems presented by the Piraic-stone walls 12–13, 14, and 15. Julius does not hesitate

---

* It is interesting to note that the position of wall 10–11 is nearly, if not exactly, in accord with the rules which Vitruvius gives (V. 7. 1) for the position of the scene in a Greek theatre; that is, if we accept the arc upon which the front line of the marble chairs is set as the circumference of the orchestra circle.

† See Strack, *Das altgriechische Theatergebäude*, p. 4 and Plate III.; also Donaldson's *Theatre of the Greeks*, p. 254 ff.

‡ *Zeitsch. f. bildende Kunst*, XIII., p. 236.

§ The wall 6–8 now extends beyond the line of 3, as in the plan; but this could not have been the case in Hellenic times.

to assign them to the time of Lycurgus,* and he believes them to have been erected to strengthen the older walls in front of them, so that the foundations might thus be fitted to carry the stone building which was then erected in place of a previous wooden one. But these walls stand distinctly by themselves, and do not at all form a united whole with 10–11, as they should do if they were intended to bear the renovated structure of the fourth century. Except the wall 14 (which, owing to the incomplete condition of the excavation at this point, cannot be thoroughly examined), these walls are very carelessly built, though the blocks of stone are large. In view of these facts, I think it is very doubtful whether they date from any time when good Hellenic work was in vogue. The opinion that the first scene-structure was built of wood, though it is held by Julius and many other scholars, and possibly may be correct, is still a theory, which many refuse to accept.†

The wall 20–22 is the foundation wall of the postscenium. At the back of this runs the wall 23–24, consisting at present of a single course of Piraic stone, which rests upon the foundations of 20–22 (as shown in Fig. 1). The theory which Julius has proposed in explanation of walls 12–13, 14, and 15, that they were added at the time of Lycurgus to strengthen the older foundation, he applies also to wall 23–24. This, in his opinion, was added to make the foundation of the postscenium suitable for the more perfect building which it is supposed was erected upon them during the fourth century. In any case, it is evident that the wall 20–22 must always have had some kind of a facing on the south side, since the structure, as shown in the cross section, plainly betokens this. Accepting for the moment the theory of Julius, that the wall 23–24 belongs to the building of Lycurgus, the width of the block *h* shows that, from the very beginning, it supported a broader wall than 20–22. The addition of so broad a supporting wall as 23–24 would have necessitated a widening of the foundation; so that, if 23–24 was added in the fourth century B.C., the block *g* must date from the same time. As to walls 12–13,

---

* See p. 237.

† For Julius's view, cf. Uhrlichs in *Verhandl. der* 20 *Philol-Vers.*, 1861, pp. 45 f.; and Bursian, *Allgemeine Encyklopädie: Griechische Kunst*, Sec. LXXXII. p. 449; and, for the opposite view, C. Curtius in *Philogus*, XXIV. pp. 261–283, *Zum Redner Lycurgus*, section on the Theatre.

14, and 15, I have previously expressed the opinion that the theory of Julius is not a very probable one. I cannot, therefore, think that these walls furnish any basis for an argument as to the origin of wall 23–24; and I believe, further, that there are no sufficient grounds for the theory that the additions of Piraic stone behind the foundation

FIG. 1.

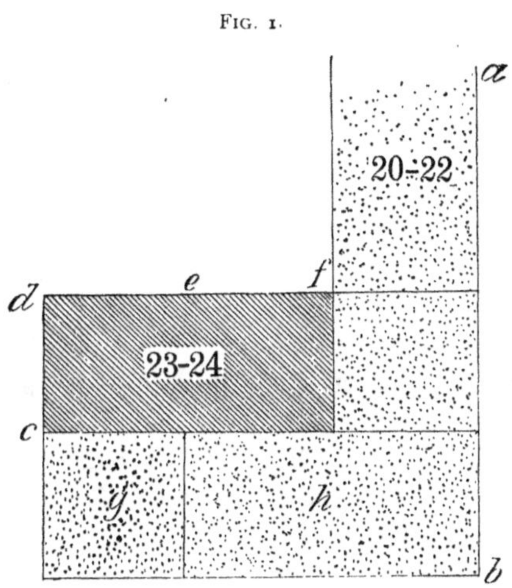

The above is a rough sketch of a section of the two walls, showing the relative position of the blocks of stone. The line *ab* represents the inner or northern side of the wall 20–22, the line *d–c* the outer or southern side of the wall 23–24. The thickness of 20–22 is 0.70 m., and that of 23–24 is 1.40 m.

of the ancient scene and those at the back of the postscenium are corresponding parts of the renovated structure of the fourth century. There are, however, some other facts, not alluded to by Julius, which make it probable that the wall 23–24 was a part of the structure of this date. In the first place, a line in the stone is visible which runs the whole length of the wall 23–24 at the point *e* (Fig. 1). This line marks the limit of a course of stone which once occupied the space between *e* and *f*. Next, following the same wall along to the angle at 24 (plan of theatre), we find a block of Hymettian marble (marked black), divided on the southern surface by a vertical line into two parts, so that it has the appearance of two blocks; and this block exactly fills the space at this point between *e* and *f* (Fig. 1). A little farther to the west, upon the same wall, stand three or four blocks of Piraic stone (not indicated upon the plan), narrower than the block of Hymettian marble. These at first sight look as if they could not be *in situ;* but a closer observation removes all doubt, and we find traces of iron clamps, which must have been used to fasten on another course of stones in front. Clamps were also used to bind together the Piraic blocks themselves. From these facts we reach the conclusion, that the single broad course of Piraic stone, of which the wall 23–24 at present consists, was never carried higher at its present width than it now is; that above this, the wall 20–22 was covered by a wall of Piraic stone of the thickness of the blocks of this stone just mentioned; and that this wall was faced by slabs of Hymettian marble, which concealed the Piraic stone and gave the wall sufficient thickness to fill up the space between *e* and *f* (Fig. 1).

It is a fact worth noticing, that the eastern division of the block of Hymettian marble which fits into the corner at 24 is not finished smoothly upon the southern surface, and that the width of this portion exactly corresponds with a line which is visible upon the Piraic-stone wall 24–26. We have therefore ground for supposing that the facing of Hymettian marble extended around the corner at 24, and that thus the unfinished part of the marble block was originally covered. This use of Hymettian marble points to work not earlier than the fourth century;* but the character of these walls, and their close connection with an essential part of the theatre, seem to me to indicate that they are of this earlier date, rather than later. It is probable, therefore, that in this wall 23–24, built up with 20–22, we have the postscenium wall of the fourth century B.C. To the same period belong also the walls 29, 25–26, and 24–26 with its continuation 31, which lie in close connection with 23–24. These are of Piraic stone, built on foundation of conglomerate stones. It is impossible to determine exactly what was the nature of the structure to which these walls served as foundations, though their general character strongly suggests that a stoa of some kind was erected at this southern side of the theatre. The fact that these walls seem to form an essential part of the main scene-structure would seem to show that they might

* See Koehler, *Mittheilungen des deutschen archäol. Institutes in Athen*, III. p. 234.

be the foundation of a stoa which had been added at the time of Lycurgus;* but, on the other hand, the great number of fragments of a later date which are scattered about suggest that we may have here the stoa of Eumenes, which was "post scaenam."† I rather incline to the former view, but admit frankly that sufficient evidence to establish it is still wanting.

Of the wall 31, which extends in a southerly direction from 25–26, and of the wall 18, I can offer no explanation; they seem, however, to lie in close connection with an Hellenic structure. The little piece of wall, too, which cuts into 25–26 at an angle (30 in the plan), gives no hint of its purpose; it is later than the wall into which it is built, as its construction and position plainly show. The wall 27–28 also must be passed by without explanation, as the destruction of the building is so complete at this point as to leave no room even for conjecture.

All other existing remains of the scene-structure date from Roman times, and there is evidence that even as early as the beginning of the Christian era extensive additions were made to this part of the building. Julius has aptly pointed out the close resemblance between certain monolith arches of Hymettian marble, found among the ruins, and those of the aqueduct at the back of the Tower of the Winds, which carried water from the Acropolis to the Clepsydra,‡ and was built shortly before the Christian era.§ The resemblance between

---

* Dyer, in *Ancient Athens* (p. 341), quotes a passage from Andocides, *De Myst.*, § 38: *ἐπεὶ δὲ παρὰ τὸ προπύλαιον τοῦ Διονύσου ἦν* (sc. ὁ Διοκλείδης), *ὁρᾶν ἀνθρώπους πολλοὺς ἀπὸ τοῦ ᾠδείου καταβαίνοντας εἰς τὴν ὀρχήστραν.* This, he thinks, refers to a "propylaeum or screen" attached to the theatre on the south. But *τὸ προπύλαιον* may refer simply to the gateway of the enclosure sacred to Dionysus, which need not have been very imposing to have this name applied to it. (Cf. Mr. Dyer's own note 1, p. 341, on the expression "*ἐν Διονύσου.*") The statement of Mr. Dyer's views of the condition of the theatre previous to the time of Lycurgus is, moreover, hardly consistent with his deduction from the words of Andocides. He speaks of the early theatre (p. 83) as being "a rude construction in comparison with what Lycurgus the orator made it," and afterwards states his belief that, in the time of Andocides, ninety years before Lycurgus finished the theatre, a "magnificent propylaeum or screen" existed upon the south side of the building. Cf. also Die Enneakrunosepisode bei Pausanias: G. Loeschke, *Dorpati Livonorum.* Schnakenburg, 1884.

† See Vitruv., V. 9, quoted on page 126 (above).

‡ *Zeitschrift für bild. Kunst*, XIII. p. 238.

§ E. Curtius, in *Sieben Karten z. Topog. v. Athen*: Text, p. 44.

these arches — or, one might perhaps with more correctness say, their identity of pattern — is certainly very striking, and makes it highly probable that both constructions are of the same date. Upon wall 19, a structure of late date, rests a double pier of Hymettian marble, evidently not *in situ*. This was doubtless used to support the monolith arches; and it also corresponds exactly in pattern to the piers which support the arches of the aqueduct just mentioned. We have, further, the wall 5, of Hymettian marble, and the little stylobate with its columns at 3, to which a structure at 4 on the other side of the scene (σκηνή) corresponded. These columns, which have their stylobate on a level with the floor of the orchestra, seem to have formed a part of a Roman scene; it is, however, quite uncertain how they were connected with it.

The marble reliefs, moreover, which are built into the stage of Phaedrus (1–2 in plan) cannot date from a period when Greek art was flourishing; on the other hand, they cannot be as late as the structure into which they have been built. It will appear later that originally they were not intended to occupy their present place. These, therefore, also point to early Roman work. It is possible too that the theatre may have stood in need of some restoration shortly before the Christian era, since in 86 B.C. Sulla besieged the tyrant Aristion in the Acropolis, and during this siege we know that the Odeum of Pericles suffered serious damage.* It is not at all improbable, therefore, that the contiguous theatre was damaged at the same time.

It remains to consider the walls 6–7 and 1–2, with the marble reliefs built into the latter, before we pass on to the orchestra. The wall 6–7 is finished on the top, for about half its width on the southern side, with slabs of Hymettian marble (marked black in the plan), upon which traces of columns are visible. This wall at first sight seems to be closely connected with the stylobates and columns at 3 and 4; but it is undeniably of much inferior construction, and very probably of much later date.† It is built of loose irregular stones, carelessly heaped together. I cannot attempt to say how it was con-

* *C. I. G.*, No. 357; Vitruv., V. 9. 1. See Appian, *Mithrid.*, § 38: *καὶ Ἀριστίων αὐτοῖς συνέφευγεν, ἐμπρήσας τὸ ᾠδεῖον ἵνα μὴ ἑτοίμοις ξύλοις αὐτίκα ὁ Σύλλας ἔχοι τὴν ἀκρόπολιν ἐνοχλεῖν.*

† Cf. Julius's article, p. 238, where he inclines to the belief that the wall 6–7 dates from the middle ages.

Reliefs below the Stage of Phaedrus.

The Silenus and the second group are repeated.

nected with the original scene-structure of the theatre, if indeed it is early enough to have formed a part of it at all.*

The wall 1–2, the so-called hyposcenium of Phaedrus, is the latest addition to the theatre of which we have any knowledge. Its position alone would prove it to be extremely late work, even if bad construction and other evidence did not betray its date. The line of this structure was so far advanced into the orchestra as to cut off exit and entrance by the two πάροδοι, thus completely shutting in the orchestra. The western half only of this ruined stage is preserved, with the flight of steps by which it was reached from the orchestra. The upper step bears the following inscription : —

Σοὶ τόδε καλὸν ἔτευξε, φιλόργιε, βῆμα θεήτρου
Φαῖδρος Ζωΐλου βιοδώτορος Ἀτθίδος ἀρχός.†

"Phaedrus, Zoïlus' son, in life-giving Attica ruler,
Built in thine honor this beautiful stage, O God of the orgy."

Archaeologists are inclined to identify this Phaedrus with the one whose name, with the addition of the designation Παιανιεύς, *the Paeanian*, appears on a sun-dial which is now among the Elgin Marbles of the British Museum.‡ The inscription upon the dial is referred by Boeckh to the reign of Septimius Severus (193–211 A.D.); § and if the identity of Phaedrus is assumed as established, our hyposcenium must date from the same period. Dittenberger, in the *Corpus Inscriptionum Atticarum*, assigns it without hesitation to this or even a later period; and this is well supported by the character of the letters of the inscription.

The half of the stage of Phaedrus which remains is adorned with four groups of figures in high-relief,‖ each group being separated from its neighbor by an unoccupied space, while in the middle, separating the groups into two pairs, is the crouching figure of a Silenus in a deep niche. Upon the eastern side of the steps, a second

---

* The two dotted lines between 6–7 and 1–2 represent a mediæval wall which has been removed by the Archaeological Society of Athens.

† *C. I. A.*, III. 1, No. 239.

‡ For some discussion of this point, cf. Dyer's *Ancient Athens*, p. 311; also Vischer, *Neues Schweizerisches Museum*, 1863, III. p. 70.

§ *C. I. G.*, No. 522.

‖ See the opposite plate, in which the steps of the stage and the reliefs are shown in two lines.

figure of a Silenus has been found, which undoubtedly was once the companion of the other, but now lies disengaged upon the ground. There can be no question that these reliefs are of older and better workmanship than the stage, and the clumsy way in which they have been introduced into their present position is clear proof that they were not originally intended for it. Julius points out that the edges of the separate slabs are so dressed that we must suppose them to have been originally set up contiguously, without niches or dividing spaces.* Further, the slabs have evidently been cut down at the top, so that the heads of the figures are now higher than the background to which they belong as reliefs. The Silenus, too, is still more evidently out of place; and the fact (which can be observed on the disengaged figure) that both Sileni are completely finished at the back perhaps argues that they were not designed to stand in niches.

These reliefs have been specially treated in an able article by F. Matz,† which presents so reasonable a theory of their various subjects that I propose in the main to follow it in what I have to say about them.

The first two groups almost immediately suggest their own subjects. In the group on the left ‡ a seated male figure first attracts our notice. Above the waist it is naked, but the lower part of the body is covered by a loosely draped garment. The figure, like all the others except the Silenus, is headless, and the left arm is broken off near the shoulder, while the right arm is wanting from the elbow. Before the seated figure is a standing one, evidently of a younger man, over whose left shoulder a garment is thrown, which falls down behind as far as the knee-joint, and in front covers the left breast and most of the left arm. His right arm is wanting below the elbow, and the right leg also is gone. Upon his left arm he bears the figure of an infant, which is much mutilated, the lower part of the body, slightly draped, being alone preserved.

---

* *Zeitschr. für bild. Kunst*, XIII. p. 239: Als technische Grund für eine ursprünglich andere Verwendung ist anzuführen, dass die Seitenflächen Stosskanten tragen, also nicht, wie jetzt, die Seitenwände von Nischen gebildet haben können.

† *Annali dell' Instituto*, 1870.

‡ Throughout this description the terms "left" and "right," when applied to the position or arrangement of the groups, refer to the spectator as he stands facing the reliefs, unless it is otherwise specified.

It need hardly be said that we have here a representation of the birth of Dionysus. The seated figure is Zeus, from whom the youthful god Hermes has just taken the new-born child. The subject was a favorite one with the ancients, as is shown by the frequency of the scene in bronzes, gems, and coins, besides the other instances in sculpture.* The two figures upon either side of Zeus and Hermes are more difficult to explain, though they evidently stand as guards over the birth of the infant. The legs of the figure upon the extreme left of the group are entirely destroyed, and of the lower parts of the body only portions of the feet remain. The right arm is wanting below the elbow, but with the left the figure holds aloft a round shield. The figure upon the other side of the group has suffered less, and, with the exception of the lower right arm, it is in good preservation. With his left arm this guardian also holds a shield, but does not raise it aloft as his companion does. Matz suggests that these figures have been introduced at the birth of Dionysus in imitation of the Cretan myth about the infant Zeus, and remarks: "The Orphic bards thenceforth assigned the same protectors (*i.e.*, as to Zeus) to Dionysus Zagreus, son of Zeus and Persephone (Lobeck, *Aglaophamus*, p. 555), to defend him from the wiles of the Titans, whence the transfer to the son of Semele is very easy." †

The next group also can be interpreted with tolerable certainty. Upon each side of a small altar stands a male figure. The one upon the right is clad in a short garment, over which is cast an animal's skin; he wears also a cothurnus. Behind him is the graceful figure of a young man, over whose left shoulder and arm hang a light mantle, caught together just below the right shoulder. His right arm, now gone below the elbow, was extended; and the hand, as Matz suggests, may have shaded his face. The figure upon the left of the altar is more simply clad in a short tunic; with his right arm, now destroyed, he was evidently dragging a goat,‡ which is seen

* Cf. *Journal of Hellenic Studies*, April, 1882, p. 107; and an article in the same number, by A. H. Smith, upon the Hermes of Praxiteles, in which, although the author has collected a large number of representations of the birth of Dionysus, our relief has been overlooked.

† Upon the subject of the Curetes and Corybantes, and their relations to the myth of Dionysus, cf. A. Brown, *The Great Dionysiack Myth*, Vol. I. p. 128 ff. Cf. Gerhard, *Antike Bildwerke*, CIV.; and Müller-Wieseler, *Denkmäler der alten Kunst*, II. XXXV. 412.

‡ Verg. *Georg.*, II. 380: Non aliam ob culpam Baccho caper omnibus aris caeditur.

behind him hanging back, and in his left arm he bears a bunch of grapes. Behind him walks a woman, clad in a long tunic, who bears a dish of sacrificial fruit. At the back of the relief is seen a crouching hound, and above the altar is a vine with hanging bunches of grapes. There can hardly be any doubt that the group represents Icarius about to sacrifice a goat to Dionysus, at the time when the worship of that God was first introduced into Attica. The legend runs as follows. When Dionysus, in company with Demeter, came into Attica, he was welcomed by Icarius, whom he taught vine-culture and the making of wine.* Upon one occasion Icarius gave wine to some peasants, who became intoxicated, and, supposing that he had poisoned them, slew him, and buried him under a tree. His daughter Erigone hunted long for her father, and was at last directed to his grave by her faithful dog Maera. She then hanged herself on the tree. In our relief, then, we have Icarius, the figure upon the left of the altar, about to offer a sacrifice to the god who stands upon the right, with his attendant Satyr, the graceful figure described above, ready to receive the honor tendered to him. Behind Icarius comes the daughter Erigone, bearing sacrificial fruits, and the crouching dog is the faithful Maera.

The explanation of the third and fourth groups on the right of the Silenus is far more difficult, and certainty here is not attainable. In the absence of any more satisfactory theory, I have generally followed that of Matz, which, though it may be open to objections, has also much to recommend it. The third group lacks one figure, which has apparently been cut away by a chisel; what it may have been it is idle to conjecture. The first thing that strikes one who examines the two reliefs is their similarity. We find the three figures of the third group repeated in inverted order in the fourth. In the third, a young man, entirely naked, but carrying a small garment on his left arm, — in the fourth, a similar youth, with a light covering about the loins, — stand each with a female figure on either side. Traces of something like a club, which the central figure of the fourth group held in his right hand, are visible on the background; and similar traces may also be seen in the other group, though less distinctly. The presence of a club gives Matz his first clew to the interpretation of the relief. He thinks that the young man is Theseus. In the

* Apollod., III. 14, 7.

third group, the female figure on the right seems to me to present great difficulty. She is clad in a gracefully draped double chiton, and in her left hand bears a large cornucopia. This symbol would suggest that we have here a representation of Tyche. To carry out Matz's idea, however, the figure should be Eirene, the Goddess of Peace; and he finds evidence in the position of the right arm, now wanting below the elbow, that she held in her hand a sceptre, a symbol which would accord with his theory. As he points out, the arm is in such a position that we cannot suppose the figure to have supported anything which was above; but it seems to me extremely doubtful whether we are justified in assuming that a sceptre must have entered into the composition. The cornucopia would undoubtedly be an appropriate symbol for the Goddess of Peace, as well as for Tyche. The other female figure in this group is still more difficult to explain, for really no distinguishing characteristics are preserved. She also is dressed in a double chiton; and, as Matz suggests, she may, like the other, have held a sceptre. "Of the small number of divinities," he writes, "from whom we can select, none is more suitable to the subject than Hestia. The tutelary divinity of the sacred hearth of the individual family, as well as of the common hearth of the state, corresponds very well to the goddess who guarantees the security and well-being of the citizens." This is certainly true, and is very likely correct in its bearing upon the argument; but we should remember that we have no right to build very much here upon the identity of Eirene, and further, that the subject ought to be deduced from the characteristics of the relief rather than the relief from the characteristics of the subject.

But we must not forget the seated figure in the fourth group, for it is an important link in explaining Matz's theory. It is much mutilated, the left leg being entirely destroyed and both the arms greatly injured. The chair upon which the figure sits is carved with considerable elegance, and is supported in front by a lion's legs and paws. A sceptre rested once between the legs of the figure; and just above, at the back of the relief, are seen eight columns of a temple upon a rocky eminence. The small portion of the columns that is visible is additional proof that the slabs were at one time higher than at present. This temple is probably the Parthenon, and the scene which is represented is in the enclosure sacred to Dionysus at the foot of the Acropolis. If this be granted, the explanation of this relief immediately becomes easy, though the absence of one figure in the third group makes it impossible to say more of that. In this fourth plaque, the city renders homage to Dionysus in his sacred enclosure. Theseus typifies the united city, and the two goddesses Eirene and Hestia, on either side of him, whose statues stood together in the Prytaneum,* represent the *κοινὴ ἑστία* of the city. Surely there is much beauty in Matz's explanation: Athens the city and Athens in her home-life pay a tribute to the great God to whose worship she was so devoted. It will be noticed that we have a regular progress of events in the reliefs: the first is the birth of the God; the second is the first acknowledgment in Attica of his supremacy; and in the fourth we see him as receiving the worship of the city which has become his own. The general character of the sculpture in the reliefs is good, though far below the standard of the best period of Greek art. Still they exhibit no such barbarity as the hyposcenium into which they are built. Almost all who have studied the sculptures are agreed in assigning them to an early period of the Roman Empire; though the Sileni, which are finer pieces of work than the reliefs, are very likely of an earlier date. It is quite possible that they were brought from an older and somewhat higher hyposcenium, except, of course, the Sileni, which probably did not belong originally to any series of reliefs.

THE ORCHESTRA.

The orchestra† of the theatre at Athens is not shaped like a horse-shoe, as is often the case in Greek theatres,‡ but the arc upon which its boundary is traced is continued by tangents parallel to the main axis of the theatre. The ruins, as we at present see them, show the orchestra to have been completely shut in upon the southern side by the stage of Phaedrus, so as to preclude entrance to it through the

---

* Πλησίον δὲ Πρυτανεῖόν ἐστιν, ἐν ᾧ νόμοι τε οἱ Σόλωνός εἰσι γεγραμμένοι, καὶ θεῶν Εἰρήνης ἀγάλματα κεῖται καὶ Ἑστίας. Paus. I. 18, 3.

† See plan of the theatre.

‡ A familiar example of this is found in the theatre near Epidaurus (Lessa), a good plan of which is to be found in this year's (1883) *Proceedings* (Πρακτικά) *of the Archæological Society of Athens.*

πάροδοι, and a balustrade of upright marble slabs* separates it from the κοῖλον. The slabs are 1.10 m. high, the upper edges being rounded off smoothly; and each one is bound to its neighbor by an iron clamp. Along the inside of the balustrade runs a gutter, which served to carry off the water that would otherwise have gathered in the orchestra; its outlet was under the scene-structure, and it can be easily traced until it pierces wall 23–24. The original covering of this gutter seems to have been of Piraic stone; but in places large slabs of Pentelic marble were inserted, through which a rosette-shaped opening was cut.† The present covering consists largely of Pentelic and Hymettian marble, and is probably of a late date.

The entire enclosure of the orchestra is paved with small slabs of Pentelic and Hymettian marble, a line of red stone being occasionally introduced. The general direction of this pavement is in lines parallel to the hyposcenium of Phaedrus; and it is bounded by a narrow strip of Pentelic marble, laid along the inner edge of the gutter. At a distance of about a metre and a half in front of the steps of Phaedrus, the regular pavement of the orchestra is interrupted by a large rhombus-shaped figure, the outline of which is traced by two enclosing lines, — the outer of Pentelic and Hymettian marble, the inner of Hymettian marble alone. The separate stones within the large figure are rhombus-shaped, and, like the rest of the pavement of the orchestra, are of red, Pentelic, and Hymettian marble. In the centre of the figure is a block of Pentelic marble, 1.05 m. in length and 0.70 m. in breadth, in which is cut a shallow circular depression, 0.51 m. in diameter and 0.02 m. in depth. It has been suggested that this depression marks the place of the image of Dionysus which was introduced in some of the ceremonies of his worship; ‡ but this, though possibly correct, is not supported by any evidence, and it seems more probable that an altar of some kind was erected here. Some small figures of late date have been found cut upon the pavement,§ but their purpose is unknown. At the western end of wall 1–2 a cistern is drawn in the plan: this has now been removed.

---

* Shown on the plan by a black line.

† See plan. Three of these rosettes are still preserved.

‡ *Philologus*, XXIII. p. 496. Benndorf, *Beiträge zur Kenntniss des attischen Theaters*, pp. 2 ff.

§ A representation of these figures, with their measurements, may be found in the second article of Ch. Kirchhoff cited on p. 129.

The question remains, To what period are we to assign this orchestra? The fact that it is completely shut in by the hyposcenium of Phaedrus (see p. 136) is clear evidence of late work, though it is hardly probable that the whole is to be assigned to as late a date as the hyposcenium itself. Leopold Julius thinks that the stage was later than the pavement, for the reason that it was erected without reference to the general direction in which the slabs are laid,* — a fact which I did not remark. The pavement is a good piece of work, however; and we shall probably not be far wrong in classing it with those additions to the theatre which were made about the beginning of the Christian era.† The balustrade around the orchestra, moreover, cannot be earlier than Roman times, since the orchestra of a Greek theatre was never separated in this way from the *κοῖλον*, and the nature of Greek dramatic representations can suggest no reason for such a separation. Two passages, one from Dio Chrysostomus (100 A.D.), the other from Philostratus (230 A.D.), seem to throw some light on the matter.‡ These writers allude to the disgrace of holding gladiatorial shows in the theatre; and, if such a custom had grown up among the people, it is clear that the orchestra would have to be separated in some way from the *κοῖλον*. There are some remains of a rubble support behind the balustrade, which have given rise to the suggestion that the orchestra may at some time have been used as a basin for water in such entertainments as *ναυμαχίαι*. This theory, however, lacks support. In the gutter which drains the orchestra we have a piece of work which agrees with that found in the oldest parts of the building, and may therefore with little doubt be assigned to the fifth century before Christ.

---

* *Zeitschr. f. bild. Kunst*, p. 204: Der Fussboden wurde aber jedenfalls vor Entstehung des Hyposkenion des Phaedros gelegt, da ersterer sich in seiner Zeichnung gar nicht nach letzterem richtet, letzteres aber ersteren willkürlich zerschneidet.

† Pp. 135 ff., above.

‡ Dio. Chrys., *Orat.*, XXXI. § 121: *νῦν δὲ οὐδέν ἐστιν ἐφ' ὅτῳ τῶν ἐκεῖ γιγνομένων οὐκ ἂν αἰσχυνθείη τις· οἷον εὐθὺς τὰ περὶ τοὺς μονομάχους οὕτω σφόδρα ἐζηλώκασι Κορινθίους, . . . ὥστε οἱ Κορίνθιοι μὲν ἔξω τῆς πόλεως θεωροῦσιν ἐν χαράδρᾳ τινὶ, πλῆθος μὲν δυναμένῳ δέξασθαι τόπῳ, ῥυπαρῷ δὲ ἄλλως καὶ ὅπου μηδεὶς ἂν μηδὲ θάψειε μηδένα τῶν ἐλευθέρων, 'Αθηναῖοι δὲ ἐν τῷ θεάτρῳ θεῶνται τὴν καλὴν ταύτην θέαν ὑπ' αὐτὴν τὴν 'Ακρόπολιν, οὗ τὸν Διόνυσον ἐπὶ τὴν ὀρχήστραν τιθέασιν, ὥστε πολλάκις ἐν αὐτοῖς τινα σφάττεσθαι τοῖς θρόνοις, οὗ τὸν ἱεροφάντην καὶ τοὺς ἄλλους ἱερεῖς ἀνάγκη καθίζειν.* Philos., *Vit. Apoll. Tyan.*, IV. 22: *σὺ δὲ, Διόνυσε, μετὰ τοιοῦτον αἷμα ἐς τὸ θέατρον φοιτᾷς; κἀκεῖ σοι σπένδουσιν οἱ σοφοὶ 'Αθηναῖοι; μετάστηθι καὶ σὺ, Δίονυσε· Κιθαιρὼν καθαρώτερος.*

In the orchestra, as a whole, we have little left of the Greek theatre. It is essentially a Roman structure, and little or no light is thrown by it upon any of the vexed questions of Greek choric arrangements.* It is really the one part of the theatre in which scarcely a trace of the ancient building of the fifth century B.C. is to be found.

THE ΚΟΙΛΟΝ.

The κοῖλον (*cavea* or *auditorium*) of the Dionysiac Theatre was built upon an arc of about 250°, with its open side toward the south. At each end of the arc, if we may judge from the ruins which are left on the western side, the retaining walls were continued by straight walls, which made an angle (measured on the outside) of about 150° with the curve.† The arc is, however, by no means a regular one. It is compressed at the point where it meets the projecting rock of the Acropolis, while a further irregularity is noticeable in the retaining wall of the eastern πάροδος, which is about 7 m. longer than that of the western πάροδος. The radius, therefore, of the east side of the κοῖλον — at least, of the more southerly part of it — was considerably longer than that of the west side. From the point *i* to the point *k* (see plan) upon the western side still runs a strong retaining wall, from which project lateral arms towards the interior of the space. These meet a second wall, following the line of the outer one, at the distance of about 2 m., and are carried through it, those which abut upon *j–k* converging towards the middle of the κοῖλον, while those which abut upon *j–i* run from that wall in parallel lines. The inner wall, of conglomerate stone, is the real retaining wall; and the outer one, of Piraic stone, seems only to serve as a support and cover to the inner structure. Whether the eastern side of the κοῖλον had a similar construction cannot be determined, since this side is now in an utterly

---

* Dyer, in the appendix to his *Ancient Athens*, has a short but able discussion of the Greek orchestra in classical times, in which he regards the rhombus-shaped figure in the orchestra as defining in some way the position of the chorus, and searches for evidence in the existing ruin to support his view of the arrangement of the orchestra in classical times. I believe, however, that the orchestra has been too completely Romanized to make speculations of this nature based upon its ruins of any value.

† See walls *j–i* and *j–k* on the plan of the theatre.

ruined state. There can be no doubt, however, that the eastern retaining wall was mainly like the western one, though the proximity of the Odeum of Pericles, which lay upon the slope of the Acropolis just north-east of the great theatre, may have led to some modifications on that side. At the point *k*, a wall *l* of Piraic stone, closely connected with *k–j*, is carried out some distance in a westerly direction; and a short distance towards the north is a wall *m* of conglomerate stone, slightly convergent with *l*. Between these walls, the main retaining wall of the theatre is discontinued. In close connection with wall *m*, the northern part of the retaining wall, built of conglomerate stone, is continued to the Acropolis; but in this part there is no inner structure, and the line of the wall corresponds not with the true inner retaining wall of the southern half, but with the outer wall of Piraic stone. The traces of one lateral arm, projecting towards the inside, still remain. Upon the western side, toward the Asklepieion, the retaining wall was faced with a light covering of Piraic stone. At the point *n* seats were built, outside of the true boundary of the κοῖλον, upon the rocky slope of the Acropolis; and the wall *n*, projecting from the main retaining wall, afforded them support. If we trace the boundary of the κοῖλον further, we reach that part which was known as the κατατομή, where the rock of the Acropolis has been hewn into a curve of fair regularity. Just below this point, ledges have been cut in the rock, which were either seats themselves, or served as supports for seats. From this part of the theatre, slightly east of its main axis, we enter the grotto of the Panagia Spiliotissa, the front of which was formerly adorned by the Choragic monument of Thrasyllus. Stuart and Revett, in *The Antiquities of Athens*, give a representation of this monument, which was still in a fair state of preservation at the time of their visit; and the female figure which surmounted the structure, now headless, is to be seen among the Elgin Marbles of the British Museum.

The walls of the πάροδοι, *i–i* and *h–h*, are the southern retaining walls of the κοῖλον. They are faced, like the other retaining walls, with Piraic stone, which seems to be laid directly against the conglomerate stone within, and not simply connected with it by lateral arms, as is the case with the walls *j–k* and *j–i*. It is a fact worthy of notice, that these walls of the πάροδοι do not run at right angles with the main axis of the theatre, but, if continued, would meet in the orchestra at an obtuse angle.

Restoration of part of the sixth *κερκίς* on the left; showing the outer *κλῖμαξ*, the balustrade of the orchestra, the marble chairs, and the four lowest steps (with their divisions). See pages 147, 148.

From the *Zeitschrift für bildende Kunst.*

Such are the chief characteristics of the exterior of the κοῖλον. Within the enclosed space the spectators' seats, now largely destroyed, were constructed up to the very foot of the rock of the Acropolis. They were of hewn Piraic stone, and were, for the most part, imbedded in the earth, though in the upper part of the κοῖλον there are traces of conglomerate-stone foundations. This system of seats was divided into 13 κερκίδες (cunei), *wedges*, by 14 κλίμακες, or flights of steps, which are 0.70 m. in breadth, the two outer flights leading up close against the walls of the πάροδοι. The axis of the theatre does not pass through a κλῖμαξ dividing the κοῖλον into halves, — an arrangement frequently found in Greek theatres, — but through the middle of the central κερκίς. There is no trace of a διάζωμα (*praecinctio*), or concentric passage, dividing the seats; but the way which led through the theatre obliquely from the point *o* on the east side, and had its exit into the Asklepieion between walls *l* and *m* on the west side, may have served the purpose of a more regular passage, and also have afforded an entrance to the theatre from above.

The lowest step, along the outer edge of which the balustrade of the orchestra runs, has the depth of two slabs of stone. It is slightly inclined toward the orchestra, that water may not collect upon it. Toward the ends it is 3 m. in depth, but in the middle only 2 m.: a result of this is, that the row of marble chairs which follows the inner edge of the step is not concentric with the balustrade which follows the outer edge of the step. These chairs are a striking feature of the theatre, and I shall discuss them specially in Part III.

Just behind the marble chairs is a second step, which served as a sort of passage-way; it varies in width from 0.85 to 0.87 m. At the back of this is a narrow step,* which served as the foot-rest for those who sat upon the third step above. With this third step, the rows of ordinary seats begin. The rectangular holes which occur at regular intervals in the passage-way behind the marble chairs and in the lowest row of ordinary seats, are worthy of notice. They were probably cut to receive poles which supported an awning of some kind. The ordinary seats are about 0.32 m. high, and 0.85 m. in depth. Their surface is divided into three parts: (1) the seat proper, (2) a depression made to receive the feet of the person who sat on the seat above, and (3), at the back, a narrow edge of the same level

---

* This foot-rest is not reckoned as a step in numbering the rows of seats.

as the seat. These parts measure respectively about 0.33 m., 0.42 m., and 0.10 m. The steps of the stairways are of the same height as the seats, but they slope downward so that the front edge of the step is only 0.22 m. in height, while the back is 0.10 m. higher; and we ascend as we pass over the step, which is grooved to prevent slipping.

It remains now to determine the period to which the building of the *κοῖλον* is to be assigned. I have already stated the belief that the theatre was largely built during the fifth century B.C.; and this view is strongly supported by what has been found in the *κοῖλον*. The character of this entire structure points to an early date, and the various parts of it all seem to have been erected at the same time. Julius takes what seems to me a most reasonable view of the matter,* and rejects C. Curtius's statement † that retaining walls of various ages have been uncovered on the west side of the theatre. The ruins of the *κοῖλον* are certainly uniform in character. We can fix approximately one date, previous to which the *κοῖλον* could not have been finished. In the Piraic-stone facing of the western *πάροδος*, at the corner *i*, a block of stone has been built into the wall which bears an obscure inscription.‡ According to Kirchhoff, judging by the style of certain letters, the inscription is to be assigned to a time about Olymp. 93 (408 B.C.). Julius does not concur in this opinion, but inclines to the belief that the stone dates back to the middle of the fifth century B.C. The presence of the stone shows us that the *κοῖλον* could not have been finished (even upon Julius's theory) before the middle of the fifth century B.C., and probably was still unfinished at about 408 B.C. We cannot be greatly mistaken, I think, in ascribing its completion to the later part of the fifth century B.C. The character of the entire structure supports this view,

---

* *Zeitschr. für bild. Kunst*, XIII. p. 202. † *Philologus*, XXIV. pp. 270 ff.

‡ *C. I. A.*, I. No. 499.

Ο Χ
ΒΟΛΗΣ
ΥΠΗΡΕΤΟΝ

Βουλῆς ὑπηρετῶν, *i.e.*, [*seats*] *of the servants of the Senate.*

Kirchhoff says (*l. c.*): Videtur autem lapis olim scriptus esse ad locum designandum, in quo spectabant senatus apparitores, post recentiore tempore sede motus et muro exaedificando adhibitus. The interpretation of the inscription is doubtful, and it is impossible to be at all sure that the stone was ever one of the seats of the theatre. It is built into the wall with the inscription inverted.

and the different parts of it seem all to have been erected at the same time. Julius is without doubt right in rejecting Carl Curtius's statement that walls of various ages have been uncovered on the western side of the κοῖλον. Dyer, in his *Ancient Athens*, cites a passage from the *Thesmophoriazusae* of Aristophanes (vs. 395), in which the word ἴκρια is used, to show that there must have been wooden seats in the theatre at the date of this play, 411 B.C., and that consequently the building then could not have been finished. But the interpretation of the passage, and of the Scholia upon it, is very doubtful; and it is even uncertain whether the poet had in mind ἴκρια of the Dionysiac Theatre at all. The ruins of this part of the theatre, in marked contrast to those of the scene-structure and orchestra, show no diversity of character, and we may confidently believe that they are substantially the remains of the κοῖλον as it was in the best days of the Attic drama. The line of marble chairs in the first row, and the statues which were erected in different places among the seats, are unquestionably of later date.

Before passing to the consideration of the marble chairs in the theatre and the inscriptions upon them, mention must be made of the bases found in several κερκίδες of the κοῖλον, which originally bore statues erected in honor of Hadrian. Three of these bases, with a fragment of a fourth, have been found in the four κερκίδες marked on the plan A., 1 *r.*, 1 *l.*, and 6 *l.** The one in κερκὶς A. bears a long Latin dedication addressed to Hadrian as Consul, with numerous other titles; and at the end of this is a brief inscription in Greek to the Archon Hadrian.† Upon the other bases the inscription, which is the same upon all three, except that a different tribe is recorded as having erected each statue, addresses Hadrian as Emperor.‡

If now we count the κερκίδες, beginning at κερκὶς 6 *l.*, in which the fragment of the base of the statue erected by the tribe Erechtheïs

---

* The central κερκίς is marked A on the plan; and the others 1 *r.*, 2 *r.*, 3 *r.*, etc. (on the right of a person facing the stage), and 1 *l.*, 2 *l.*, 3 *l.*, etc. (on the left). The bases are marked with the letters e, c, f, g, upon the plan.

† See *C. I. A.*, III. 1, 464. For the Latin inscription, see *Annali dell' Instituto*, 1862, pp. 137 ff. The Greek inscription is as follows: Ἡ ἐξ Ἀρείου πάγου βουλὴ καὶ ἡ τῶν ἑξακοσίων καὶ ὁ δῆμος ὁ Ἀθηναίων τὸν ἄρχοντα ἑαυτῶν Ἀδριανόν.

‡ *C. I. A.*, III. 1. 466–469: Αὐτοκράτορα Καίσαρα, θεοῦ Τραιανοῦ Παρθικοῦ υἱὸν, θεοῦ Νέρουα υἱωνὸν Ἀδριανὸν Σεβαστὸν, ἡ ἐξ Ἀρείου πάγου βουλὴ καὶ ἡ βουλὴ τῶν χ′ καὶ ὁ δῆμος ἐπιμελουμένης τῆς Οἰνηΐδος (Ἀκαμαντίδος, Ἐρεχθηΐδος) φυλῆς.

has been found, it will appear that the statues erected by the Akamantis and Oineïs stood respectively in the sixth and eighth *κερκίδες*. It was immediately perceived by the Athenian archæologists that the numbers corresponded with the numbers of these tribes in the official tribal list of the age of Hadrian, and it was plausibly argued that each of the tribes must have erected a statue to Hadrian in a *κερκίς* of the theatre. It was further assumed that the statue which stood in the middle *κερκίς* (A.) was the offering of the tribe Hadrianis, named for Hadrian himself,* since this occupied the seventh place in the tribal list, although the base which stands in this *κερκίς* does not record the name of any tribe. Against this it might be argued, that not only does this omission of the tribal name seem very strange, but it is almost inconceivable that a tribe, in erecting a statue to its eponymous hero, should omit his highest title, and address him as Archon when he was in reality Emperor. Vischer, however, adduces other and more conclusive arguments, which prove that the Hadrianis could have had nothing to do with the erection of any of these statues. Each base records the fact that the statue which stood on it was erected by the Senate of Six Hundred. But when the Hadrianis was established, the number of the Senate was reduced from six hundred to five hundred,† and the basis of representation underwent a radical change; moreover, we must suppose that this change was made as soon as the Hadrianis came into existence, since otherwise the tribal representation would have become much confused. Hence we are forced to conclude that the statues of which we now have the bases must have been erected previous to the establishment of the Hadrianis. This theory being set aside, the question arises when the erection of these statues did take place. Hadrian was archon of Athens in 112 A.D., and we are quite safe in assuming that the statue whose base now stands in *κερκὶς* A. was set up in his honor at that time, and was not the offering of any one tribe.‡ As to the others, there is more uncertainty. Dr. Vischer expresses the opinion that the Athenians would have been most likely to make such an exhibition of flattery

---

* Ἀρχαιολογικὴ Ἐφημερίς, 1862, p. 181.

† *C. I. G.*, I. pp. 323 and 902. Cf. also Vischer, *N. Schweiz. Museum*, III. p. 63; *Hermes*, I. 417 ff.; Herzberg, *Griech. u. d. Röm.*, II. 344.

‡ This is now universally accepted. See Wachsmuth, *S. A.*, 694, N. 1; Mommsen, *C. I. Lat.*, III. 550; *Hermes*, I. 418; Vischer, *Kleine Schriften*, II. p. 375, N. 2.

and adulation as the erection of these statues implies at the time when Hadrian, after finishing the Olympieium, presided as Archon at the great Dionysia.* The Olympieium was probably finished in 129 A.D., and it is quite likely that the statues date from this year.† The only difficulty with this view is one which Dr. Vischer himself recognizes, namely, that the establishment of the Hadrianis has usually been referred to Olymp. 225, 1, or 121–122 A.D., ‡ and therefore a senate of five hundred must have existed in 129 A.D. Later investigations, however, have shown that much of the chronology of Hadrian's reign has been very imperfectly understood; and even now there are many uncertain points about it. §

Another theory in respect to the erection of these statues suggests itself, which may not be altogether without foundation. Dittenberger has shown, in his article in the *Hermes* (VII. pp. 213–229), that it is quite possible, and even probable, that Hadrian may have been honored with the office of archon in 112 A.D. without coming to Athens; and he quotes Th. Mommsen, who seems inclined to favor his view. If this be so, it is not at all unreasonable to suppose that the statues which were dedicated to Hadrian *as emperor* may have been erected in honor of his becoming emperor, after the death of Trajan in 117 A.D.,‖ although probably he did not visit Athens as emperor until about 124 or 125 A.D. at the earliest. This view would remove all difficulty connected with the date of the establishment of the Hadrianis, although it seems pretty clear that this tribe was instituted at a later date than was formerly supposed.¶

---

* Dion Cass., LXIX. 16; Herzberg, II. 316.

† Cf. Wachsmuth, *S. A.*, 688, N. 6.

‡ Corsini, *Fasti Attici*, IV. 167.

§ *Hermes*, Vol. VII. pp. 213–229; Herzberg, II. 301, N. 2.

‖ Previous to the establishment of the Hadrianis, the Oineïs was the seventh in the tribal list; but since the statue in *κερκὶς* A. was not the offering of a tribe, this *κερκίς* is not to be reckoned in comparing the numbers of the tribes with the numbers of the *κερκίδες* in which bases have been found; and the base which bears the name of the Oineïs will thus be in the seventh and not in the eighth *κερκίς*.

¶ See *C. I. A.*, III. 1, No. 83: Hadrianidis tribus nomen titulum anno 126 post Chr. recentiorem esse indicat. Dittenberger (*Hermes*, I. 417 ff.) discusses the establishment of the Hadrianis and the change in the number of the Senate. He assigns these to the year 132 A.D. Certainty seems to be impossible.

PART III.

THE MARBLE CHAIRS.

THE following account of the marble chairs in the theatre is largely based upon the commentary of the *C. I. A.*, III. 1, pp. 77 ff.; but, in addition to what is found there, quotations from other authorities have been given and references made, with the object of explaining something of the nature of the various offices held by those who were honored with chairs in the theatre. These will not be sufficient for the complete understanding of any particular cult in the Greek worship; but it is hoped that they may bring students into contact with the best authorities on the subject of the Athenian hierarchy, and thereby prepare the way for more exhaustive study. Dr. Vischer's article is most helpful for the study of the chairs; but, as many important works which are referred to in this paper have been published since his report of the excavations was made, it is natural that this should not be entirely satisfactory at the present time.

It is impossible to determine with certainty when these chairs were placed in the theatre. The inscriptions upon them are nearly all as late as the beginning of the Christian era, though on several an earlier inscription of some kind has evidently been cut away to make room for the present one.* This of course shows that at least some of the chairs are older than the present inscriptions would indicate.† The chairs can hardly have belonged to the original theatre of the fifth century B.C.; and we must therefore place them either among the additions of Lycurgus or among those of the early Roman imperial period. The sculpture on the chair of the Priest of Dionysus may

* The following chairs show traces of an obliterated inscription: Nos. 2, 5, 9, 10, 11, 12, 13, 30, 33, 34, 37, 43, 45, 56.

† The allusion in Aeschin. *in Ctes.*, § 76, to the προεδρία is too indefinite to be of authority in determining the age of the chairs.

seem to make the latter supposition the more probable; but even should we suppose this chair to be of early Roman times, it would not prove with certainty that the other chairs were of the same date. We must, therefore, be content to leave the question unsolved. The number and probable date, according to the *Corpus Inscriptionum Atticarum*, are given with each inscription, together with its number in Dr. Vischer's article. Two articles in the *Philologus* (Vol. XXIII. pp. 212–259, 592–622; and Supplement-Band II. pp. 628 ff.), by K. Keil, which have not been specially referred to in the following pages, are valuable contributions to the literature of this subject: they are entitled *Attische Culte aus Inschriften.*

EXPLANATION OF ABBREVIATED REFERENCES.

C. I. A., Corpus Inscriptionum Atticarum. Whenever these letters are used without designation of the volume, Vol. III. Part I. is always to be understood.
C. I. G., Boeckh's Corpus Inscriptionum Graecarum.
V., Vischer, in Neues Schweizerisches Museum, III., 1863; the article is also in Vischer's Kleine Schriften, II. pp. 324–390.
W., *S. A.*, Wachsmuth's Stadt Athen im Alterthum.
Sch., *Gr. Alt.*, Schoemann's Griechische Alterthümer.
M., *Heor.*, Aug. Mommsen's Heortologie.
Gh., *Gr. Myth.*, Gerhard's Griechische Mythologie.
Pauly, *R. E.*, Pauly's Real Encyclopädie.
Rang., *Antiq. Hell.*, Rangabé's Antiquités Helléniques.
H., *Gr. u. R.*, Herzberg's Griechenland unter Rom.
Martha, *Sacer. Ath.*, Martha, Les Sacerdoces Athéniens.
B., *Geog. v. Griech.*, Bursian's Geographie von Griechenland.
Welck., *Gr. Götterl.*, Welcker's Griechische Götterlehre.

Κερκὶς Α΄. FIRST ROW.

No. 1. — Ἱερέως | Διὸς Ὀλυμπίου.

C. I. A. 243 : V. 32. Date : Hadrian's reign.

The seat of the Priest of Olympian Zeus, whose temple was finished by Hadrian about 129–130 A.D. See W., *S. A.*, p. 688, N. 6.

No. 2. — Πυθοχρήστου | Ἐξηγητοῦ.

C. I. A. 241 : V. 33. Date : Not before Hadrian.

The seat of the interpreter appointed by the Pythian Oracle.

Very little is known about this office. See Sch., *Gr. Alt.*, I. p. 455 : "Einen amtlichen Charakter haben nur die sogenannten Exegeten, ein Collegium von drei Personen an die man sich um Belehrung in allen das Religionsrecht betreffenden Fragen, auch wohl um Deutung von Diosemien, d. h. von Himmelserscheinungen und andern schicksalsverkündenden Zeichen wenden konnte. Ueber ihre Ernennungsart ist nichts bekannt. Ob dabei das delphische Orakel eine Mitwirkung gehabt, wie Einige aus der von Plato für seinen Musterstadt getroffenen Anordnung geschlossen haben, müssen wir dahin gestellt sein lassen." Cf. Plat. *Leg.* 759 C, *Rep.* 427 C.

V. inclines to the belief that Timaeus, *Lex. Plat.*, is wrong in saying Ἐξηγηταὶ τρεῖς γίγνονται Πυθόχρηστοι, and that, though he is probably right in speaking of three ἐξηγηταί, it is likely that only one was Πυθόχρηστος. Cf. M., *Heor.*, p. 245, note, and the references there given.

We know of two other Ἐξηγηταί, the one chosen from the Eupatridae by χειροτονία of the people (*C. I. A.* 267, note), and the ἐξηγητής of the Eumolpidae (*C. I. A.* 720 ; *C. I. G.* 392) ; Boeckh refers to Plut. *Vit. X. Orat.* 843 B, where this office is mentioned. See also Sch., *Gr. Alt.*, II. pp. 46, note 5, 308, 347.*

---

* The following is the commentary of the *C. I. A.*, No. 241 : Exegetae tres sunt ; praeter hunc is qui ex Eupatridarum numero totius populi suffragiis eligitur (Nro. 267) et tertius ex gente Eumolpidarum. Recte sine dubio Vischerus Timaeum in lexico Plat., ubi dicit Ἐξηγηταὶ τρεῖς γίγνονται Πυθόχρηστοι, erasse iudicavit, quum potius dicendum fuerit tres exegetas publicos, inter quos unus sit πυθόχρηστος, *i.e.*, Apollini Pythii oraculo designatus. Ceterum Aelium Zenonem πυθόχρηστον habes, Nro. 684. See also *C. I. G.* 765 for evidence on this whole question.

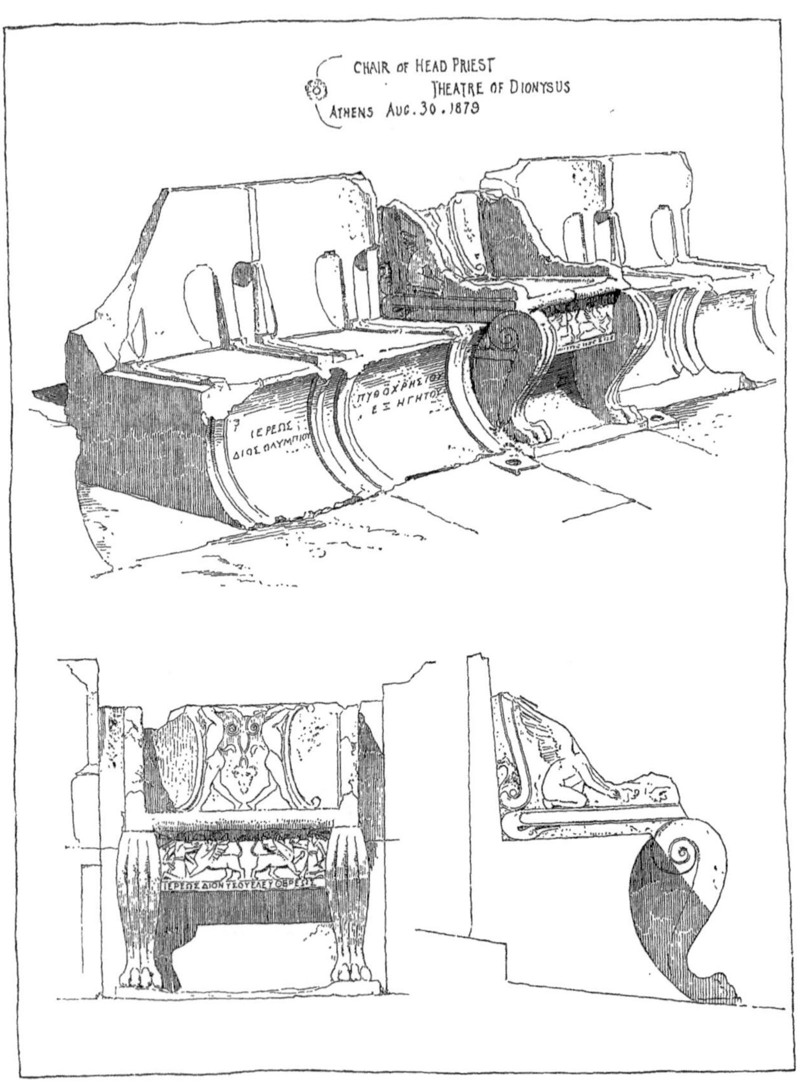

FIVE CHAIRS IN THE FRONT ROW OF THE CENTRAL *κερκίς.*

Two enlarged views of the middle chair, that of the Priest of Dionysus of Eleutherae, are given below.

No. 3. — Ἱερέως Διονύσου Ἐλευθερέως.

C. I. A. 240 : V. 34. Date : First century A.D.

This is the central chair, the seat of the Priest of Dionysus of Eleutherae, to whom the theatre was sacred. Eleuthereus was the favorite designation of Dionysus at Athens. The name comes from Eleutherae, a town on the Attic slopes of Cithaeron. Here was a famous ancient temple of Dionysus, whence the *ξόανον* of the God was brought to Athens: see Paus., I. 38, 8, and I. 2, 5; for the temples of the God at Athens, see I. 20, 3. Pegasus of Eleutherae introduced the deity to the Athenians, and was in consequence highly honored: cf. Paus., I. 2, 5.*

This chair is the largest and by far the finest in the theatre. (See the opposite plate.) The sculpture upon it is extremely elegant. Upon the back are carved in low-relief the figures of two satyrs, who bear bunches of grapes over their shoulders; and upon a little frieze just below the seat in front are two figures clad in Eastern dress, who are fighting with lions. There is some conventionality about the style of the sculpture, but it produces the effect of great richness. But far more beautiful than the carving upon the front of the chair are the reliefs upon the outside of the arms. A bending figure with wings is holding between his hands a cock, which he is about to let go for the fight. The head and upper part of the body of the opposing cock are visible opposite; but the chair is broken at this point, and it is impossible to supply the rest of the picture. The outlines of the winged figure are wonderfully graceful, and nothing of the conventionality which marks the other reliefs is to be found here. Aelian (*Var. Hist.*, II. 28) says that there was a law at Athens which provided for an annual cock-fight, to be held in the theatre at the public expense. This was done in remembrance of the occasion when Themistocles, before the battle of Salamis, showed to the Athenians two cocks which were fighting, and exhorted them to imitate the fowls in their vigor and bravery. There is a good article by Beulé (*Revue Archéologique*, Vol. VI., No. 3, pp. 349, 350), which treats of this chair, with an engraving. Beulé thinks that the winged

* See Dyer's *Athens*, pp. 41–43; and Ger., *Gr. Myth.*, § 442. 2, 3. For various forms of worship, cf. M., *Heor.* (index).

figure represents Agon, the God of the palaestra (cf. Gh., *Gr. Myth.*, I. 606), but it has been supposed by some to be a Nike. Dyer follows the *Ephemeris* in the following amusing explanation of the figure: *ἐδῶ* (*i.e.*, *εἰς τὰ ἐξωτερικὰ πλάγια τῆς ἀνακλίσεως*) *βλέπεις ἀναγεγλυμμένην γυμνὴν ὅλως ὡραίαν Νίκην, σύμβολον τῆς ἀκαλύπτου καὶ φανερᾶς ἁπανταχοῦ τοῦ Διονύσου νίκης, ἀναπεπταμένας ἔχουσαν τὰς πτέρυγας καὶ ταπεινῶς ὑποβάλλουσαν ἀντὶ προσκεφαλαίου πυρφόρον τοῦ Διὸς κεραυνόν, ὡς εἰκάζω, εἰς τὴν γένεσιν τοῦ Διονύσου ἀναφερόμενον.* — *Ἀρχαιολογικὴ Ἐφημερίς*, 1862, p. 142.

No. 4. — Ἱερέως | Διὸς Πολιέως.

C. I. A. 242 : V. 35. Date : Probably a little before the Christian era.*

The seat of the Priest of Zeus Polieus (protector of the city).

This is the Zeus who is associated with Athena Polias as guardian of the city, and his worship dates from the earliest times. M., *Heor.*, pp. 449 f. His altar was on the Acropolis: cf. Paus., I. 24, 4; I. 28, 11; and Gh., *Gr. Myth.*, § 193. 3, *a* and *b*; § 207. 6, *c*; § 200. 6.

No. 5. — *Θυηχόου.*

C. I. A. 244 : V. 36. Date : Not before Hadrian.

The seat of the Sacrificer.

Little or nothing is known about this office. Associated with the Erechtheum was an altar of the *θυηχόος*, but exactly what the office was is not known. Pausanias does not mention it. The word occurs *C. I. G.*, I. 160, col. 1, line 79, col. 2, line 95; also *C. I. A.*, I. No. 324, frag. *c*, col. 1, line 62. Cf. Dyer's *Athens*, pp. 143, 420; also M., *Heor.*, p. 195, note ***.†

---

* Aetas eorum (*i.e.*, 242, 247, 276) quin initium aerae Christianae aliquanto superet, non videtur dubitandum esse; accuratius definire satis difficile est, sed mihi alterius potissimum a Chr. saeculi esse videntur. *C. I. A.*

† Non probanda videtur Keilii conjectura qui *ἱερέως* | *θυηχόου* scriptum fuisse putat. Nam quae supra hanc vocem exsculpta sunt, ea non eiusdem tituli fuisse videntur sed antiquioris. *C. I. A.*

Κερκὶς Α΄. SECOND ROW.

No. 6. — Ἱερέως | Ὀλυμπίας | Νίκης.

C. I. A. 245 : V. 70. Date : Hadrian's reign.

The seat of the Priest of the Olympian Victory.

As Vischer says, it is very likely that this priest was connected with the cult of the Olympian Zeus in Athens. It is known that Hadrian introduced a new system of Olympiads ; and it is quite probable that, as there was an altar to Nike at Olympia (Paus., V. 14, 6), there may have been one at Athens in connection with the worship of Olympian Zeus. See *C. I. G.* 342 ; *C. I. A.*, III. 1, 127 ; Pauly, *R. E.*, *s. v.* Victoria.

No. 7. — Δαδούχου.

C. I. A. 246 : V. 69. Date : Not before Hadrian's reign.

The seat of the Torch-bearer (in the Eleusinian Mysteries). See Sch., *Gr. Alt.*, II. p. 383. Cf. M., *Heor.*, pp. 233 f., p. 63, note. This seat and the next are not *in situ*.

No. 8. — Ἱερέως | Ἀπόλλωνος Πυθίου.

C. I. A. 247 : V. 68. Date : Cf. No. 4.

The seat of the Pythian Apollo. This cult needs no comment. The Πύθιον at Athens stood near the Ilissus. Paus., I. 19, 1 ; Thuc., II. 15. Cf. No. 34.

Κερκὶς Α΄. THIRD ROW.

A double chair, with seats 9 and 10 ; not *in situ*.

No. 9. — Στρατηγοῦ.

The seat of the Strategus.

C. I. A. 248 : V. 71. Date : Not before Hadrian.

Vischer says that this inscription is decidedly older than those of the Archons.* The *C. I. A.* does not speak decidedly on this point.

* See V., p. 45 : Dass nur für einen Strategen ein Sitz da ist, darf uns nicht zu der Vermuthung verleiten, es seien andere verloren gegangen. Denn obgleich in der Zeit der Freiheit und Grösse Athens es zehn an Rand einander gleiche Strategen gegeben hatte, war doch unter der römischen Herrschaft allmälig einer von ihnen στρατηγὸς ἐπὶ τὰ ὅπλα, zum wichtigsten Beamten in Athen emporgestie-

Upon the back of this chair is this obscure inscription: KYPIAIB.*

No. 10. — Κήρυκος.

C. I. A. 250: V. 72. Date: Not before Hadrian.

The seat of the Herald. See Pauly, *R. E.*, VI. 1, p. 1, and II. p. 287.

V., p. 45: Ohne Zweifel der Herold des Volks und Raths, den wir wiederholt in Inschriften neben den ersten Magistraten genannt finden, und wohl derselbe der in ganz später Zeit bloss Herold des Raths heisst.

M., *Heor.*, p. 234, n. **: Den Herold, welcher mit dem Strategen einen Doppelthron im Lenaeon hat, kann man füglich als einen weltlichen Beamten ansehen.

In the *C. I. A.* it is maintained that the seat was that of the Herald of the Council of the Areopagus, on the ground that the chair is closely connected with that of the Strategus, and that, in *C. I. A.*, III. 1, No. 10, the Herald of the Areopagus is mentioned in connection with the Strategus and the Archon Eponymus. Cf. also No. 21 (below).

Κερκὶς 1. LEFT.

No. 11. — Ἱερομνήμονος.

C. I. A. 251: V. 37. Date: Not before Hadrian.

The seat of the Hieromnemon.

See *C. I. A.:* Etsi fuerunt Athenis etiam alii hieromnemones, quorum unus ad Herculis cultum spectabat, tamen hunc qui simpliciter hieromnemon audit, dei nomine non addito, ad amphictioniam Delphicam referendum esse demonstravit H. Sauppe.†

---

gen, neben dem die andern kaum mehr in Betracht kommen, wenn sie überhaupt existirten. Cf. Pauly, *R. E.*, VI. 2, p. 1456, where are abundant references on the point; also, H., *Gr. u. R.*, II. 339 and note, I. p. 311.

* See Rhousopoulos in 'Αρχαιολ. 'Εφημ., 1862, pp. 99, 100: *ἄνω περὶ τὸ μέσον τῆς ἀνακλίσεως κεῖται ἐγγεγραμμένη μικροτέροις γράμμασιν ἐκ χρόνων ὑστερωτέρων ἴσως καὶ ἄλλη ἐπιγραφή*: **ΚΥΡΙΑΙΒ**, *ἤτοι κύρια (ἑδώλια ? δώδεκα?). τὸ πρὸ τοῦ* B *γράμμα ἴνε ἀσαφὲς ἐπὶ τοῦ λίθου καὶ μᾶλλον τῷ ἰῶτα ὅμοιον ἢ τῷ ἄλφα.*

Cf. *C. I. A.* (note on 249): Hae reliquiae incertissimae sunt, neque veri similis est Rhusopuli conjectura, *κύρια ιβ'*, *i.e.*, *κύρια (ἑδώλια) δώδεκα* scripta fuisse; nam quid significet *κύρια ἑδώλια* vix assequi possis.

† See the valuable treatise of Sauppe, *De amphictionia Delphica deque*

No. 12.—Ἱερέως | καὶ ἀρχιερέως | Σεβαστοῦ Καίσαρος.

C. I. A. 252 : V. 38. Date : Reign of Augustus (Octavianus).

See *C. I. A.*: Non in universum accipiendum esse videtur Σεβαστοῦ Καίσαρος, ut de eius qui quoque tempore fuit imperatoris sacerdote intelligatur, sed ad Caesarem Augustum imperii auctorem referendus videtur titulus, cuius sacra peculiaria atque a caeterorum imperatorum defunctorum cultu separata mansisse credibile est; distinguendus igitur hic sacerdos ab eo qui dicitur ἀρχιερεὺς τῶν Σεβαστῶν.

This view is substantially Vischer's, who says: Den zu diesem gehörigen Priester haben wir vermuthlich in dem Nro. 38 genannten "Priester und Erzpriester des Caesar Augustus" zu erkennen. Aus dem Umstande, dass der Name von Rom fehlt, möchte ich nicht auf ein Wegfallen ihres Cultus schliessen, sondern nur eine Abkürzung des vollen Titels darin sehen. Bemerkungswerth ist die Verbindung ἱερέως καὶ ἀρχιερέως. Sonst finden wir sehr oft den ἀρχιερεὺς θεῶν Σεβαστῶν oden τῶν Σεβαστῶν erwähnt (z. B. *C. I. G.* 382, 383; Ross *Archäolog. Aufs.* I. s. 123), aber für eine solche Verbindung weiss ich im Augenblick kein Beispiel. See also Vischer's remarks on No. 20 (below).*

No. 13.—Ἱερέως | Ἁδριανοῦ | Ἐλευθεραίως.

C. I. A. 253 : V. 39. Date : Hadriani aetatis esse titulum (praeter versum tertium) ex ipsius argumento patet.†

The other two chairs which were originally in this κερκίς have been destroyed.

---

hieromnemone Attico, Götting., 1873, p. 10; also Rang., *Antiq. Hell.*, pp. 308, 563, 325. Sch. (*Gr. Alt.*, Vol. II., p. 37) holds that there were two amphictyonic hieromnemons, but this hardly seems susceptible of proof. In the early times the hieromnemon was chosen by lot, but later very probably by χειροτονία, and possibly for life. Cf. V., p. 57.

* Cf. H., *Gr. u. R.*, I. p. 519, where valuable references will be found; also II., p. 12, Anm. 12, and p. 523. See W., *S. A.*, p. 674, with N. 1.

† See note in *C. I. A.*: Extremum vocabulum non modo ceteris recentius sed etiam aliquanto post Hadriani mortem incisum esse cum litterarum forma, tum scriptura αι pro ε indicat; nam quae eius orthographiae exempla Hadriani et Antonini Pii aetate inveniuntur veluti Φηγεεύς, Πειρεεύς similia, alius generis sunt. Quare additamentum illud ad alterius p. Chr. saeculi finem aut tertii initium rettulerim; cur tum demum hoc cognomen adscriptum sit, obscurum est. See also V., p. 56. The existence of a priesthood whose object was the worship of Hadrian has long been known. Cf. H., *Gr. u. R.*, pp. 332 ff.; *C. I. G.*, Nos. 3832, 3833.

Κερκὶς 2. LEFT.

No. 14. — Three seats: (*a*) Ἄρχον[τος]. (*b*) Βασιλέω[ς]. (*c*) Πολεμάρχου.

C. I. A. 254, 255, 256: V. (*a*) and (*b*) not numbered; (*c*), 46.

(*a*) The seat of the Chief Archon. (*b*) The seat of the King Archon. (*c*) The seat of the Polemarch.

In the five chairs of this κερκίς and the first four of the next, we have the seats of the nine Archons. The two other chairs of κερκὶς 2 have perished; but there can be no doubt that they belonged to two of the six Thesmothetae, since the seats of the four others are found in κερκὶς 3 (No. 15).*

Κερκὶς 3. LEFT.

No. 15. — Four seats: (*a*) Θεσμοθέτου. (*b*) Θεσμοθέτου. (*c*) Θεσμοθέτου. (*d*) Θεσμοθέτου.
Γορ . . . . .

C.I.A. 257, 258, 259, 260: V. 47–50. Date: Not earlier than Hadrian.

The seats of four Thesmothetae. We have noticed under No. 14 the two vacant places in κερκὶς 2, in which the seats of the other two Thesmothetae must have stood.

V., p. 45: Die sämmtlichen Archonteninschriften gehören auffallender Weise einer sehr späten Zeit an. Das bei einem Thesmotheten Nro. 50 noch mit kleinen Buchstaben Γορ untergeschrieben ist, mag vielleicht mit Rusopulos (*Eph.* s. 156) so zu erklären sein das einmal ein Thesmothet, dessen Name so anfing, etwa Γοργίας, den Sitz noch speziell als den seinigen bezeichnen wollte. Doch ist dies bei dem jährigen Wechsel des Amtes nicht eben wahrscheinlich. Eine bessere Erklärung weiss ich freilich nicht wenn, nicht etwa die Buchstaben der Rest einer früheren oder der Anfang einer späteren Inschrift sind.

* For the tendencies of the Athenian constitution under Roman rule, cf. H., *Gr. u. R.*, II. pp. 339 ff.; and Ahrens, *De Statu Athenarum politico sub Romanis*. (Unfortunately I have not been able to obtain the latter work.)

No. 16. — Ἱεροκήρυκος.

C. I. A. 261 : V. 51. Date : Age of Hadrian.

The seat of the Sacred Herald.*

Κερκὶς 4. LEFT.

The chairs have all perished.

Κερκὶς 5. LEFT.

Of five chairs, the first three have perished.

No. 17. — Ἱερέως | Ἰακχαγωγοῦ.

C. I. A. 262 : V. 60. Date : Age of Hadrian.

The seat of the leader of the Eleusinian procession, and the carrier of the Iakchos, or representation of the God.†

No. 18. — Ἱερέως | Ἀσκληπιοῦ | Πα[ί]ω[ν]ος.

C. I. A. 263 : V. 61. Date : Age of Hadrian.

The seat of the Priest of Asklepios, the Healer.

Παίωνος is the emendation of the *C. I. A.*, but the whole matter is rather uncertain.

V. says, p. 53 : Priester des Asklepios sind zwei da, Nro. 16 und Nro. 61. Auf der ersten Inschrift hat der Gott keinen näher bestimmenden Beinamen, auf der zweiten sehr schlecht geschrieben steht dagegen allerdings unter Ἀσκληπιοῦ noch eine Zeile die aber nicht sicher zu lesen ist und von der sogar fraglich bleibt, ob und wie weit sie zu den Worten Ἱερέως Ἀσκληπιοῦ gehört, da hier eine ältere Inschrift ausgemeisselt ist.‡

---

* See Sch., *Gr. Alt.*, II. p. 419 ; Martha, *Sacer. Ath.*, p. 158, 3° ; M., *Heor.*, p. 324 and notes. Cf. also the remarks on Nos. 10 and 21.

† See Sch., *Gr. Alt.*, II. p. 389 ; Pollux, I. 35 ; K. F. Hermann, *Gottesdienstliche Alterthümer*, § 55, 27 ; *C. I. A.*, III. 162, 163 ; M., *Heor.*, p. 236. For further references, see Martha, *Sacer. Ath.*, p. 170, N. 131. The Ἰακχεῖον was in the Ceramicus (Paus., I. 2, 4). B., *Geog. v. Griech.*, I. p. 279.

‡ *C. I. A.*, note on No. 263 : Tertii versus vestigia Rhusopulos interpretatur

Κερκὶς 6. LEFT.

No. 19.—Ἱερέως | πυρφόρου | ἐξ Ἀκροπό|λεως.

C. I. A. 264: V. 62. Date: Age of Hadrian.

The seat of the Fire-bearing Priest from the Acropolis.

V. says, p. 58: Ferner der Priester Feuerträger aus der Akropolis. Feuerträger, πυρφόροι gab es überall, und namentlich wurde so der Priester genannt, der das heilige Feuer zum Anzünden der Opfer im Kriege mittrug. Bei den einzelnen Heiligthümern scheinen solche πυρφόροι als besondere Bedienstete gewesen zu sein, wie Euripides πυρφόρος des Apollon Zosterios gewesen sein soll (*Vit. Eurip. anon*). Der hier genannte wird durch den Beisatz ἐξ Ἀκροπόλεως näher bezeichnet und gehörte vermuthlich zu dem Tempel der Polias, wie der Opferpriester. In einer Inschrift aus der Zeit des Septimius Severus finden wir einen Pyrphoros unter den Aeisiten des Prytaneions, vielleicht den von der Burg. (*C. I. G.* 353; vgl., Nro. 186, wo auch einer genannt ist, und Boeckh daselbst I. p. 325). Da er aber unmittelbar nach den Eleusinischen Priestern steht, gehört er möglicherweise auch zum Personal jenes Cultus.*

ἥρωος, Vischerus non modo de ea re dubitat, sed omnino hunc versum ad antiquiorum titulum conicit quem inscriptum fuisse et deletum esse vestigia quaedam in versus 2 conspicua demonstrant. At mihi haec sententia minus probatur cum propter litterae sigma figuram tum quia alium Aesculapii sacerdotem habemus Nro. 287; quare hic cognomine dei addito ab illo distinguatur necesse est. Ut Παίωνος potissimum supplerem inprimis eo permotus sum quod litterarum reliquiae quales Kumanudis invenit cum illo ἥρωος conciliari nequeunt. Et hoc cognomen (sive geminam eius formam Παιάν) Aesculapio cum patre Apollini commune esse etiam titulus Nro. 171 docet.

See also Gh., *Gr. Myth.*, § 507 and note. Vischer says further (p. 54): Aber auch in Eleusis hatte er eine bedeutungsvolle Stätte, wo die mit den Eleusinien eng verbundenen Epidaurien gefeiert wurden (Paus., II. 26, 7; Philos., *Vit. Apoll.*, IV. 18). Man darf vielleicht bei Nro. 61 an den Priester des Eleusinischen Asklepios denken, da daneben der Iakchagogos sitzt. Cf. *C. I. G.* 511, line 1, and 3158. See No. 41 (below).

* *C. I. A.*, note on No. 264: In his πυρφόρου non dei vel herois nomen alicuius est, sed sacerdotis officium significat ut λιθοφόρος, Nro. 296, Βουζύγης, Nro. 273, 274: cf. adn. ad N. 268. See also Sch., *Gr. Alt.*, I. pp. 260, 300; II. p. 419.

No. 20.—Ἱερέως Δήμου | καὶ Χαρίτων | καὶ Ῥώμης.

C. I. A. 265. Date: Age of Augustus.

The seat of the Priest of Demos and the Graces and Roma.

Martha, *Sacer. Ath.*, p. 160, No. 74: Le téménos du Peuple et des Grâces, mentionné dans un inscription (*C. I. A.*, II. 605) était sans doute dans l'enceinte même du Prytanée; car le jour où les éphèbes se réunissaient dans le Prytanée pour prêter le serment civique et recevoir leurs armes, le prêtre du Peuple et des Grâces assistait à la cérémonie (*C. I. A.*, II. 470, ligne 5. 6: ἐπειδὴ οἱ ἔφηβοι θύσαντες ταῖς ἐγγραφαῖς τὰ εἰ[σιτ]ήρια ἐν [τῷ] πρυτανείῳ ἐπὶ τῆς κοινῆς ἑστίας τοῦ δήμου μετά τε τοῦ κοσμητ[ο]ῦ καὶ τῶν ἐξηγητῶν καὶ τοῦ ἱερέως [τ]οῦ τε Δήμου καὶ τῶν Χαρ[ί]των. Cf. p. 164, No. 93.

V. says, p. 56: Wahrscheinlich in Augustus Zeit wurde nun in Athen dem Demos und den Chariten noch die Roma beigefügt. Bekanntlich hatte sie mit Augustus zusammen ein Heiligthum auf der Burg östlich vom Parthenon.

For the priest of Roma, see references in H., *Gr. u. R.*, No. 12.

No. 21. — Κήρυκος παναγοῦς | καὶ ἱερέως.

C. I. A. 266: V. 64. Date: Age of Hadrian.

The seat of the most holy Herald and Priest.

C. I. A.: Ad idem Sacerdotium, quod accuratius definiri non potest, jam Vischerus recte rettulit ἱερέα παναγῆ in titulo Herennii Dexippi, Nro. 716. Nunc accessit alter n. 717.

M., *Heor.*, p. 234, n. **: Im Lenaeon hat sich nicht bloss ein Sessel des ἱεροκήρυξ sondern auch einer mit der Aufschrift κήρυκος παναγοῦς καὶ ἱερέως gefunden. Ueber die Unterschiede dieser Heroldsämter, welche beide die Mysterien (eleusinischen) angehen, dürfte so viel zu vermuthen sein, dass der Hierokeryx an Rang der vornehmere war. Cf. Nos. 16 and 10.

The three other chairs in κερκὶς 6 (left) have perished.

Κερκὶς 1. RIGHT.

No. 22. — Ἐξηγητοῦ | ἐξ Εὐπατριδῶν χειρο|τονητοῦ ὑπὸ τοῦ | Δήμου διὰ βίου.

C. I. A. 267 : V. 27. Date : Not much after Augustus.

The seat of the Interpreter, chosen from the Eupatridae for life by vote of the people. See remarks under No. 2.

No. 23. — Ἱερέως Χαρίτων | καὶ Ἀρτέμιδος | Ἐπιπυργιδίας | πυρφόρου.

C. I. A. 268 : V. 28. Date : Not before second century A.D.

The seat of the Priest of the Graces and Artemis Epipyrgidia, [and] of the fire-bearing (priest).

C. I. A.: Dianem hanc eandem esse, quae Ἑκάτη ἐπιπυργιδία dicitur a Pausania II. 30, 2, verissime dicit Vischer. Minus recte idem de voce πυρφόρος (sic cum ipse scripsisset in tituli verbis, miro errore in disputatione φως-φόρου substituit). Ea vox non ad Ἀρτέμιδος, sed ad ἱερέως referenda est ut Nro. 264. Collocatio verborum plane eadem est Nro. 294. Cf. Welck., *Gr. Götterl.*, II. p. 405.

Pausanias, in the passage cited above, tells us that there was a statue of Hecate Ἐπιπυργιδία which had three faces, and that it stood on the Acropolis near the temple of Athena Nike (or "Wingless Victory"). This temple stands on a large pier or abutment known as the Πύργος, which projects in front of the south wing of the Propylaea, whence the name ἐπιπυργιδία.

No. 24. — Ἱερέως | Ποσειδῶνος | φυταλμίου.

C. I. A. 269 : V. 29. Date : Not before the second century A.D.

The seat of the Priest of Poseidon, the giver of fruitfulness.

As an Attic cult this is not otherwise known, but Poseidon was doubtless worshipped under this title at Athens. Pausanias (II. 32, 8), in describing Troezen, says : Ἔστι δὲ ἔξω τείχους καὶ Ποσειδῶνος ἱερὸν φυταλμίου. Cf. Hartung, *Relig. der Griechen*, III. 214. See M., *Heor.*, 322.

No. 25. — Ἱερέως | Ἀπόλλωνος | Δηλίου.

C. I. A. 270 : V. 30. Date : Not before Hadrian.

The seat of the Priest of the Delian Apollo.

Little is known of the worship of the *Delian* Apollo at Athens, or of the time of its introduction. It was probably not of an early date, however. There is no record of a temple. Mommsen discusses the question in his remarks on the Θαργήλια (*Heor.*, p. 50) : Die Thargeliendarbringung war in älterer Zeit nicht städtisch. So lange Athen mit Apoll bloss durch die lockeren Bande der Amphictyonie in Bezug stand, scheint ihm wenig eingeräumt zu sein. Hätte die Stadt damals den (delischen) Apoll recipirt, so würde sie ein Delion gehabt haben und ein altes Priesteramt des delischen Apoll. See No. 34.

No. 26. — Ἱεροφάντου.

C. I. A. 271 : V. 31. Date : Not before the second century A.D.

The seat of the Hierophant.

See Sch., *Gr. Alt.*, II. p. 382 : Zunächst aus dem Geschlechte der Eumolpiden der Hierophantes, dessen Amtsname schon andeutet, dass ihm oblag den eingeweihten die geheimnissvollen Heiligthümer dieses Cultus (des eleusinischen) zu zeigen. Ohne Zweifel hatte er dabei auch liturgische Gesänge anzustimmen.

The office of the Hierophant was one of the most important of those connected with the Eleusinian Mysteries.

Excellent treatment of the subject of the mysteries generally and of this office is to be found in M., *Heor.*, p. 233.

Κερκὶς 2. RIGHT.

No. 27. — Ἱερέως | Διὸς Βουλαίου | καὶ Ἀθηνᾶς | Βουλαίας.

C. I. A. 272 : V. 22. Date : Not before Hadrian.

The seat of the Priest of Zeus Boulaios and Athena Boulaia. These were the guardian divinities of the Βουλή, and their altar was in the Βουλευτήριον. When the senator entered upon his duties, he made an offering to these divinities, known as the εἰσιτήρια. Paus., I. 3, 4 ; Dem. 19, 190. Cf. Welck., *Gr. Götterl.*, II. p. 206 ; and *C. I. A.*, III. 683.

No. 28. — Βουζύγου | ἱερέως Διὸς ἐν | Παλλαδίῳ.

C. I. A. 273 : V. 23. Date : Later than Hadrian.

The seat of the Bouzyges, the Priest of Zeus in the Palladium.

For the office of Bouzyges, see M., *Heor.*, p. 76 ; Sch., *Gr. Alt.*, II. p. 487 ; Hermann, *Lehrbuch d. Gr. Antiq.*, II. § 62, 16.

This order of priests probably took its name from Epimenides, who was called Bouzyges. Their office was connected with the worship of the Eleusinian Demeter ; and they also took part in some form of the worship of Athena and of Zeus, as this inscription implies. K. O. Müller (*Kleine deutsche Schriften*, II. 147) says that the Palladium was in charge of the Bouzygai.

"Zeus in the Palladium" is a divinity known only in late inscriptions (Rang., *Antiq. Hell.*, II. 819) ; but it is quite possible that he may have been worshipped there at an early date. The Palladium was of course under the protection of Athena ; but, as Rangabé says, Zeus may have been invoked by the judges of the court. See *C. I. G.* 491, where the title appears. Cf. M., *Heor.*, pp. 429, 432 ; Pauly, *R. E.*, V. pp. 1084, 1085 ; B., *Geog. v. Griech.*, I. 302.

No. 29. — Ἱερέως | Μελπομένου | Διονύσου | ἐξ Εὐνειδῶν.

C. I. A. 274 : V. 24. Date : Not earlier than Hadrian.

The seat of the Priest of Dionysus the Singer, chosen from the race of the Euneidae.

Διόνυσος μελπόμενος * had his sanctuary in the Ceramicus, probably just outside the Piraïc gate (Paus., I. 2, 4 and 5). The house of Polytion, where some of the mimicking of the Eleusinian Mysteries by Alcibiades and his friends took place, was confiscated and dedicated to this worship (B., *Geog. v. Griech.*, I. p. 279 and references) ; cf. also M., *Heor.*, 266, 268.

For the Euneidae, cf. Suidas, s.v. ; also, Hesychius and Harpocration. The latter says : Γένος ἐστὶ παρ' Ἀθηναίοις οὕτως ὀνομαζόμενον Εὐνεῖδαι· ἦσαν δὲ κιθαρῳδοὶ πρὸς τὰς ἱερουργίας παρέχοντες τὴν χρείαν. Cf. Pollux, VIII. 103. They often acted as heralds in processions.

* Paus., I. 2, 5 : Διόνυσον δὲ τοῦτον καλοῦσι Μελπόμενον ἐπὶ λόγῳ τοιῷδε ἐφ' ὁποίῳ περ Ἀπόλλωνα Μουσαγέτην.

No. 30. — Ἱερέως | Ἀρτέμιδος | Κολαινίδος.

C. I. A. 275 : V. 25. Date : Not before Hadrian.

The seat of the Priest of Artemis Kolainis.

This goddess had a ξόανον, and was worshipped in the deme Μυρρινοῦς (Paus., I. 31, 2–4). The cult may have become more general afterward. Ross, *Demen von Attika*, says (No. 98) : Μυρρινοῦς, An der Ostseite des Landes (*Strab.*, IX. p. 399), mit einem Heiligthum der Artemis Kolänis; also, wahrscheinlich bei dem zerstörten Dorfe Merenda, zwischen Markopoulos und Prasiä oder Porto Raphti, wo Fourmont ausser andern Inschriften (*C. I. G.* 28, 490) auch ein Psephisma der Myrrhinusier gefunden (*C. I. G.* 100), welches ἐν τῷ ἱερῷ τῆς Ἀρτέμιδος τῆς Κολαινίδος aufgestellt war.

No. 31. — Ἱερέως | Ποσειδῶνος | Γαιηόχου καὶ | Ἐρεχθέως.

C. I. A. 276 : V. 26. Date : Probably a little before the Christian era. Cf. No. 4.

The seat of the Priest of Poseidon Gaieochos (Holder of the Earth) and Erechtheus, *i.e.*, of Poseidon in his two forms of Gaieochos and Erechtheus.

The altar of Poseidon Erechtheus stood in the Erechtheum on the Acropolis. Vischer speaks of the Priest of Poseidon *and* Erechtheus; but these two are not to be separated.*

Κερκὶς 3. RIGHT.

No. 32. — Ἱερέως | Εὐκλείας καὶ | Εὐνομίας.

C. I. A. 277 : V. 17. Date : Not before Hadrian's time.

A. Mommsen (*Heor.*, p. 410) says : Der Tempel der Eukleia, aus der marathonischen Beute gestiftet (Paus., I. 14, 5), galt wohl ursprüng-

* See *C. I. A.*, note on 276 : Erechtheum hunc eundem esse atque Neptunum, neque cum Vischero ita titulum intelligendum, ut ille sacerdos Neptuni simul et Erechthei fuerit, titulus C. Iuli Spartiatici (v. ins.) docet, ubi ἱερεὺς Ποσειδῶνος Ἐρεχθέως γαιηόχου est. Nam haec duo diversa sacerdotia esse quis tandem credit? See *C. I. A.*, I. 387; Paus., I. 26, 5. For a discussion of the association of Poseidon with Erechtheus, cf. Welck., *Gr. Götterl.*, II. 284 ff.; M., *Heor.*, pp. 27, note, and 34, note.

lich der Artemis als Eukleia, weil unter Artemis Schutze (p. 212) die Schlacht geschlagen war, späterhin mag Eukleia eine besondere Gottheit geworden sein. V., p. 54; *C. I. G.* 258; see, further, W., *S. A.*, p. 273.

No. 33. — Ἱερέως | Διονύσου | Μελπομένου | ἐκ τεχνειτῶν.

C. I. A. 278: V. 18. Date: Age of Hadrian, possibly later.

The seat of the Priest of Dionysus the Singer, chosen from the τεχνῖται.

In respect to Διόνυσος Μελπόμενος, cf. No. 29. The τεχνῖται were a guild of actors, who were of the nature of a religious caste because of the religious character of the Greek Drama. Cf. Rang., *Antiq. Hell.*, II. 813; *Athenaeus*, V. p. 212 D; *C. I. G.* 349; M., *Heor.*, p. 266; *Die Dionysischen Künstler*, von Otto Lüders.

No. 34. — Ἱερέως Ἀπόλλωνος Πατρ[ῴ]ο[υ].

C. I. A. 279: V. 19. Date: Not before Hadrian.

The seat of the Priest of Apollo Patroos.*

The Pythian Apollo was the Patroos of the city, and there were two places sacred to him, — the Πύθιον and the Δελφίνιον.†

No. 35. — Ἱερέως | Ἀντινόου | χορείου ἐκ τε|χνειτῶν.

C. I. A. 280: V. 20. Date: Hadrian's Reign.

The seat of the Priest of Antinous, the leader of the dances, chosen from the Artists.

Hadrian, as is well known, established a cult for the worship of Antinous after the unlucky youth was drowned in the Nile. Cf. H., *Gr. u. R.*, II. p. 345. For the τεχνῖται, see remarks under No. 33.

---

* For this surname of Apollo, see Maury, *Religions de la Grèce Antique*, II. p. 3. For a longer discussion, see Welck., *Gr. Götterl.*, I. 491 ff.; M., *Heor.*, p. 51 ff.; Sch., *Gr. Alt.*, II. p. 548 f.

† See Demosth., *Cor.*, § 141; *Aristid. Panath.*, p. 112 (Jebb); Paus., I. 3, 4. Mommsen believes the cult to have been of rather late introduction. The inscriptions are all of imperial times. *C. I. A.*, III. 1, 647, 687, 707.

No. 36.—Ἱερέως | Διὸς (Διὸς) Σωτ[ῆ]ρος | καὶ Ἀθ[η]νᾶς Σωτείρας (written ΣΩΤΕΡΟΣ and ΑΘΕΝΑΣ).

C. I. A. 281 : V. 21. Date : Later than the reign of Hadrian.

C. I. A.: Vocis Διός repetitionem, id quod Vischerus negat, a mera lapicidae socordia profectam esse patet; nam quaenam alia causa excogitari potest? Eandem neglegentiam in scriptura ε pro η bis redeunte agnosco, quam ille potius affectationem antiquitatis esse vult.

M., *Heor.*, p. 454, n.: Der Zeus Eleutherios oder Soter ist erst nach dem Perser-Krieg mit Bezug auf die Schlacht bei Plataeae (Thucy., II. 71) aufgestellt, und als Soterienopfer muss demnach von a. Chr. 479 an aufgenommen sein. Cf. also the remainder of the note.

That there was a cult of Zeus Soter associated with Athena is well known, though it is difficult to determine the exact place of the sanctuary. In the Piraeus there was certainly a τέμενος (*Strabo*, IX. p. 396; Paus., I. 1, 3); and there seems to have been one in Athens also, but it is uncertain where it stood.*

Κερκὶς 4. RIGHT.

No. 37.—Φαιδυντοῦ | Διὸς ἐκ Πείσης.

C. I. A. 283 : V. 12. Date : Not before the second century A.D.

The seat of the Phaidyntes of Zeus from Pisa.

The Phaidyntai were those who had charge of the God's statue, and attended to the cleaning of it. The word is usually written φαιδρυνταί, coming from the verb φαιδρύνειν, *to wash or cleanse*. The descendants of Phidias were Phaidryntai at Olympia (Paus., V. 14, 5); cf. Martha, *Sacer. Ath.*, p. 54. It is impossible to say when this cult of Ζεὺς ἐκ Πείσης was introduced into Athens. The presumption is that it is late. Cf. *C. I. A.*, III. 5; M., *Heor.*, p. 236.

---

* Cf. Lycurg., *Leocr.*, § 17: οὐδὲ τὴν ἀκρόπολιν καὶ τὸ ἱερὸν τοῦ Διὸς τοῦ Σωτῆρος καὶ τῆς Ἀθηνᾶς τῆς Σωτείρας ἀφορῶν. Cf. also §§ 136, 137.

Vischer, who refers § 17 to a sanctuary on the Acropolis (p. 48), suggests in a note that it may refer to the one in Piraeus. Cf. Rang., *Antiq. Hell.*, II. pp. 410, 411; Welck., *Gr. Götterl.*, II. p. 184; Plut., *Demos.*, 27; Boeckh, *Staatsh. d. Alt.*, II. pp. 130, 139; *C. I. A.*, II. 325, 326.

No. 38.—Ἱερέως | Δώδεκα θεῶν.

C. I. A. 284: V. 13. Date: Not before the second century A.D.

The seat of the Priest of the Twelve Gods.

An altar to the Twelve Gods was erected in the Agora by Peisistratus, the son of Hippias. Herod., VI. 108; Thucyd., VI. 54. Mommsen (*Heor.*, p. 394), in the chapter on the städtische Dionysien, says: Auf dem Markt hielt die Pompe an, damit ein cyclischer Chor den Zwölf-Götter-Altar umtanze. Die Bedeutung dieses Altars stimmt zu der über Athen hinausreichenden allgemein griechischen Bedeutung des Festes. Cf. Welck., *Gr. Götterl.*, II. 168, 169 ff.; and *Zwölfgötteraltar aus Athen*, in Mittheil. d. deutsch. Arch. Inst. in Athen, IV. 337.

No. 39.—Ἱερέως Διὸς φιλίου.

C. I. A. 285: V. 14. Date: During the first century A.D.

Whether Zeus Philios had a sanctuary in Athens is not known; but in other cities he is often mentioned. Cf. Welck., *Gr. Götterl.*, II. pp. 202, 203.

No. 40.—Ἱερέως Μουσῶν.

C. I. A. 286: V. 15. Date: Not before the second century A.D.

The seat of the Priest of the Muses.

In Athens the Muses were worshipped in several places; and the Μουσεῖον hill, overlooking the Acropolis, was sacred to them.*

No. 41.—Ἱερέως Ἀσκληπιοῦ.

C. I. A. 287: V. 16. Date: Not before the second century A.D.

The seat of the Priest of Asklepios. Cf. No. 18.

The whole enclosure which was sacred to Asklepios upon the south slope of the Acropolis was excavated a few years ago. See Paul Girard, L'Asclépieion à Athènes d'après de récentes découvertes, in the *Bibliothèque des Écoles Françaises d'Athènes et de Rome;* also Mittheil. d. deutsch. Ins. in Athen (cf. Register to Voll. I.–V.).

---

* See Paus., I. 19, 5; 25, 7; 26, 1; 30, 2; III. 6, 6. Cf. also Dr. Hermann Deiters, *Ueber die Verehrung der Musen bei den Griechen.*

Κερκὶς 5. RIGHT.

No. 42.—Ἱερέως | Ἡφαίστου.

C. I. A. 288: V. 7. Date: Not before the second century A.D.

The seat of the Priest of Hephaestus.

The festivals celebrated in honor of Hephaestus at Athens were very important, since they were the special honors paid by the phratries at the Apaturia to the ancestor of the Erechtheidae: cf. Sch., *Gr. Alt.*, II. p. 546; and especially M., *Heor.*, chapter on the Apaturien und Chalkeen.

The temple of Hephaestus at Athens was in the neighborhood of the Agora. Paus., I. 14, 6: Ὑπὲρ δὲ τὸν Κεραμεικὸν καὶ στοὰν τὴν καλουμένην βασίλειον ναός ἐστιν Ἡφαίστου. Cf. also W., *S. A.*, p. 177, and Stephan. Byzant., *s. v.*, Ἡφαιστιάδαι. There was an altar of Hephaestus in the Erechtheum (Paus., I. 26, 5).

No. 43.—Ἱερέως | Οὐρανίας | Νεμέσεως.

C. I. A. 289: V. 8. Date: Not before the second century A.D., and very likely later.

The seat of the Priest of the heavenly Nemesis.

Nemesis was especially adored at Rhamnus, where she had a temple, the ruins of which may still be seen (B., *Geog. v. Griech.*, I. p. 341). The goddess was undoubtedly worshipped in some form at Athens, since we find that the γενέσια were also called νεμέσια: cf. M., *Heor.*, p. 209. See also Welck., *Gr. Götterl.*, I. 576; III. 25.

Vischer, pp. 51, 52, says: An Artemis reiht sich die ihr nah verwandte Nemesis, die Göttin von Rhamnus, die hier, wenn ich nicht irre, zum ersten Mal das Epitheton der himmlischen οὐρανία hat. Es soll damit vielleicht das nämliche bezeichnet werden, was sonst ihre Verbindung mit Zeus, sei es als Gattin, sei es als Tochter, ausdrückt, das Walten des in ihr enthaltenen ethischen Begriffs unter den himmlischen Göttern, ähnlich wie Sophokles (*El.*, 1064) die Themis himmlisch nennt. Doch beruht wohl ursprünglich das Epitheton auf ihrem Zusammenhang mit der Aphrodite Urania.

No. 44. — Ἱερέως | Ἀνάκων | καὶ ἥρωος | Ἐπιτεγίου.

C. I. A. 290 : V. 9. Date : Not before the second century A.D.

Seat of the Priest of the Anakes and of the Hero Epitegios.

The Anakes were the Dioscuri, and were worshipped in a temple which stood just north of the Acropolis and was known as the Ἀνάκειον (Paus., I. 18, 1 : Thucyd., VIII. 93 ; Cic., *De Nat. Deor.*, III. 21 ; Welck., *Gr. Götterl.*, II. 433–435 ; W., *S. A.*, p. 221). Nothing is known of the Hero Ἐπιτέγιος.*

No. 45. — Φαιδυντοῦ | Διὸς Ὀλυμπίου | ἐν Ἄστει.

C. I. A. 291 : V. 10. Date : Hadrian's reign.

The seat of the Phaidyntes of the Olympian Zeus in the city. Cf. No. 37.

This Phaidyntes was doubtless the one who had charge of the statue in the temple of the Olympian Zeus which Hadrian completed. Cf. No. 1.

No. 46. — Ἱερέως | Ἀπόλλωνος Λυκήου.

C. I. A. 292 : V. 11. Date : Time of Augustus (Octavian).

The seat of the Priest of the Lycean Apollo. For an excellent discussion of this surname of Apollo, see Welck., *Gr. Götterl.*, I. 476–482. The Λυκεῖον at Athens was east of the gate of Diochares, on the right bank of the Ilissus, probably near the present Rizareion. See W., *S. A.*, 232, 233 ; B., *Geog. v. Griech.*, I. 321, 322 ; Paus., I. 19, 3.

* Vischer says (p. 55) : Nie erwähnt aber wird der Heros Epitegios, dessen Name von τέγος, Dach und überhaupt Haus, hergeleitet, eigentlich den auf oder an dem Dache oder Hause bedeutet. Es fällt einem dabei Adonis ein, der auf den Dächern bejämmert wurde (Aristoph., *Lysist.*, 388, ὅ τ' Ἀδωνιασμὸς οὗτος οὑπὶ τῶν τεγῶν), und zu dessen Erinnerung man auf den Dächern die Adonisgärtchen zog. Doch ist nicht einzusehen, warum dann nicht Adonis selbst genannt sein sollte, auch nicht, wie dieser mit den Anakes in Verbindung kommt. Es ist daher wohl an einem Heros zu denken, der zum Dache oder Hause gehört, und da bieten sich zum Vergleiche die Epitheta ἐποικίδιος und ἐπιθαλαμίτης. Ἐποικιδία hiess Demeter in Korinth nach Hesychios, wohl als Schützerin des Hauses wie ἑστιοῦχος; ἐπιθαλαμίτης Hermes in Euboea nach demselben Gewährsmann, gewiss auch als Schützer des Innern des Hauses (θάλαμος) und nicht mit Beziehung auf die Schiffahrt. Da nun ursprünglich wenigstens nach Cicero's bestimmter Angabe die Anakes drei waren, bei ihrer Verschmelzung mit den Dioskuren aber auf zwei beschränkt wurden, scheint es gar nicht unwahrscheinlich dass der dritte als ein besonderer Heros von ihnen unterscheiden wurde, aber doch im Cultus mit ihnen vereint blieb. Und ein Schutzherr des Hauses passt in diesem Verein durchaus.

Κερκὶς 6. RIGHT.

No. 47.—Ἱερέως Δήμητρος | καὶ Φερρεφάττης.

C. I. A. 293 : V. 1. Date : Not before the second century A.D.

The seat of the Priest of Demeter and Pherrephatte (Persephone).

This is presumably the seat of the priest who had charge of the Lesser Mysteries, which were celebrated in the month Anthesterion (about February) : cf. Sch., *Gr. Alt.*, II. p. 385. Very little is known of the celebration, except that the exercises were begun in a temple of Demeter and Persephone which lay in the suburb Agra, beyond the Ilissus. Whether this was the Φερρεφάττιον mentioned by Demosth. *in Con.*, § 8, is uncertain. See Forchhammer, *Topogr. von Athen;* cf. M., *Heor.*, p. 377 ; W., *S. A.*, p. 273 ff.

No. 48.—Ἱερέως | Διὸς Τελεί|ου καὶ Βουζούγου.

C. I. A. 294 : V. 2. Date : Not before the second century A.D.

The seat of the Bouzyges, the Priest of Zeus Teleios. Cf. No. 28.

Zeus Teleios is, in general, the *Accomplisher*, and was particularly the God of Marriage, in which character he is connected with the sacred ploughing festival (Βουζύγιον), over which a Bouzyges presided. See Plut., *Conjug. Praec.*, c. 42. Cf. also M., *Heor.*, p. 221, note, p. 76, note ; Gh., *Gr. Myth.*, §§ 200. 8, 248. 5.

No. 49.—Ἱερέως | Θησέως.

C. I. A. 295 : V. 3. Date : Not before the second century A.D.

The seat of the Priest of Theseus.

The worship of Theseus was, as is well known, of ancient date : cf. M., *Heor.* (chapter on the Theseus-Feste). The identification of his temple with the so-called "Theseum" is doubted by many : cf. W., *S. A.*, pp. 357–365.

No. 50.—Ἱερέως | Λιθοφόρου.

C. I. A. 296 : V. 4. Date : Not before the second century A.D.

The seat of the Stone-bearing Priest.

Vischer (p. 58) says : Ohne Zweifel ist es der Priester der bei einem Feste, etwa an einer Procession einen Stein zu tragen hatte, wie wir sonst auch einen Korb- oder Wannenträger (λικνοφόρος, λικναφόρος) erwähnt finden. Was für einen Stein und bei welchem Feste, müssen wir freilich dahingestellt sein lassen. Am ehesten möchte man mit Beziehung auf eines der Zeusfeste oder die Kronia an jenen stein denken, den Rhea dem Kronos zu verschlingen gab. Oder sollte etwa das Βαλλητύς, Steinwerfen genannte Fest in Eleusis hieher gehören? (Athenaeus, IX. p. 406, D sq.)*

No. 51. — Ἱερέως | Αὐλωνέως | Διονύσου.

C. I. A. 297 : V. 5. Date : Not before Hadrian.

The seat of the Priest of Dionysus Auloneus. Nothing definite is known of this cult.†

No. 52. — Ἱερέως Ἀπόλλω|νος Δαφνηφόρου.

C. I. A. 298 : V. 6. Date : Not before the second century A.D.

The seat of the Priest of Apollo Daphnephoros (Laurel-wearer).

Nothing is known about this cult in Athens. Vischer (pp. 50, 51) says : Weniger häufig genannt ist in Athen der Apollon Daphnephoros, der Lorbeerträger, obwohl uns vom Lorbeertragen an Festen des Apollon in Athen berichtet wird. Ihm weihte nach der Schlacht bei Artemision Lykomedes das Bildzeichen eines eroberten Schiffes.‡

---

* *C. I. A.*, note on 296: Etiam hic Λιθοφόρου sacerdotis epitheton non herois cujusdam nomen, cuius ille sacerdotio fungeretur, esse videri Vischer (p. 58) recte monuit. Nescio an cum hoc sacerdotio aliqua ratio intercedat homini illi qui nr 702 M. Ἀυρήλιος Λιθοφόρος Πρόσδεκτος Πιστοκράτους Κεφαλῆθεν audit.

† See *C. I. A.*: Idem dei cognomen habes nr. 193. Ac recte quidem illud cognomen ab Aulone derivarunt Vischer et Keil; qui locus terrae Atticae commemoratur etiam in titulo nr. 61. Sed mea quidem sententia nulla est causa, cur eum locum in pagorum sive demorum Atticae numero fuisse indicemus cum E. Curtio in *Archaeol. Zeitung*, XXIX. (1871) p. 7. For the place called Ἀυλών, cf. B., *Geog. v. Griech.*, I. p. 353 and note; also, *Mittheil. d. deutsch. Inst. in Athen*, V. p. 116.

‡ Plut., *Them.* 15; *Herod.*, VIII. 11. Sintenis has corrected Plutarch's error of "Salamis" for "Artemision." Theophrastus (Athen., X. 424 F) mentions a Daphnephoreion in the Attic deme Φλυή or Φλυεῖς. See B., *Geog. v. Griech.*, I. pp. 348, 333 n. 2; Ross, *Demen v. Attika*, No. 153.

The two following inscriptions are on a fragmentary double chair which stands in the fourth row of *κερκὶς* A. : —

(*a*) No. 53. — *Διογένους* | *Εὐεργέτου.*

The seat of Diogenes the Benefactor.

C. I. A., No. 299 : Hunc esse phrurarchum Macedonicum, qui in anno 229. a. Chr. mortuo Demetrio Antigoni f. Macedonum rege ex castellis terrae Atticae praesidius deductis libertatem Atheniensibus restituisset, Koehler argumentis gravissimis demonstravit. See *Hermes*, VII. p. 2.

(*b*) No. 54. — *Ἱερέως Ἀττάλου ἐπωνύμου.*

The seat of the Priest of Attalus the Eponymus.

C. I. A., No. 300 : Etsi litterarum formae, quales Rhusopulos exhibet, aliquanto recentiorem aetatem indicare videntur, tamen dubitandum non videtur quin hi tituli ipsa Attali Diogenisque aetate incisi sunt.

This is Attalus, the king of Pergamus, who visited Athens in 200 B.C., and received the most distinguished honors. A tribe was named Attalis, as a compliment to him ; hence his title *ἐπώνυμος*. Cf. Clinton, *Fasti Hell.*, III. p. 52 (200 B.C.).

No. 55.

A fragment of a seat of Pentelic marble, found in the Stoa of Hadrian. It corresponds in character to the seats in the theatre, and in all probability was originally one of these. The inscription upon it is as follows : —

Ἱερέως | *Ἀπόλλωνος* | *Ζωστηρίου.*

C. I. A. 301 : V. 75.

The seat of the Priest of Apollo of Zoster.

The title *Ζωστήριος* comes from Cape Zoster, upon the south-west coast of Attica, where Apollo had an altar in connection with Leto, Artemis, and Athene. Cf. Paus., I. 31, 1 ; B., *Geog. v. Griech.*, I. p. 359.

No. 56.

In the third row of κερκὶς 1 (right), a large high-backed chair has been found, undoubtedly not *in situ*, upon the front of which the claws and part of the legs of a lion are carved, as a support to the seat. It bears the following inscription: —

Ἡ πόλις
Μάρκῳ Οὐλπίῳ
Εὐβιότῳ, τῷ λαμ-
προτάτῳ ὑπατι-
κῷ καὶ ἐπωνύμῳ
ἄρχοντι, τῷ εὐερ-
γέτῃ αὐτῷ καὶ τοῖς
ὑειοῖς αὐτοῦ Τεισαμέ-
νῳ καὶ Μαξίμῳ.

C. I. A. 688: V. 73. Date: Probably the time of Hadrian.

"The city to Marcus Ulpius Eubiotus, the most illustrious Consularis and Eponymous Archon, — to the benefactor himself, and to his sons Teisamenus and Maximus."

The Eubiotus mentioned is probably the same as the one referred to in *C. I. G.* 378, *C. I. A.*, III. 1, 687, where he appears to have helped the city materially when a famine was imminent. The inscription in the *C. I. G.* is referred to the reign of Hadrian, when the Athenians were sorely afflicted with a famine (Philostr., *Vit. Soph.*, p. 225, § 23). But, although the inscription belongs to this period, the chair itself is probably older, since some traces of an older, obliterated inscription are still visible under the later one.

No. 57.

In the fourth row of κερκὶς 3 (right) has been found the fragment of a fine chair, evidently no longer *in situ*. The back has been entirely destroyed. On each side, a snake is carved; and in front, flanking the seat, are two heads in low relief. It bears the following inscription: —

Ἱερίας Ἀθηνᾶς Ἀθηνίου.

C. I. A. 282: V. 74.

The seat of the Priestess of Athena Athenion.

It is impossible to give any satisfactory explanation of this inscription. Nothing really is known of such an official, though we have ἐπὶ ἱερείας ἡστ Ἀθηνᾶς Ἀθηνίου (*C. I. A.*, III. 1, 668) upon the base of a statue, found near the Propylaea, which was erected in honor of Claudius Atticus, who was probably the son of Herodes Atticus. This raises a presumption that the priestess lived in the latter half of the second century A.D. The chair cannot be *in situ*. In *C. I. A.*, III. 1, 61, we find (A. I., line 11) Ἀρρία [Ἀ]θήνιον.

It is worthy of notice that this chair and the one inscribed to Eubiotus (No. 56) were placed in the theatre in honor of individuals, and were not seats of the holders of particular offices.

In different parts of the κοῖλον of the theatre, inscriptions have been cut into the ordinary seats of Piraic stone. The cutting is very careless, and most if not all of the inscriptions are as late as the time of the Roman emperors. These inscriptions are of no great interest, being, for the most part, designations of seats for priests or priestesses. They are given in *facsimile* in the plates at the end of Vol. III. 1 of the *C. I. A.*, and brief remarks on most of them may be found in the text, Nos. 303–384.

Before closing, a few words on some of the pieces of sculpture and bases of statues which have been found in or near the theatre, may not be out of place.

I have avoided discussing the inscriptions found in the theatre, except those upon the official chairs and the bases of the statues of Hadrian, chiefly because they have no special bearing upon the history of the theatre and most of them are of little interest. They have all been published with at least some commentary in the *C. I. A.* That there were a multitude of statues in the theatre, erected to distinguished persons, we have ample testimony from the number of inscribed bases that have been found. Some, without doubt, had their places in the κοῖλον, as the bases marked **a**,* **b**, **d**,† on the plan;

---

* To Marcus Aurelius.

† It has been suggested that this large base may once have borne a throne for the Emperor Hadrian, when he presided over the Dionysia.

others stood against the sides of the *πάροδοι*, as p and other smaller bases indicate. There were statues erected to the tragic poet Thespis, to the comic poets Eupolis and Timostratus; and we know from Pausanias (I. 21, 1–3) that statues were erected there in honor of Aeschylus, Sophocles, and Euripides. A base has been found bearing Menander's name, which is subscribed with the names of Cephisodotus and Timarchus, the sons of Praxiteles.* This latter base has been supposed to fit the statue of Menander which is now in the Vatican; but Overbeck, in the *Geschichte der greichischen Plastik*, denies that this is possible, and says that the measure of the statue does not correspond to that of the base. I have not been able to investigate this question. Fragments of two colossal Atlantes were found among the ruins of the scene-structure. Two Caryatids also of similar dimensions were found. An altar (marked "Thymele" on the plan), of great beauty, now lies just south of the ruins of the scene-structure. Its height is about 1.20 m., and upon it in low-relief are carved four Silenus-masks, from each of which hang festoons of leaves and grapes, each of the spaces between the masks being ornamented by a rose-like flower.† The sculpture probably dates from an early period in the Empire, if not from a still earlier time, and gives us one more proof that work was done upon the theatre at that period. It is to be remarked that the rose-like ornament between the masks upon the altar is almost exactly like the ornament that is found in the spandrels of the monolith arches which have been already noticed (see p. 135, above).

In the Central Museum at Athens there are two beautiful reliefs, representing dancing girls. These were found at the theatre, but it is impossible to say what connection they may have had with the building.

---

* Cf. Pervanoglu in the Ἀρχαιολογικὴ Ἐφημερίς, p. 244.

† The altar bears the following inscription (*C. I. A.* 97): Πιστοκράτης καὶ Ἀπολλόδωρος Σατύρου Αὐρίδαι πομποστολήσαντες καὶ ἄρχοντες γενόμενοι τοῦ γένους τοῦ Βακχιαδῶν ἀνέθηκαν. "Pistocrates and Apollodorus, sons of Satyrus of Auridae (a deme, cf. Ross, *Demen v. Attika*, 25, p. 62), having led the procession and being presidents of the clan of the Bacchiadae, dedicated (this altar)." Mr. Dyer says that only five words of this inscription are legible, — a strange mistake, since there is not the slightest difficulty in making out the whole. Cf. *Bull. dell' Instit.*, 1868, p. 69.

In conclusion, we will give a brief summary of our study of the ruins of the theatre, that we may more concisely assign to the various historical periods the parts which properly belong to them.

We have been able to trace five different periods in which the history of the theatre may be said to fall:

I. *The period of the fifth century B.C.* To this belongs the κοῖλον, with the subterranean gutter which drains the orchestra, and certain of the conglomerate-stone walls of the orchestra; viz., Nos. 10–11, 6–8, and 7–9 (at right angles with 10–11), and 20–22.

II. *The period of the Orator Lycurgus.* To this it seems probable that the wall 23–24 belongs, together with the Hymettian marble facing of the postscenium wall 20–22, which rested upon it. Here, too, in all probability should be placed the structure in close connection with the postscenium, which had as its foundation walls 25–26, 29, and 24–26. I have expressed doubt as to the theory of Julius, that walls 12–13, 14, and 15 are to be assigned to this period, and have left many questions regarding these walls unsettled. Vischer thinks that the marble chairs also date from this period; but this is, to say the least, very doubtful.

III. *The period about the beginning of the Christian era, or a little later.* The monolith arches found in the ruins of the scene-structure point to the erection of galleries or some works of that nature at this period; and it seems likely, as is shown by the structures at 3 and 4, that some extensive alterations were made in the scene at this time. It has been remarked that the theatre may have suffered during Sulla's siege of the Acropolis in 86 B.C. The marble reliefs in the hyposcenium of Phaedrus may also be assigned to this period, and very probably the pavement of the orchestra. The upright marble slabs which enclose the orchestra are probably of a little later date than the pavement. It is also possible that the marble chairs belong to this period.

IV. *The period of Hadrian.* The theatre was doubtless adorned with many statues at this time; but it is not probable, as was supposed when the excavations were first made, that any radical changes were effected in the structure itself.

V. *The period of Septimius Severus* (193–214 A.D.). To this period is to be assigned the hyposcenium of Phaedrus.

THE OLYMPIEION AT ATHENS.

BY

LOUIS BEVIER.

THE OLYMPIEION* AT ATHENS.

AMONG all the ruins of ancient Athens, there are none, excepting alone the Parthenon, that sooner attract the attention of the traveller than the group of columns between the Acropolis and the Ilissos. Standing on the large open plateau, isolated from all other buildings,

* The Greek Mss. present five forms of this word; viz., 'Ὀλυμπιεῖον, 'Ὀλυμπίειον, 'Ὀλυμπεῖον, 'Ὀλύμπειον, and 'Ὀλύμπιον, making it an exact analogue of the word 'Ἀσκληπιεῖον, which occurs with the same variations. Those who have discussed this word most fully (Lobeck, *Phrynichus*, p. 370 ff.; Poppo, *Proleg. ad Thuc.*, II. p. 514; L. Dindorf, in Stephanus's *Thesaurus*) agree in recognizing the pentasyllabic properispomenon form as the correct one. The penult is accented, not only from the general analogies of the language, but in deference to the express testimony of the ancient grammarians. This is unequivocal, though their own Mss. do not follow out their rules. Stephanos Byzantios (*s.v.* Καπετώλιον) formulates the rule as follows: Καπετώλιον· . . . Εἰρηναῖος προπαροξύνει διὰ τὸ ι γράφων. Ἡρωδιανὸς δὲ Καπετωλιεῖον ἐν ἓξ συλλαβαῖς, καὶ ἐν συναιρέσει Καπετωλεῖον. Ὅσα γὰρ ἔχει προϋπάρχον τὸ ι καὶ εἰς **ος** λήγει καθαρὸν, παραληγόμενα ἢ μόνῳ τῷ ι, ἢ προηγουμένου αὐτοῦ τοῦ **α**, ὥστε εἶναι πρὸ τέλους τὴν **αι** δίφθογγον, προπερισπᾶται· ἢ καὶ ὅσα κτητικά. 'Ἀσκληπιεῖον, 'Ἀσκληπιὸς γάρ· Πτολεμαεῖον, Πτολεμαῖος γάρ· 'Ὀλυμπίεια τὰ 'Ἀθήνησιν, 'Ὀλύμπιος γάρ. Though his Mss. give 'Ὀλυμπίεια, it is evident that he must have written 'Ὀλυμπιεῖα. Perhaps the copyist, not taking pains to understand the rule, associated the place of the accent in the derivative with that of the word from which it comes. Thus, 'Ἀσκληπιός, 'Ἀσκληπιεῖον; but 'Ὀλύμπιος (with recessive accent), 'Ὀλυμπίειον. Again, Theognostus (*Canon.*, p. 129, 27): προπερισπῶνται δ' ὁμοίως (τὰ) διὰ τῆς **ει** διφθόγγου γραφόμενα καὶ ὅσα ἀπὸ τῶν εἰς **ος** καθαρῶν τῷ ι παραληγομένων κύρια καὶ κτητικά· . . . οἷον 'Ἀσκληπιεῖον, 'Ἀσκληπιὸς γάρ· 'Ὀλύμπιος, 'Ὀλυμπίειον. Here the same mistake of the copyist must be assumed, for it is evident that the author could not have written 'Ὀλυμπίειον, in direct contradiction to his rule. The authority of the grammarians then is in favor of 'Ὀλυμπιεῖον. As 'Ὀλυμπεῖον and 'Ὀλύμπειον are recognized by all as spurious, it remains to decide between 'Ὀλυμπιεῖον (properispomenon) and 'Ὀλύμπιον. Here a passage of Photius is in point (*s.v.* 'Ὀλύμπια): 'Ὀλύμπια· τὰ ἐν Πίσῃ 'Ὀλύμπια. 'Ἀθήνησι· καὶ τὸ ἱερὸν 'Ὀλυμπιεῖον πενταυσυλλάβως ὡς 'Ἀσκληπιεῖον. The Ms. has 'Ὀλύμπιον, but 'Ὀλυμπιεῖον must evidently be restored. Most scholars now accept this; but a few, as Rhusopulos (*Arch. Eph.*, 1862, pp. 31 ff.) and Dyer (*Ancient Athens*, p. 272) still defend 'Ὀλύμπιον.

The inscriptions give little evidence. In *C. I. G.*, 1052, where the temple at Megara is mentioned, we find ΟΛΥΜΠΙΕΙΟΝ. The date of the inscription falls

and reaching to a height of nearly sixty feet, they form one of the most conspicuous objects in the whole city. Indeed, to the Athenians themselves they have long been a sort of landmark, and a designation for the part of the city in which they stand, called in colloquial speech simply "The Columns" (αἱ Στῆλαι). The ruins, as they now are, consist of sixteen columns of Pentelic marble in two groups. To the eastward stand thirteen, which are comparatively intact and, for the most part, still bear their architraves. Separated from these columns by a gap of about 100 feet, are three others, — two erect,

---

after the founding of Megalopolis, and before Greece became a Roman province, *i.e.*, between 371 B.C. and 168 B.C. Again, in another inscription (Boeckh, *C. I. G.*, 3847 *b*), the letters ειον, evidently forming the end of the name of a temple, remain, and the restoration to 'Ολυμπιεῖον made by Boeckh is rendered certain by the words τοῦ Διὸς 'Ολυμπίου in the next line. The form 'Ολύμπιον does not seem to occur in any inscription that we have. The temple of Asklepios is mentioned in Boeckh (*C. I. G.*, 3582), the form being 'Ασκληπείῳ, but this is probably a slip of the stonecutter for the longer form 'Ασκληπιείῳ.

In the Mss. there is, as I have said, the greatest confusion; but we have at least a settled point to start from in Thucydides. In every passage where the word occurs in Thucydides, the weight of Ms. authority is in favor of the pentasyllabic form; although the variants 'Ολυμπίου (VII. 37 and 42), 'Ολυμπίῳ (VI. 64, and VII. 4), 'Ολυμπείῳ (VI. 64), 'Ολύμπιον, and 'Ολυμπεῖον, are met with in the poorer Mss. There can, however, be no doubt that the author used the pentasyllabic form exclusively. Plato (*Phaedr.*, 227 B) and Aristotle (*Polit.*, V. 11) have 'Ολυμπίου once each, on the authority of all the Mss. Theophrastos (*Caus. Pl.*, V. 14, 2) uses the short form 'Ολύμπιον. Polybius (XXVI. 10, 12, quoted by Athen., V. 194 A) has 'Ολυμπιείου with the variant 'Ολυμπίου. The Ps. Dikaearchos (Müller, *Frag. Hist. Gr.*, II. p. 254) has 'Ολύμπιον; so also Strabo, IX. p. 396; and Diod. Sic., XIII. 6, 4, and 82, 1; XVI. 83, 2; XX. 29, 3; but in XVI. 68, 1, occurs also the form 'Ολυμπεῖον, *i.e.* 'Ολυμπιεῖον. In Plutarch (*Solon*, 32, 1) all Mss. but one have 'Ολυμπιεῖον, while in *Nicias*, 16, 6, they vary between 'Ολυμπείου, *i.e.* 'Ολυμπιείου, and 'Ολυμπίου. In Ps. Plutarch (*Vit. X. Orat.*, p. 837 B) the Mss. give 'Ολυμπίῳ ὡς, where the ὡς is evidently false, and most editors emend to 'Ολυμπιείῳ. Lucian (*Icaromen.*, 24) and Dion Cass. (LXIX. 19) have the short form. In Pausanias there is a good deal of diversity. In I. 40, 4, all Mss. give 'Ολυμπίειον, *i.e.* 'Ολυμπιεῖον; and in VII. 2, 9, this reading is pretty certain. The Mss. of Pausanias give all five forms, with the weight of authority about equally divided between 'Ολυμπιεῖον and 'Ολύμπιον. In II. 7, 3, however, all have 'Ολύμπιον; and in I. 41, 1, 'Ολυμπίου. In later writers the form 'Ολύμπιον is almost exclusively found.

From this it appears that 'Ολυμπιεῖον is the old and genuine Attic form. It is true the genitive 'Ολυμπίου is given by the Mss. of Plato and Aristotle; but it must be noted that this is not the case with the nominative. On various grounds (cf. Blass, *Ausspr. d. Griech.*, p. 51) it is clear that the diphthong ει became very early little more than a simple ι-sound. This is amply proved by the numerous

with one prostrate companion between them which was overthrown by a violent storm in 1852.* With the help of the pillars which remain in their original positions, and this fallen one, which gives a scale of measurement, it is comparatively easy to form a picture of the perfect temple; and we cease to wonder at the number of ineffectual attempts of the ancients to finish it.

First of all, it is necessary to review the notices of earlier travellers, in order to determine, first, what the last four centuries have done to these ruins, and, secondly, how and when their identification with the famous temple of Zeus Olympios took place, and on what grounds it rests.

The earliest notice in modern times is that of Cyriacus of Ancona, who was in Athens in April, 1436. He says: "Ad domos Hadriani principis marmoreis et immanibus columnis sed magna ex parte collapsis; extant utique adhuc integris et directis suis cum epistyliis c. XXI." (cf. Wachsmuth, p. 727). We observe that he calls the ruins of the temple the palace of Hadrian, and this seems to have been the popular name at that time. We shall find the same designation recurring over and over again, until the real name was scientifically discovered. The most valuable part of this notice is the information about the number of the columns. There were, it seems, "about twenty-one" then standing; so that but few have disappeared in the last four centuries.

---

orthographical errors in the inscriptions. That being the case, the difference between Ὀλυμπιείου and Ὀλυμπίου, Ὀλυμπιείῳ and Ὀλυμπίῳ, would in common speech almost or quite disappear; and consequently it is probable that the genitive and dative became very early confused with forms of the adjective Ὀλύμπιος. Not so, however, with the nominative; and even if Plato could have written Ὀλυμπίου, this is by no means proof for the nominative Ὀλύμπιον. From 100 B.C. on, the longer form gradually disappears, though we meet it occasionally in Plutarch and Pausanias. It seems to me that Ὀλυμπιεῖον is the only legitimate form. Later writers no doubt used Ὀλύμπιον, and it must therefore be kept in their texts; but I hold it to be a spurious form, which arose by false analogy after the genitive and dative Ὀλυμπιείου and Ὀλυμπιείῳ had become confounded with the genitive and dative of Ὀλύμπιος. Ὀλυμπιεῖον, according to the natural development of the language, could not become anything but Ὀλυμπῖον. This reasoning from the oblique cases is such a common phenomenon of language that it needs no illustration here.

* See Rhusopoulos in Ἀρχαιολ. Ἐφημ., 1862, pp. 31 ff. Beulé (*L'Acropole*, II. 274) says that the column was thrown down by the same earthquake which destroyed a part of the Erechtheion on the Acropolis; but this seems to be an error.

Next comes the *Anonymus* of Vienna, whose date Ross (*Aufs.*, I. 250) determined to be about 1460. There is a short paragraph on the Olympieion, which we can easily identify by the words referring to the arch of Hadrian:* ἵσταται δὲ κατὰ ἀνατολὰς τούτου καμάρα μεγίστη καὶ ὡραία. εἰσὶ δὲ τὰ ὀνόματα Ἀδριανοῦ καὶ Θησέως· εὑρίσκεται δὲ ἔνδον τῆς αὐλῆς [here a gap of several words] μεγίστη ἐτύγχανεν· εἰς ἣν οἶκος Βασιλικὸς ὑπῆρχε πλείστοις κίοσιν ὑποκάτωθεν στηριζόμενος (-ομένη Ms.), ὅστις ἐλεπτουργήθη πρὸς τῶν δύο καὶ δέκα Βασιλέων τῶν τὴν ἄκραν οἰκοδομησάντων. The text is untrustworthy, and but little can be made of it; still, it is not altogether without value. In designating the ruins, he also calls it the palace of Hadrian. It is not very strange that the name of Zeus should, in the popular tradition, have had to yield to that of Hadrian, for, from the very first, the temple was the glorification of the Emperor rather than the God. What the last clause of the quotation refers to, I do not know. Ross takes it to be a dim reminiscence of the attempt made under Augustus to finish the temple; but this does not seem very probable, for it is difficult to see how a tradition affecting the temple of Zeus Olympios could have clung to ruins which were regarded as remains of the palace of Hadrian; and, as Ross himself remarks, the number δύο καὶ δέκα is suspicious.

A little later, but in the same century (cf. Wachsmuth, p. 61), is the short notice of the *Anonymus* of Paris; but this adds nothing whatever to our knowledge of the state of the ruins. Nearly a century now passes without giving us any further information, until the publication of *Turco-Graecia* by Martin Kraus (Basel, 1584). In it there appears a letter addressed to the author by one Simeon Karbasilas, a native of Akarnania. It bears no date, but letters that precede it indicate that it belongs to the year 1578. In describing the various parts of the city in his time, he says: τοῦ δ' ἐξωτέρου (ἐν ᾧ καὶ βασίλεια διὰ μαρμάρου καὶ κιόνων μεγίστων· ἐφ' ὧν τῆς πύλης ἐπιγέγραπται μονόστιχον καὶ ἔστι σωζόμενον· Αἵδ' εἴσ' Ἀθῆναι, Θησέως ἡ πρὶν πόλις) τὸ τρίτον οἰκούμενον (Laborde, p. 55 ff.).

The next mention that is of interest brings us down to the latter part of the next century, viz., to Oct. 8, 1672, the date of the famous letter of the Jesuit Babin (Laborde, I. 185 ff.), where we find the

* A facsimile of the Ms. is published by de Laborde, *Athènes aux XVe., XVIe., et XVIIe. siècles.*

following (p. 204): "Ce même empereur fit faire pour soy un palais fort magnifique dont on void encore des restes dans un champ entre la ville et une petite rivière. On dit qu'il y avoit autrefois six vingt colomnes de marbre. Il en reste encore environ seize, extrêmement hautes, et si grosses que deux hommes n'en sauraient embrasser une, et sur chacune desquelles on void des restes d'une petite gallerie voûtée. Entre quatre de ces colomnes il y a une petite chapelle des Grecs toute entière." He understates the number of columns by one; for seventeen were standing four years later, and remained until after the visit of Stuart to Greece in 1753.

To a German belongs the honor of having first discovered what the so-called pillars of Hadrian really were. Joh. G. Transfeldt (cf. Wachsmuth, p. 71) was a prisoner of the Turks in the years 1673 and 1674, and occupied a part of his time in archæological investigations. He recognized the Olympieion from the descriptions of Pausanias and Vitruvius. His work was not published, and so we find later travellers making the same old mistakes.

Guillet, in 1675 (cf. Laborde, I. pp. 223, 224), calls it again by the traditional name: "Le jeudy matin," he writes, "25 avril nous sortîmes pour aller voir les ruines du stadion Panathenaïcon, et celles du Palais d'Adrien. . . . Au dehors de la porte de Raphti nous laissâmes le Palais d'Adrien à main gauche et à costé le lieu qu'ils appellent 'ta mnimouria' [τὰ μνημούρια], c'est le cemetière des Turcs." After describing his visit to the Stadion, he continues: "Nous entrasmes dans celuy d'Agrae. De là tournant à main droite nous fûmes admirer les superbes colomnes et le magnifique portail qui restent du Palais d'Adrien. Le Vulguaire l'appelle *Didascalion.*"

To an Englishman is due the first description that makes any claim to accuracy in detail. Francis Vernon wrote a letter from Smyrna in 1676 which was translated into French, and published by Spon in his *Voyage.* The passage that concerns this subject is as follows: "Toutes les colomnes qui restent du portique de l'empereur Hadrien sont magnifiques, elles sont d'ordre Corinthien d'environ 52 pieds de hauteur et 19½ du circonférence. Elles sont cannelées et il y en a sur pied dix-sept entières avec une partie de leurs corniches. J'ay mesuré l'enceinte du bâtiment auquel elles appartenoient, le plus juste que j'ay pu, et j'ay trouvé qu'elle a environ 1000 pieds de longueur et 680 de largeur." These measurements are not very exact; but they are not purposely inaccurate, and we learn at least the exact number of columns.

Two years later, the memorable journey of Spon and Wheler was made; and I quote a portion of Spon's account, because, while rejecting the traditional name, he sets up a most curious theory in its place. After describing the size of the columns, he says: "Ce n'est pas qu'elles ne pussent avoir servi à l'ornement des palais que cet empereur avoit fait bâtir en ces quartiers là, néantmoins elles n'étoient qu'une espèce de portique, sous lequel on joüissoit agréablement de la promenade. . . . La petite église qui est dessous, bien loin d'être le temple de Jupiter et Junon Panhelléniens, que le même empereur avoit fait bâtir, n'est qu'un amas presque sans chaux de pièces de colonnes, dont l'on a fait cette chapelle, que les Grecs appellent *Agios Ioannis eis tais colonnais*, S. Jean sous les colonnes. Il n'y a point de fabrique ancienne."

In the great work of Stuart and Revett, *Antiquities of Athens* (1762–1816), the matter was for the first time investigated scientifically. Stuart gives an exact and full account of the state of the remains at the time when he wrote, and the plan given by Revett in the third volume is in the main correct. The foundations then, as now, were covered with earth; but the dimensions and general plan of the temple were accurately determined from the columns which then remained. Besides the sixteen which are still in their places, — counting the fallen one, — there was another, separated by some distance from the rest, and belonging to the west end, or back, of the temple. Stuart himself was in error in his conclusions as to this column, and the plan that he gives in the second volume is consequently false. He found by measurement that it stood in the seventh place from the south side, and in the twentieth from the east end, or front. As he did not excavate to determine the size of the stereobate, and the temple was manifestly decastyle, he naturally thought that it had one more than twice as many columns on the side as in front, as is usual in Greek temples. He concluded, therefore, that the isolated column standing in the twentieth place was in the second row from the west end. Revett observed more accurately, and proved that we have here an exception, and that the number of columns in the flank was but twenty. This he did by actual measurement of the bases, which, as we shall see later, are different in the inner and outer rows. The seventeenth column had the base peculiar to the outer row, and must consequently have been on the outside of the west end. Between the years 1753, when Stuart and Revett were together in Athens, and 1765, when Revett repeated his visit, this column was thrown down by the Turkish governor, who wanted the marble to make lime for the new mosque that he was building (cf. Stuart, III. 2). A curious superstition sprang up in connection with this, which Dodwell relates in his *Tour through Greece* (I. 390): "The Pasha of Egripos inflicted a fine of seventeen purses (8500 Turkish piastres) for having destroyed those venerable remains. The Athenians relate that after this column was thrown down the three nearest to it were heard at night to lament the loss of their sister; and these nocturnal lamentations did not cease to terrify the inhabitants till the sacrilegious Voivode, who had been appointed governor of Tetoun, was destroyed by poison."

As to the plan of the temple, later measurements have amply confirmed the position taken by Revett. The temple is no longer surrounded by the marble steps that once adorned it and led up to the temple floor (cf. Rhusop., *Arch. Eph.*, 1862, p. 31 ff.); but the outside of the foundation descends perpendicularly and presents a surface of rough, coarse Piraic stone. We see, then, that the last four centuries have done very little to damage the scanty remains of this once magnificent temple. The earliest travellers found little more than we see to-day. There was a small church beneath, built from the fragments of the ruins, and there was also a sort of building on the top, that had served as a dwelling for a Stylites hermit; but we cannot prove the existence of more than "about" twenty-one columns, and there certainly were not many more even four centuries ago.

Though the identification of the Olympieion was made by Transfeldt in 1673, it was not scientifically proved until the great work of Stuart was written. It remains to review briefly the grounds on which this identification rests.

The great size of the ruins, which surpass in that respect every other building in Athens, would of itself be strong evidence that the temple of which they are the remains was no other than that which Livy* cites as unum in terris inchoatum pro magnitudine Dei (Jovis),

* Liv., XLI. 20, 8.

which Vitruvius (VII. *praef.* 17) mentions as one of the four most famous examples of marble architecture, and which Aristotle (*Polit.*, V. 11) compares to the works of the Kypselidae in Corinth, the pyramids of Egypt, and the public works of Polykrates of Samos. Again, the ruins lie in a south-easterly direction from the Acropolis, and we know from Thucydides * that the Olympieion was one of the old temples in the southern part of the city. It was, moreover, near the fountain Kallirrhoe, or Enneakrunos.† Thirdly, Vitruvius (VII. *praef.* 15 and 17) says that the temple of Zeus was dipteral and of the Corinthian order, which agrees exactly with what we find. It is true, in another place (III. 1, 8), in defining a hypæthral temple, he seems to cite it as octastyle; but the passage presents difficulties in several particulars, and probably is corrupt. Fourthly, Pausanias (I. 18, 6) mentions that the peribolos was full of statues of Hadrian, which the colonial cities of Athens had set up. A large number of these bases with their dedicatory inscriptions have been found at various times, many of them among the ruins. (Cf. *C. I. A.*, III. 1, 472–486.) Again, we learn from Vitruvius (VII. *loc. cit.*) that under Antiochos Epiphanes (175–164 B.C.) the architect of the Olympieion was a Roman citizen named Cossutius. Near the present ruins a block was found, presumably the base of a statue, with the inscription Δέκμος Κοσσούτιος Ποπλίου Ῥωμαῖος (cf. Boeckh, *C. I. G.*, 363). There can be no doubt that this is the same man; and it seems quite certain that Boeckh is right in supposing a statue of the architect to have been erected in the peribolos of the temple which he had

* Thuc., II. 15: τὸ δὲ πρὸ τούτου ἡ ἀκρόπολις ἡ νῦν οὖσα πόλις ἦν καὶ τὸ ὑπ' αὐτὴν πρὸς νότον μάλιστα τετραμμένον. . . . καὶ τὰ ἔξω πρὸς τοῦτο τὸ μέρος τῆς πόλεως μᾶλλον ἵδρυται, τό τε τοῦ Διὸς τοῦ Ὀλυμπίου καὶ τὸ Πύθιον καὶ τὸ τῆς Γῆς καὶ τὸ ἐν Λίμναις Διονύσου· . . . καὶ τῇ κρήνῃ τῇ νῦν μὲν τῶν τυράννων οὕτω σκευασάντων Ἐννεακρούνῳ καλουμένῃ, τὸ δὲ πάλαι φανερῶν τῶν πηγῶν οὐσῶν Καλλιρρόῃ ὠνομασμένῃ, ἐκεῖνοί τε ἐγγὺς οὔσῃ τὰ πλείστου ἄξια ἐχρῶντο, κ.τ.ἑ. The natural interpretation of this passage is to make ἡ ἀκρόπολις ἡ νῦν οὖσα and τὸ ὑπ' αὐτήν together the subject of πόλις ἦν (see Classen's note); and if this be correct, then Thucydides vouches also for the fact that Ἐννεάκρουνος, or Καλλιρρόη, was on the south of the Acropolis, *i.e.*, near the Olympieion. But see Dyer's *Ancient Athens*, pp. 517 ff.; opposed by Wachsmuth, pp. 174 ff.

† Hierokles, *Hippiatr.* (Meursius, *Cecropia*, p. 32): Ταραντῖνος ἱστορεῖ τὸν τοῦ Διὸς νεὼν κατασκευάζοντας Ἀθηναίους Ἐννεακρούνου πλησίον εἰσελαθῆναι ψηφίσασθαι τὰ ἐκ τῆς Ἀττικῆς εἰς τὸ ἄστυ ζεύγη ἅπαντα. Here Dyer (pp. 517 ff.), in order to support his theory, is forced to take Ἐννεακρούνου πλησίον with εἰσελαθῆναι.

begun to rebuild. This is much more likely than Dodwell's idea (*Tour through Greece*, p. 391) that the inscription formed part of an epitaph. However that may be, its presence is another proof of the correctness of the identification. Sixthly, the four sides of the peribolos, according to the accurate measurements of Rhusopulos (*Arch. Eph.*, 1862, pp. 30 ff.), are together 668 m. in length, which is equal to about 3⅝ Olympic stadia. This agrees with the statement of Pausanias (I. 18, 6) : Ὁ μὲν δὴ πᾶς περίβολος σταδίων μάλιστα τεσσάρων ἐστίν. Considering that Pausanias is never very accurate with figures, this is as close an agreement as could be expected. Here he adds the word μάλιστα, showing that he had no intention of giving anything more than a rough approximation. Lastly, the arch of Hadrian with its inscriptions shows that the site of our ruins was the so-called New Athens, or Athens of Hadrian. This is likewise indicated by an inscription found in the large water-pipe; and we know that this section received its name chiefly because this great temple, the crown of all Hadrian's work in Athens, stood in it. All these points make the identification of the Olympieion absolutely certain.

Perhaps the most interesting matter in connection with this temple is the history of its erection. In constructing this history we have as evidence the direct statements of the ancients, and the ruins themselves, which by exact study can be made to supplement the direct tradition. Notwithstanding this, the narrative will be far from complete. Even the statements of the ancient authors, few as they are, present several points of difficult interpretation.

The site of the ruins was one of the oldest hallowed spots in Athens. On it stood a temple in honor of Zeus, long before the famous temple was begun. The Attic tradition mentioned Deukalion himself as its founder; and the fact that his grave was pointed out in the immediate vicinity is cited by Pausanias as the evidence usually adduced to prove that he really lived at Athens. Nor was this the only link that connected this temple enclosure with the hero Deukalion, for in the same paragraph (I. 18, 7) Pausanias says: ἐνταῦθα ὅσον ἐς πῆχυν τὸ ἔδαφος διέστηκε, καὶ λέγουσι μετὰ τὴν ἐπομβρίαν τὴν ἐπὶ Δευκαλίωνος συμβᾶσαν ὑπορρυῆναι ταύτῃ τὸ ὕδωρ, ἐσβάλλουσί τε ἐς αὐτὸ ἀνὰ πᾶν ἔτος ἄλφιτα πυρῶν μέλιτι μίξαντες. Of this cleft no traces remain; and though Forchhammer (*Topog.*, p. 95) identifies this with a large underground cistern connected with the fountain Kallirrhoe, no one will follow him in supposing that this is what Pausanias meant. Of what style the old temple may have been we have no means of knowing; but the fact of its existence does not rest on a popular report or a superstitious rite, since we have the express testimony of Thucydides in the passage already cited. He asserts that the Acropolis and the southern part originally formed all that there was of the city, which after the political unification of Attica under Theseus spread out to its later large dimensions. As proof of this he shows that all the old temples, such as those on the Acropolis, the Olympieion, those of the Pythian Apollo, of Earth, and of Dionysos, were situated here, demonstrating that in this, as in so many other cases, the later large and magnificent temple was but a substitute for an older and simpler one. There is still another passage which may refer to this older temple. Among the most notable antiquities which stood in the peribolos when Pausanias visited it was a bronze statue of Zeus, which may have been the sacred image of the antique temple.* Anything more it is impossible to learn, and the history of the Olympieion properly begins with the Peisistratidae. It is clear at the outset that the main work of its erection was done at three widely different epochs. First, under the tyrant Peisistratos and his sons; secondly, under the Syrian king Antiochos Epiphanes; and thirdly, under the Roman emperor Hadrian. Besides this, something may have been done in the reign of Augustus, nor is it impossible that the work was taken up at other times also; but of such work there are no traces and no records.

It was not until about the year 541 B.C. that the reign of Peisistratos really began. Twice before he had seized the supreme power by various stratagems; but twice the union of the two other factions under Lykurgos and Megakles had driven him from the city, the second time to an exile of more than ten years in Eretria. The third return he effected by force of arms, and he then took measures to render his expulsion impossible for the future. The first part of his reign was full of active enterprises abroad, having in view the aggrandizement of Athens and the legitimatization of his own title to power, — such were the purification of Delos, the restoration of Lygdamos

* Paus., I. 18, 7: ἔστι δὲ ἀρχαῖα ἐν τῷ περιβόλῳ Ζεὺς χαλκοῦς, κ.τ.ἑ.

to Naxos, and the contest with the Mytileneans for the possession of Sigeion on the Hellespont. These are of importance here, because they render it probable that the domestic improvements, which we hear of in connection with his achievements, belong to the latter part of his reign. Such are the cutting of new streets in Athens; the renewal of the Panathenaic festival on a grander scale; the patronage of art and letters, which brought so many distinguished men to his court; and, lastly, his design to perpetuate the memory of his reign by monumental works of architecture. Among these are mentioned a temple of Apollo, the gymnasium of the Academy, and, lastly, the temple of Zeus Olympios, which was to be his grandest work. For the reasons assigned, it is not probable that the work was begun before 535 B.C., at the earliest; and it certainly could not have been continued after the expulsion of his son Hippias in 510 B.C., for we are informed by Vitruvius that the undertaking was interrupted by the political disorders of that time.* Probably the giant work was looked upon even then as a monument of tyranny, and shared a part of the odium that was bestowed on the expelled tyrant. Aristotle, speaking nearly two centuries afterwards, says (V. 11): *καὶ τὸ πένητας ποιεῖν τοὺς ἀρχομένους τυραννικόν, ὅπως ἥ τε φυλακὴ τρέφηται καὶ πρὸς τῷ καθ' ἡμέραν ὄντες ἄσχολοι ὦσιν ἐπιβουλεύειν· παράδειγμα δὲ τούτου αἵ τε πυραμίδες αἱ περὶ Αἴγυπτον, καὶ τὰ ἀναθήματα Κυψελιδῶν, καὶ τοῦ Ὀλυμπίου ἡ οἰκοδόμησις ὑπὸ τῶν Πεισιστρατιδῶν, καὶ τῶν περὶ Σάμον ἔργα Πολυκράτεια· πάντα γὰρ ταῦτα δύναται ταὐτόν, ἀσχολίαν καὶ πενίαν τῶν ἀρχομένων.* He thus makes the building of this temple characteristic of the most odious features of tyranny. To execute his plan, Peisistratos engaged four architects, Antistates, Kallaeschros, Antimachides, and Porinos.†

In connection with the work of Peisistratos and his sons, three questions present themselves for consideration. First, what was the size of the temple as begun by his architects? second, in what style of architecture was it planned? and third, how far did the building advance at this period?

---

* Vitruv., VII. praef. 15: Post mortem autem eius propter interpellationem reipublicae incepta reliquerunt.

† Vitruv., VII. praef. 17. Pormos is found as a variant in the Mss. Callaeschros also is not quite certain. These are merely names to us, for they are nowhere mentioned except in this passage.

As to the first, it is probable from various indications that the ground-plan was the same as that of the finished temple. In the passage of Aristotle just quoted he cites the Olympieion as the characteristic work of the tyranny of the Peisistratidae, dwarfing all its other architectural undertakings. Now, at the time of Peisistratos, foremost among the centres of culture were Samos, then under Polykrates, and Ephesos. In each of them was a colossal temple, — that of Hera in the former, and that of Artemis in the latter. These temples, the glories of their respective cities, were widely known at that time, and attracted visitors from all sides. It has been noticed as a remarkable fact (cf. *Antiquities of Ionia*, IV. p. 15) that the largest temples of Greece were almost exactly of the same size; viz., about 360 by 170 ft. The temples at Samos and Ephesos measured respectively, as nearly as can now be determined, 362 by 167 ft., and 342 by 163 ft.; while the dimensions of the Olympieion were 354 by 171 ft. Such a close agreement can hardly have been accidental; and it seems more than probable that Peisistratos had in mind these great buildings, and intended to equal or outdo them by his temple of the Olympian Zeus at Athens.

I approach with greater diffidence an architectural question bearing on this point; that is, the much-discussed question of horizontal curvature as a principle of Greek architecture.* If we accept the conclusions first reached by Penrose as the result of his measurements, we must admit the existence of this curvature in the Olympieion. In measuring the Olympieion, he found that the centre of the line along the upper step of the crepidoma is three inches above a right line from end to end.† On the front of the temple there are but three columns left; but there too the inner one is appreciably higher than the one at the corner. This small amount of curvature in so large a temple would naturally refer it to an early date. Now, there is little reason to suppose that the principle of horizontal curvature continued in use, even at Athens, as late as the time of Antiochos Epiphanes. Certainly there is no corresponding finesse in the plumbing of the columns. No inward inclination is observable in them, nor does it appear from the measurements attainable that there was any

---

* See on this subject, beside the work of Penrose, the exhaustive discussions of Bötticher and Ziller, and also Reber's *Geschichte der Baukunst*.

† *Principles of Athenian Architecture*, p. 26.

artistic accommodation of the epistyle (Penrose, p. 70). Again, the passage of Vitruvius above cited gives, I think, a slight support to the view here advanced. He says: Namque Athenis Antistates et Callaeschros et Antimachides et Porinos architecti Pisistrato aedem Jovi Olympio facienti fundamenta constituerunt; and then gives an account of what Antiochos Epiphanes contributed, implying by the immediate connection that the work of the latter was a mere continuation of the former on the old foundations.

Secondly, what was the style of architecture chosen? As the Corinthian order was not in use at that early date, we have here to decide between Doric and Ionic; and on the following grounds it seems to me certain that the Doric was the style adopted. In the first place, we should naturally expect that in that age a colossal temple of Zeus would be built in the severe Doric style rather than in the lighter Ionic. In fact, among all the temples of Zeus, I know of no instance of the Ionic order until long after the best period. Still more cogent is a passage of Pliny (XXXVI. 5, 45), where he says: Columnis demum utebantur in templis nec lautitiae causa (nondum enim ista intelligebantur) sed quia firmiores aliter statui non poterant. Sic est inchoatum Athenis templum Iovis Olympii, ex quo Sulla Capitolinis aedibus advexerat columnas. The first part of this passage is very clear. Stability, he says, was the principle held in view in early architecture: it was much later that the idea was conceived of making the columns ornaments as well as supports. The Athenian temple of Zeus was begun in the early style; from this it follows almost of necessity that the order was Doric, for of no other could the stability be so emphasized, in contrast with the ornamental character of later architecture. On the last clause, ex quo Sulla Capitolinis aedibus advexerat columnas, there has been much difference of opinion; but this is largely due, I believe, to its being considered apart from its connection. When rightly understood, it is perfectly intelligible, and renders the conclusion drawn from the main clause still more forcible. Pliny says: "In this way, *i.e.*, with a view to stability rather than ornament, was begun the temple of Zeus at Athens, some columns from which Sulla conveyed to Rome for the Capitoline temple." Only one interpretation is at all natural, viz., that Sulla carried to Rome some of the columns placed in the temple by Peisistratos; and the passage has been so understood by several authorities (see Hirt,

Gesch. d. Baukunst, I. p. 225; Müller, in Ersch & Gruber's *Encycl.* I. vi. p. 233; Hertzberg, *Griechenland unter d. Römern*, I. p. 384; Wachsmuth, *Stadt Athen*, p. 666), even by Leake (*Top. of Athens*), though he supposed the columns to have been Ionic and not Doric. On the other hand, Penrose (p. 71), Stark (*Augsb. Allgem. Zeit.*, 1872, p. 5398), and Dyer (p. 165) think that the columns removed by Sulla were the work of Antiochos Epiphanes. This, however, is a pure assumption, and our only evidence, the passage of Pliny, tells directly against it; nor does any one of these authorities attempt to support his opinion by any arguments. Assuming then that Sulla, after the capture of Athens in 86 B.C., carried away some of the columns which were used by Peisistratos and laid aside when the work was again taken up in a different style and on a different scale, a further argument bearing on the main point may be drawn from this clause of Pliny. These columns were taken to ornament the Capitoline temple at Rome; and this temple, as we know, belonged originally to the Tuscan order, which was nothing more than the Grecian Doric after its adoption and modification by the Etruscans. (Guhl und Koner, *Leben d. Gr. u. Röm.*, II. pp. 8, 9.) It was burned down in the time of Sulla, who rebuilt it, reproducing the old temple with all its main peculiarities. The order that he employed was probably the Doric, and therefore the columns of which he plundered Athens for its adornment were also of this order. To my mind, this passage of Pliny renders it practically certain that the Olympieion was begun by Peisistratos in the Doric order, and further, that the columns carried away by Sulla were his work. Possibly, as has been suggested, they were remarkable as long monolith shafts, or for the rare quality of the marble. It is to be doubted whether a large column of many drums could be taken down, transported, and set up again, without clipping the edges and marring irreparably the niceness of the joints (cf. Penrose *loc. cit.*). On the other hand, Leake, followed by Penrose, thinks that the original order was Ionic. Leake considers this probable because the Ionic was the national order; and because, if the temple were begun in the Ionic, its continuation and completion in the nearly related Corinthian style would be more easily explained. These arguments have very little weight. The first needs no answer; and the final choice of the Corinthian order is amply explained by the taste of the time.

The third question, as to the degree of advancement to which the building was brought under the Tyrants, does not admit of so definite an answer. How much of the period that I have marked out (535–510 B.C.) was employed in active building we cannot tell; and it must always be borne in mind that the means at the disposal of the most powerful Greek tyrant of that time were far less than those at the command of such an absolute Eastern despot as the Syrian king Antiochos Epiphanes, to say nothing of a Roman emperor. But it is safe to conclude from the amply-proved energy of Peisistratos and Hippias that they pushed the building of this characteristic monument with all possible speed; and there can be little doubt that it was soon advanced far enough at least to be used for purposes of worship. That it actually was advanced considerably is evident from Vitruvius and Aristotle,* but more from their general tone than their definite words, although one or two particular indications must not be neglected. All that we can prove to have existed at any time between 510 and 175 B.C. is probably to be referred to the earliest period, for we have no information of any additions during the subsequent three and a half centuries. It is true, Hesychios, speaking of this temple, says: *τοῦτο ἀτελὲς ἔμεινεν Ἀθήνησιν οἰκοδομούμενον, πολλάκις ἀρχὰς λαβὸν τῆς κατασκευῆς*,† but *πολλάκις* need not be taken too strictly. The passage of Pliny ‡ discussed at length above (p. 195) is of importance here, because it makes it highly probable that some of the columns at least had been set up in the time of the Peisistratidae. In Plato's time the temple must have been a conspicuous object, for he speaks of the house of Morychos as "near the Olympieion" (*Phaedr.* 227 B). Whether it was partially demolished by the Persians during their occupation of the city, it is impossible to say. If so, it must have been repaired sufficiently to allow of its continued use.§

* See Vitruvius, quoted p. 198; and Aristotle, quoted p. 193. For Strabo, IX. p. 396, see below, p. 200.

† These words are taken from some of the lexicographer's sources, perhaps from Pamphilos.

‡ Leake cites Plin. XXXV. 8, to prove that the cella must have been far enough advanced to admit of ornamentation, reading cum Phidiam ipsum initio pictorem fuisse tradatur *Olympiumque* Athenis ab eo pictum. But the better Mss. read *eliptumque* and *clipeumque*, and the reading now accepted is *clipeumque*. This, however, does not seem to me certain; and *Olympiumque* may possibly be right, or Pliny may have written something different from either.

§ Besides the work on the temple itself, Semper (*Der Styl*), on purely stylistic

The time from the expulsion of the tyrants to the reign of Antiochos IV. (510–175 B.C.) is a blank in the history of the Olympieion. Its very size was its curse. While Athens was being adorned by the most perfect works of art, and temples were springing up on every side, it lay there as Hippias left it, with no prospect of completion. It was the fate of the temple of Zeus to be a monument, not of the liberty of Athens, but of her slavery and degradation. Begun by a tyrant, it had to wait for its completion until Athens was subject and degraded, and looked for favors, not to the energy and self-sacrifice of her citizens, but to the good-will of foreign princes. In 175 B.C., about 350 years after the temple was begun, Antiochos Epiphanes came to the throne of Syria. He seems to have had a true love for Hellenic culture and art, for he not only won the gratitude of Rhodes, Kyzikos, Delos, Tegea, Megalopolis (cf. Hertzberg, I. 177), and, more than all, of Athens, by his generosity, but he adorned his own capital, Antioch, with copies of the Greek masterpieces, among which was the great Athena of Pheidias (cf. Michaelis, *Parthenon*, pp. 42 and 282, 27). To Athens he was especially munificent; but what chiefly marks his activity here is his renewal of the work upon the unfinished Olympieion. This is attested by so many independent witnesses, representing different periods, that there can be no manner of doubt about the great significance of his work. The most explicit information is obtained from Vitruvius (VII. *praef.* 15), who, after speaking of the work of Peisistratos as quoted above, continues as follows: Itaque circiter annis quadringentis* post Antiochus rex cum in id opus inpensam esset pollicitus, cellae magnitudinem et columnarum circa dipteron conlocationem, epistyliorumque et ceterorum ornamentorum ad symmetriam distributionem magna sollertia scientiaque summa civis Romanus Cossutius nobiliter est architectatus. Id autem opus non modo vulgo sed etiam paucis a magnificentia nominatur. Again (17): In asty vero Olympium in amplo modulorum comparatu Corinthiis symmetriis et proportionibus, uti supra scriptum est, architectandum Cossutius suscepisse me-

---

grounds, refers the wall of the peribolos also to this period. On the other hand, Stark (*loc. cit.*) attributes this wall to the time of Augustus. The opinion of Semper has naturally greater weight.

* Quadringentis is an emendation of Meursius for ducentis, which the Mss. give; and it seems a certain one.

moratur. From this we learn that a Roman architect, Cossutius, was appointed by the king to carry out his design; that he made a plan of the entire temple,—cella, columns, epistyle, and ornamentation,—choosing the Corinthian order of architecture, and surrounding the cella by a double row of columns. How far he really carried out all this, Vitruvius does not tell us; but the fact that he makes this temple of so much importance raises the presumption at least that it was well advanced toward completion when he wrote. Hirt, however, is not entirely justified in assuming that all the parts mentioned were really executed, as when he says (II. p. 150 f.): So dass zur Vollendung in den Zeiten Hadrians höchstens die Aufstellung der Säulen im Innern und die dazu passende Auszierung noch übrig war. In the account of Vitruvius it strikes us at once as singular that a Roman architect should be chosen by a Syrian king to build a temple at Athens; and this is especially remarkable, as Cossutius is the earliest Roman architect whose name has been handed down to us (Hirt, *loc. cit.*). Of him we know nothing further, excepting from the single inscription already mentioned (see p. 190), which is valuable as an independent confirmation of Vitruvius. The choice of the Corinthian order is no doubt due to the fact that the architect was a Roman, since the Romans were, as is well known, very fond of that order. Other notices are less important, but a short review of them is necessary. Polybios (XXVI. 10, 12, cited by Athenaeos, V. p. 194 A), as a contemporary of Antiochos, is especially valuable. After speaking of the general character of the King and his idiosyncrasies, he continues: ἐν δὲ ταῖς πρὸς τὰς πόλεις θυσίαις καὶ ταῖς πρὸς τοὺς θεοὺς τιμαῖς πάντας ὑπερέβαλλε τοὺς βεβασιλευκότας· τοῦτο δ' ἄν τις τεκμήραιτο ἔκ τε τοῦ παρ' Ἀθηναίοις Ὀλυμπιείου, κ.τ.ἑ. Livy (XLI. 20, 8), in very similar phraseology, says: magnificentiae in deos vel Iovis Olympii templum Athenis, unum in terris inchoatum pro magnitudine dei, potest testis esse.* . . . et alia multa in aliis locis pollicitus, quia perbreve tempus eius fuit, non perfecit. Here belongs also a passage in the short description of Athens by the Ps. Dikaearchos (Müller, *Frag. Hist. Gr.*, II. p. 254): Ὁ καλούμενος Παρθενὼν . . . μεγάλην

* The Mss. do not give *testis*, which was added by the first Basil. Livy seems to have written with the passage of Polybios in mind; and *testis* is a very slight emendation, and probably correct.

καταπληξιν ποιεῖ τοῖς θεωροῦσιν· Ὀλύμπιον, ἡμιτελὲς μέν, κατάπληξιν* δ' ἔχον τὴν τῆς οἰκοδομίας ὑπογραφήν, γενόμενον ἂν βέλτιστον εἴπερ συνετελέσθη· with a few words from Strabo (IX. p. 396) : τὸ Ὀλύμπιον, ὅπερ ἡμιτελὲς κατέλιπε τελευτῶν ὁ ἀναθεὶς βασιλεύς. This, according to some, refers to Peisistratos; but Strabo is describing Greece in his own day, and he applies the epithet ἡμιτελές, used likewise by the Ps. Dikaearchos, to the building as it then stood. The expression ὁ ἀναθεὶς βασιλεύς presents some difficulty. Ἀνατίθημι generally means *to set up*, for example, a statue or temple, implying its completion; more rarely, *to consecrate* or *dedicate*. Leake proposes to read Ἀντίοχος, but this could hardly have been corrupted into ἀνατιθείς. Perhaps the building really did advance far enough under Antiochos to allow of its dedication (cf. Stark, *loc. cit.*), and this supposition is rendered plausible by a passage in the scanty remains of the historian Licinianus Granius (28, p. 6, Bonn ed.; 36, p. 26, Berlin ed.). That which concerns Antiochos Epiphanes is extremely full of gaps. He evidently described in some detail the work of the King on the Olympieion, for the words *mures, lapidem, columnas aliquot, circumdederat,* are apparently certain. But we are chiefly concerned with the first word in the paragraph. In the Ms. stands the senseless DEORCA-TUR, of which Mommsen by a very slight change makes *dedicatur*. The weight of an emended passage is not great, and probability is all that can be claimed. The passage ends with the words: Aedes nobilissima Olympii Iovis Atheniensis diù imperfecta permanserat.† From these passages it is clear that King Antiochos practically began the temple anew,‡ merely using the old foundations; that he carried the building rapidly forward, at least so far that it could be called "half-finished"; and it is further probable that a dedication took place under his name. The work

* Many emendations have been suggested for κατάπληξιν, though Osanu defends it as it stands. The most plausible is that of Usener (*Rhein. Mus.*, 1875, p. 607 f.), who reads κατάδηλον. Cf. *Rhein. Mus.*, 1866, p. 217; and Müll., *Hist. Gr. Frag.* (*loc. cit.*). For my purpose the passage is clear, and none of the emendations materially affect it.

† The text as given in the Berlin ed. is as follows: DEORCA—TURETATHEN ISOLUMPIO—ETMURESLAPIDEM1AS—. ONE INSULUERATNAM—COLUMNAS ALIQUOT NU-MEROCIRCUMDEDERAT — EDESNOBILISSIMAOLUMPIIOUIS ATHENIENSISDIUINPERFECTAPERMANSERAT.

‡ Cf. Vell. Pater., I. 10: Antiochus Epiphanes qui Athenis Olympieum inchoavit.

was interrupted by his death in 164 B.C., after which the enormous sums necessary to carry on the work were no longer at command.

The examination of the present remains makes our knowledge a little more definite. We have in Athens two buildings in the Corinthian style known to date from the time of Hadrian, viz., the arch in the immediate vicinity of the Olympieion and the stoa just west of the market. It is only necessary to compare the temple with these works to be convinced that they cannot be contemporaneous. The temple retains much of the simplicity of the earlier Greek taste, in contrast with the excessive ornamentation and effeminacy of the later time (Stark, *loc. cit.*). To mention some particulars among many,—the carving of the capitals of the temple is bolder and of better workmanship, while the later work gives rather the effect of being "picked out"; the cusps of the leaves belong to the oldest Corinthian (Penrose, p. 70; Woods, II. 263); and the curves of the abacus are much better managed, so as to avoid the extreme prolongation of the corner angles observable in the arch and in the stoa. Both Stark and Penrose testify that the columns now existing cannot belong to the time of Hadrian. These columns represent almost the entire south side, and are all of the same workmanship; so that we can safely conclude that the entire peristyle was set up by the Syrian king. Penrose, while recognizing the difference between the work of Hadrian and that shown in the ruins, is led into grave error by supposing that the columns removed by Sulla were the work of Antiochos Epiphanes. Assuming that to be the case, he is obliged to refer the present columns to the reign of Augustus.

Before proceeding, I must devote a few words to this subject, to see on what grounds such a supposition rests. Augustus did bestow on Greece, and especially on Athens, many marks of his favor; and not only the Emperor himself, but also several Philhellenic kings connected with the Roman empire,—foremost among whom was Herod the Great,—delighted in adorning Athens with works of art; but to claim for this period any material contribution toward the building of the Olympieion is not warranted. All that suggests the name of Augustus in connection with the temple is a single passage of Suetonius (*Aug.*, 60): Reges amici atque socii et singuli in suo quisque regno Caesareas urbes condiderunt, et cuncti simul aedem Iovis Olympii Athenis antiquitus inchoatam perficere communi sumptu *destina-*

verunt, genioque eius dedicare. There is not a syllable to show that the idea of completing the temple bore any practical fruit. Though in general it is dangerous to argue from negative evidence, in this case I think it is justified; for while the contributions of Antiochos and Hadrian toward the finishing of the temple are each attested by several independent witnesses, there is no testimony for those of Augustus but a single passage of Suetonius, and even that does not say that anything substantial was accomplished. We must bear in mind, too, that, among those who speak of the work of Antiochos upon the building, Vitruvius, Livy, and Strabo are all contemporaries of Augustus; and we should certainly expect some notice, at least in Vitruvius, if Augustus really accomplished anything of importance. The fact, then, which is commonly recognized, that the present columns do not belong to the time of Hadrian, seems to refer them of necessity to that of Antiochos Epiphanes.

Much, however, remained to be done; the roofing, the finishing of the interior, together with the sculptural adornment of the whole, in the case of so large a temple were no small task. Almost three entire centuries passed, leaving the half-finished temple substantially unchanged. The idea that it would ever be completed seems to have been almost given up. Plutarch (*Sol.*, 32) says: ὡς ἡ πόλις τῶν Ἀθηναίων τὸ Ὀλύμπιον, οὕτως ἡ Πλάτωνος σοφία τὸν Ἀτλαντικὸν ἐν πολλοῖς καλοῖς μόνον ἔργον ἀτελὲς ἔσχηκεν. And Lucian (*Icaromen.*, 24), represents even Zeus as getting impatient to know when the Athenians intend to finish his temple. At last, however, Hadrian was declared emperor of Rome, and in his reign it was destined to be completed.

Here the problems that meet us are chronological; for the reign of Hadrian, while familiar enough in its main features, has long been a bone of contention to chronologists. This uncertainty affects almost all of Hadrian's journeys in the various provinces of his empire; but all that concerns us here are his visits to Athens after he was emperor. Whether he was in Athens in 112 A.D., when he held his archonship, does not matter here, for he was not then in a position to undertake the completion of the temple. The date of his first visit to Athens as Emperor is probably also the date at which the work on the Olympieion was resumed; but this date is not accurately determined. The older investigations on the subject generally placed this visit in 122 or 123 A.D.; though Gregorovius decides for 124 or 125 A.D., and Keil for 125 A.D.* Now, however, since the investigation of Dittenberger (*Hermes*, VII., 1873, 213 ff.), it seems almost certain that the latest date is the only tenable one. Dittenberger himself thinks the year 125–126 A.D. the most probable.

The next point is perhaps even more difficult, that is, to determine when the final dedication took place. There are two passages in which an attempt is made to fix this date. The first is in Philostratos (*Vit. Soph.*, I. 25, 6): *τὸ δὲ Ἀθήνησιν Ὀλύμπιον δι' ἑξήκοντα καὶ πεντακοσίων ἐτῶν ἀποτελεσθὲν καθιερώσας ὁ αὐτοκράτωρ ὡς χρόνου μέγα ἀγώνισμα.* There seems to be no various reading here, but one is much tempted to believe that *ἑξακοσίων* was written instead of *πεντακοσίων*. Assuming 530 B.C. as the date of the beginning, 660 years would bring it down to 130 A.D., or almost the exact time at which the dedication is generally placed. If the writer were giving the date in round numbers, he might have said 600, but it is hard to see on what grounds he could have written 560. The other is the scholium on the passage of Lucian cited above (*Scholia*, III. 57, Jacob.): *τὸ Ὀλύμπιον, ὅπερ ἐστὶν ἱερὸν τοῦ Ὀλυμπίου Διὸς ἐν Ἀθήναις, διὰ μεγαλουργίαν ἀπορούντων Ἀθηναίων χρημάτων εἰς τὴν κατασκευήν, πλεῖον τῶν τ' ἐτῶν παρέτεινε κτιζόμενον, ὡς καὶ ὁ ἐν Κυζίκῳ νεώς· καὶ οὐκ ἂν συνετελέσθησαν ἄμφω, εἰ μὴ Ἀδριανὸς ὁ αὐτοκράτωρ Ῥωμαίων δημοσίοις ἀναλώμασι συναντελάβετο τῶν ἔργων.* The three hundred years here are evidently reckoned from Antiochos Epiphanes (175 B.C.), and this is entirely correct; still, we have merely an approximation. In the life of Hadrian by Spartianus, however, occurs a passage from which something more definite can be gained: Ad orientem profectus per Athenas iter fecit, atque opera quae apud Athenienses coeperat dedicavit, ut Iovis Olympii aedem et aram sibi (§ 13). Here we learn that the dedication took place on one of his journeys to the East, and this at once brings us again to the chronology of his travels. Almost all chronologists agree that Hadrian visited Athens at least three times as Emperor; and the problem is to determine the dates of his last two visits, and to decide on which one the dedication took place. On this point opinions vary considerably (Hertzberg, II. 329). Lenormant (*Recherches Arch. à Eleusis: Rec. d'inscr.*, p. 179), Clinton (*Fast. Rom.*, p. 124), and Eckhel (*Doctr. Num.*, VI. p.

* See the full collation of the various views in Hertzberg, II. p. 301 ff.

482), who place the ceremony as late as 135 A.D., assign it of course to the last visit of Hadrian to Athens; as do also Corsini (*Fast. Att.*, II. p. 105), Boeckh (*C. I. G.*, 1072, cf. 342), Franz (*Elem. Epigr. Gr.*, p. 286), and Keil (*Philologus*, Suppl.-Bd. II., 1863, p. 596), although these place this journey as early as 132 A.D. This was until lately the most widely accepted opinion, although Flemmer (*de itin. et rebus gestis Hadr. Imp.*, p. vi., and pp. 2, 30, 46, 53–58) thinks that the temple was dedicated during the visit before the last, in the summer of 130 A.D.; and lastly, Haakh (Pauly, *Real-Encyc.*, III. 1033 ff.) assigns this visit and the dedication to the year 129 A.D. The result of Flemmer has been rendered very probable by a most ingenious combination of Renier. (Lebas-Foucart, p. 34 of the *Exeg. of the Megarian Inscr.*) The following is the substance of his argument. In an inscription found in the province of Lambaesa is an order of the day addressed by the Emperor Hadrian to the auxiliary troops of the African army while Q. Fabius Catullinus was Imperial Legate in that province. Now the latter was made consul for the year 130 A.D., and must therefore have left his province before the autumn of 129 A.D. But the visit of Hadrian took place in the rainy season, *i.e.*, autumn (Spart., *Hadr.*, c. 22), so that the order cannot be later than the autumn of 128. Again, we learn from Spartianus (*Hadr.* 13) that Hadrian on leaving Africa betook himself immediately to Rome, where he remained but a short time, and departed shortly after for the East, visiting Athens on his way, in order to dedicate the works which he had begun there, among them the Olympieion. Lastly, we learn from an Egyptian inscription (Boeckh, *C. I. G.*, 4727) that the Emperor arrived in Thebes in November of the fifteenth year of his reign, *i.e.*, 131 A.D. Accordingly, the dedication must have taken place in the time between 129 and 131 A.D., probably in 130 A.D. If we can trust Spartianus in details, this is almost complete demonstration; and the fact that Haakh and Flemmer, independently of each other and on somewhat different grounds, had already arrived at almost the same result, adds to it no little force.

* Renier follows Boeckh in placing the date of the Egyptian inscription in November, 130 A.D., and consequently fixes the dedication in 129 or the beginning of 130 A.D. But the inscription is dated Nov. 20 *of the fifteenth year* of Hadrian's reign, which is 131 and not 130 A.D., for he was proclaimed emperor on the 11th of August, 117 A.D.

At the end of this historical review, I must emphasize once more the main result. The temple, architecturally considered, was the work not of the second century A.D., but of the second century B.C. This has been very often forgotten, and consequently the temple has not been studied with the care which it deserves.

Its completion and dedication had a very marked effect on the religious life of Athens. The ceremony itself was made as imposing as possible, and the most popular orator of the day was engaged to deliver the oration. This was the famous sophist Polemon (Philostr., *Vit. Soph.*, I. 25, 6), who, as we know from his principal biographer Philostratos, enjoyed an exceptional reputation during the reigns of Trajan, Hadrian, and Antoninus Pius, especially for the extemporaneous declamations which were then so popular. Upon the completion of the temple Hadrian wished to create at Athens a worship of Zeus Olympios to rival or surpass in brilliancy that at Olympia. So we find that he instituted quadrennial Olympic games like those at Olympia (cf. Boeckh, *C. I. G.*, 342), beginning therewith a new series of Olympiads. The priest of Zeus Olympios at Athens, and the Phaedyntes, whose duty it was to cleanse the colossal image of the god which stood in the cella of the temple, had each a seat of honor in the Dionysiac theatre, like the corresponding officials of the temple of Zeus in Elis.* But even at Olympia the worship of Zeus had long ceased to be genuine; and the galvanic revival at Athens was even a far worse mockery, being little more than a half-concealed servile adulation of the Roman emperor himself by the Athenians. Ever since the time of Augustus it had been customary to pay divine honors to the Roman emperors, even during their lives, generally in connection with a god or hero with whom the emperor might fancifully be identified (Hertzb., I. 529); and when the allied kings entertained the plan of completing the Olympieion in honor of Augustus, they proposed to dedicate it to his genius (*loc. cit.*). And now Hadrian identified himself with Zeus, assuming the title of Ὀλύμπιος, causing a statue of himself and a symbol of his own divinity to be placed within the temple,† devoting a separate altar

* Vischer, *N. Schweiz. Mus.* (1863), pp. 36, 37, 49, 59. See above, pp. 154, 169, 172.

† Dio. Cass., LXIX. 16: Ἁδριανὸς δὲ τό τε Ὀλύμπιον τὸ ἐν ταῖς Ἀθήναις ἐν ᾧ καὶ αὐτὸς ἵδρυται ἐξεποίησε, καὶ δράκοντα ἐς αὐτὸ ἀπὸ Ἰνδίας κομισθέντα ἀνέθηκε (cf. Wachsmuth, *S. A.*, p. 688).

there to his worship (Spart., *Hadr.*, 13), and claiming for himself all the honors of the god from the priests. The first, or among the first, of these priests was the famous Herodes Atticus of Marathon (Boeckh, *C. I. G.*, 335, 336; cf. Dittenb., *C. I. A.*, 476, 485); and the name of another, Statius Quadratus, who probably officiated some years later, is handed down to us.* In its subsequent history, the temple, or at least a part of it, seems to have become the special property of the reigning emperor. In the time of Septimius Severus a statue of his son Caracalla was probably erected here on the occasion of his elevation to the rank of Augustus (Boeckh, *C. I. G.*, 353; cf. Hertzb., II. 426).

When the heathen temples of Athens were converted into Christian churches, the Olympieion became a church of St. John (p. 188 above, and Hertzb., III. 447). It henceforth disappears from history until the fifteenth century, when it reappears, under the name of the Palace of Hadrian, in almost as ruined a state as that in which it appears to-day. When Pausanias came to Athens, on his tour through Greece (about 170 A.D.), the temple had recently been finished, and he saw it in its full beauty; for though it suffered in comparison with the smaller and more perfect works of the better days of art, it was, nevertheless, one of the most remarkable and imposing buildings of Athens. For size, it had no rival in the city, and but few in the world. There are only five to be mentioned with it: viz., the great temple at Selinus, 359 by 167 feet; the temple of Zeus at Agrigentum, —which was destroyed by the Carthaginians when half-completed,— 357 by 170 feet; the great Samian temple of Hera, 362 by 167 feet; that of Apollo at Didyma, 366 by 163 feet; and that of Artemis at Ephesos, 342 by 163 feet.† The Olympieion itself measured 354 by 171 feet; and though it was built in the Corinthian order, it must have presented an effect of solidity almost Doric, for the columns are far more massive than is usual in the Corinthian order, the height being but 8½ diameters, instead of the 9⅔ that Vitruvius (IV. 1) gives as the rule. The entasis of the columns of the Olympieion is

* Boeckh, *C. I. G.*, 337; Dittenberger, *C. I. A.*, 486. Dittenberger (*Hermes*, VII. 1873, p. 213 ff.) shows that in the Athenian inscriptions it was only after the death of the emperor that the word θεός was placed directly before his name, without his imperial titles. He consequently assigns this inscription to a year after the death of Hadrian. For another point of resemblance between the worship of Zeus at Athens and that at Olympia, cf. Dittenb., *C. I. A.*, 487.

† *Antiquities of Ionia*, IV. p. 15.

carefully made; but it is still decidedly inferior, in exactness and uniformity of curvature, to the work of the Periclean age. In amount it is not excessive, being far less than was common in late Roman times, but, on the other hand, greater than in any of the older temples at Athens. The comparative amounts of the entasis in the Erechtheion, Theseion, Parthenon, Propylaea (small and large order), and the Olympieion, are to each other very nearly as the numbers 4, 6, 8, 9, 11, and 12, respectively. The entasis of the large order in the Propylaea is therefore nearly as great as that of our temple (for details, see Penrose, pp. 40–43). In still another way the outline of the columns betrays their comparatively late date; they do not begin to taper until they have reached nearly a quarter of their height, the diameter so far remaining precisely the same, whereas in all the older temples the diminution of the diameter begins at the base. The individual columns present the following dimensions (cf. Rhusop., *Arch. Eph.*, 1862, p. 33 f.). The entire height is 17.25 m. (56 ft., 7 in.), of which 2.02 m. (6 ft., 7½ in.) belongs to the capital, and 1.16 (3 ft., 9⅔ in.) to the base. The diameter at the base is 1.70 m. (5 ft., 7 in.), and at the top, directly beneath the capital, 1.49 m. (4 ft., 10⅝ in.). In the middle it is 1.63 m. (5 ft., 4⅙ in.). These diameters are measured from the bottom of the flutings, which are twenty-four in number. The inside row of columns differs slightly from the outside row, the base, both plinth and mouldings, being a little higher, and the shaft consequently a little shorter. The temple was decastyle, dipteral, and probably hypæthral. The passage of Vitruvius which defines an hypæthral temple (III. 1, 8) is self-contradictory and probably corrupt; but it is clear that if there existed any hypæthral temples at all, as is now generally admitted, an enormous decastyle, dipteral temple would certainly have been so constructed. Vitruvius could hardly have used the Olympieion at Athens as an example in any case, because at his time it was almost certainly not roofed at all. The cella, which no doubt did not differ materially from the ordinary type, was surrounded by 124 columns; for, besides the two rows of twenty on each side and three rows of six (10–4) both in front and behind, there were four columns between the antae at each end. The temple was adorned with sculpture; but all trace of this has disappeared excepting some clamp-marks, which may still be seen along the architrave where the marble blocks were fastened.

The passage of Pausanias giving an account of his visit to the Olympieion, which I have already cited more than once, is concerned chiefly with the peribolos and its contents, and it remains still to discuss it a little more in detail. The words of Pausanias are as follows (I. 18, 6–8): *πρὶν δὲ ἐς τὸ ἱερὸν ἰέναι τοῦ Διὸς τοῦ Ὀλυμπίου,—Ἀδριανὸς ὁ Ῥωμαίων βασιλεὺς τόν τε ναὸν ἀνέθηκε καὶ τὸ ἄγαλμα θέας ἄξιον, οὗ μεγέθει μὲν, ὅτι μὴ Ῥοδίοις καὶ Ῥωμαίοις εἰσὶν οἱ κολοσσοὶ, τὰ λοιπὰ ἀγάλματα ὁμοίως ἀπολείπεται,* πεποίηται δὲ ἔκ τε ἐλέφαντος καὶ χρυσοῦ καὶ ἔχει τέχνης εὖ πρὸς τὸ μέγεθος ὁρῶσιν,—ἐνταῦθα εἰκόνες Ἀδριανοῦ δύο μέν εἰσι Θασίου λίθου, δύο δὲ Αἰγυπτίου. χαλκαῖ δὲ ἑστᾶσι πρὸ τῶν κιόνων ἃς Ἀθηναῖοι καλοῦσιν ἀποίκους πόλεις. ὁ μὲν δὴ πᾶς περίβολος σταδίων μάλιστα τεσσάρων ἐστὶν, ἀνδριάντων δὲ πλήρης· ἀπὸ γὰρ πόλεως ἑκάστης εἰκὼν Ἀδριανοῦ βασιλέως ἀνάκειται, καὶ σφᾶς ὑπερεβάλοντο Ἀθηναῖοι τὸν κολοσσὸν ἀναθέντες ὄπισθε τοῦ ναοῦ, θέας ἄξιον. ἔστι δὲ ἀρχαῖα ἐν τῷ περιβόλῳ Ζεὺς χαλκοῦς καὶ ναὸς Κρόνου καὶ Ῥέας καὶ τέμενος Γῆς ἐπίκλησιν Ὀλυμπίας. ἐνταῦθα ὅσον ἐς πῆχυν τὸ ἔδαφος διέστηκε, καὶ λέγουσι μετὰ τὴν ἐπομβρίαν τὴν ἐπὶ Δευκαλίωνος συμβᾶσαν ὑπορρυῆναι ταύτῃ τὸ ὕδωρ, ἐσβάλλουσί τε ἐς αὐτὸ ἀνὰ πᾶν ἔτος ἄλφιτα πυρῶν μέλιτι μίξαντες. κεῖται δὲ ἐπὶ κίονος Ἰσοκράτους ἀνδρίας· . . . κεῖνται δὲ καὶ λίθου Φρυγίου Πέρσαι χαλκοῦν τρίποδα ἀνέχοντες, θέας ἄξιοι καὶ αὐτοὶ καὶ ὁ τρίπους. τοῦ δὲ Ὀλυμπίου Διὸς Δευκαλίωνα οἰκοδομῆσαι λέγουσι τὸ ἀρχαῖον ἱερὸν, σημεῖον ἀποφαίνοντες ὡς Δευκαλίων Ἀθήνησιν ᾤκησε τάφον τοῦ ναοῦ τοῦ νῦν οὐ πολὺ ἀφεστηκότα.*

There are several things in this narrative that deserve notice. It is strange at the outset that Pausanias makes no reference whatever to the Arch of Hadrian, for it is probable that in entering the peribolos he passed under it. Wachsmuth suggests that the arch may not yet have been built; but this is not very probable, since it seems to have been the work of Hadrian himself. The propylaeon, which was laid bare in 1861 in making a road, is semicircular in form, and built of the same material as the rest of the peribolos wall. It was no doubt clothed with marble steps, leading up from the level of the arch to that of the peribolos. So far as can be seen from the walls

* The emendation of *οὐ . . . ἐπιδείκνυται* to *οὗ . . . ἀπολείπεται*, which is adopted by Dindorf, Walz, Bekker, and Schubart, appears to be necessary. It is evident from this whole passage, and from II. 27, 2, that the size is just what Pausanias is emphasizing. Siebel and Boeckh (*C. I. G.*, 331) keep the Mss. text and understand the passage, "not on account of its size, for even disregarding the colossi of Rhodes and Rome the other images are as large."

of the peribolos in their present condition, this was the only entrance; and through this Pausanias probably passed. Leake has observed (mistaking, however, the arch for the entrance) that the first view of the temple included both the side and the west end, as in the case of the Parthenon when one passes the Propylaea. Of the temple itself Pausanias gives no description, and adds nothing to our knowledge of it; but of the great image of the god we learn something. It was of enormous size, only excelled by the colossi of Rhodes and Rome, and was, as he informs us in another place (II. 27, 2), more than twice as large as that of Asklepios at Epidauros. In his opinion it was of fine workmanship, considering its size. It was of gold and ivory, and on its base were reliefs representing the battle of the Athenians with the Amazons* (Paus., I. 17, 2). After disposing of the temple and its contents in a parenthesis, Pausanias goes on to describe the statues of Hadrian, of which there was a great multitude in the peribolos. First of all, there were four, made of specially valuable marbles, two of Thasian and two of Egyptian. Just where these stood we do not know, for Pausanias' words bear several interpretations. Besides these, a great number of Greek cities, both of the mainland and beyond the sea, caused statues of the Emperor to be set up in the peribolos of the newly-finished temple, to signify their gratitude for the favors which he had bestowed on them. Among these were Abydos, Aegina, Amphipolis, Anemurion in Kilikia, Keramos in Karia, Kyzikos, Laodikeia on the Sea, Miletos, Pale in Kephallenia, Pompeiopolis, Sebastopolis on the Black Sea, Sestos, Smyrna or Ephesos, and Thasos.† The dedicatory inscriptions from

---

* Πρὸς δὲ τῷ γυμνασίῳ Θησέως ἐστὶν ἱερόν· γραφαὶ δέ εἰσι πρὸς Ἀμαζόνας Ἀθηναῖοι μαχόμενοι. πεποίηται δέ σφισιν ὁ πόλεμος οὗτος καὶ τῇ Ἀθηνᾷ ἐπὶ τῇ ἀσπίδι καὶ τοῦ Ὀλυμπίου Διὸς ἐπὶ τῷ βάθρῳ. Editors have generally referred this to the Zeus at Olympia, but they find a discrepancy between this remark and the extended description of that statue in the Fifth Book. Schubart refers it with great plausibility to the statue in Athens; and certainly, if *σφίσιν* is to be interpreted exactly, it can mean nothing else.

† There is much difference of opinion as to the interpretation of this clause of Pausanias; as the Mss. give it, χαλκαῖ δὲ ἑστᾶσι πρὸ τῶν κιόνων ἃς Ἀθηναῖοι καλοῦσιν ἀποίκους πόλεις. The old Latin translation, which is adopted by most of the editors, paraphrases it as follows: Ad templi vero columnas urbium quas colonias Athenienses appellant ex aere erecta sunt simulacra. According to this, Pausanias would say that the colonial cities had set up statues of themselves personified. Such personifications occur quite early in the history of Greek art, and were very com-

these cities have been found on marble bases, mostly near the ruins. They are all practically the same, and one example will suffice. (Boeckh, *C. I. G.*, 332) Αὐτοκράτορα Καίσαρα Τραϊανὸν Ἀδριανὸν Σεβαστὸν Ὀλύμπιον καὶ ἀρχηγέτην ἡ πόλις ἡ Αἰγειντῶν τὸν ἑαυτῆς σωτῆρα καὶ εὐεργέτην διὰ ἐπιμελητοῦ Σωσικλείδου. Some of these seem to have been set up close against the columns of the temple, a disposition of which several other examples may be cited among both the Greeks and the Romans (Ross, *Arch. Aufsätze*, I. 192). An immense statue of Hadrian, overtopping all the others, was erected by the Athenians themselves and placed behind the temple, that is at the west end.

---

mon in Roman times (cf. Overbeck, *Gesch. d. Gr. Pl.*, II. 435), so that on that score there is no objection to this interpretation, which is adopted by Ross (*Arch. Auf.*, *loc. cit.*) and by Dyer (p. 277). Dyer urges that in the next sentence the statues of Hadrian are mentioned, and that therefore we are to suppose that each city erected a statue of the Emperor and also one of herself. But it must be observed that the second clause would not in any case be a repetition. After speaking of the bronze statues which stood in front of the columns, he continues: "The whole peribolos indeed is full of statues, for a statue of Hadrian was erected by *each* city." Here it is very evident that the emphasis is on ἑκάστης. It was very common for a number of cities to club together and, at their joint expense, to erect a statue of an emperor who had aided or befriended them; for example, the cities of Asia Minor, when Tiberius helped them to repair the damages caused by a severe series of earthquakes (Overbeck, *loc. cit.*). Pausanias calls attention to the great number of statues, and naturally explains why there were so many. Even were it a mere repetition, that would by no means exclude it from the text of Pausanias. There are, moreover, some positive arguments to be urged against the above-mentioned interpretation. Pausanias begins with the statues of Hadrian. "Here there are statues of Hadrian," he says, "two of Thasian and two of Egyptian marble; and bronze ones stand before the columns," etc. It is the only natural interpretation to let εἰκόνες Ἀδριανοῦ continue as the subject to be supplied in the next sentence. Two lines further on we find him again speaking of the statues of Hadrian. It would certainly be very harsh to suppose that he thrust in here, without explanation, a reference to a numerous class of very different statues. Again, in other places, when Pausanias mentions such personifications of cities, he adds an explanation rendering his meaning clear (cf. II. 16, 3; III. 18, 5; X. 18, 7). It is needless to add that among the inscriptions, etc., found in the peribolos, nothing has appeared which gives the slightest support to this interpretation. From an æsthetic point of view, no doubt, the effect would be improved, if among the crowd of Hadrians, big and little, were scattered a few graceful female forms; but, unfortunately, their existence cannot be proved, and some other interpretation of the words of Pausanias must be attempted. Most scholars agree in understanding them to refer to statues of Hadrian erected by the colonies; but here also we find some difference of opinion. Boeckh (*C. I. G.*, 331) sets forth a most elaborate explanation: Ad introitum περιβόλου pro antis haud dubie Hadriani duae statuae Thasii et totidem Aegyptiaci lapidis collocatae

Other and older statues also occupied various places in the enclosure, among which was a statue of Isocrates, erected by his adopted son, Aphareus. This is mentioned also by the Ps. Plutarch (*Vit. X. Orat.*, p. 839 B: ['Αφαρεὺς] εἰκόνα αὐτοῦ ἀνέθηκε πρὸς τῷ 'Ολυμπιείῳ ἐπὶ κίονος καὶ ἐπέγραψεν·

> 'Ισοκράτους 'Αφαρεὺς πατρὸς εἰκόνα τήνδ' ἀνέθηκε
> Ζηνί, θεούς τε σέβων καὶ γονέων ἀρετήν.

Pausanias closes the list of the statues with the mention of a fine group consisting of some Persians upholding a bronze tripod, and the archaic statue of Zeus already mentioned. In the peribolos was

---

erant; intus vero ad murum περιβόλου in stoa positae erant Imperatoris imagines a Graecis civitatibus dedicatae; et ante huius stoae columnas sub dio statuae eiusdem a coloniis Romanis dicatae, eaeque aheneae. The two clauses χαλκαῖ δὲ ἑστᾶσι πρὸ τῶν κιόνων, etc., and ἀπὸ γὰρ πόλεως ἑκάστης εἰκὼν 'Αδριανοῦ, etc., according to him refer to two different sets of statues; the latter, dedicated by Greek cities, stood in a corridor along the wall of the peribolos, and the former, set up by Roman colonies, stood before the columns of this corridor. The corridor is purely a creation of Boeckh's fancy; but in proof of the assumption that Roman colonies erected statues in the temple enclosure, he cites the following inscription, copied by Spon, and later by Dodwell: Imperatori Caesari, Divi Traiani Parthici filio, Divi Nervae nepoti, Traiano Hadriano Augusto, . . . Olympio, etc. (cf. Dittenberger in *C.I.A.*, III. 1, 471). This has precisely the Latin form which corresponds to the Greek inscriptions found in the peribolos, and it belongs certainly to a statue of Hadrian erected in Athens by a Roman colony in 132 A.D., after the dedication of the Olympieion; but it was not found in the temple enclosure, and there is no proof that it ever stood there. Even if it did, this by no means justifies such a violent interpretation of the words of Pausanias. Boeckh does not emend the text; but how he gets the required sense from it he does not say, and I do not understand. Wachsmuth (p. 226) refers the words to statues of Hadrian, but does not go into the question of the exact exegesis of the text; and Hertzberg (II. 327) seemingly dissents from the explanation of Boeckh. There is, however, considerable difficulty in the text as it stands. Literally translated the words would mean: "Bronze statues of Hadrian, which the Athenians call colonial cities"; and it is hard to get the required sense from this. Leake felt this difficulty, and proposed to remedy it by an emendation. The text of Pausanias is not good, and in many places one or more words have fallen out. Leake supposes this to be the case here, and would insert before the words ἃς 'Αθηναῖοι the similar ones ἃς ἀνέθεσαν, making the passage read, χαλκαῖ δὲ ἑστᾶσι πρὸ τῶν κιόνων ἃς ἀνέθεσαν ἃς 'Αθηναῖοι καλοῦσιν ἀποίκους πόλεις. This, however, introduces a scarcely less harsh construction, and does not seem probable. He has not been followed, I believe, by any editors. The interpretation given in the text seems to me the only plausible one; but it is probable that Pausanias did not write the words as they now stand. The passage has resisted the endeavors of so many learned critics that it seems hopeless to attempt its emendation.

also a temple of Kronos and Rhea; but its temenos, *i.e.* the enclosure sacred to the deities, must have extended to a considerable distance outside the peribolos, down to the Ilissos, as Wachsmuth (p. 227) shows in detail. It must be remembered that before the time of Pausanias the city wall on the east side had been levelled. There was, lastly, a temenos of the Olympian Earth (Γῆ); * and this also probably extended beyond the peribolos in a south-westerly direction, till it approached the city wall near the Itonian Gate (Wachsmuth, p. 228; cf. Plut. *Thes.*, 27).

During the excavations in 1861, Rhusopulos took occasion to examine the peribolos much more closely than had before been done; and he laid bare a large portion of the northern boundary wall, the exact position of which was hitherto unknown. The temple did not lie, as was supposed, directly in the centre of the enclosure, but was considerably nearer the north wall. (For a more detailed description of the peribolos, cf. Rhusopulos in the *Arch. Eph.*, 1862, p. 31 ff.)

In our knowledge of the Olympieion there are many gaps; and many questions suggest themselves, which, for the present at least, cannot be answered. Nevertheless, its remarkable history, its large dimensions, and the beauty and picturesqueness of its ruins, will always make it one of the most interesting of the architectural remains of Greek antiquity.

* The emendation Γῆς ἐπίκλησιν for τὴν ἐπίκλησιν, in Paus. I. 18, 7, is now universally accepted, and seems certain.

THE ERECHTHEION AT ATHENS.

BY

HAROLD N. FOWLER.

INTRODUCTORY NOTE.

So much has been written upon the Erechtheion that I have hesitated to swell the list of writers upon the subject. I hope, however, that my article may be of some slight service to those who wish to understand the arrangement of this remarkable building. I take pleasure in expressing my thanks for kind suggestions to Dr. Wilhelm Dörpfeld, of the Imperial German Archæological Institute at Athens, and Mr. Francis H. Bacon, of the American Expedition to Assos. There are some questions relating to the Erechtheion which can be settled, if at all, only after more complete and careful excavations than have yet been made. It is greatly to be desired that this task should be undertaken soon by some one of the Archæological Institutes in Athens.

The Erechtheion was the most venerated temple of Athens, containing the sacred olive of Athena (Paus., I. 27, 2), the well of Poseidon (Paus., I. 26, 5), and the ancient statue of Athena, which was said to have fallen from heaven (Paus., I. 26, 6; *Corpus Inscript. Graec.*, No. 160). No fixed date can be given for either the beginning or the completion of the present edifice. The older temple was burnt by the Persians in 480 B.C. (Herod., VIII. 53 and 55; Paus., I. 27, 2). When the Athenians returned to their ruined city, it is highly probable that one of their first undertakings was to rebuild the sacred structure in some way; but no definite record of the erection of any such building remains. But Herodotus (VIII. 55) says of the Acropolis of Athens, ἔστι ἐν τῇ ἀκροπόλι ταύτῃ Ἐρεχθέος τοῦ γηγενέος λεγομένου εἶναι νηός, which seems to mean that when Herodotus wrote, in the early part of the Peloponnesian war, a building called the temple of Erechtheus stood on the Acropolis. The inscription in *C. I. G.*, 160, and *C. I. A.*, I. 323, bears the date of the archonship of Diocles (Olymp. 92, 4; 408 B.C.); and that in *C. I. A.*, I. 324, dates from Olymp. 93, 1; 407 B.C. At this time the temple was clearly approaching completion. Xenophon (*Hellen.*, I. 6, 1) says that "the ancient temple of Athena" (ὁ παλαιὸς τῆς Ἀθηνᾶς νεώς) in Athens was set on fire in the archonship of Kallias, the year when Kallikratidas succeeded Lysander as Spartan admiral, *i.e.*, in 406–405 B.C. It has been maintained that by the expression ὁ παλαιὸς νεώς the Erechtheion cannot be meant, as a temple not yet completed could not be called "ancient"; but the word νεώς is used to signify not only the building, but the sacred site together with the building. The Erechtheion is constantly called ὁ ἀρχαῖος νεώς (Schol. in Arist. *Lys.*, 273; Strabo, IX. 396; *C. I. A.*, II. 464); and the expression παλαιός is certainly justifiable, even if we do not assume, what is not unlikely, that some part of the ancient building may have been preserved. Whether the Erechtheion was very much injured by the fire of B.C. 406 we have no means of determining; nor have we any records of subsequent repairs. The temple is mentioned by several ancient writers, but none except Pausanias attempt to give a description of it. In early Christian times, as the remains show, the building was used as a church, probably of the Saviour, τοῦ Σωτῆρος (cf. Mommsen, *Athenae Christianae*, p. 40; Pittakis, *Eph. Arch.*, No. 1102 sq., p. 640 sq., and No. 1204, p. 742), and divided into a nave and two side aisles. Under the Turks it was used as a dwelling-house (Wheler, *Journey into Greece*, p. 364), and also as a powder magazine. When Stuart and Revett saw the building (1751–1753), it was already in a very ruinous condition. During the war of Greek independence (1821–1828), the Erechtheion suffered greatly. In 1838 the building was repaired under the direction of Pittakis; but a violent storm in 1852 threw down all but one of the columns of the western wall, and they are now lying in the interior of the building. The latest excavations, made in 1852, left the Erechtheion in its present condition.

I subjoin a list of papers upon the Erechtheion. I have attempted to give a complete bibliography of all articles which can claim to be considered the result of independent research, and I hope nothing of importance has been omitted. Some books or parts of books are mentioned which do not claim originality, but which present the views of others in an easily accessible form.

SPON AND WHELER. *Voyage d'Italie, de Dalmatie, de Grèce, et du Levant.* Lyon, 1678; La Haye, 1724.

GEORGE WHELER. *Journey into Greece.* London, 1682.

STUART AND REVETT. *Antiquities of Athens.* Vol. II., Chap. II. London, 1787.

EDWARD DODWELL. *A Classical and Topographical Tour through Greece during the Years* 1801, 1805, *and* 1806.

W. WILKINS. *Atheniensia, or Remarks on the Topography and Buildings of Athens:* p. 75 ff. London, 1816.

W. WILKINS. *Memoirs of Robert Walpole.—Memoirs relating to European and Asiatic Turkey, etc.* London, 1818.

R. WALPOLE. *Travels in Various Countries of the East.* London, 1820.

K. O. MÜLLER. *Minervae Poliadis Sacra et Aedes in Arce Athenarum, etc.* Göttingen, 1820.

ALOYS HIRT. *Geschichte der Baukunst bei den Alten.* II. 24. Berlin, 1821.

W. H. INWOOD. *The Erechtheion of Athens.* London, 1827.

AUGUST BÖCKH. *Corpus Inscriptionum Graecarum,* No. 160. Berlin, 1828.

W. WILKINS. *Prolusiones Architectonicae.* London, 1834.

CHRISTOPHER WORDSWORTH. *Athens and Attica: Notes of a Tour.* London, 1836.

ALEXANDER FERDINAND VON QUAEST. *Das Erechtheion zu Athen.* Berlin, 1840.

W. M. LEAKE. *Topography of Athens.* Vol. I. Ed. 2. London, 1841.

FRIEDRICH THIERSCH. *Ueber das Erechtheum auf der Akropolis zu Athen.* München, 1843.

P. W. FORCHHAMMER. *Ueber Alte Königsgräber, etc.* In *Allgemeine Zeitung,* 1843, No. 256.

CARL BÖTTICHER. *Tektonik der Hellenen.* Potsdam, 1844.

A. R. RANGABÉ. Article in the *Revue Archéologique,* 1845.

HAUSEN. In the *Wiener Allgemeine Bauzeitung,* 1851.

TÉTAZ. In the *Wiener Allgemeine Bauzeitung,* 1851: pp. 342 ff.

TÉTAZ. In the *Revue Archéologique,* 1851: viii. Année, pp. 1–12, 81–96; pl. 158–159.

CARL BÖTTICHER. *Der Polias-tempel als Wohnhaus des Königs Erechtheus, nach der Annahme von Fr. Thiersch.* Berlin, 1851.

RAOUL-ROCHETTE. In the *Journal des Savants,* 1852.

Πρακτικὰ τῆς ἐπὶ τοῦ Ἐρεχθείου ἐπιτροπῆς, ἢ ἀναγραφὴ τῆς ἀληθοῦς καταστάσεως τοῦ Ἐρεχθείου, κ.τ.λ. Ἀθήνησιν, 1853.

FRIEDRICH THIERSCH. *Ueber die neuesten Untersuchungen des Erechtheums auf der Akropolis zu Athen. Ein Sendschreiben an Herrn Geheimrath August Böckh.* München, 1853.

FRIEDRICH THIERSCH. *Ueber das* οἴκημα *bei Pausanias. Eine Beilage zur Epikrisis der neuesten Untersuchungen des Erechtheums.* München, 1857.

FRIEDRICH THIERSCH. *Epikrisis der neuesten Untersuchungen des Erechtheums auf der Akropolis zu Athen.* München, 1857.

P. W. FORCHHAMMER. *Hellenica.* I. pp. 31 ff. Berlin, 1857.

CARL BÖTTICHER. In the *Zeitschrift für Bauwesen.* Berlin, 1859.

E. M. BEULÉ. *L'Acropole d'Athènes.* Paris, 1862.

CARL BÖTTICHER. *Bericht über die Untersuchungen auf der Akropolis von Athen im Frühjahre,* 1862. Berlin, 1863.

ERNEST BRETON. *Athènes décrite et dessinée.* Ed. 2. Paris, 1868.

THOMAS HENRY DYER. *Ancient Athens; its History, Topography, and Remains.* London, 1873.

P. W. FORCHHAMMER. *Daduchos, Eine Leitung in das Verständniss der Hellenischen Mythen, Mythensprache, und mythischen Bauten.* Kiel, 1875.

ADOLPH MICHAELIS. *Bemerkungen zur Periegese der Akropolis von Athen.* In *Mittheilungen des deutschen Institutes in Athen,* 1877, 1.

LEOPOLD JULIUS. *Ueber das Erechtheion.* München, 1878.

JAMES FERGUSSON. *The Erechtheum and the Temple of Athena Polias in Athens.* In *Transactions of the Royal Institute of British Architects,* 1875–6. Republished with an appendix in 1879.

A. S. MURRAY. *The Erechtheum.* In *Journal of Hellenic Studies.* Vol. I. p. 224. 1880.

R. BORRMANN. *Neue Untersuchungen am Erechtheion zu Athen.* In *Mitth. d. deutschen Inst. in Athen,* 1881, p. 372.

JAMES FERGUSSON. *Stairs to Pandroseum at Athens.* In *Journal of Hellenic Studies.* Vol. II. p. 83. 1881.

A. R. RANGABE. *Das Erechtheion.* In *Mitth. d. deutschen Inst. in Athen,* 1882, p. 258.

For Inscriptions, see *Corpus Inscriptionum Graecarum,* No. 160; *Corpus Inscriptionum Atticarum,* I. Nos. 321, 322, 324; **Ἀθήναιον,** VII. p. 482; **Ἐφημερὶς Ἀρχαιολογική,** November, 1837 (Rangabé); *Kunstblatt,* 1836, No. 39 ff. (Ross); *Antiquités Helléniques,* 1842, No. 56 ff. (Rangabé); C. T. Newton's *Collection of Ancient Greek Inscriptions in the British Museum,* London, 1874; and Otto Jahn's *Pausaniae Descriptio Arcis Athenarum,* ed. 2, revised by Michaelis. Bonn, 1880.

On the excavations of 1832 and the following years, see **Ἐφημερὶς Ἀρχαιολογική**; *Kunstblatt,* 1835, No. 78; *Allgemeine Zeitung,* July, 1835.

The four plans of the Erechtheion given with this paper are taken from the **Πρακτικά** of the Archæological Society of Athens, 1853.

THE ERECHTHEION.

THE Erechtheion is a rectangular edifice 20.30 m. in length and 11.21 m. in breadth. Seen from the east, it has the appearance of an Ionic hexastyle temple. The southern wall stands half a metre from a terrace about 3 m. high, which is continued for some distance both east and west of the building. The space between this terrace and the wall of the Erechtheion is filled with earth. On account of this arrangement, the building appears about 3 m. lower from the south than from the north, where there is no terrace. The eastern front of the building is on the same level as the southern side, while the stereobate of the north and west sides is about 3 m. lower than that of the east and south sides. At the north-west corner is a portico with six Ionic columns, four on the front, and one behind each corner column. At the south-west corner is a small porch, the roof of which is supported by six Κόραι (*maidens*) or Karyatids standing on the high wall which encloses the porch. Each of these two porches communicates by a doorway with the interior of the building. Besides these two doors and the main entrance at the east, there is another door under the base of the second (counting from the south) of the engaged columns of the western wall. The antiquity of this last door has been doubted on account of the roughness of its sides and the fact that the threshold is not made, as we should expect, of one stone. The lintel, however, is formed of one block, equal in height to two courses of the stones of which the temple is built, and it extends the same distance on each side of the door. As this stone could have been inserted for no other purpose than as a lintel, the antiquity of the door admits of no reasonable doubt. (See Plate II., *a.*) The rough work on the sides may date from the time when the Christians used this as the main entrance to their church.

In the interior of the building are the foundations of three walls. One was a cross-wall from north to south, just east of the great doorway R, which opens upon the northern porch F. The other two ran at right angles to the first, extending from it to the east end of the building.* The first of these walls was part of the original building. The two others were late additions, built probably by the Christians to support the pillars by which the nave of the church was separated from the side aisles, and their late date is evident from the workmanship. The space from the ancient cross-wall to the western wall of the building is occupied by a cistern, which was once covered by a brick vault.† This vault, a small part of which is preserved, rises above the threshold of the great northern door, and was, of course, not a part of the original building. This fact has led many to affirm positively that the cistern itself was a late addition. This, however, is not the case. The two upper steps of the western stereobate, instead of being formed by two layers of stones, consist of one course of blocks about 0.45 m. thick. These blocks are not cut off so as to form part of the surface of the wall within the building; but they project over the edge of the cistern. They are now roughly broken off, so that none of them project more than 0.20 m.; but this is enough to show that these heavy blocks were not employed without a purpose. Now the only possible purpose of such blocks can have been to bridge over a hollow space. The space occupied by the cistern was therefore always hollow. The cistern itself is partly cut out of the solid rock, and it was evidently very carefully made. Everything speaks for its antiquity; and the only argument to the contrary, the height of the brick vault which at one time covered it, falls to the ground as soon as it is shown that the original covering was not the brick vault, but the horizontal pavement of heavy marble blocks, portions of which are still to be seen projecting over the edge of the cistern. It seems therefore hardly possible to deny that the cistern is as old as the blocks; that is, as old as the building. This cistern was probably the *θάλασσα* of Poseidon.‡

The wall *d*, on the eastern side of the cistern, built of the so-called Piraic stone and founded upon the solid rock, supported the cross-wall A. Directly above this, in the eleventh and fourteenth courses

---

* See Plate I. (2), A and *b*, *b*.

† Plate III. and IV., *g*; Plate I., *μ*, *μ*, *μ*.

‡ Apoll., III. 14, 1, 2: *ἀνέφηνε θάλασσαν, ἣν νῦν Ἐρεχθηίδα καλοῦσι.* See Paus., I. 26, 5.

of the northern wall,* are projecting stones, 0.65 m. in width, to which corresponds a hole, also 0.65 m. wide, in the southern wall.† The present wall east of the cistern was then the foundation of a wall of some sort, probably of the same age as the temple, which divided the building from top to bottom.

There was a second cross-wall about half way between the last-mentioned wall and the eastern front of the temple.‡ At this point the stones of both the north and south wall show clearly that a cross-wall existed, for their surfaces were evidently prepared to receive such a wall; § but no foundations remain.

The Erechtheion was thus divided into three parts, the two eastern rooms being nearly equal in size, while the western division was much narrower than the others. The eastern apartment had its entrance from the east, while the other two must generally have been entered through the great door opening on the northern portico. There was the same difference of level between the floors of the rooms to which these entrances gave admission which has been noticed between the entrances themselves. There was no basement under the eastern cella, nor was the building in any part two-storied. The floor of the eastern cella was raised one step above the threshold, and joined the side walls where they are patched with modern brick work. (Pl. III.) If it had been lower than this, it must have left visible traces; and it is hardly conceivable that it should have been higher. The space under this floor was filled with a foundation of Piraic stone like that now remaining in the corners. When the Erechtheion was altered to suit the demands of the Christian worship, the floor of the whole edifice was placed at the level of the ancient floor of the two western divisions. All the inner foundations of the eastern cella were torn away, except a few stones in the corners; and part of the foundation of the eastern porch was removed to make room for the apse of the church (Pl. I., *y*). The Piraic stones which remain show by their position, as well as by their dressed edges, that they did not originally form the face of a wall, but were embedded in a solid foundation, which probably filled all, or at least a great part, of the space under the floor of the eastern cella (cf. Borrmann in *Mitth. d. deutsch. Inst.*,

* See Pl. IV., ϵ, ϵ; and Fig. 1, p. 223. The two rectangular holes in the first and third courses are, as their workmanship show, of late origin.

† Pl. III., *r*. ‡ Pl. I., B. § Pl. III, *p*, *o*; Pl. IV., *m*, *n*.

1881, p. 383). Moreover, whereas the northern and southern walls of the building west of the eastern cross-wall are both of marble down to the level of the floor of this part, east of the eastern cross-wall they are built of marble only where they can be seen from the outside, since they were not intended to be seen from the inside below the level of the eastern entrance. (See Plates III. and IV.)

There is no good reason for supposing that the building had two stories west of the eastern cross-wall, where the floor was lower. Carl Bötticher, the chief supporter of the theory of two stories, says that the faces of some of the stones of the southern wall show that there was a division into two stories (*Bericht*, p. 199 ff.). I can only say that I have been unable to find any traces of such a construction, nor has any one since Bötticher been able to discover any. In the north and south walls are five small slits or windows, which Bötticher calls cellar windows, and which he uses as a chief argument for his theory. He says: "Wo Souterrain-Fenster sind, muss auch ein Souterrain dahinter vorhanden sein;" but, as has been justly remarked, before we prove the existence of a cellar from cellar windows, we must first be sure that we have the cellar windows. I am strongly of the opinion that these openings are neither cellar windows nor ancient windows at all. They were not made by the builders of the temple, for they are not found at the joints between the blocks, but in the middle of the blocks. It would be no more difficult to cut them here than at the joints, after the stones were in place; but the original builders would surely have left such openings between the stones when they put them in place, as was done in the case of the similar openings in the stoa of Attalus, in the Arsenal of Philon, and elsewhere. Besides, the inferior workmanship of these openings makes it highly improbable that they belonged to the original building. It is not unlikely that they were made by the Christians to light the side aisles of their church, a purpose for which similar openings are still in use. While then there is no valid argument for the theory that the Erechtheion was a two-storied building in any part, the rough Piraic stones below the eastern cella show plainly that there at least such a division into stories did not exist.

The eastern cross-wall was probably a solid wall, with a door near the southern end. At this point the Piraic stones of the southern wall give place to marble; not, however, all at once on the same vertical line, but each course of Piraic stone is continued further than the one above it, giving it the appearance of a flight of steps. (See Plate III.) This arrangement makes it probable that the steps connecting the eastern cella with the rest of the edifice were at this point; though, as there are no actual traces of them, we may suppose them to have been built of wood. There must have been some mode of communication between the eastern cella and the rest of the building; and this seems the most probable place for the stairs.

The western cross-wall was not a solid wall, like the eastern one. Fig. 1, copied from Borrmann, gives a view of the northern wall where it was joined by this cross-wall. In the eleventh and fourteenth courses of stone are still seen the rough ends of the stones of the cross-wall (ε, ε) projecting from the main wall. Below these the wall is roughened, as if a wall had been built against it here; but this rough surface is only half as wide as the projecting stones above. Up to these stones, then, the wall had only half the thickness which it had above. It is by no means improbable that, as Julius suggests, this division consisted of little or nothing more than a row of columns with an architrave, in which case there would merely have been an anta set up against the wall where the roughness is. This appears all the more probable from the nature of the roughening of the stones. They do not seem to have projected so as to form part of a cross-wall, except those of the eleventh and fourteenth courses, but are merely roughened on the surface.

FIG. 1.

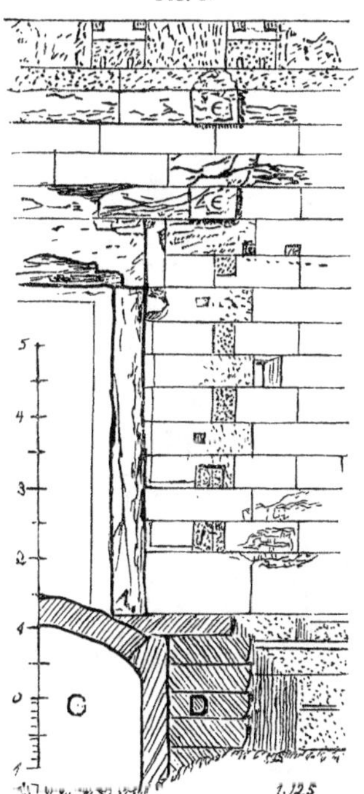

The western wall of the Erechtheion was not solid in its upper portion, but had four openings in it, — one between each pair of engaged columns, and one between the southern column and the anta which adjoined the southern portico. This last opening is shown to have existed by the finish of the anta. The first three courses of stone above the line of the bases of the engaged columns have dressed joints, showing that a wall 0.29 m. thick was built against them; but above this point there is no trace of any wall. This agrees with the inscription (Ἀθήναιον, VII. p. 482), *διαφάρξαντι τὰ μετακιόνια τέτταρα ὄντα τὰ πρὸς τοῦ Πανδροσείου.* In the drawings of Stuart and Inwood this space is left open, and it seems never to have been built up. The purpose of this opening may have been to admit light to the singular niche in the southern wall close to the corner anta. This niche is 1.72 m. long and 0.36 m. deep, and reaches from the line of the top of the western wall to the top of the building; *i.e.*, it is about 3.40 m. high. (See Fig. 2.) The stones which form its back are not smoothed, but are finished as if for the reception of a coating of stucco. The large stone just below the niche is roughly hewn off, and seems to have projected to form a platform, upon which a statue may have stood. There is no reason to suppose that there was any room or flooring in front of this niche beyond the projecting shelf just mentioned. As Borrmann suggests (*Mitth. d. deutsch. Inst.*, 1881, p. 387), the opening between the southern column of the western wall and the corner anta is in painful disagreement with the windows between the columns, which are represented by Stuart and others, and leads us to doubt whether these windows, as seen by Stuart, were part of the original plan of the building. This doubt is strengthened by the fact that the window casings were almost too large for the space between the columns, inasmuch as they seem to have projected so far as to hide part of the fluting. Moreover, where the window cases were fitted in, the columns are hewn away more roughly than elsewhere. It is, on the whole, probable that all four openings in the western wall were originally alike, and that the windows were inserted at some subsequent period.

Fig. 2.

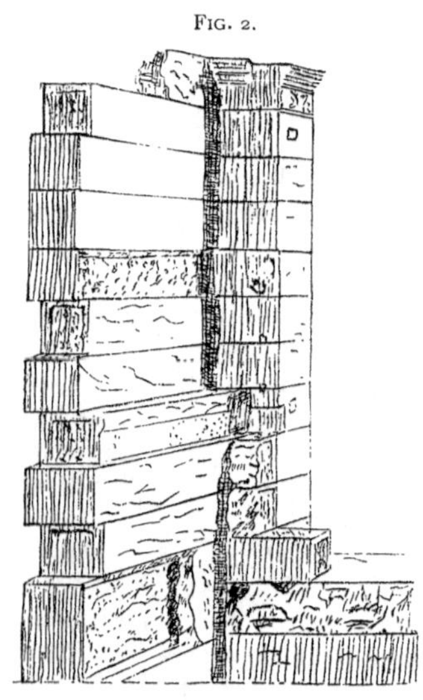

South-west anta and niche. After Borrmann.

In the western wall, in the corner where the temple meets the terrace wall which runs under the porch of the Κόραι, is a large break in the wall, now filled with rough modern masonry. A break at this point was part of the original design, as is shown by the fact that the whole length of the modern masonry is spanned by one gigantic stone (Plate II., *t*), which extends the same distance north and south of the break. This great stone was intended to hold up the superincumbent weight of the anta; but this would not have been necessary if the place now filled with the rubble masonry had been originally part of the solid wall. If, as has been maintained by Murray (*Journal of Hellenic Studies*, I. 224), Borrmann, and others, the present rubble work marks the place where a broad flight of steps joined the building, the large lintel-like stone was quite unnecessary, for the stairs, with their foundations, would be built into the wall as solidly as any other stones, and would serve like other stones to support the weight of the anta. Nor is there anything in the disposition of the stones of the terrace or those of the portico to show that a flight of steps existed here; though it does seem very probable that the terrace was continued at least one course of stone further to the north than it now is. On the other hand, if some building joined the Erechtheion at this point, it would be necessary to keep off the weight of the anta from the smaller building, and the great stone (Plate II., *t*) would then be of use. What the shape of this building may have been, whether it was a long stoa, as suggested by Fergusson, or merely a small edifice which occupied the corner, it is impossible to tell, as no foundations have been found. It is very desirable that this corner be thoroughly and carefully excavated. On the western end of the porch of the Κόραι, the egg and dart moulding of the railing stops about half way between the two figures, and there is at this point the mark of a railing which met that of the porch from the west. The fine lines which adorn the bases of the engaged columns of the western wall and the course of stone immediately beneath them are not continued south of the north side of the southern column. The presumption is, therefore, that the comparatively unornamented space between these two points was not ordinarily visible. (See Plate II.) This is another argument for the existence of a building in this corner. The wall between these two points cannot well have been an interior wall, for it has all the main lines of the other parts of the external wall. Any building which stood in the corner would probably have been low, with a railing around its roof which hid the western wall of the Erechtheion at least to the height of the railing of the porch of the Κόραι. The platform formed by this roof with its railing would naturally be accessible from the interior of the small building. The south-west corner of the Erechtheion is called in the inscription (*C. I. G.* 160, *C. I. A.*, I. 322, § 2) ἡ γωνία ἡ πρὸς τοῦ Κεκροπίου, *the corner by the Kekropion*. We may then safely affirm that the low building in the corner was the Kekropion.

From the great pier which terminates the northern wall of the Erechtheion at the south-west corner of the north porch (Pl. I., E), a wall ran toward the west or south-west, which probably turned toward the south, and met the southern terrace at some distance west of the Erechtheion. The enclosure thus formed was entered from the north through the small door S, which leads from the porch through the northern wall just outside of the western wall. The lower part of the pier which terminates the northern wall is not finished in a line parallel to the length of the building, but slants toward the terrace, and it is clearly to be seen that a double wall met the building here (Pl. II., *h* and *h'*). Fergusson thinks that this enclosed a covered passage, being led to this opinion by the flat stone which covers the small door by the pier. But as nothing positive is known of any buildings in this direction, and as a covered passage can be accounted for only by supposing it to lead to some building, the assumption involves us in too many complicated hypotheses. We can confidently assert only the existence of a wall at this place; and the small door leading from this great porch justifies us in assuming that this wall belonged to an enclosure or τέμενος, to which the door formed the entrance.

In the second step of the stereobate, under the great pier just mentioned, and in a stone now lying near it, are the remains of an ancient drain discovered by Bötticher in 1862, the purpose of which has always been more or less enigmatical. The direction of the drain is from the corner by the porch of the Κόραι. This corner was, as we have seen, probably occupied by a building, the water from the roof of which must have run off into the enclosed court-yard west of the Erechtheion. The drain was probably intended merely to carry off this rain-water.

The porch of the Κόραι K communicated with the interior of the temple by a door (Plates I. and III., *a*) and a flight of steps, part of which still remains; but there appears to have been at least no public passage-way from the porch to the outside. At the north-east corner of the porch, where it joins the building, is an opening in the wall or railing of the porch, about 1 m. in width. This opening has evidently existed from the beginning, for the curve in the base of the anta and also that of the railing are continued around the corner, showing that the opening was never built up. The evidently ancient character of this opening has led Michaelis and Julius to assume an entrance at this point, and to base their arguments in no small degree upon its existence. If, however, any such entrance existed, it must have been a strictly private one for the priests and other functionaries; for on the stone which forms the threshold of this supposed entrance (the upper stone of the foundation) the ornamentation is continued across the opening. Now this elaborate ornamentation, which consists not only of curved but also of sharply-cut edges, would be exposed to injury from the feet of every one who passed over it. In fact, the ornamented edge has suffered very severely at this point where sight-seers now scramble over it, while other parts are much better preserved. Moreover, in order to use this opening as an entrance, it is necessary to mount a step 0.50 m. in height, that is, fully twice as high as any other step in the building. These arguments against the existence of a public entrance at this point have been advanced by A. S. Murray (*Journal of Hellenic Studies*, I. 224), and they seem to me conclusive.

It remains to speak of the crypt *n* under the northern porch F. (Plate I., 2.) This is a small apartment entered from the interior of the building through a small door in the stone foundations of the north wall. (Plates I. and IV., X.) In its north-west corner is a small round cistern *c*. This Beulé dug out, and found to be not very deep: it is now again choked up. The eastern opening into the square magazine is roughly broken through the foundations of the porch, and cannot be older than the magazine, which is of modern construction; while the crypt and the entrance thereto from the interior of the building are evidently of the same date as the temple itself. In the rocky floor of the crypt are some irregular fissures in the rock, which have been supposed to be the marks shown in antiquity as those of Poseidon's trident.* Beulé (*Acropole d' Athènes*) is the chief supporter of this theory, and Bötticher (*Bericht*) is its chief opponent. It is difficult to believe that these irregular fissures could have been shown by the ancient guides as marks of a trident; on the other hand, the purpose of the little chamber under the porch has never been explained on any other theory. This may possibly have been the dwelling of the sacred serpent,† though there is really no sufficient reason for the supposition.

The Erechtheion, then, consisted of three apartments. The western one had a public entrance from the great northern porch, and small doors opening into the porch of the Κόραι and the enclosure on the west of the building. The eastern apartment was entered from the eastern portico. The middle room had no direct entrance from the outside; but it communicated with the eastern apartment by a door and a flight of steps, while probably it was separated from the narrower western apartment only by a row of columns supporting an entablature. Besides these three apartments, there was a small crypt under the north porch, which was entered from the middle apartment. Under the western apartment was a cistern. West of the building was an enclosure, entered by a door in the western wall and by another door leading from the north porch. In the south-east corner of this enclosure, adjoining the south-west corner of the Erechtheion, there appears to have been a low building, probably the Kekropion.

Such being the arrangement of the parts of the building, it remains to consider to what use its various parts were devoted, and what was the relative position of the several sanctuaries which it contained. For this purpose we must consult the inscriptions, and also the notices of ancient writers, especially of Pausanias.‡

Leaving Pausanias for the present, let us first examine our other authorities.

---

* Paus. I. 26, 5; Apollod. III. 14, 1, 2; Strabo, IX. p.396.

† Aristoph., *Lysistr.* 758; Herod. VIII. 41; Plut. *Themist.* 10.

‡ All the inscriptions, as well as the passages of ancient writers relating to the Erechtheion, are collected in the appendix and foot-notes of Jahn's work: *Pausaniae Descriptio Arcis Athenarum in usum Scholarum edidit Otto Jahn. Editio altera recognita ab Adolfo Michaelis, aucta cum aliis tabulis tum forma arcis ab J. A. Kaupert descripta. Bonnae: ap. A. Marcum*, 1880.

C. I. A., I. 322, lines 44, 45 : *τῶν κιόνων τῶν ἐπὶ τοῦ τοίχου τοῦ πρὸς τοῦ Πανδροσείου.* Again, *'Αθήναιον*, VII. p. 482, lines 32–33 : *διαφάρξαντι τὰ μετακιόνια τέτταρα ὄντα τὰ πρὸς τοῦ Πανδροσείου.* The wall *πρὸς τοῦ Πανδροσείου* was then a wall with columns upon it, and with four intercolumniations. Now this corresponds exactly with what we have seen to be the case with the western wall, for there were four engaged columns with open spaces between them, and also a fourth open space between the southern column and the anta at the southwest corner of the building. The western wall, then, was the wall *πρὸς τοῦ Πανδροσείου.*

Philochorus, frag. 146 (apud Dionys. Hal. *de Din.* 3) : *κύων εἰς τὸν τῆς Πολιάδος νεὼν εἰσελθοῦσα, καὶ δῦσα εἰς τὸ Πανδρόσειον, ἐπὶ τὸν βωμὸν ἀναβᾶσα τοῦ Ἑρκείου Διὸς τὸν ὑπὸ τῇ ἐλαίᾳ, κατέκειτο.* Also Apollodorus, III. § 14, 1, 2 : *μετὰ δὲ τοῦτον ἧκεν 'Αθηνᾶ καὶ ποιησαμένη τῆς καταλήψεως Κέκροπα μάρτυρα ἐφύτευσεν ἐλαίαν, ἣ νῦν ἐν τῷ Πανδροσείῳ δείκνυται.* The olive tree was then in the Pandroseion. Now, since the western wall was *πρὸς τοῦ Πανδροσείου*, the Pandroseion either must be just east of this wall, that is, it must be the narrow western hall of the temple, or it must be west of the wall,— that is, it must be the outer enclosure just west of the temple. The latter alternative seems from the first preferable. We should certainly expect to find the olive tree under the open sky. Moreover, the dog of Philochorus mounted upon the altar of Zeus Herkeios (*Zeus of the court*) which stood *under the olive tree.* The altar of Zeus Herkeios could hardly have been within any building. The Pandroseion was, then, the enclosure P west of the Erechtheion. (Pl. I.)

C. I. A., I. 322, lines 69–72 : *τοῦ τοίχου τοῦ ἐκτὸς* ἀκατάξεστα* [*γο*]*γγύλου λίθου τετραποδίας* ΠΙΙΙ · *τοῦ ἐν τῷ προστομιαί*[*ῳ*] *τετραποδίας* Δ[ΙΙ]. *Of the wall in the προστομιαῖον* (the inscription says) *twelve* (?) *tetrapodies were unpolished.* This wall, whatever view is taken of the preceding sentence of the inscription, must be an inside wall. Now a *προστομιαῖον* can be nothing but a place where *προστόμια* are the most prominent feature. The *προστομιαῖον* is *the place by the door* or *the place with the doors.* The most conspicuous and

---

* In the *C. I. A.* and elsewhere, *ἐκτός* is changed to *ἐντός*. In the *C. I. A.* and in Jahn's *Pausaniae Descriptio Arcis*, *τοῦ τοίχου τοῦ ἐ(ν)τὸς ἀκατάξεστα* is made a general heading, under which four items (two besides those quoted above) are included. The stone reads *ἐκτός*, and also Boeckh, *C. I. G.* 160.

beautiful door of the Erechtheion was that of the northern porch (R in Plates I. and IV.), which opened into the western hall. Of the three other doors, two opened from this same hall. This western hall, then, was probably the προστομιαῖον. This gives additional proof that the Pandroseion was the outer enclosure west of the temple; for if the space east of the wall πρὸς τοῦ πανδροσείου was known as the προστομιαῖον, the Pandroseion must lie on the west of the wall.

C. I. A., I. 322, col. 1, lines 83–87: ἐπὶ τῇ προστάσει τῇ πρὸς τῷ Κεκροπίῳ ἔδει τοὺς λίθους τοὺς ὀροφιαίους τοὺς ἐπὶ τῶν κορῶν ἐπεργάσασθαι ἄνωθεν, κ.τ.λ. *In the portico by the Kekropion, the roof stones over the Maidens needed finishing.* The porch of the Maidens was, then, πρὸς τῷ Κεκροπίῳ. This can hardly mean that the porch itself was the Kekropion, and held the tomb of Kekrops; but the Kekropion was probably, as we have seen, contiguous to this porch. We cannot suppose, with Michaelis and others, that the porch was merely a place for the stairway (a "Treppenhaus"), by which the western chamber was entered from the south; for, as we have seen, there can hardly have been a public entrance by this way. What was the purpose of the porch, I am, however, unable to determine.

C. I. A., I. 322, col. 1, lines 73–74: τῆς παραστάδος τετραποδίας I[II]. What is this παραστάς, of which "three tetrapodies were unpolished"? The word παραστάς cannot refer to a solid wall; nor can it here refer to any one of the porches, for they are all otherwise designated. One thing only remains: the row of columns which divided the western chamber from the central room was the παραστάς.

C. I. A., I. 322, col. 1, lines 75, 76 (the two lines following those last quoted): τοῦ πρὸς τὠγάλματος τετραποδίας [Δ]I, *In the wall by the statue, eleven tetrapodies* (*unpolished*). The only wall to which this can refer is the cross-wall half way between the παραστάς and the east end of the building. By that wall, then, stood the ancient heaven-descended statue of Athena.* Now, as the statue, according to the universal Greek custom, must have faced the east, it must have stood in the eastern room, which was therefore the special sanctuary of Athena. The rest of the building appears to have been used mainly as a place for displaying ἀναθήματα, or votive offerings and relics.

---

* Paus., I. 26; Plutarch, *de Daedal. Plat.*, fr. 10: ξύλινον δὲ τὸ τῆς Πολιάδος, κ.τ.λ.; Apollod., III. 14, 6, 6: Ἐριχθόνιος . . . τὸ ἐν Ἀκροπόλει ξόανον τῆς Ἀθηνᾶς ἱδρύσατο.

C. I. A., I. 324*c*, col. 1, lines 34–36 : *ῥαβδώσεως τῶν κιόνων τῶν πρὸς ἕω, τῶν κατὰ τὸν βωμόν*. This is repeated in lines 63–65 ; and again in col. 2, 46–48, with the change of *κατά* to *παρά*. In each case follows an enumeration of special columns, the fluting of which was provided for. What altar now is this which is thus mentioned as "the altar" *par excellence?* The only altars mentioned by name in the inscriptions are the altar of the *θυηχοῦς* and the altar of Dione. The first cannot be the altar in question, for *C. I. A.*, I. 322, lines 77–80, reads *ἐν τῇ προστάσει τῇ πρὸς τοῦ θυρώματος· τὸν βωμὸν τοῦ θυηχοῦ ἄθετον*, *in the porch at the doorway the altar of the θυηχοῦς was not set up.* The porch at the doorway is of course the northern porch, from which the great door opens into the western chamber; consequently, the altar mentioned as *the altar*, near which stood "the columns towards the east," must have been distinct from this. The altar of Dione cannot have been "the altar"; for, whereas all the eastern columns are collectively called *κατὰ τὸν βωμόν* or *παρὰ τὸν βωμόν*, they are then counted separately as the first, second, etc., "from the altar of Dione." * If the altar of Dione were meant by the simple *βωμός*, these double references to it, thrice repeated, would be impossible. The altar mentioned under the simple appellation of *βωμός*, at which the eastern columns are said to stand, was probably the altar of *Ζεὺς Ὕπατος*, the Supreme Zeus, with which Pausanias begins his description of the Erechtheion. But before discussing Pausanias, it may be well to restate briefly the results which we have thus far reached.

The Erechtheion was divided by a cross-wall and by a difference of level into two unequal parts. The eastern part consisted of a single chamber, which contained the statue of Athena Polias. The western part was divided (probably only by a row of columns with an entablature) into two rooms, one of which was little more than an entrance hall (*προστομιαῖον*). Under this entry was a cistern. West of the building was the Pandroseion, in which was the sacred olive tree of Athena.

The description of Pausanias † agrees perfectly with this arrangement. It begins as follows : *Ἔστι δὲ καὶ οἴκημα Ἐρέχθειον καλούμενον·*

* See *C. I. A.*, I. 324: the words immediately following the three passages cited above from this inscription.

† See Paus., I. 26, 5—27, 2.

πρὸ δὲ τῆς ἐσόδου Διός ἐστι βωμὸς Ὑπάτου, ἔνθα ἔμψυχον θύουσιν οὐδὲν, πέμματα δὲ θέντες οὐδέν τι οἴνῳ χρήσασθαι νομίζουσιν. *Now there is also a building called the Erechtheion; and before the entrance is an altar* of Zeus Hypatos, at which they sacrifice nothing which has life, but offer cakes, making no use of wine.* Pausanias, if he saw things on the Acropolis in the order in which he describes them, approached the Erechtheion from the east. From the inscriptions we know that there was an altar, called "the altar," on the east of the Erechtheion. When now Pausanias says, "Before the entrance is an altar of Zeus Hypatos," what is more natural than to identify this with the βωμός of the inscriptions? Of course Pausanias might have entered the Erechtheion by the north porch, in which case the altar of Zeus Hypatos must be sought at that entrance; but in this supposition he must have passed the eastern entrance without noticing it, in order to reach the north porch, which is hardly probable. As there was no regular entrance by the porch of the Maidens, it is most natural to suppose that Pausanias entered the Erechtheion from the east.

Pausanias proceeds: Ἐσελθοῦσι δέ εἰσι βωμοὶ, Ποσειδῶνος, ἐφ' οὗ καὶ Ἐρεχθεῖ θύουσιν ἔκ του μαντεύματος, καὶ ἥρωος Βούτου, τρίτος δὲ Ἡφαίστου. γραφαὶ δὲ ἐπὶ τῶν τοίχων τοῦ γένους εἰσὶ τοῦ Βουταδῶν. *Upon entering, there are three altars; one of Poseidon, upon which they sacrifice also to Erechtheus, according to some oracle; one of the hero Butes; and one of Hephaestos. And there are upon the walls pictures of the family of the Butadae.* These three altars must have been near the eastern entrance, in the cella where stood the most sacred image of Athena. Pausanias nowhere mentions an altar of Athena. Were there then in the cella with the ancient statue altars of Poseidon, Butes, and Hephaestos, but none of Athena? This seems hardly possible. An altar of Athena must have been there, and it was probably quite as conspicuous as any of those mentioned. But an altar of Athena was a necessary part of the temple of Athena, the presence of which Pausanias quietly assumes without taking the trouble to mention it; whereas the presence of the other three altars

---

* This was probably the altar founded by Kekrops. See Paus., VIII. 2, 3: ὁ μὲν γὰρ (Κέκροψ) Δία τε ὠνόμασεν Ὕπατον πρῶτος, καὶ ὁπόσα ἔχει ψυχὴν τούτων μὲν ἠξίωσεν οὐδὲν θῦσαι, πέμματα δὲ ἐπιχώρια ἐπὶ τοῦ βωμοῦ καθήγισεν, κ.τ.λ. Eusebius, *Praep. Evang.*, X. 9, 22: πρῶτος δὲ Κέκροψ λέγεται Ζῆνα κεκληκέναι τὸν θεὸν, μὴ πρότερον οὕτω παρ' ἀνθρώποις ὠνομασμένον· ἔπειτα βωμὸν παρ' Ἀθηναίοις ἱδρῦσαι πρῶτος.

in the chamber of the goddess was something remarkable. The altar of Butes and the pictures of Butadae were, however, not out of place in the temple, for Butes and his descendants were Athena's priests quite as much as Poseidon's.* The official name of the temple, ὁ νεὼς ἐν ᾧ τὸ ἀρχαῖον ἄγαλμα (*C. I. A.*, I. 322, line 1), shows that the building was regarded as a temple of Athena, in which the other divinities were but guests. It is, therefore, not to be wondered at that no separate cella appears to have been set apart for Poseidon-Erechtheus, whose altar stood in the eastern chamber.

Having mentioned the altar of Poseidon, Pausanias proceeds to mention the other objects connected with that god before saying anything about Athena: Καὶ (διπλοῦν γάρ ἐστι τὸ οἴκημα) καὶ ὕδωρ ἐστὶν ἔνδον θαλάσσιον ἐν φρέατι (τοῦτο μὲν θαῦμα οὐ μέγα· καὶ γὰρ ὅσοι μεσόγαιαν οἰκοῦσιν ἄλλοις τε ἔστι καὶ Καρσὶν Ἀφροδισιεῦσιν· ἀλλὰ τόδε τὸ φρέαρ ἐς συγγραφὴν παρέχεται κυμάτων ἦχον ἐπὶ νότῳ πνεύσαντι) καὶ τριαίνης ἐστὶν ἐν τῇ πέτρᾳ σχῆμα. ταῦτα δὲ λέγεται Ποσειδῶνι μαρτύρια ἐς τὴν ἀμφισβήτησιν τῆς χώρας φανῆναι. *The building is double; and there is therein sea-water in a well. Now this is no great wonder, for the Karian Aphrodisians and others who inhabit the interior have the same. But the well in question is noted for giving forth a sound of waves when the south wind blows. There is also the mark of a trident in the rock. These are said to have appeared as signs for Poseidon when he was contending for the country.*

Pausanias does not mention the objects of interest in the Erechtheion in the order in which he saw them, that is, in a purely local order, but rather in the order in which they would naturally present themselves to the mind of one who knew their mythical relations. Immediately after mentioning the altars which he saw upon entering, he remarks that "the building is double," and then mentions the well of sea-water; this must mean that the altars were in one part of the double building and the well in the other. This agrees exactly with what has been said above concerning the cistern under the Prostomiaeon. The expression "the building is double" offers no difficulty. Although there are remains of two cross-walls, the western one was, as has been explained above, probably little more than a row of

---

* Apollod., III. 15, 1: Πανδίονος δὲ ἀποθανόντος οἱ παῖδες τὰ πατρῷα ἐμερίσαντο καὶ τὴν μὲν βασιλείαν Ἐρεχθεὺς λαμβάνει, τὴν δὲ ἱερωσύνην τῆς Ἀθηνᾶς καὶ τοῦ Ποσειδῶνος τοῦ Ἐρεχθέως Βούτης. Similar statements are found elsewhere.

columns with antae at the ends; whereas the division of the building at the eastern cross-wall was much more marked by the great difference in the level of the floor east and west of that wall. The marks of the trident may or may not be the fissures now seen in the small chamber under the northern porch. These fissures do not look much like trident marks, nor is their position with relation to the cistern consistent with the account of Pausanias. On the whole, it is not likely that they were ever exhibited as the marks of Poseidon's trident. The trident marks must have been somewhere near the cistern; but more than this we cannot determine.*

After mentioning the signs which bore witness to Poseidon's might, Pausanias turns his attention to Athena: Ἱερὰ μὲν τῆς Ἀθηνᾶς ἐστὶν ἥ τε ἄλλη πόλις καὶ ἡ πᾶσα ὁμοίως γῆ (καὶ γὰρ ὅσοις θεοὺς καθέστηκεν ἄλλους ἐν τοῖς δήμοις σέβειν, οὐδέν τι ἧσσον τὴν Ἀθηνᾶν ἄγουσιν ἐν τιμῇ), τὸ δὲ ἁγιώτατον ἐν κοινῷ πολλοῖς πρότερον νομισθὲν ἔτεσιν ἢ συνῆλθον ἀπὸ τῶν δήμων ἐστὶν Ἀθηνᾶς ἄγαλμα ἐν τῇ νῦν ἀκροπόλει, τότε δὲ ὀνομαζομένῃ πόλει· φήμη δὲ ἐς αὐτὸ ἔχει πεσεῖν ἐκ τοῦ οὐρανοῦ, καὶ τοῦτο μὲν οὐκ ὑπέξειμι, εἴτε οὕτως εἴτε ἄλλως ἔχει. *Now the rest of the city and the whole country likewise is sacred to Athena, for those whose custom it is to worship other deities in the demes hold Athena none the less in honor; but the most sacred statue, which was worshipped in common many years before the union of the demes was made, is the statue of Athena in what is now called the Acropolis but was then called the Polis; and the story goes that it fell from heaven. And this question I will not discuss, whether it be so or otherwise.*

Then follows the description of the lamp of Kallimachos: Λύχνον δὲ τῇ θεῷ χρυσοῦν Καλλίμαχος ἐποίησεν. ἐμπλήσαντες δὲ ἐλαίου τὸν λύχνον τὴν αὐτὴν τοῦ μέλλοντος ἔτους ἀναμένουσιν ἡμέραν· ἔλαιον δὲ ἐκεῖνο τὸν μεταξὺ ἐπαρκεῖ χρόνον τῷ λύχνῳ κατὰ τὰ αὐτὰ ἐν ἡμέρᾳ καὶ νυκτὶ φαίνοντι. καί οἱ λίνου Καρπασίου θρυαλλὶς ἔνεστιν, ὃ δὴ πυρὶ λίνων μόνον οὐκ ἔστιν ἁλώσιμον. φοῖνιξ δὲ ὑπὲρ τοῦ λύχνου χαλκοῦς ἀνήκων ἐς τὸ ὄροφον ἀνασπᾷ τὴν ἀτμίδα. *Kallimachos made a golden lamp for the Goddess. When they have filled this lamp with oil,*

* The author's statement here is perhaps somewhat too strong. The fissures, half choked with earth and rubbish as they are, do look very like what one might imagine the mark of a tremendous trident stroke to be. The presence of the door and passage leading to these fissures from the temple, in the absence of any other reasonable explanation, creates a strong presumption that the fissures were looked upon in antiquity as the trident stroke. — T. W. L.

they wait until the same day of the next year; and the oil lasts all the intervening time, though the lamp burns day and night alike. It has a wick of Karpasian flax, which is the only flax that is not destroyed by fire. And a bronze palm-tree over the lamp reaches to the roof and carries off the smoke. This lamp must have burnt before the sacred statue of Athena in the eastern cella.

Then follows the enumeration of the other objects of interest in the temple (I. 27, 1) : Κεῖται δὲ ἐν τῷ ναῷ τῆς Πολιάδος Ἑρμῆς ξύλου, Κέκροπος εἶναι λεγόμενον ἀνάθημα, ὑπὸ κλάδων μυρσίνης οὐ σύνοπτον. ἀναθήματα δὲ ὁπόσα ἄξια λόγου, τῶν μὲν ἀρχαίων δίφρος ὀκλαδίας ἐστὶ, Δαιδάλου ποίημα, λάφυρα δὲ ἀπὸ Μήδων Μασιστίου θώραξ, ὃς εἶχεν ἐν Πλαταιαῖς τὴν ἡγεμονίαν τῆς ἵππου, καὶ ἀκινάκης Μαρδονίου λεγόμενος εἶναι. *There stands in the temple of (Athena) Polias a Hermes of wood, said to be an offering of Kekrops, which is hidden from sight with myrtle boughs. And among the more ancient votive offerings worthy of note, is a folding arm-chair, the work of Daedalos; and with the spoils taken from the Persians are the breast-plate of Masistios, who commanded the cavalry at Plataea, and a short sword, said to be that of Mardonios.* We have no means of determining the position of any of these objects.

After mentioning these objects of interest within the temple, Pausanias goes on : Περὶ δὲ τῆς ἐλαίας οὐδὲν ἔχουσιν ἄλλο εἰπεῖν ἢ τῇ θεῷ μαρτύριον γενέσθαι τοῦτο ἐς τὸν ἀγῶνα τὸν ἐπὶ τῇ χώρᾳ. λέγουσι δὲ καὶ τάδε, κατακαυθῆναι μὲν τὴν ἐλαίαν ἡνίκα ὁ Μῆδος τὴν πόλιν ἐνέπρησεν Ἀθηναίοις, κατακαυθεῖσαν δὲ αὐθημερὸν ὅσον τε ἐπὶ δύο βλαστῆσαι πήχεις.* *But about the olive tree they have nothing to say but that it sprang up as a sign for the goddess in her struggle for the country. But they say also that the olive was burnt when the Persian set fire to the city of the Athenians, and that after being burnt down it sprang up the same day to a height of some two cubits.*

This olive tree stood, as we have already seen, in the Pandroseion. Pausanias says : Τῷ ναῷ δὲ τῆς Ἀθηνᾶς Πανδρόσου ναὸς συνεχής ἐστι· καὶ ἔστι Πάνδροσος ἐς τὴν παρακαταθήκην ἀναίτιος τῶν ἀδελφῶν μόνη. *Contiguous to the temple of Athena is the temple of Pandrosos. Now*

* Herod., VIII. 55 : ταύτην ὦν τὴν ἐλαίην ἅμα τῷ ἄλλῳ ἱρῷ κατέλαβε ἐμπρησθῆναι ὑπὸ τῶν βαρβάρων· δευτέρῃ δὲ ἡμέρῃ ἀπὸ τῆς ἐμπρήσιος Ἀθηναίων οἱ θύειν ὑπὸ βασιλέος κελευόμενοι ὡς ἀνέβησαν ἐς τὸ ἱρὸν, ὥρων βλαστὸν ἐκ τοῦ στελέχεος ὅσον τε πηχυαῖον ἀναδεδραμηκότα. Pausanias doubles the single cubit here mentioned by Herodotus.

Pandrosos is the only one of the sisters who was not false to her trust.

The Pandroseion was just west of the Erechtheion, which is here called the temple of Athena. The sacred statue of Athena stood in the eastern cella, to which the Pandroseion was not συνεχές; but the whole building now generally called the Erechtheion was a joint temple of Athena and Poseidon, or rather a temple of Athena in which Poseidon-Erechtheus had a share. The name by which the temple is mentioned in the inscription quoted above (*C. I. A.*, I. 322, line 1), *the temple in which is the ancient statue*, is enough to show that Athena was regarded as the chief divinity of the whole temple; so that the Pandroseion is very properly called "contiguous to the temple of Athena," although the special cella of Athena was at the other end of the building.

There is then nothing in the description of Pausanias which does not agree with the conclusions at which we have arrived from an examination of the ruins of the building and the study of the inscriptions.

The roof of the Erechtheion was undoubtedly framed of wood, as is proved by *C.I.A.*, I. 324*a*, col. 1, lines 35–37: πρίσταις . . . καλύμματα εἰς τὴν ὀροφήν, and by the subsequent mention of τέκτονες, *carpenters*, in connection with parts of the roof.

It is not my purpose to describe or discuss the beautiful ornamentation and architectural details of the Erechtheion. Suffice it to say that the work is everywhere characterized by extreme richness of design and delicacy of execution, and that the effect was doubtless much heightened by the free use of color and gilding. It is not probable that the pediments were filled with sculptures.* No mention of any such figures is found in the inscriptions, nor have any fragments of them been found among the ruins.

* The middle block of the pediment of the north porch, much broken, stands on the ground, against a mass of modern wall and rubbish, back outward, apex upward, immediately north of the porch. — T. W. L.

Plate I

Ground Plan of the Erechtheion.

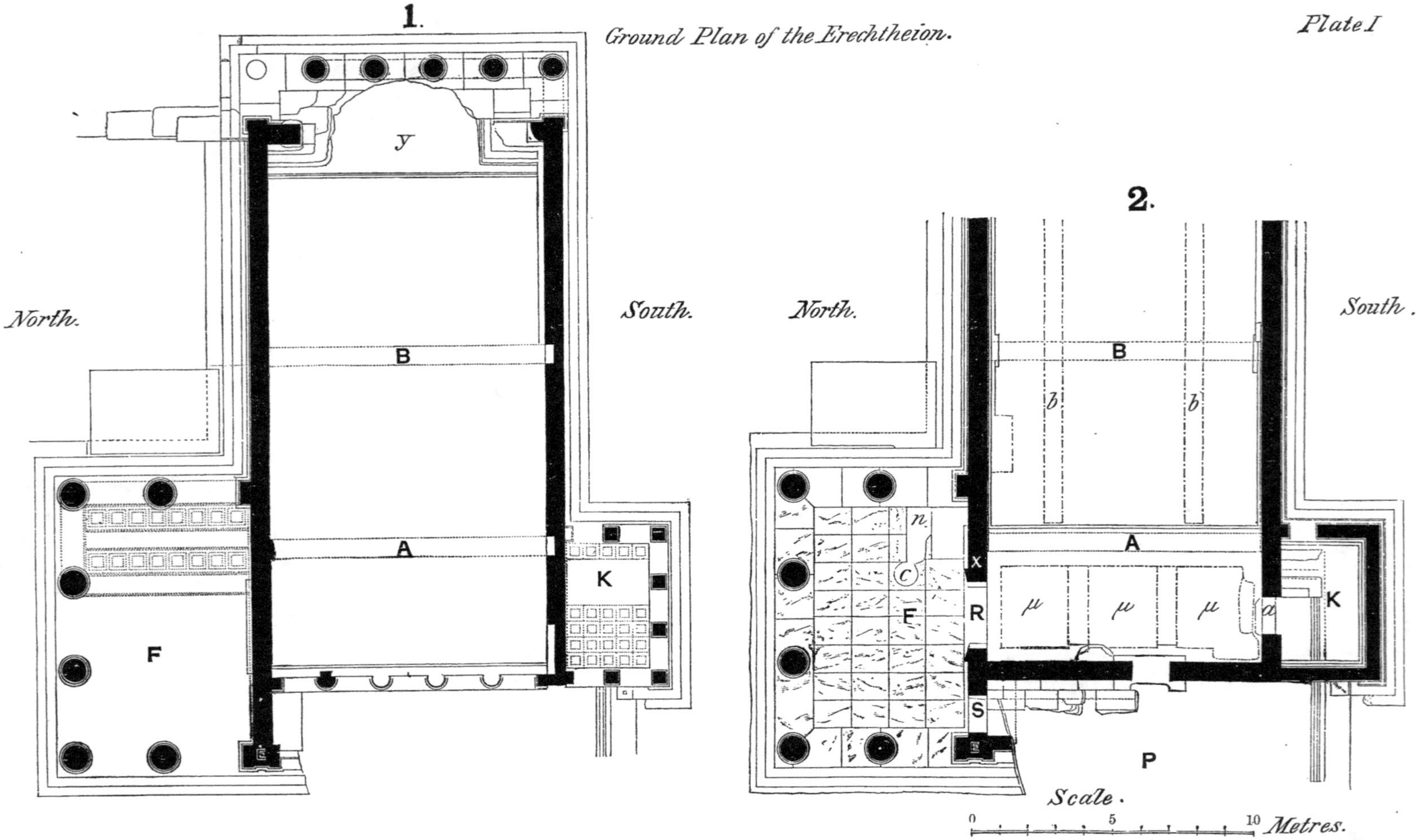

View of the Erechtheion from the West. Plate II.

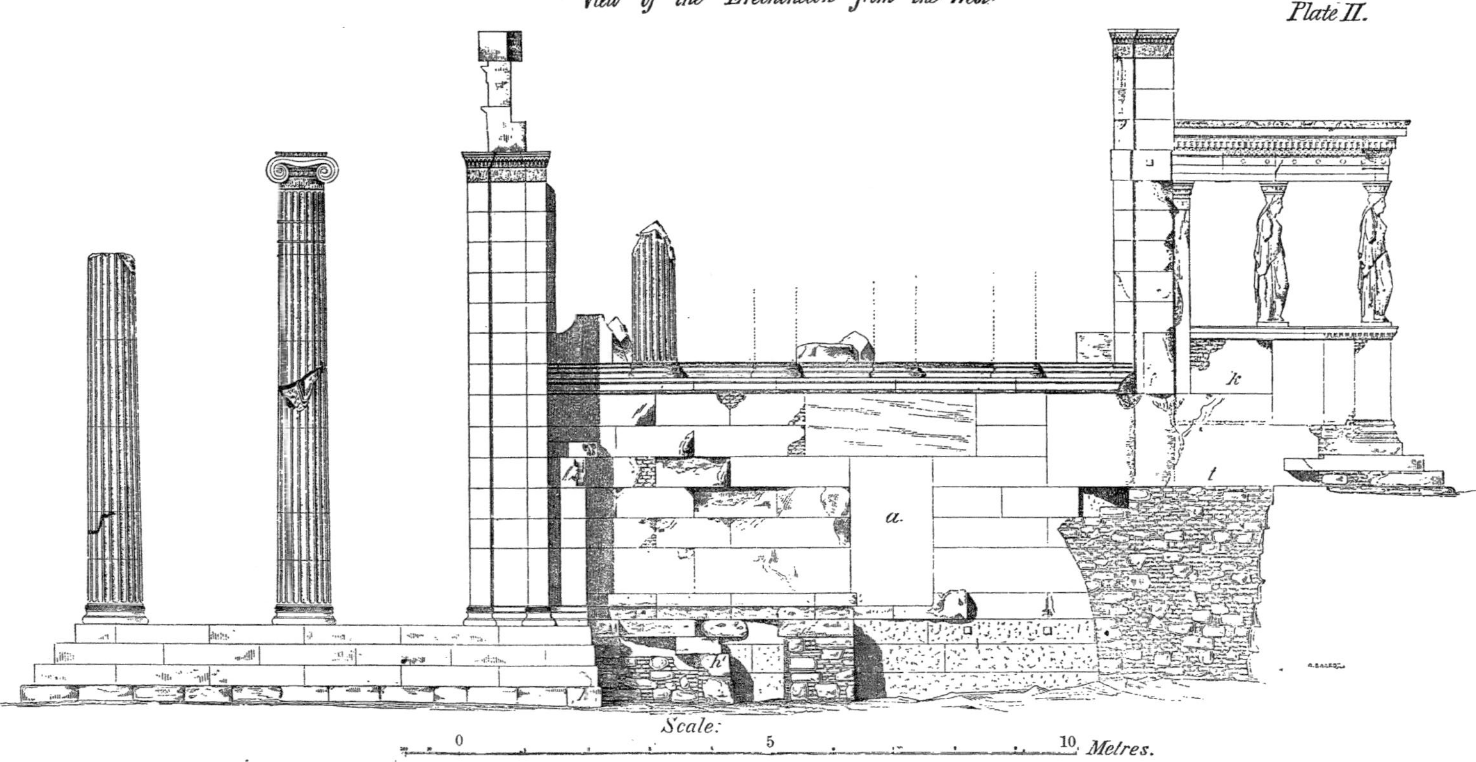

Plate III.

Inner Southern Wall of the Erechtheion.

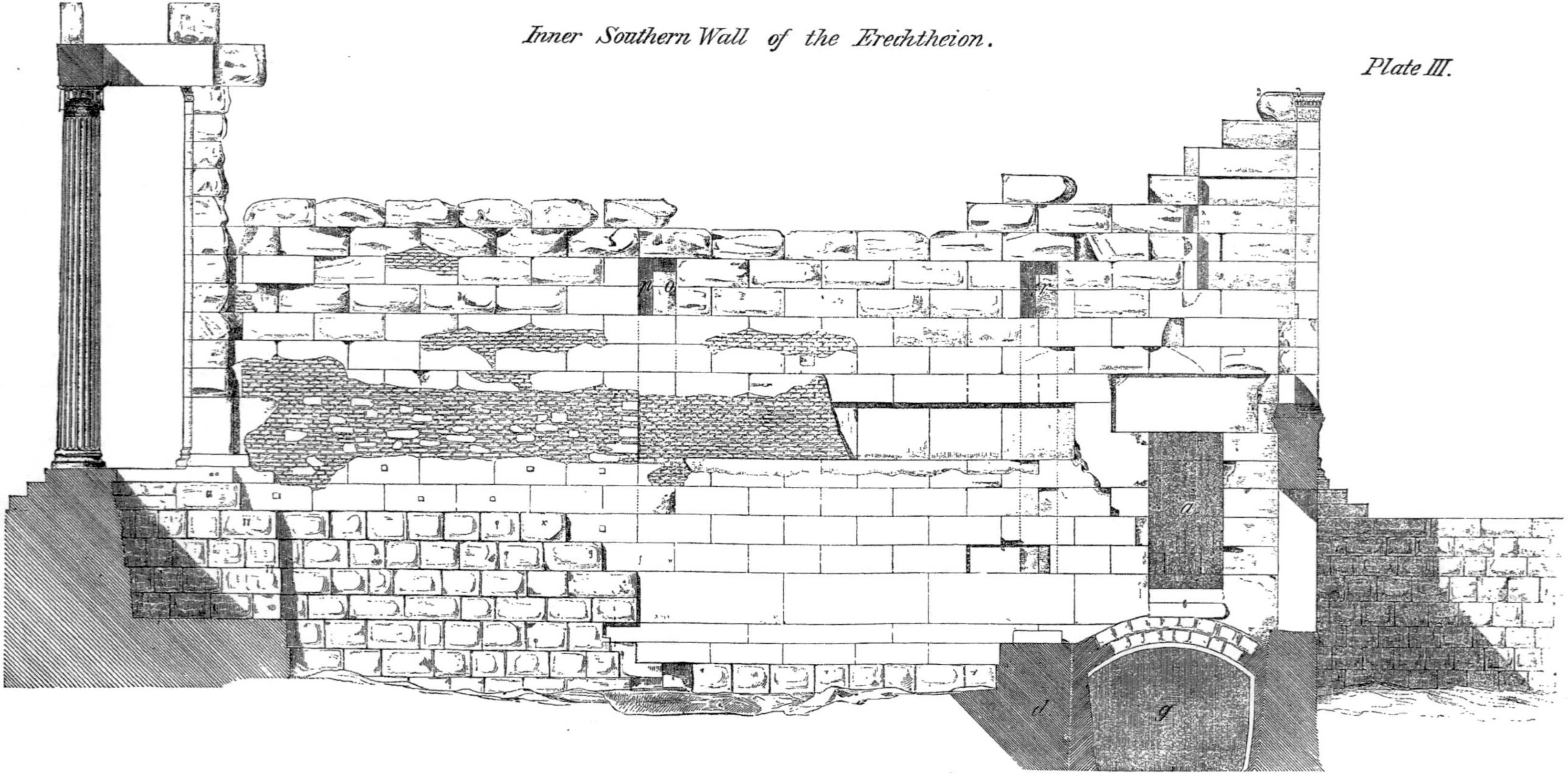

Plate IV.

Inner Northern Wall of the Erechtheion

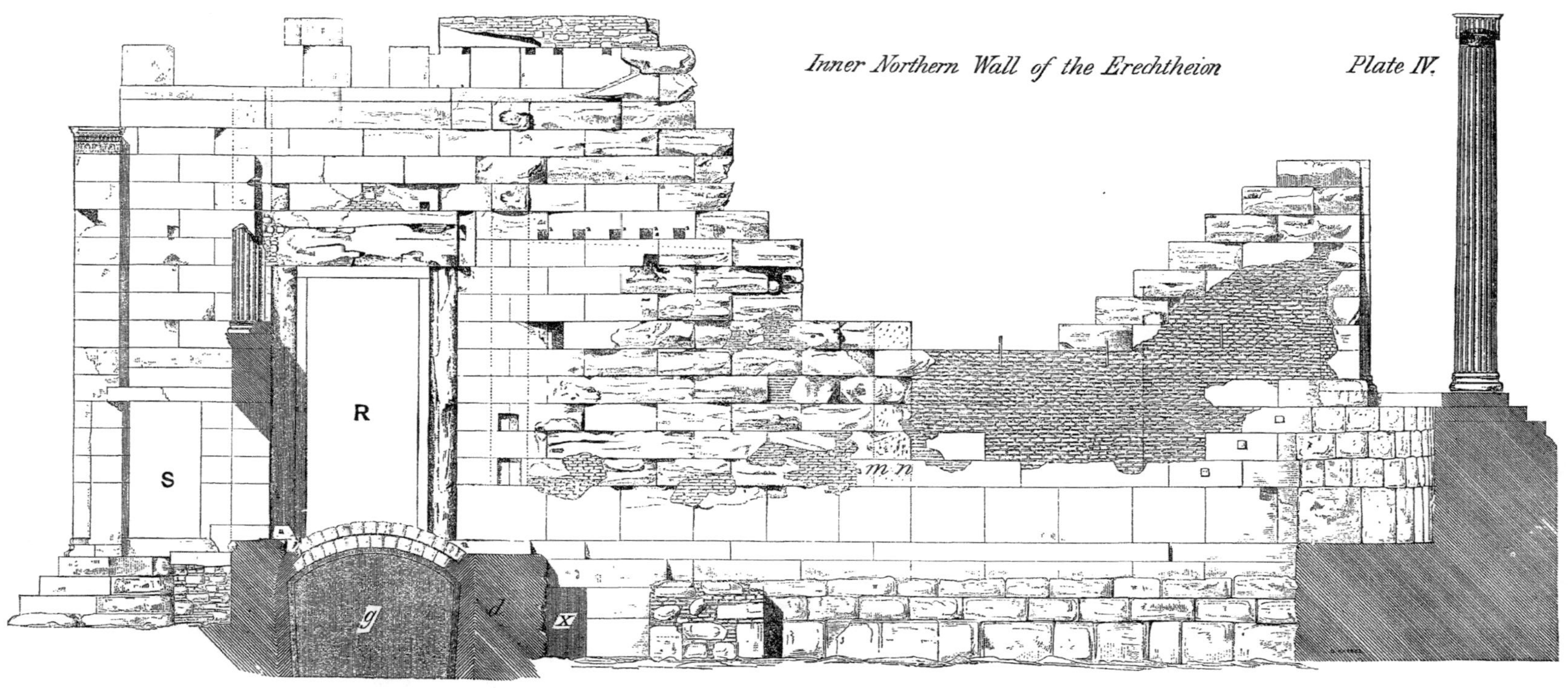

THE BATTLE OF SALAMIS.

BY

WILLIAM W. GOODWIN.

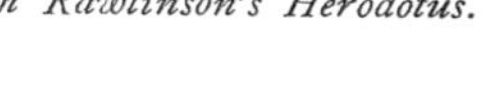

VIEW OF THE STRAITS AND BAY OF SALAMIS, FROM MOUNT AEGALEOS.

From Rawlinson's Herodotus.

SOUTH.

Coast of Attica. [Join.]

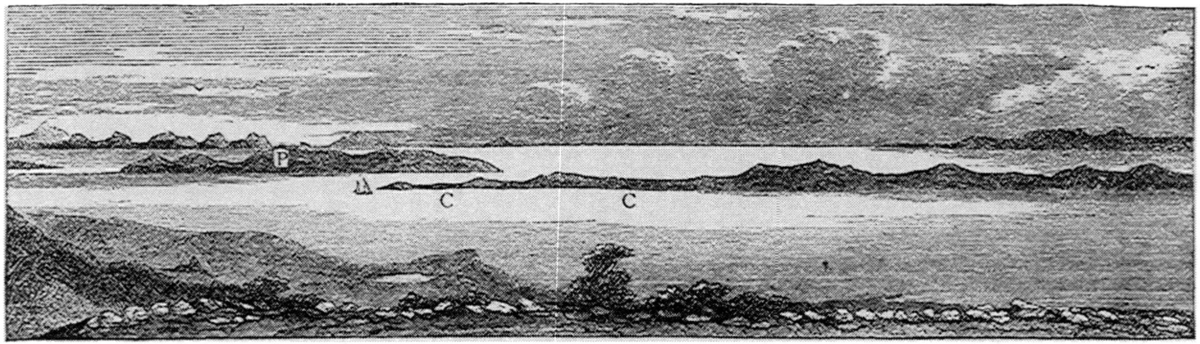

P. *Island of Psyttaleia.* C . . . C. *Point of Salamis* (*Cynosoura*).

WEST.

[Join.] *Salamis.*

S . . . S. *Town of Salamis.* G. *Island of St. George.* sh. *Shoal.*

THE BATTLE OF SALAMIS.

In this paper on the Battle of Salamis I propose to discuss chiefly questions which relate to the positions and movements of the two hostile fleets before the battle and during its progress, with other topographical matters, leaving untouched many interesting historical points which are not directly connected with the topography. During the autumn of 1882 and the spring of 1883 I made frequent excursions to Salamis and to the Attic shores opposite the island, and thus had the advantage of reading the ancient accounts of the battle and considering the various modern theories of the positions and movements of the two fleets amid the scenes of the contest.[1] The view of land and water which these memorable scenes present to-day is essentially the same as that upon which Xerxes looked when he took his seat on Mt. Aegaleos on that eventful September morning in 480 B.C. which decided the fate of Hellas. The barren island of Psyttaleia, one of the central points in the combat; the

[1] Many of the views expressed in this paper upon the possibility of reconciling the accounts of Aeschylus and Herodotus were the result of an earlier visit to Athens, and were published in brief notes on Herod. VIII. 76 and 85 in my Greek Reader in 1871 (pp. 141–143). Since the paper was read in Athens, I have revised it in the light of several articles on the subject to which I did not have access when it was first written, especially the following: Loeschke, *Ephorus-studien*, I., *die Schlacht bei Salamis*, in *Jahrb. d. Phil.*, 1877, pp. 25 ff.; Busolt (reply to the last), in *Rhein. Mus.*, 1883, pp. 627 ff.; Sihler, *The Battle of Salamis*, in *Trans. of Am. Phil. Assoc.*, 1877, pp. 109 ff.; Lolling, *Meerenge v. Salamis*, in *Hist. u. Phil. Aufsätze, Festgabe an E. Curtius*, 1884. The article of Loeschke is specially valuable in presenting the view of Aeschylus as the only one to be accepted; but he seems to me to be in error in ascribing to Herodotus (unless his text is changed) a view absolutely irreconcilable with this. He places the Greek line outside of the straits, facing south, running westward from the so-called *Thieves' Harbor* (Φωρῶν Λιμήν), marked Φ on the map, near which he places the Heracleum. Dr. Sihler's object is chiefly literary, and he agrees with most scholars in taking for granted the chief point which I have disputed, the arrangement of the Persian fleet opposite the town of Salamis before the battle.

rough Silenian rocks, at the end of the long sharp point of Salamis, where "Artembares, leader of ten-thousand horse"[1] found his grave; the hill on which the town of Salamis stood, in its commanding position, boldly projecting into the bay; the rocky and inhospitable coast of the mainland of Attica, with its steep height of Aegaleos rising opposite the town; the bright clear waters of the straits of Salamis, still as ready as of old to change from a glassy calm to a lively swell in the morning sea-breeze;[2] — all these are still familiar sights to every one who sails or rows from the Piraeus over to the bay of Salamis.

In most histories of Greece and in most commentaries on Herodotus an account of the battle of Salamis is given, chiefly or wholly on the supposed authority of Herodotus, which seems to me to neglect or to contradict some of the most obvious facts of the topography, as well as the best testimony of the ancients. Nearly all modern writers represent the Greek fleet at the beginning of the battle as drawn up in a curved line around the great bay of Salamis, sometimes outside the hill on which the town stood and the high island of St. George north of the town, sometimes with the line broken by one or both of these formidable obstructions; while the Persian fleet is arranged (often in three lines) directly opposite the Greeks, extending from the entrance of the gulf of Eleusis almost to the Piraeus. Indeed, it is generally assumed that the principal movement by which the Persians endeavored to cut off the escape of the Greeks, after the message of Themistocles to Xerxes, consisted in bringing a large part of their fleet into this position. It is said that, under cover of the night and without the knowledge of the Greeks, they rowed several hundred ships quietly through the narrow passages between the Attic coast and the two opposite points of Psyttaleia and Salamis, and formed their line from the neighborhood of the Piraeus along the main land through the straits of Salamis, until their northern wing was pushed beyond Aegaleos so as to close the passage from the straits into the gulf of Eleusis.[3] If this move-

---

1 Aesch. *Pers.* 302. 2 Plut. *Them.* 14.

3 Grote, V. p. 172, says: During the night, a portion of the Persian fleet, sailing from Peiraeus northward along the western coast of Attica, closed round to the north of the town and harbour of Salamis, so as to shut up the northern issue from the strait on the side of Eleusis. Curtius, *Griech. Gesch.* II. p. 69, makes

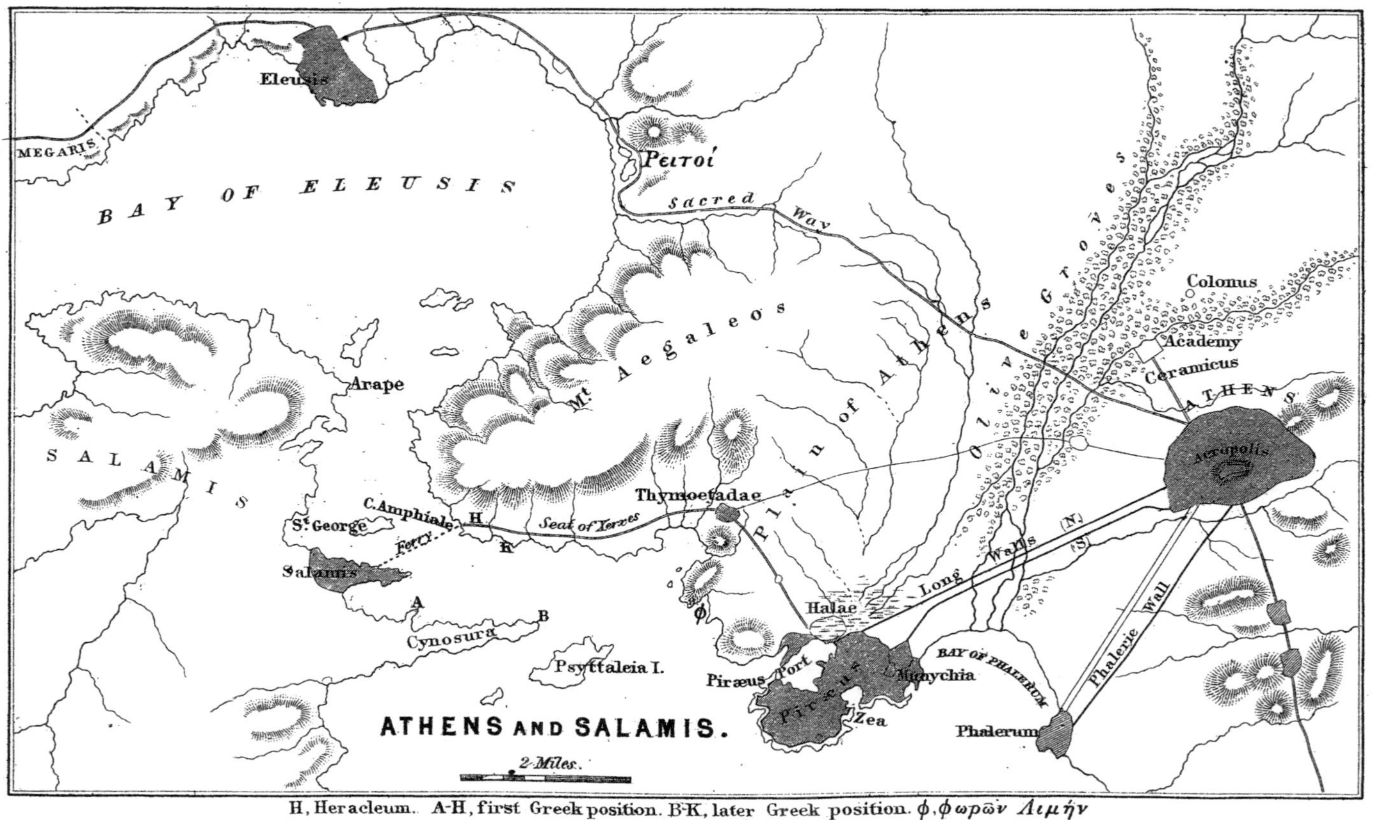

ATHENS AND SALAMIS.

H, Heracleum. A-H, first Greek position. B-K, later Greek position. φ, φωρῶν Λιμήν

ment, which is commonly supposed to be an essential feature in the account of Herodotus, is once admitted, the plan of the next day's battle becomes very simple. The Greeks, who had spent the night on shore at Salamis, would have embarked on their ships soon after daybreak and formed their line in the bay of Salamis directly in the face of the enemy; so that little would remain but for each of the fleets to advance a few hundred yards and engage the opposite enemy. According to this plan, Xerxes must have intended that his long left wing should take no active part in the battle, and that the Persian nobles shut up on Psyttaleia should remain idle spectators of a distant conflict. As this night-movement is believed to be the decisive stroke upon the success of which Xerxes risked his whole plan of attack, it becomes the fundamental question, to be settled at the outset, whether it really took place, — whether, in short, the Persian fleet entered the straits of Salamis at all before the morning of the battle. Several objections to the supposed movement at once suggest themselves.

1. The straits and bay of Salamis are very narrow at some points. The passage between the shore of Attica and Psyttaleia is less than 4000 feet wide. The foot of Aegaleos is hardly 4500 feet from the point of Salamis, and hardly 3500 feet from the island of St. George in the bay north of the town. Moreover, this last passage is broken by a large shoal,[1] which must have been not only very dangerous in night navigation, but also a serious obstruction to naval movements, practically reducing the width of the channel here to about 1800 feet. Can we now believe that the Greek fleet was allowed to form quietly in line of battle in the two passages last mentioned, in the very face of the Persian fleet only a few hundred yards distant? It is worth remembering here that our eye-witness, Aeschylus, implies that it was only after the Greeks had rowed forward from their first

---

the Persian fleet enter the straits on the morning of the day before the battle: Als es tagte, sah man auch schon von Phaleros her die feindliche Flotte heranrudern, um sich am eleusinischen Strande den Griechen gegenüber zu lagern. See also Cox's *Hist. of Greece*, I. 534, and especially the opposite map, with the supposed positions of the two fleets marked.

[1] This rocky shoal can hardly have been formed in recent times. Dr. H. Lolling, *Die Meerenge von Salamis*, p. 7 (in *Hist. u. Phil. Aufsätze, Festgabe an E. Curtius*, 1884), recognizes the smaller of the Pharmacussae islands in this "Klippe," and the larger in the adjacent island of St. George.

position that they were fairly seen by the Persians.[1] Themistocles, we are informed, harangued the Greek crews on the shore of Salamis after day-break, when (on the common theory) the enemy's fleet must have been in plain sight just across the bay. After this the Greeks embarked;[2] then, after waiting for the arrival of the Aeginetan trireme sent the day before to summon the Aeacidae from Aegina to their aid,[3] or (as Plutarch relates) for the morning sea-breeze to blow,[4] they began their advance. Is it likely that the Persians, who if they were within the straits were there eager to capture the Greek fleet, which they believed to be anxious to elude them by flight, would have lost this opportunity to anticipate the Spartan tactics at Aegospotami[5] by seizing the Greek ships while the crews were getting ready to embark, or would have failed at least to attack them before the line of battle could be formed?

2. It is agreed on all hands that the Persian movement, whatever it was, by which the Greeks were actually surrounded and their escape was cut off was executed by night so secretly and silently that none of the Greeks at Salamis (except, of course, Themistocles) even suspected it until they heard of its accomplishment from Aristides and afterwards from the crew of a Tenian ship which had deserted from the Persians.[6] Is it possible now to conceive of such carelessness on the part of the Greeks at this momentous crisis, that the long line of Persian ships, which is commonly believed to have faced them in the morning, could have passed directly by their camp at Salamis and within hearing distance of the town without attracting the least attention? And although we cannot trust Plutarch's statement that the battle was fought at the time of full moon, on the sixteenth of Munychion,[7] especially in the face of the more probable date also given by Plutarch, "about the twentieth" of Boëdromion[8] (about our twen-

---

[1] Aesch. *Pers.* 398: θοῶς δὲ πάντες ἦσαν ἐκφανεῖς ἰδεῖν. This point is strongly emphasized by Loeschke, *Jahrb. d. Phil.*, 1877, pp. 29, 30.

[2] Herod. VIII. 83: παραινέσας δὲ τούτων τὰ κρέσσω αἱρέεσθαι καὶ καταπλέξας τὴν ῥῆσιν, ἐσβαίνειν ἐκέλευε ἐς τὰς νεῦς. καὶ οὗτοι μὲν δὴ ἐσέβαινον, καὶ ἧκε ἡ ἀπ᾽ Αἰγίνης τριήρης ἡ κατὰ τοὺς Αἰακίδας ἀπεδήμησε.

[3] See last note, and Herod. VIII. 64.

[4] Plut. *Them.* 14.

[5] Xen. *Hellen.* I. 2, 27; Grote, VIII. p. 296.

[6] See Herod. VIII. 79–82; Plut. *Them.* 12, *Arist.* 8.

[7] Plut. *de Glor. Athen.* 7: τὴν δὲ ἕκτην ἐπὶ δέκα τοῦ Μουνυχιῶνος Ἀρτέμιδι καθιέρωσαν, ἐν ᾗ τοῖς Ἕλλησι περὶ Σαλαμῖνα νικῶσιν ἐπέλαμψεν ἡ θεὸς πανσέληνος.

[8] Plut. *Camill.* 19: ἐν δὲ Σαλαμῖνι περὶ τὰς εἰκάδας (ἐνίκων). On this whole question see Boeckh, *Mondcyclen der Hellenen*, pp. 73, 74.

tieth of September), still the tradition that a moonlight night preceded the battle is most likely to be authentic. As the Athenian calendar was based almost wholly on the moon's phases, the months being as nearly as possible exact lunar months, it is impossible that the nineteenth of the month should be long after the full moon; and the September moon, even six days after it is full, rises before ten P.M. A cloudy night at that season is hardly to be thought of. There is therefore every reason to believe that during the greater part of the night in question the straits of Salamis were illumined by moonlight, so that every movement along the Attic shore must have been visible from the opposite town. Aristides, it will be remembered, returning from exile at this critical moment, made the passage from Aegina to Salamis during this night with great danger, and immediately informed Themistocles that the Greeks were completely shut in by the enemy. Themistocles saw by this that his stratagem was successful, and he explained to Aristides that the Persian movement was made by his own advice. But he shows by his language (as Herodotus[1] reports it) that he had no information on the subject before the coming of Aristides: if, however, the chief Persian movement had been made within the bay of Salamis, it could never have escaped his vigilance. His first reply to Aristides, *τὰ γὰρ ἐγὼ ἐδεόμην γενέσθαι, αὐτὸς αὐτόπτης γενόμενος ἥκεις*,[2] shows plainly that the movements which Aristides had witnessed on the west and southwest of Salamis, out of sight of the Greek camp, were those which he was expecting. Aristides was then introduced to the council of the Greek commanders, to whom he told his story, saying that he had come over from Aegina and had with great difficulty eluded the blockading ships of the enemy, for the whole Greek encampment was encompassed by the ships of Xerxes.[3] Plutarch quotes Aristides as saying: "The sea about us *and behind us* is full of the enemy's ships";[4] and he himself relates that the Persian ships "sailed out by night, and surrounded and beset the straits on all sides and the islands, no one being aware of move-

---

[1] Herod. VIII. 80.

[2] *Ibid.*

[3] Herod. VIII. 81: *φάμενος ἐξ Αἰγίνης τε ἥκειν καὶ μόγις ἐκπλῶσαι λαθὼν τοὺς ἐπορμέοντας· περιέχεσθαι γὰρ πᾶν τὸ στρατόπεδον τὸ Ἑλληνικὸν ὑπὸ τῶν νεῶν τῶν Ξέρξεω.*

[4] Plut. *Arist.* 8: *τὸ γὰρ ἐν κύκλῳ καὶ κατόπιν ἤδη πέλαγος ἐμπέπλησται νεῶν πολεμίων.*

ment" (*i.e.* until Aristides came).[1] Is it credible that Aristides should thus dwell so strongly on the swarm of ships between Salamis and Aegina as his chief proof that the Greeks were wholly shut in, if a large Persian fleet had already pushed in between Salamis and the Attic coast and was actually lying less than a mile distant from the town? It seems to me that the expressions of Aristides, as well as those of Herodotus and Plutarch, plainly refer to a blockade of both outlets of the bay of Salamis, so that the escape of the Greeks was completely cut off on the north as well as on the south; and to the stationing of ships at other points around Salamis where escape might be attempted. They also refer to the landing of troops on Psyttaleia and perhaps on some smaller islands. But they cannot reasonably be made to imply anything like filling the straits of Salamis themselves with Persian ships.

3. Aeschylus, Herodotus, and Plutarch concur in the statement that Xerxes landed a body of Persians on Psyttaleia because he thought that this island would be a central point in the sea-fight.[2] This certainly implies that he expected to meet the Greek fleet at the southern outlet of the straits, by which he thought it would attempt to escape. If he had formed his plan to pen the whole Greek fleet into the bay of Salamis by stretching his own ships through the straits beyond Aegaleos, he must have expected that the battle would be fought within the bay; and nothing short of a successful breaking of his blockade by the Greeks could have made Psyttaleia the scene of a serious contest. Aeschylus and Herodotus[3] agree that the Persians on the island were to save Persians and slaughter Greeks who might be driven ashore there in the battle. Herodotus speaks of the probability of both men and wrecks being brought there, since the island lay directly in the line of the expected battle.[4] Plutarch says expressly that about Psyttaleia appears to have been the scene of the greatest struggle and the hardest fighting.[5] Does not all this show that Xerxes

---

[1] *Ibid.:* *αἱ βαρβαρικαὶ τριήρεις νύκτωρ ἀναχθεῖσαι καὶ περιβαλοῦσαι τόν τε πόρον ἐν κύκλῳ καὶ τὰς νήσους κατεῖχον, οὐδενὸς προειδότος τὴν κύκλωσιν ἧκεν ὁ Ἀριστείδης, κ.τ.λ.*

[2] Aesch. *Pers.* 441–464; Herod. VIII. 76, 95; Plut. *Arist.* 9.

[3] Aesch. *Pers.* 450–453; Herod. VIII. 76.

[4] *Ibid.:* *ἐν γὰρ δὴ πόρῳ τῆς ναυμαχίας τῆς μελλούσης ἔσεσθαι ἔκειτο ἡ νῆσος.*

[5] Plut. *Arist.* 9: *ὁ γὰρ πλεῖστος ὠθισμὸς τῶν νεῶν καὶ τῆς μάχης τὸ καρτερώτατον ἔοικε περὶ τὸν τόπον ἐκεῖνον γενέσθαι.*

had no idea of catching the Greeks in the bay as in a trap, and capturing them all together by a single move; but fully expected the chief conflict to be in the straits near Psyttaleia?

These considerations, I maintain, fully justify us in rejecting the idea that the Persian fleet passed the straits during the night before the battle, unless we find the most positive testimony in support of such a movement. Let us now see what the testimony is which has generally proved so convincing. It must be found in Herodotus alone, for those who adopt this view defend it on the ground that Herodotus is the highest authority for the history of the battle and must be followed in preference to others. The only passages of Herodotus from which this view could possibly be derived are these two: viii. 76, *ἀνῆγον μὲν τὸ ἀπ' ἑσπέρης κέρας κυκλούμενοι πρὸς τὴν Σαλαμῖνα*, and viii. 85, *κατὰ μὲν δὴ Ἀθηναίους ἐτετάχατο Φοίνικες (οὗτοι γὰρ εἶχον τὸ πρὸς Ἐλευσῖνός τε καὶ ἑσπέρης κέρας)· κατὰ δὲ Λακεδαιμονίους Ἴωνες (οὗτοι δ' εἶχον τὸ πρὸς τὴν ἠῶ τε καὶ τὸν Πειραιέα)*. As these passages, especially in their relation to each other, are confessedly obscure in meaning, we will postpone the consideration of them until we can discuss them in connection with others which describe the position of the two fleets in and before the battle, in order that we may then see whether they can be so interpreted as to agree with the view which on the whole seems most probable, or whether we must decide (as many have done) that Herodotus gives an account which is irreconcilable with that of our other authorities.

Besides Herodotus, who wrote his history about fifty years after the battle, our prose authorities are Plutarch and Diodorus Siculus, with scattered passages in other writers bearing on special points. Diodorus is understood here to be copying Ephorus, so that his testimony is really only about a century later than that of Herodotus. But in the poet Aeschylus we have an eye-witness of the battle, and probably an actual combatant. According to Ion of Chios (said to be a friend of the poet),[1] Pausanias,[2] and the Medi-

[1] Scholia on Aesch. *Pers.* 429: *Ἴων ἐν ταῖς Ἐπιδημίαις παρεῖναι Αἰσχύλον ἐν τοῖς Σαλαμινιακοῖς φησι.* Plutarch, *de Prof. in Virt.*, 8, reports a story of Aeschylus sitting with Ion at the Isthmian games, and *nudging* him as he made the remark, "The man who is hit keeps quiet, but the spectators cry out." Ion was at all events a younger contemporary of Aeschylus.

[2] Pausan. I. 14, 5: *Αἰσχύλος . . . δόξης ἐς τοσοῦτον ἥκων ἐπὶ ποιήσει καὶ πρὸ Ἀρτεμισίου καὶ ἐν Σαλαμῖνι ναυμαχήσας.*

cean Life of Aeschylus,[1] the poet actually fought on one of the Athenian ships at Salamis. In any case his testimony is unimpeachable; and although he is a poet, to whom it would be absurd to look for a detailed and accurate history of the battle, it is at least safe to say that nothing can be accepted as historic which *distinctly contradicts* any plain statement of Aeschylus regarding the contest. In 473–472 B.C., less than eight years after the battle, Aeschylus wrote his tragedy, *The Persians*, in which he puts a most graphic narrative of the fight of Salamis into the mouth of a Persian messenger, who bears the report of the great defeat to Atossa, the mother of Xerxes, at Susa. The account begins (*Pers.* 353) with the crafty message sent by Themistocles to Xerxes, through his servant Sicinnus, which tells the king that the Greeks are about to make their escape in the coming night from the bay of Salamis, where they have been lying since their return from Artemisium. The king at once gives orders to all the officers of his fleet to make two movements to shut up the Greeks within the bay, so that escape shall be impossible. When night shall come, they are first to "station a squadron of ships in three lines, to guard the exits and the rushing straits of the sea" (*i.e.* the southern outlet of the straits of Salamis), and secondly to station "others round about the island of Ajax."[2] He threatens that, if the Greeks escape this blockade and take to flight, all the commanders shall lose their heads. When night comes on, the movement proceeds, and the Persian ships are kept rowing about all night,[3] taking their positions and eagerly watching for the expected flight of the Greeks. The landing of a large force of the noblest Persians on Psyttaleia, though it is not mentioned here, is described in another place.[4] The poet, addressing an audience composed in great part

---

[1] *Vit. Aeschyl.* p. 2 (Dind.): γενναῖον δὲ αὐτόν φασι καὶ μετασχεῖν τῆς ἐν Μαραθῶνι μάχης σὺν τῷ ἀδελφῷ Κυνεγείρῳ, τῆς τε ἐν Σαλαμῖνι ναυμαχίας σὺν τῷ νεωτάτῳ τῶν ἀδελφῶν Ἀμεινίᾳ, καὶ τῆς ἐν Πλατειαῖς πεζομαχίας.

[2] *Pers.* 364–368:—

εὖτ' ἂν φλέγων ἀκτῖσιν ἥλιος χθόνα
λήξῃ, κνέφας δὲ τέμενος αἰθέρος λάβῃ,
τάξαι νεῶν στῖφος μὲν ἐν στοίχοις τρισὶν,
ἔκπλους φυλάσσειν καὶ πόρους ἁλιρρόθους·
ἄλλας δὲ κύκλῳ νῆσον Αἴαντος πέριξ.

[3] *Pers.* 382, 383:—

καὶ πάννυχοι δὴ διάπλοον καθίστασαν
ναῶν ἄνακτες πάντα ναυτικὸν λέων.

[4] *Pers.* 441–464.

of those who had witnessed the battle or had fought in it, does not mention the reason assigned by the historians for the failure of the Greeks to carry out their plan of retreat to the Isthmus, that Aristides and the Persian deserters informed them of the blockade; indeed he wisely omits all mention of the ignominious resolution of the previous day. Aeschylus next describes the disappointment of the Persians as the night advanced and no signs of flight appeared, and their consternation when at day-break they heard the solemn paean — the signal for battle — chanted by the Greeks in their fleet and loudly echoing from the hills of Salamis.[1] At the trumpet's sound the Greeks advanced to meet the enemy, who were evidently supposed by the poet to be just entering the straits, outside of which they had been posted during the night. As the Greeks rowed forward, "they all quickly appeared in full sight" to the Persians.[2] The right wing first advanced in good order, and soon the whole line was in motion. A loud cry burst forth from all the ships at once, "Children of the Greeks, advance; free your country; free your children, your wives, and the shrines of your fathers' Gods and the tombs of your sires. Now ye are to fight for your all." The conflict was soon begun by a Greek ship (elsewhere said to be that of Ameinias, the youngest brother of Aeschylus) attacking a Phoenician vessel and breaking off her prow;[3] and now "ship dashed against ship its brazen-pointed beak. At first the *stream* (ῥεῦμα) of the Persian host held out; but when a mass of ships were crowded *in the narrows* and they could give no help to one another," they dashed into their own vessels and crashed the banks of oars with their own beaks,[4] while the Greeks skilfully rushed upon them from every side. The Persian ships attempted to escape by flight; but their fleet was in

---

[1] *Pers.* 384–394. [2] *Pers.* 398. See note 1 on p. 242.

[3] *Pers.* 409–411. The mention of the Phoenician ship in vs. 410 shows that the Greek ship was an Athenian (Herod. VIII. 85). Ameinias is called a brother of Aeschylus by Diodorus, XI. 27, and in the Life of Aeschylus (see note 1 on p. 246). But Plutarch, *Them.* 14, calls him a Decelean; and Herodotus, VIII. 84, 93, calls him a Pallenian; whereas Aeschylus was an Eleusinian.

[4] *Pers.* 412–416: —

τὰ πρῶτα μὲν δὴ ῥεῦμα Περσικοῦ στρατοῦ
ἀντεῖχεν· ὡς δὲ πλῆθος ἐν στενῷ νεῶν
ἤθροιστ', ἀρωγὴ δ' οὔτις ἀλλήλοις παρῆν,
αὐτοὶ δ' ὑφ' αὑτῶν ἐμβόλοις χαλκοστόμοις
παίοντ' ἔθραυον πάντα κωπήρη στόλον.

utter disorder; "their hulls lay upturned; and the water was no longer to be seen, filled with wrecks of ships and slaughtered mortals. The shores and the rocks were full of the dead." The Greeks, it is said, speared the Persians in the sea with broken oars and pieces of wrecks, "as men spear tunnies." Night alone ended the slaughter.[1]

In this account there is nothing that looks like a line (or three lines) of Persian ships between Salamis and the shore of Attica. On the contrary, we have three lines of ships set by Xerxes to guard the exit of the straits of Salamis (ἔκπλους φυλάσσειν καὶ πόρους ἁλιρρόθους), which certainly is the same movement as that described by Herodotus in the words (viii. 76), κατεῖχον μέχρι Μουνυχίης πάντα τὸν πορθμὸν τῇσι νηυσί, *they held the whole passage* (evidently from the straits) *to Munychia with their ships.* The movement mentioned by Aeschylus in vs. 368, ἄλλας δὲ κύκλῳ νῆσον Αἴαντος πέριξ (sc. τάξαι), *and (set) others round about the island of Ajax,* must include what Diodorus describes as "sending out the Egyptian naval force with orders to block the passage between Salamis and the coast of Megara."[2] Plutarch, without mentioning the Egyptians, but evidently having this movement in mind, speaks of a blockading force of two hundred ships sent out by night.[3] Two hundred, according to Herodotus, was just the number of the Egyptian ships.[4] Whether Herodotus recognizes this precaution of Xerxes, is a question which may be postponed for the present. These ships sent to guard the northwest passage near Megara, as well as the force landed on Psyttaleia, were, as it proved, practically out of the battle; and the ships which met the Greek fleet as it set forth from the bay of Salamis in the morning were those which were stationed in the night at the southern entrance

---

[1] *Pers.* 417–428.

[2] Diod. XI. 17: εὐθὺς οὖν τὸ τῶν Αἰγυπτίων ναυτικὸν ἐξέπεμψε, προστάξας ἐμφράττειν τὸν μεταξὺ πόρον τῆς τε Σαλαμῖνος καὶ τῆς Μεγαρίδος χώρας.

[3] Plut. *Them.* 12: τὰς μὲν ἄλλας πληροῦν καθ' ἡσυχίαν, διακοσίαις δ' ἀναχθέντας ἤδη περιβαλέσθαι τὸν πόρον ἐν κύκλῳ πάντα καὶ διαζῶσαι τὰς νήσους, ὅπως ἐκφύγοι μηδεὶς τῶν πολεμίων. Cf. *Arist.* 8: περιβαλοῦσαι τόν τε πόρον ἐν κύκλῳ καὶ τὰς νήσους κατεῖχον. Plutarch with his usual carelessness seems to suppose that the blockade of both outlets of the straits and, indeed, of the whole island was effected by these two hundred ships. But he evidently understands that the main body of the fleet, which was to be manned at leisure, is to remain outside of the southern outlet until morning. He certainly places the battle in the narrows (see *Them.* 14).

[4] Herod. VII. 89.

of the straits. Diodorus states simply that Xerxes, after sending the Egyptians to block the Megarian channel, "sent the rest of his multitude of ships to Salamis, with orders to attack the enemy and settle the contest by a sea-fight."[1] But it is obvious from what follows that he places the Persian fleet, before its advance in the morning, outside of the straits; for he thus describes the movement made after Xerxes gave the order for an attack: "The Persians at first sailed on keeping their line, having plenty of room; but when they came into the narrows, they were forced to withdraw some ships from the line, and this caused great confusion.[2] The admiral led the line, and was the first to join battle; but he fell after a brilliant struggle. When his ship was sunk, the whole fleet of the barbarians fell into disorder." He then describes the Persians' attempts to retreat into the open sea, and the skilful attacks of the Athenians by which their ships were destroyed. This agrees perfectly with the account of Aeschylus, who speaks of the *stream* (ῥεῦμα) of the Persian ships entering the narrows and falling into confusion there. We may add here the testimony of Thucydides and Plutarch to the fact that the battle was fought *in the straits*. Thucydides makes the Athenian orator at Sparta speak of Themistocles as αἰτιώτατος ἐν τῷ στενῷ ναυμαχῆσαι, *chiefly responsible for fighting in the narrows*, which, it is added, did most of all to ensure the victory.[3] Plutarch gives Themistocles credit for great sagacity in beginning the battle just when the morning sea-breeze drove a swell into the narrows;[4] this swell would have caused no trouble to ships well inside of the long point of Salamis, but it did annoy the Persians greatly. All these accounts of the battle become sheer nonsense if we believe that the Persian fleet was arranged along the Attic shore within the straits before daybreak. On that supposition Aeschylus and Diodorus (*i.e.* Ephorus) do not give *another* account of the matter; they simply tell an impossible story.

Let us now examine the evidence on which it is so generally and so confidently asserted that this was the position of the Persians when the day opened. Thus far we have found substantial agreement

---

[1] Diod. XI. 17.

[2] Diod. XI. 18: οἱ δὲ Πέρσαι τὸ μὲν πρῶτον πλέοντες διετήρουν τὴν τάξιν, ἔχοντες πολλὴν εὐρυχωρίαν· ὡς δ' εἰς τὸ στενὸν ἦλθον, ἠναγκάζοντο τῶν νεῶν τινας ἀπὸ τῆς τάξεως ἀποσπᾶν, καὶ πολὺν ἐποίουν θόρυβον.

[3] Thucyd. I. 74.

[4] Plut. *Them.* 14.

among all our authorities, including Herodotus, upon the main point, the stationing of a large body of Persian ships *outside* the straits of Salamis during the night before the battle. According to Aeschylus and Diodorus (Ephorus) this was the only naval force with which the Greeks came in conflict; it has generally been thought, however, that Herodotus makes this of less importance, and represents the Greeks as fighting mainly with another body of ships, which was sent into the bay of Salamis during the night. If this is so, the evidence must be found in the two passages of Herodotus the consideration of which we postponed (p. 245). Remembering always that this interpretation must bring Herodotus and Aeschylus into irreconcilable opposition on a question of fact, in which Aeschylus is an eyewitness of unimpeachable authority, let us examine the passages of Herodotus (viii. 76 and 85), and see whether there is really any disagreement at all.

We first hear of the Persian fleet, after the battle of Artemisium, as sailing to Histiaea in Euboea, then passing through the Euripus, and at last assembling at Phalerum, at that time the only port of Athens.[1] Here Xerxes came down to the fleet from the ruins of Athens, which he had just destroyed, and held the council of war described by Herodotus.[2] The result of this conference was that Xerxes resolved to attack the Greek fleet, which was already lying in the bay of Salamis, without further delay. It was just at the time when Themistocles had persuaded the Spartan admiral to remain and risk a sea-fight at Salamis instead of sailing away with the remains of the Greek fleet to defend the Peloponnesus.[3] As soon as Xerxes had resolved to fight, the Persians brought up their ships from Phalerum towards Salamis and arranged them in order of battle, although it was too late to make an attack the same day.[4] This must be the movement which brought the Persians to the position which Herodotus supposes them to occupy when he speaks in chapter 76 of the further movements during the night by which the Greeks were shut in. The movement from Phalerum towards Salamis, he tells us, so terrified the Peloponnesian Greeks, that in a panic the earlier vote to fight at Salamis was reversed, and it was now voted to sail away to the

[1] Herod. VIII. 66. [2] Herod. VIII. 67–69. [3] Herod. VIII. 56–63.

[4] Herod. VIII. 70: ἀνῆγον τὰς νέας ἐπὶ τὴν Σαλαμῖνα καὶ παρεκρίθησαν διαταχθέντες κατ' ἡσυχίην.

Isthmus. It was at this time, apparently in the afternoon before the day of the battle, just after the sudden approach of the Persian fleet to Salamis, that Themistocles sent Sicinnus to Xerxes, warning him of the intended flight of the Greeks.[1] Xerxes immediately fell into the trap, and ordered the movements which Herodotus describes in somewhat obscure language in chapter 76. He first (as all agree) placed a strong force of Persians on Psyttaleia, to save Persians and destroy Greeks during the battle. Then, after midnight, Herodotus proceeds, the Persians "brought their west wing up to Salamis so as to encircle it" or "by a circuitous movement" (κυκλούμενοι).[2] This by itself would never have suggested a movement *into* the bay of Salamis. Its most obvious meaning is surely, that the ships which formed the west wing (τὸ ἀφ' ἑσπέρης κέρας) as the fleet lay before night-fall were now sent to blockade the island of Salamis, to cut off all escape for the Greeks in the direction of Aegina, and especially to guard the passage between Salamis and Megara, by which it was thought the Greeks might attempt to escape when they found the southern straits closed. It corresponds in fact to what Aeschylus describes (vs. 368) as stationing "other ships round about the island of Ajax," and to the sending of two hundred ships to the northwest of Salamis which is described by Diodorus. It was this force which made the night passage of Aristides from Aegina to Salamis so dangerous. It seems hardly possible that Herodotus should omit all mention of this important movement, which is clearly described by Aeschylus and Diodorus; and I submit that, unless the discussion of the other passage of Herodotus gives strong ground for a contrary opinion, this is the most rational and consistent explanation of the words in question. We have no knowledge of the position of the Persian fleet when this west wing was sent off, except that it was brought up from Phalerum to Salamis and arranged in order,[3] probably southeast of Salamis and south of the long point and of Psyttaleia. With this interpretation of the clause referring to the west wing, the following statement of Herodotus becomes plain and perfectly consistent with the accounts of Aeschylus and Diodorus. He says: ἀνῆγον δὲ οἱ ἀμφὶ τὴν Κέον τε καὶ τὴν Κυνόσουραν τεταγμένοι, κατεῖχον

[1] Herod. VIII. 74, 75.

[2] ἀνῆγον μὲν τὸ ἀπ' ἑσπέρης κέρας κυκλούμενοι πρὸς τὴν Σαλαμῖνα.

[3] Herod. VIII. 70 (see note 4 on page 250).

τε μέχρι Μουνυχίης πάντα τὸν πορθμὸν τῇσι νηυσί, *those stationed about Ceos and Cynosura sailed up, and held the whole passage with their ships as far as Munychia.*[1] This means that the greater part of the fleet, after the Egyptians had been sent round Salamis, blocked the straits with a squadron which extended to the mouth of the harbor of Piraeus. Next is mentioned the landing of Persian troops on Psyttaleia. Thus interpreted, the narrative of Herodotus in chapter 76 simply repeats in less plain language the account of the three Persian movements related by Aeschylus (vs. 366–368, and 447 ff.).

The other passage (viii. 85)[2] presents somewhat greater difficulties, though the language is plain. Herodotus is describing the Persian line as it was after the battle was begun. "Opposite the Athenians," he says, "were posted the Phoenicians, who held the west wing towards Eleusis; and opposite the Lacedaemonians were the Ionians, who held the east wing towards Piraeus." Here at last we find the evidence for the supposed Persian position east of Salamis. It is assumed that τὸ ἀφ' ἑσπέρης κέρας in chapter 76 and τὸ πρὸς Ἐλευσῖνός τε καὶ ἑσπέρης κέρας here must be the same body of ships; and it follows that the part of the fleet which the Persians brought up to Salamis κυκλούμενοι during the night must have formed a line extending through the

[1] The names Κέος and Κυνόσουρα are nowhere else applied to any places in the neighborhood of Salamis. But Κυνόσουρα, *dog's tail*, is a general name for any long point, and is no more to be confined to any one such *dog's tail* than our word *spit* to any one sharp point of sand. Here it must refer to the long eastern point of Salamis. Perhaps the oracle in Herod. VIII. 77,

ἀλλ' ὅταν Ἀρτέμιδος χρυσαόρου ἱερὸν ἀκτὴν
νηυσὶ γεφυρώσωσι καὶ εἰναλίην Κυνόσουραν,

which the historian thinks was fulfilled by *bridging* the space between Munychia, where there was a famous temple of Artemis, and the point of Salamis by the Persian ships, may have caused him to give the perfectly proper but little used name Κυνόσουρα to the point. Anyone who has ever looked back towards the Piraeus from the straits of Salamis will not wonder that Munychia is mentioned here by Herodotus. From this point the harbor of Piraeus and all the lower land of the peninsula almost disappear from view, and the high hill of Munychia remains a most conspicuous landmark.

Κέος, certainly not the well-known island Κέως, was probably also some place on Salamis, perhaps some part of the same long point, though (as Dr. Sihler points out) the repetition of τήν is opposed to the latter view. Lolling (*Meerenge v. Sal.*, p. 5) proposes Λέρον for Κέον, as the large island just northeast of Salamis is still called Λέρος. The Persians would thus be said to have their west wing stationed at Leros, and to bring it down into the bay of Salamis during the night.

[2] See the passage quoted, p. 245.

straits at least as far as the bay of Eleusis. Furthermore, Diodorus states that the Phoenicians were on the right Persian wing, and the Ionians on the left;[1] that the Athenians and Lacedaemonians were on the Greek left, opposite the Phoenicians, and the Aeginetans and Megarians on the right.[2] Diodorus is probably in error here about the position of the Lacedaemonians, who on account of their ἡγεμονία must have been with their sixteen ships on the right wing;[3] but it is clear that the Persian "west wing towards Eleusis" was also the right wing; that the Athenians were opposed to them on the left wing of the Greeks; and that the Persian "east wing towards Piraeus" was also the left wing. It is obvious that, if we have rightly explained τὸ ἀφ' ἑσπέρης κέρας in chapter 76, it is hardly possible to refer this expression and τὸ πρὸς Ἐλευσῖνός τε καὶ ἑσπέρης κέρας to the same body of ships, since no part of the Persian fleet on the afternoon before the battle could have been at once on the right wing, towards the west, and towards Eleusis.[4] There is certainly no strong reason, apart from the similarity of the two expressions, for referring them to the same thing. There is an interval between them of nearly nine chapters in Herodotus; and while the former refers to the Persian fleet as it lay before Xerxes received the message of Themistocles, the latter describes the fleet as it was manœuvring after the battle was actually begun the next day. Xerxes, it must be remembered, changed his whole plan of operations in this short interval, and it is not at all unlikely that what was his left wing in the afternoon should be sent off on some new expedition before daybreak. It is to be noticed, further, that the two hundred Egyptian ships, which we have supposed to be on the left wing in the afternoon, and to be sent round Salamis in the night, do not appear to have taken part in the next day's battle.[5]

---

[1] Diod. XI. 17. [2] Diod. XI. 18.

[3] The little squadron of sixteen Lacedaemonian ships (Herod. VIII. 43) might easily have been overlooked in presence of the 180 Athenian vessels.

[4] Loeschke, *Jahrb. für Philol.*, 1877, p. 31, proposes to read πρὸς Σαλαμῖνος for πρὸς Ἐλευσῖνος in Herod. VIII. 85 (to make 85 accord with 76); but, as he himself remarks (p. 32), this change brings the Phoenicians on the left Persian wing, in opposition to Diodorus, XI. 17.

[5] There is nothing impossible in the supposition that some or all of the Egyptian ships may have sailed through the gulf of Eleusis and entered the battle in the morning, if the evidence is thought to show their presence. It is common to refer to Herod. VIII. 100, and to Aesch. *Pers.* 311 and 321, for evidence of

Let us now consider under what circumstances, consistently with probability and with our other authorities, the Persian fleet could have been in such a position that its right wing was towards the west and also towards Eleusis.[1] This description, it will be remembered, refers to the time when the two hostile lines were just meeting at the beginning of the battle. If we follow what must be accepted as the account of Aeschylus as well as of Diodorus (Ephorus), the Persians entered the straits of Salamis and immediately found themselves in conflict with the Greeks. Aeschylus calls their line as they entered a *stream* (ῥεῦμα); and Diodorus speaks of them as keeping their line at first, while there was plenty of room, but falling into confusion in the narrows, where they were obliged to withdraw some ships from their line to enable it to enter. As the passage between Psyttaleia and the mainland is less than four thousand feet wide, it is absurd to think of a fleet of at least eight hundred ships passing between the rocky shores in three lines. Even in eight lines they would have had less than forty feet of space for each ship, with no allowance for reefs and shoals on the sides of the channel. The graphic word *stream* used by Aes-

Egyptians in the battle. But the vague allusion in Herodotus, where Mardonius tells Xerxes that it is no disgrace to the real Persians "if Phoenicians and Egyptians, Cyprians and Cilicians, proved cowards," can hardly be called evidence of the actual presence of Egyptians (in any numbers, or at all) at Salamis. The supposed evidence of Aeschylus is rather comic. "Arcteus, who dwells near the sources of the Egyptian Nile" (?), is mentioned in vs. 311 among the victims of the sea-fight, being one of four "who fell from the same ship" (vs. 313). Arcteus himself is called leader of the "luxurious Lydians" in vs. 44; and two of his fellow-sufferers, Adeues and Pheresseues, are said by the scholiast to have names which are not of the Egyptian style, but poetic inventions. Ariomardus, who is called in vs. 38 "ruler of Ogygian Thebes," is said in vs. 321 to have brought mourning upon Sardes by his untimely death. We must remember that Persian officers did not always command the troops of their own country, and also that high-sounding names which fitted the anapaestic verse must have been at a high premium when Aeschylus was writing the πάροδος of *The Persians*. See Hermann's note on *Pers.* 316, which ends thus: Quare maneat posthac Aeschyli Ariomardo et imperium Aegyptiorum et patria Sardes. These Egyptians certainly seem a little mixed!

[1] Duncker, *Gesch. d. Alterthums*, IV. pp. 793 ff., attempts to reconcile Herodotus with geography by supposing that the right Persian wing (as the fleet lay at Phalerum), consisting of the Phoenician division, was sent round Salamis in the night by the northwest passage, to block the entrance from the bay of Salamis to the bay of Eleusis, and that it united with the main body of ships sent northward through the straits beyond Aegaleos, and thus again formed the Persian right wing, which was opposed to the Athenians in the battle. For the similar view of Dr. Lolling, see note 1 on p. 252.

chylus shows that they entered in a column rather than in an extended line, probably with the intention of facing about and forming a new line of battle after passing the two narrow places, although their want of skill in passing those points prevented them from executing their plan, whatever it may have been. The right wing, where the Phoenicians were placed, would naturally lead the way; and if we suppose the line to have sailed by the points of Psyttaleia and of Salamis in the same direction before it met the Greeks and began its retreat, it was then running precisely as Herodotus describes it, from N.N.W. to S.S.E., the right directed towards Eleusis and the left towards Piraeus.[1] In this position it was attacked by the Greeks, probably before the new line of battle could be formed; and after this the Greeks had merely a disorderly mass of ships to deal with. Herodotus speaks of the Greeks as "fighting in good order in line of battle, while the barbarians were no longer in regular line and showed no sense in anything they did."[2]

Where now did the Greeks form their line at the beginning of the battle? The common belief that the Persians occupied the eastern side of the bay has made it necessary to drive the Greek line back upon the shore of Salamis. But if the Persians were not in the bay at all, the Greeks could choose their position at pleasure. We have only one ancient statement as to the Greek position. Diodorus, after describing the order of battle on each side, says that the Greeks "sailed out" (probably from the inner bay of Salamis, south of the town) "in the order just described, and occupied the passage between Salamis and the Heracleum."[3] We must therefore attempt to fix the position of this Heracleum. This must be the *τετράκωμον Ἡράκλειον*, the sanctuary of Heracles which was the bond of union of four Attic demes, the *τετρακωμία* of Piraeus, Phalerum, Xypete, and Thymoetadae.[4] It has usually been identified with the ruins seen by Leake

---

[1] A glance at the map will show that a line running literally from west to east and also pointing towards Eleusis and the Piraeus is a geographical impossibility. Herodotus is often still more inaccurate in giving directions; as when he makes the pass of Thermopylae run north and south (VII. 176). In making the Hellespont run westward to the Aegean (VII. 36) he is as exact as he is here.

[2] Herod. VIII. 86: *ἅτε γὰρ τῶν μὲν Ἑλλήνων σὺν κόσμῳ ναυμαχεόντων κατὰ τάξιν, τῶν δὲ βαρβάρων οὔτε τεταγμένων ἔτι οὔτε σὺν νόῳ ποιεόντων οὐδέν.*

[3] Diod. XI. 18: *οὗτοι μὲν οὖν τοῦτον τὸν τρόπον συνταχθέντες ἐξέπλευσαν, καὶ τὸν πόρον μεταξὺ Σαλαμῖνος καὶ Ἡρακλείου κατεῖχον.*

[4] Steph. Byzant. *s.v.* Ἐχελίδαι.

near the little bay on the south of Aegaleos, nearly east of the opposite town of Salamis. Kiepert places Thymoetadae in this immediate neighborhood. But this position does not agree with the ancient authorities for the site. Ctesias, after speaking of the burning of Athens by Xerxes, thus proceeds: ὁ δὲ Ξέρξης αὐτόθεν ἐλθὼν ἐπὶ στεινότατον τῆς Ἀττικῆς (Ἡράκλειον καλεῖται) ἐχώννυε χῶμα ἐπὶ Σαλαμῖνα, πεζῇ ἐπ' αὐτὴν διαβῆναι διανοούμενος,[1] i.e. *Xerxes came from Athens to the place in Attica, called Heracleum, where there is the narrowest* (or *a very narrow*) *passage, and undertook to build a causeway across to Salamis, with the intention of passing over to the island by land.* Strabo, after mentioning the Thriasian Plain (north of Aegaleos) and the deme of Thria, says: εἶθ' ἡ ἄκρα ἡ Ἀμφιάλη καὶ τὸ ὑπερκείμενον λατόμιον καὶ ὁ εἰς Σαλαμῖνα πορθμὸς ὅσον διστάδιος, ὃν διαχοῦν ἐπειρᾶτο Ξέρξης, ἔφθη δὲ ἡ ναυμαχία γενομένη καὶ φυγὴ τῶν Περσῶν,[2] i.e. *next is the headland Amphiale with the stone quarry above it, and the ferry to Salamis about two stadia wide, which Xerxes attempted to dam over, but the sea-fight and the retreat of the Persians prevented.*[3] Herodotus speaks of the preparations of Xerxes to build a causeway to Salamis as a device of the king to conceal his real intention to retreat *after the battle.*[4] Plutarch (on the authority of Phanodemus) places the seat of Xerxes, from which he watched the battle, ὑπὲρ τὸ Ἡράκλειον, ᾗ βραχεῖ πόρῳ διείργεται τῆς Ἀττικῆς ἡ νῆσος,[5] i.e. *above the Heracleum, where Salamis is separated by a narrow passage from Attica.* Herodotus speaks of Xerxes as κατήμενος ὑπὸ τῷ ὄρεϊ τῷ ἀντίον Σαλαμῖνος τὸ καλέεται Αἰγάλεως,[6] *seated on the slope of the mountain opposite Salamis, which is called Aegaleos.* From these testimonies it appears (1) that the Heracleum in question stood upon *the narrowest* (*or a very narrow*) *passage* from Attica to Salamis; (2) that this passage was that by which the ancient ferry[7] crossed; (3) that it was the place in Attica from which Xerxes undertook (or pretended to undertake) to build a causeway to Salamis; (4) that it was at the

---

[1] Ctes. *Persic.* 26 (*Phot. Bibl.* p. 39 *b*). [2] Strab. IX. p. 395.

[3] Dr. Lolling, *Meerenge v. Salamis*, p. 7, identifies this stone-quarry, which fixes the position of Amphiale as the southwest point of Aegaleos. He also maintains that διστάδιος cannot be correct in Strabo, and proposes to read δεκαστάδιος. But see note 2 on p. 257.

[4] Herod. VIII. 97. [5] Plut. *Them.* 13. [6] Herod. VIII. 90.

[7] This ferry to Salamis was and still is the regular means of intercourse between Athens and the island. See Aeschin. *in Ctes.* 158.

foot of Aegaleos, below the seat of Xerxes.[1] It seems impossible to reconcile these marks with any position on the bay near Thymoetadae; and the evidence on which the Heracleum is placed there is slight compared with the combined testimony of these passages for another site. The ancient ferry to Salamis can hardly have crossed from any other point of Attica than that from which the present ferry runs, at Cape Ἀμφιάλη. Again, the only passage over which it would not have seemed insane even for Xerxes to attempt to build a causeway to Salamis is from this point of Aegaleos (a little northwest of the ferry), over the shoal above mentioned, to the island of St. George and thence to Salamis.[2] A few minutes of the straits of Salamis in a morning sea-breeze are enough to show the madness of attempting to build a causeway from the long point of the island to the Attic shore. I cannot doubt that the Heracleum mentioned in the passage above quoted was near Cape Amphiale, at about the point marked H on the map. It is more doubtful whether we are to give up the site near Thymoetadae for the Heracleum altogether, or to assume with Dr. Lolling[3] that the whole shore from Amphiale to the site in question was called Ἡράκλειον, i.e. *a* τέμενος of Heracles, "in a wider sense."

When now Diodorus (Ephorus) states that the Greeks sailed out and formed their line of battle in the passage between Salamis and the Heracleum, we must ask whether this definite statement is consistent with our other information. Herodotus, who says nothing of the position of the Greeks, speaks of the advance of their whole fleet on the arrival of the Aeginetan trireme. As they advanced, he says, the Persians immediately attacked them. The sight of the enemy caused most of the Greeks to back water; and they would even have run their ships on shore, had it not been that the Athenian Ameinias attacked one of the enemy's ships and all hastened at once to support him. An apparition in a woman's form was said to have appeared

---

1 It is impossible now to identify any particular point of Aegaleos as the seat of Xerxes. If the battle took place at the outlet of the straits, any place on the southern slope of the hill would have commanded a full view of it.

2 If Dr. Lolling is right in identifying the shoal near Amphiale with one of the Pharmacussae, or if the present shoal was above water in ancient times, possibly Strabo's διστάδιος in p. 395 may refer to the widest single channel which Xerxes would have had to fill up. See note 1 on p. 241, and note 3 on p. 256.

3 *Meerenge v. Salamis*, p. 6. The expression Ἡράκλειον καλεῖται in Ctesias (quoted p. 256), referring to στεινότατον τῆς Ἀττικῆς, seems to favor this view.

exhorting the Greeks and reproaching them for their signs of panic.[1] If now we suppose the Greeks to have formed their first line from the Heracleum (H) to some point near A on the shore of Salamis, many of the ships would lie so near the point of Salamis town that a very slight backward movement would send them ashore on the point. This high and commanding point, moreover, is just the place where it might naturally be supposed that the apparition appeared to encourage the faltering Greeks. In fact, there is no other place on the shore of Salamis to which the description of Herodotus so well applies, especially his statement that the whole Greek fleet could hear the exhortation of the mysterious personage.[2] Aeschylus is more explicit about the order of the Greek advance. He says that the right wing first advanced in good order, and next the whole fleet sailed forth: he too makes the conflict begin almost immediately, by a Greek (*i.e.* Athenian) ship attacking a Phoenician.[3] Both Aeschylus and Herodotus appear to represent both fleets as advancing simultaneously, the Greeks leaving their position in which their right rested on the shore of Salamis, and the Persians entering the straits to meet them. As Aeschylus seems to imply that the Greek right wing advanced with greater alacrity than the rest of the fleet (for he says nothing of the slight panic before the battle opened), we may suppose that when the two fleets came into general collision, the Greeks had advanced from about the position A–H to about B–K, where they met the Persians just entering the straits. If now a line anywhere near B–K represents the position of the Greek fleet, the Persians moving to attack it would be in just the position in which Herodotus (viii. 85) represents them at this moment, with their right towards Eleusis and the west (northwest), and with their left towards Piraeus and the east (southeast). Of course, with so little positive information at our command, it is impossible to fix the position of the Greek right wing with any certainty; we can only feel sure that, assuming that the left was at first near the Heracleum (at H), we must place the right at first near the shore of Salamis, and afterwards near the entrance of the straits, where the chief contest occurred. We have the most positive testimony of both Aeschylus and Diodorus that the Persians never passed far beyond the entrance of the straits in any order of battle whatever.

[1] Herod. VIII. 84: *ὦ δαιμόνιοι, μέχρι κόσου ἔτι πρύμνην ἀνακρούεσθε;*
[2] *Ibid.*
[3] Aesch. *Pers.* 399, 409.

I have thus attempted to show how the passage of Herodotus (viii. 85) which makes the battle begin with the Persian right "towards Eleusis and the west" can be reconciled with the other authorities, especially Aeschylus, without supposing that the Persian fleet was arrayed before daybreak along the coast of Attica opposite Salamis. Let it not be forgotten that, unless some such reconciliation can be effected, we leave Herodotus in direct conflict with Aeschylus, whose plain statements on so fundamental a matter of fact cannot reasonably be questioned.

Diodorus relates that the Athenians put to flight the Phoenicians and Cyprians on the Persian right, and that these were soon followed in the panic by the Cilicians, Pamphylians, and Lycians, who were next to them.[1] But the Persian left wing made a vigorous resistance to the Aeginetans and Megarians, until the Athenians returned from the pursuit of the Phoenicians and Cyprians, whom they had driven to the shore of Attica; then the rout of the Persian fleet became complete. This is probably the point in the battle to which Herodotus refers where he says that, when the barbarians were sailing in full flight towards Phalerum, the Aeginetans stationed themselves in the narrows and destroyed Persian ships as they passed out: the Athenians, he adds, were attacking the enemy within the straits, and those which escaped them fell into the hands of the Aeginetans.[2] We must suppose the Aeginetans to be near the eastern end of Psyttaleia, and it was then that the battle raged fiercest about this island, as Plutarch describes it.[3] Herodotus confirms Diodorus again in viii. 90, where he tells of certain Phoenicians, "whose ships had been destroyed," coming to Xerxes as he sat on Aegaleos during the battle, and charging the Ionic Greeks with causing the Persian defeat by their treachery. While they were in the king's presence, a brilliant exploit of a Samothracian ship convinced Xerxes that the charge against his Greek subjects was false and malicious, and he at once ordered the heads of his Phoenician visitors to be cut off for their slanderous story. These must have been some of the Phoenicians who had been driven by the Athenians to the Attic shore and had found their way to the seat of Xerxes. Diodorus, who says nothing of the visit to Xerxes, says that the king ordered those Phoenicians who had been chiefly responsible for the flight to lose their heads, and threatened

[1] Diod. XI. 19. [2] Herod. VIII. 91. [3] Plut. *Arist.* 9.

the others with punishment; but the latter made their escape to Attica, and then by night set sail for Asia.[1]

The story which the Athenians told of Adeimantus, the Corinthian commander, that he took fright at the first approach of the Persians and sailed away from the battle, soon followed by the whole Corinthian fleet,[2] involves an interesting point of topography. Herodotus, who evidently heard the story at Athens half a century later, when Athens and Corinth were in bitter enmity, and who says expressly that it was denied by the Corinthians and by the rest of Greece, repeats the tale, that when the fugitive Corinthians were passing the temple of Athena Sciras on the shore of Salamis, they were met by a mysterious boat, believed to be directed by superhuman power, from which they were warned not to continue their flight, since the Greeks were victorious in the battle. Upon this they turned about and came into the Greek camp after the victory was assured. This ancient temple of Athena, said to be a Phoenician foundation,[3] has generally been placed, after Leake, on the northwest point of Salamis, although others have preferred a site near the Homeric town of Salamis on the south of the island. The former site is open to the objection that the retreating Corinthians would have been likely to meet the Persian squadron sent to guard the passage between Salamis and Megara; the latter assumes that the Corinthians retreated by the straits of Salamis, where at the beginning of the battle they would have met the main Persian fleet. Dr. Lolling has recently made it highly probable that the temple of Athena and the hill called Σκιράδιον were at the northeast point of Salamis near Cape Ἀράπη, just at the entrance of the bay of Eleusis.[4] If this is the correct site, the above-mentioned difficulties disappear; for Adeimantus would not have encountered any Persian ships before reaching the bay of Eleusis. The whole story was doubtless a late fabrication of the enemies of Corinth, a city which claimed to have been among the first in valor at Salamis.[5]

---

[1] Diod. XI. 19.
[2] Herod. VIII. 94.
[3] See Wachsmuth, *Stadt Athen*, pp. 440–442.
[4] *Mittheilungen d. deutsch. archaeol. Inst. in Athen*, I. pp. 127–138.
[5] Herod. VIII. 94 (end).

In conclusion, I will sum up briefly the points which I have endeavored to establish.

The account of most modern historians, that the battle of Salamis was a contest between a Greek fleet in the bay of Salamis and a Persian fleet which had been drawn up along the opposite shore of Attica during the night, is opposed to many facts of the topography, and especially to the plainest statements of Aeschylus (an eye-witness of the battle) and of other ancient authorities. Three general objections are urged. (1) The channel which is thus made the scene of the battle is so narrow in some places that, if the Persians had taken up the supposed position in the night, the Greeks could not have embarked and formed their line in the morning directly in the face of the enemy (only a few hundred yards distant) without interference. (2) It would have been impossible for the supposed movement to be effected without alarming the Greeks at Salamis, especially as it was almost certainly a moonlight night. And yet they suspected nothing of the movement (and even Themistocles, who had advised Xerxes, knew nothing of it) until Aristides informed them that they were already shut in. But Aristides had come over from Aegina to the west or the southwest side of Salamis, having escaped the Persians on his way with great difficulty; and he knew only of movements in that direction, and nothing of any enemy within the straits. (3) The occupation of Psyttaleia by Xerxes shows that he expected this island to be the centre of the sea-fight; and Plutarch gives his own opinion that it actually was so.

Aeschylus beyond doubt represents the Persians as *entering* the straits of Salamis *after daybreak* to begin the battle. This is confirmed by Diodorus (*i.e.* Ephorus) and Plutarch. Their line or "stream" fell into some confusion in entering the narrows; and they never succeeded in regaining their order of battle, being immediately met by the Greeks as they passed the long point of Salamis. In this condition they fell an easy prey to the skilful Greek seamen, and soon were eager only to escape to Phalerum.

We find nothing inconsistent with this view of the battle except the common interpretation of two passages of Herodotus. One (viii. 76) describes the Persians as bringing up their west wing to Salamis κυκλούμενοι *during the night before the battle;* the other (viii. 85) calls the Persian right *at the opening of the battle* the next day "the wing towards Eleusis and the west," and their left "the wing towards the east and Piraeus." My chief object has been to show that ἀνῆγον μὲν . . . πρὸς Σαλαμῖνα in chapter 76 must refer to sending the two hundred Egyptian ships (which probably formed the west wing of the Persian fleet as it lay near Salamis the afternoon before the battle) to the northwest point of Salamis to cut off escape through the bay of Eleusis; and that the following words, ἀνῆγον δὲ... νηυσί, then naturally refer to posting the main Persian force to guard the southern outlet of the straits, where Aeschylus places it. Then we can refer the description of the Persian line in chapter 85 to the direction in which the main Persian force (thus posted in the night) entered the straits just before the battle to meet the Greeks, who were probably drawn up in a line from northwest to southeast across the passage between Aegaleos and the long point of Salamis (Cynosura). The first Greek position, between Salamis and the Heracleum (as assigned by Diodorus, our only authority), probably from A to H, was most likely to be changed to one from B to K before the fleets really met, the right (according to Aeschylus) advancing more eagerly than the left. As the Persians approached this line, their right became the west wing towards Eleusis. This interpretation brings Herodotus into perfect harmony with Aeschylus as regards the three principal movements of Xerxes, on any of which a disagreement with Aeschylus would seem fatal to anyone's credit. In lesser details we have seen that Herodotus is in substantial agreement with Aeschylus and our other authorities, and at variance with the theory which is commonly supposed to be supported by his language.

ARCHÆOLOGICAL INSTITUTE OF AMERICA.

AMERICAN SCHOOL OF CLASSICAL STUDIES AT ATHENS.

January, 1885.

AMERICAN SCHOOL OF CLASSICAL STUDIES AT ATHENS.

1884–1885.

MANAGING COMMITTEE.

JOHN WILLIAMS WHITE (*Chairman*), Harvard University, Cambridge, Mass.

MARTIN L. D'OOGE, University of Michigan, Ann Arbor, Mich.

HENRY DRISLER, Columbia College, 48 West 46th St., New York, N. Y.

BASIL L. GILDERSLEEVE, Johns Hopkins University, Baltimore, Md.

WILLIAM W. GOODWIN, Harvard University, Cambridge, Mass.

ALBERT HARKNESS, Brown University, Providence, R. I.

THOMAS W. LUDLOW (*Secretary*), Yonkers, N. Y.

CHARLES ELIOT NORTON (*ex officio*), Harvard University, Cambridge, Mass.

FRANCIS W. PALFREY, 255 Beacon St., Boston, Mass.

FREDERIC J. DE PEYSTER (*Treasurer*), 7 East 42d St., New York, N. Y.

THOMAS D. SEYMOUR, Yale College, New Haven, Conn.

WILLIAM M. SLOANE, College of New Jersey, Princeton, N. J.

W. S. TYLER, Amherst College, Amherst, Mass.

J. C. VAN BENSCHOTEN, Wesleyan University, Middletown, Conn.

DIRECTORS.

WILLIAM WATSON GOODWIN, Ph.D., LL.D., Eliot Professor of Greek Literature in Harvard University. 1882–83.

LEWIS R. PACKARD, Ph.D., Hillhouse Professor of Greek in Yale College. 1883–84.

JAMES COOKE VAN BENSCHOTEN, LL.D., Seney Professor of the Greek Language and Literature in Wesleyan University. 1884–85.

CO-OPERATING COLLEGES.

AMHERST COLLEGE.
BROWN UNIVERSITY.
COLLEGE OF THE CITY OF NEW YORK.
COLLEGE OF NEW JERSEY.
COLUMBIA COLLEGE.
CORNELL UNIVERSITY.
DARTMOUTH COLLEGE.
HARVARD UNIVERSITY.
JOHNS HOPKINS UNIVERSITY.
UNIVERSITY OF MICHIGAN.
UNIVERSITY OF VIRGINIA.
WESLEYAN UNIVERSITY.
YALE COLLEGE.

THE AMERICAN SCHOOL OF CLASSICAL STUDIES AT ATHENS.

THE American School of Classical Studies at Athens, projected by the Archæological Institute of America, and organized under the immediate auspices of some of the leading American colleges, was opened on October 2, 1882. It occupies a house on the Ὁδὸς Ἀμαλίας, in a convenient and healthy quarter of Athens. A large room is set apart for the use of the students, is lighted in the evening, and is warmed in cold weather. In it is kept the library of the School, which includes a complete set of the Greek classics, and the most necessary books of reference for philological, archæological, and architectural study in Greece. The library contains at the present time about 2000 volumes, exclusive of sets of periodicals.

The advantages of the School are offered free of expense for tuition to graduates of colleges co-operating in its support, and to other American students deemed by the committee of sufficient promise to warrant the extension to them of the privilege of membership.

The School is unable to provide its students with board or lodging, or with any allowance for other expenses. It is hoped that the Archæological Institute may in time be supplied with the means of establishing scholarships. In the meantime, students must rely upon their own resources, or upon scholarships which may be granted them by the colleges to which they belong. The amount needed for the expenses of an eight months' residence in Athens differs little from that required in other European capitals, and depends chiefly on the economy of the individual.

A peculiar feature of the present temporary organization of the School, which distinguishes it from the older German and French schools at Athens, is the yearly change of director. That the director should, through all the future history of the School, continue to be sent out under an annual appointment is an arrangement which would be as undesirable as it would be impossible. But such an arrangement is not contemplated. When established by a permanent endowment, the School will be under the control of a permanent director, a scholar who by continuous residence at Athens will accumulate that body of local and special knowledge without which the highest functions of such a school cannot be attained. In the meantime the School is enabled by its present organization to meet a want of great importance. It cannot hope immediately to accomplish such original work in archæological investigation as will put it on a level with the German and French schools. These draw their students from bodies of picked men, specially trained for the place. The American School seeks at the first rather to arouse in American colleges a lively interest in classical archæology, than to accomplish distinguished achievements. The lack of this interest heretofore is conspicuous. Without it, the School at Athens, however well endowed, cannot accomplish the best results. It is beyond dispute that the presence in various colleges of professors who have been resident a year at Athens under favorable circumstances, as directors or as students of the School, will do much to increase American appreciation of antiquity.

The address of Professor J. W. WHITE, Chairman of the Committee, is Cambridge, Mass.; of Mr. T. W. LUDLOW, Secretary, Yonkers, N. Y.; of Mr. F. J. DE PEYSTER, Treasurer, 7 East 42d Street, New York.

REGULATIONS OF THE AMERICAN SCHOOL OF CLASSICAL STUDIES AT ATHENS.

I. The object of the American School of Classical Studies is to furnish, without charge for tuition, to graduates of American Colleges and to other qualified students, an opportunity to study Classical Literature, Art, and Antiquities in Athens, under suitable guidance; to prosecute and to aid original research in these subjects; and to co-operate with the Archæological Institute of America, so far as it may be able, in conducting the exploration and excavation of Classic sites.

II. The School is in charge of a Managing Committee, and under the superintendence of a Director. The Director of the School and the President of the Archæological Institute are *ex officio* members of the Managing Committee. This Committee, which was originally appointed by the Archæological Institute, has power to add to its membership, to administer the finances of the School, and to make such regulations for its government as it may deem proper.

III. The Managing Committee meets semi-annually, in New York on the third Friday in November, and in Boston on the third Friday in May. Special meetings may be called at any time by the Chairman.

IV. The Chairman of the Committee is the official representative of the interests of the School in America. He presents a Report annually to the Archæological Institute concerning the affairs of the School.

V. The Director is chosen by the Committee for a period of one or two years. The Committee provides him with a house in Athens, containing apartments for himself and his family, and suitable rooms for the meetings of the members of the School, its collections, and its library.

VI. The Director superintends personally the work of each member of the School, advising him in what direction to turn his studies, and assisting him in their prosecution. He conducts no regular courses of instruction, but holds meetings of the members of the School at stated times for consultation and discussion. He makes a full report annually to the Managing Committee of the work accomplished by the School.

VII. The school year extends from the 1st of October to the 1st of June. Members are required to prosecute their studies during the whole of this time in Greek lands under the supervision of the Director. The studies of the remaining four months necessary to complete a full year (the shortest term for which a certificate is given) may be carried on in Greece or elsewhere, as the student prefers.

VIII. Bachelors of Arts of co-operating Colleges, and all Bachelors of Arts who have studied at one of these Colleges as candidates for a higher degree, are admitted to membership in the School on presenting to the Committee a certificate from the instructors in Classics of the College at which they have last studied, stating that they are competent to pursue an independent course of study at Athens under the advice of the Director. All other persons desiring to become members of the School must make application to the Committee. The Committee reserves the right to modify these conditions of membership.

IX. Each member of the School must pursue some definite subject of study or research in Classical Literature, Art, or Antiquities, and must present at least one thesis, embodying the results of some important part of his year's work. These theses, if approved by the Director, are sent to the Managing Committee, by which each thesis is referred to a sub-committee of three members, of whom two are appointed by the Chairman, and the third is always the Director under whose supervision the thesis was prepared. If recommended for publication by this sub-committee, the thesis may be issued in the papers of the School.

X. When any member of the School has completed one or more full years of study, the results of which have been approved by the Director, he receives a certificate stating the work accomplished by him, signed by the Director of the School, the President of the Archæological Institute, and the other members of the Managing Committee.

XI. American students resident or travelling in Greece who are not members of the School may apply for the assistance and advice of the Director in the prosecution of their studies, and will be allowed at his discretion to use the library belonging to the School.

REGULATIONS CONCERNING THE PUBLICATIONS OF THE AMERICAN SCHOOL OF CLASSICAL STUDIES AT ATHENS.

1. There shall be published annually, after the meeting of the Managing Committee in November, a Bulletin which shall contain the reports for the previous year of the Director of the School and of the Secretary of the Committee, with any other matter relating to the School not included in those reports.

2. There shall be published also annually a volume of Papers of the School, to be made up from the work of the Director and the students during the preceding school year. This volume shall be conformed in general style to the Papers of the Archæological Institute.

3. The publications of the School shall be in charge of a permanent editor, to be elected by the Managing Committee, and shall be edited by him with the assistance of the Director under whom the papers have been written, and of the Secretary of the Committee.

4. The expense of the publications shall be met from the funds of the School to an amount not exceeding $1000 per annum.

5. The publications shall be issued to the public at a price to be fixed by the Publication Committee. They shall be sent free to the libraries of the co-operating Colleges, and to such learned bodies as the Committee may select. They may be exchanged, for the benefit of the School, with other like publications.

6. Copies of the publications may also be placed with leading booksellers for sale at a proper discount.

7. The proceeds of subscriptions and sales shall be appropriated toward the costs of publication.

www.ingramcontent.com/pod-product-compliance
Lightning Source LLC
LaVergne TN
LVHW011201110826
845150LV00006B/1283